THE
CLASSIC 1,000
CHINESE RECIPES

THE
CLASSIC 1,000
CHINESE RECIPES

EDITED BY
WENDY HOBSON

foulsham
LONDON · NEW YORK · TORONTO · SYDNEY

foulsham

The Publishing House, Bennetts Close,
Cippenham, Berkshire, SL1 5AP, England

ISBN 0-572-02849-0

Photographs by Carol and Terry Pastor
Cover photograph by Duncan Loughrey for G. Costa & Co. Ltd

With thanks to the following companies for providing items for the photographs:
China, kitchenware and tableware from **Divertimenti**, 139–141 Fulham Road,
London, SW3 6SD. Tel: 020 7581 8065. Fax: 020 7823 9429.
Also at 33–34 Marylebone High Street, London, W1U 4PT.
Tel: 020 7935 0689. Fax: 020 7224 0058. Web site: www.divertimenti.co.uk.
Decorative porcelain bowls, papers and chopsticks from **The Chinese Shop**,
Chinese Arts and Crafts, 9 St Giles Street, Norwich, NR2 1JL.
Tel: 01603 619623. Also at 82 Regent Road, Great Yarmouth, NR30 2AH.
Tel: 01493 858861. Web site: www.samarkandgifts.co.uk.

Printed in Great Britain by St Edmundsbury Press Ltd, Bury St Edmunds, Suffolk

Contents

Introduction 7

Notes on the Recipes 8

Appetisers 9

Stock and Soups 21

Seafood 34

Beef 96

Lamb 132

Pork and Ham 143

Poultry and Game 182

Eggs 250

Rice 265

Noodles and Pastry 275

Vegetables .283

Tofu 315

Sauces 321

Marinades and Condiments 328

Dips and Dressings 333

Salads 337

Desserts, Cakes and Confectionery 344

Preserves 357

Nibbles and Drinks 359

Index 362

Introduction

Everyone who loves to cook, loves to experiment with new dishes and new taste sensations. Chinese cuisine has become immensely popular in recent years because it offers a different range of flavours to enjoy. Most dishes are cooked on top of the stove, and many are quickly prepared and cooked so are ideal for the busy cook who wants to create an appetising and attractive dish when there is little time to spare. If you really enjoy Chinese cooking, you will probably already have a wok, and this is the perfect utensil for cooking most of the dishes in the book. If you have yet to be convinced that this style of cooking is for you, use a good frying pan or saucepan to try out the recipes. When you find how easy they are to prepare and how tasty to eat, you will almost certainly want to invest in a wok for your kitchen.

Notes on the Recipes

1. Do not mix metric and Imperial measures. Follow one set only.

2. Spoon measurements are level.

3. Eggs are size 3. If you use a different size, adjust the amount of liquid added to obtain the right consistency.

4. Always wash fresh foods before preparing them.

5. Peel or scrub ingredients as appropriate to the recipe. For example, onions are always peeled, so it is not listed in the recipe. Carrots can be washed, scrubbed or peeled, depending on whether they are young or old.

6. Seasoning and the use of strongly flavoured ingredients, such as onions, chilli peppers, ginger and garlic, are very much a matter of personal taste. Taste the food as you cook and adjust seasoning to suit your own taste.

7. Use freshly ground pepper, if possible. You may like to use Szechuan peppercorns which are available in most major supermarkets, or you can use black pepper.

8. You can use fresh or dried herbs in most recipes. Herbs which are commonly available in the garden or local shops, such as parsley, are best used fresh and are listed as 'chopped parsley' and so on. Other herbs are assumed to be dried. Fresh herbs are, however, becoming more widely available and if you prefer to use them chop them finely and use twice the quantity specified for dried herbs. Always use fresh herbs for garnishing or sprinkling on cooked dishes.

9. Use your own discretion in substituting ingredients and personalising the recipes. Make notes of particular successes as you go along.

10. For Chinese cooking, you need to use an oil which can be heated to high temperatures, especially for stir-fried dishes. Most people prefer groundnut oil, but you can substitute other oils if you prefer.

11. The Chinese generally use a large cleaver for all their chopping, slicing and cutting, but a large sharp knife can be used. You may have favourite kitchen gadgets which you like to use to help speed up food preparation.

12. A wok is excellent for Chinese cooking as it enables food to be cooked quickly at a high temperature. It can also be used for steaming and braising. However, you can use any utensils which you find convenient.

Appetisers

Appetisers should be simple and light in order to whet the appetite for the dishes to follow. Many Chinese dishes fit this description admirably and are also quick and simple to prepare. If you particularly like some of the dishes, you may choose to make a slightly larger quantity and serve them as part of your main meal. There is no strict distinction in Chinese cooking.

Marinated Abalone

Serves 4

450 g/1 lb canned abalone
45 ml/3 tbsp soy sauce
30 ml/2 tbsp wine vinegar
5 ml/1 tsp sugar
few drops of sesame oil

Drain the abalone and slice it thinly or cut it into strips. Mix together the remaining ingredients, pour over the abalone and toss well. Cover and refrigerate for 1 hour.

Braised Bamboo Shoots

Serves 4

60 ml/4 tbsp groundnut (peanut) oil
225 g/8 oz bamboo shoots, cut into
    strips
60 ml/4 tbsp chicken stock
15 ml/1 tbsp soy sauce
5 ml/1 tsp sugar
5 ml/1 tsp rice wine or dry sherry

Heat the oil and stir-fry the bamboo shoots for 3 minutes. Mix the stock, soy sauce, sugar and wine or sherry and add it to the pan. Cover and simmer for 20 minutes. Leave to cool and chill before serving.

Chicken with Cucumber

Serves 4

1 cucumber, peeled and seeded
225 g/8 oz cooked chicken, torn into
    shreds
5 ml/1 tsp mustard powder
2.5 ml/ ½ tsp salt
30 ml/2 tbsp wine vinegar

Cut the cucumber into strips and arrange on a flat serving plate. Arrange the chicken on top. Mix together the mustard, salt and wine vinegar and spoon over the chicken just before serving.

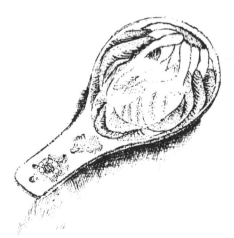

Chicken Sesame

Serves 4

350 g/12 oz cooked chicken
120 ml/4 fl oz/½ cup water
5 ml/1 tsp mustard powder
15 ml/1 tbsp sesame seeds
2.5 ml/½ tsp salt
pinch of sugar
45 ml/3 tbsp chopped fresh coriander
5 spring onions (scallions), chopped
½ head lettuce, shredded

Tear the chicken into fine shreds. Mix just enough water into the mustard to make a smooth paste and stir it into the chicken. Toast the sesame seeds in a dry pan until lightly golden then add them to the chicken and sprinkle with salt and sugar. Add half the parsley and the spring onions and toss together thoroughly. Arrange the lettuce on a serving plate, top with the chicken mixture and garnish with the remaining parsley.

Lychees with Ginger

Serves 4

1 large watermelon, halved and seeded
450 g/1 lb canned lychees, drained
5 cm/2 in stem ginger, sliced
few mint leaves

Fill the melon halves with lychees and ginger, decorate with mint leaves. Chill before serving.

Red-Cooked Chicken Wings

Serves 4

8 chicken wings
2 spring onions (scallions), chopped
75 ml/5 tbsp soy sauce
120 ml/4 fl oz/½ cup water
30 ml/2 tbsp brown sugar

Cut off and discard the bony tips of the chicken wings and cut them in half. Place in a pan with the remaining ingredients, bring to the boil, cover and simmer for 30 minutes. Remove the lid and continue to simmer for a further 15 minutes, basting frequently. Leave to cool then chill before serving.

Crab Meat with Cucumber

Serves 4

100 g/4 oz crab meat, flaked
2 cucumbers, peeled and shredded
1 slice ginger root, minced
15 ml/1 tbsp soy sauce
30 ml/2 tbsp wine vinegar
5 ml/1 tsp sugar
few drops of sesame oil

Place the crab meat and cucumbers in a bowl. Mix together the remaining ingredients, pour over the crab meat mixture and toss together well. Cover and refrigerate for 30 minutes before serving.

Marinated Mushrooms

Serves 4

225 g/8 oz button mushrooms

30 ml/2 tbsp soy sauce

15 ml/1 tbsp rice wine or dry sherry

pinch of salt

few drops of tabasco sauce

few drops of sesame oil

Blanch the mushrooms in boiling water for 2 minutes then drain and pat dry. Place in a bowl and pour over the remaining ingredients. Toss together well and chill before serving.

Marinated Garlic Mushrooms

Serves 4

225 g/8 oz button mushrooms

3 cloves garlic, crushed

30 ml/2 tbsp soy sauce

30 ml/2 tbsp rice wine or dry sherry

15 ml/1 tbsp sesame oil

pinch of salt

Place the mushrooms and garlic in a colander, pour over boiling water and leave to stand for 3 minutes. Drain and pat dry thoroughly. Mix together the remaining ingredients, pour the marinade over the mushrooms and leave to marinate for 1 hour.

Prawns and Cauliflower

Serves 4

225 g/8 oz cauliflower florets

100 g/ 4 oz peeled prawns

15 ml/1 tbsp soy sauce

5 ml/1 tsp sesame oil

Part boil the cauliflower for about 5 minutes until tender but still crunchy. Mix with the prawns, sprinkle with soy sauce and sesame oil and toss together. Chill before serving.

Sesame Ham Sticks

225 g/8 oz ham, cut into strips

10 ml/2 tsp soy sauce

2.5 ml/½ tsp sesame oil

Arrange the ham on a serving plate. Mix the soy sauce and sesame oil, sprinkle over the ham and serve.

Cold Tofu

Serves 4

450 g/1 lb tofu, sliced

45 ml/3 tbsp soy sauce

45 ml/3 tbsp groundnut (peanut) oil

freshly ground pepper

Place the tofu, a few slices at a time, in a sieve and plunge into boiling water for 40 seconds then drain and arrange on a serving plate. Leave to cool. Mix together the soy sauce and oil, sprinkle over the tofu and serve sprinkled with pepper.

Chicken with Bacon

Serves 4

225 g/8 oz chicken, very thinly sliced
75 ml/5 tbsp soy sauce
15 ml/1 tbsp rice wine or dry sherry
1 clove garlic, crushed
15 ml/1 tbsp brown sugar
5 ml/1 tsp salt
5 ml/1 tsp minced ginger root
225 g/8 oz lean bacon, cubed
100 g/4 oz water chestnuts, very thinly sliced
30 ml/2 tbsp honey

Place the chicken in a bowl. Mix 45 ml/3 tbsp of soy sauce with the wine or sherry, garlic, sugar, salt and ginger, pour over the chicken and marinate for about 3 hours. Thread the chicken, bacon and chestnuts on to kebab skewers. Mix the remaining soy sauce with the honey and brush over the kebabs. Grill (broil) under a hot grill for about 10 minutes until cooked, turning frequently and brushing with more glaze as they cook.

Chicken and Banana Fries

Serves 4

2 cooked chicken breasts
2 firm bananas
6 slices bread
4 eggs
120 ml/4 fl oz/½ cup milk
50 g/2 oz/½ cup plain (all-purpose) flour
225 g/8 oz/4 cups fresh breadcrumbs
oil for deepfrying

Cut the chicken into 24 pieces. Peel the bananas and cut lengthways into quarters. Cut each quarter into thirds to give 24 pieces. Cut the crusts off the bread and cut it into quarters. Beat the eggs and milk and brush over one side of the bread. Place one piece of chicken and one piece of banana on the egg-coated side of each piece of bread. Coat the squares lightly in flour then dip in egg and coat with breadcrumbs. Dip again into the egg and breadcrumbs. Heat the oil and fry a few squares at a time until golden brown. Drain on kitchen paper before serving.

Chicken with Ginger and Mushrooms

Serves 4

225 g/8 oz chicken breast fillets
5 ml/1 tsp five-spice powder
15 ml/1 tbsp plain (all-purpose) flour
120 ml/4 fl oz/½ cup groundnut (peanut) oil
4 shallots, halved
1 clove garlic, sliced
1 slice ginger root, chopped
25 g/1 oz/¼ cup cashew nuts
5 ml/1 tsp honey
15 ml/1 tbsp rice flour
75 ml/5 tbsp rice wine or dry sherry
00 g/4 oz mushrooms, quartered
.5 ml/½ tsp turmeric
6 yellow chilli peppers, halved
5 ml/1 tsp soy sauce
juice of ½ lime
salt and pepper
4 crisp lettuce leaves

Cut the chicken breast diagonally across the grain into fine strips. Sprinkle with five-spice powder and coat lightly with flour. Heat 15 ml/1 tbsp oil and stir-fry the chicken until golden brown. Remove from the pan. Heat a little more oil and stir-fry the shallots, garlic, ginger and cashew nuts for 1 minute. Add the honey and stir round until the vegetables are coated. Sprinkle with flour then stir in the wine or sherry. Add the mushrooms, turmeric and chilli peppers and cook for 1 minute. Add the chicken, soy sauce, half the lime juice, salt and pepper and heat through. Remove from the pan and keep warm. Heat a little more oil, add the lettuce leaves and fry quickly, seasoning with salt and pepper and the remaining lime juice. Arrange the lettuce leaves on a warmed serving dish, spread the meat and vegetables on top and serve.

Chicken and Ham

Serves 4

225 g/8 oz chicken, very thinly sliced
75 ml/5 tbsp soy sauce
15 ml/1 tbsp rice wine or dry sherry
15 ml/1 tbsp brown sugar
5 ml/1 tsp minced ginger root
1 clove garlic, crushed
225 g/8 oz cooked ham, cubed
30 ml/2 tbsp honey

Place the chicken in a bowl with 45 ml/3 tbsp of soy sauce, the wine or sherry, sugar, ginger and garlic. Leave to marinate for 3 hours. Thread the chicken and ham on to kebab skewers. Mix the remaining soy sauce with the honey and brush over the kebabs. Grill (broil) under a hot grill for about 10 minutes, turning frequently and brushing with the glaze as they cook.

Grilled Chicken Livers

Serves 4

450 g/1 lb chicken livers
45 ml/3 tbsp soy sauce
15 ml/1 tbsp rice wine or dry sherry
15 ml/1 tbsp brown sugar
5 ml/1 tsp salt
5 ml/1 tsp minced ginger root
1 clove garlic, crushed

Parboil the chicken livers in boiling water for 2 minutes then drain well. Place in a bowl with all the remaining ingredients except the oil and marinate for about 3 hours. Thread the chicken livers on to kebab skewers and grill (broil) under a hot grill for about 8 minutes until golden brown.

Crab Balls with Water Chestnuts

Serves 4

450 g/1 lb crab meat, minced
100 g/4 oz water chestnuts, chopped
1 clove garlic, crushed
1 cm/½ in slice ginger root, minced
45 ml/3 tbsp cornflour (cornstarch)
30 ml/2 tbsp soy sauce
15 ml/1 tbsp rice wine or dry sherry
5 ml/1 tsp salt
5 ml/1 tsp sugar
3 eggs, beaten
oil for deep-frying

Mix together all the ingredients except the oil and shape into small balls. Heat the oil and deep-fry the crab balls until golden brown. Drain well before serving.

Dim Sum

Serves 4

100 g/4 oz peeled prawns, chopped

225 g/8 oz lean pork, finely chopped

50 g/2 oz Chinese cabbage, finely
    chopped

3 spring onions (scallions), chopped

1 egg, beaten

30 ml/2 tbsp cornflour (cornstarch)

10 ml/2 tsp soy sauce

5 ml/1 tsp sesame oil

5 ml/1 tsp oyster sauce

24 wonton skins (page 282)

oil for deep-frying

Mix together the prawns, pork, cabbage and spring onions. Mix in the egg, cornflour, soy sauce, sesame oil and oyster sauce. Place spoonfuls of the mixture on to the centre of each wonton skins. Gently press the wrappers around the filling, tucking the edges together but leaving the tops open. Heat the oil and fry the dim sums a few at a time until golden brown. Drain well and serve hot.

Ham and Chicken Rolls

Serves 4

2 chicken breasts

1 clove garlic, crushed

2.5 ml/½ tsp salt

2.5 ml/½ tsp five-spice powder

4 slices cooked ham

1 egg, beaten

30 ml/2 tbsp milk

25 g/1 oz/¼ cup plain (all-purpose)
    flour

4 egg roll skins (page 282)

oil for deep-frying

Slice the chicken breasts in half. Pound them until very thin. Mix the garlic, salt and five-spice powder and sprinkle over the chicken. Place a slice of ham on top of each piece of chicken and roll them up tightly. Mix the egg and milk. Coat the chicken pieces lightly with flour then dip in the egg mixture. Place each piece on an egg roll skin and brush the edges with beaten egg. Fold in the sides then roll together, pinching the edges to seal. Heat the oil and fry the rolls for about 5 minutes until golden brown and cooked through. Drain on kitchen paper then cut into thick diagonal slices to serve.

Baked Ham Turnovers

Serves 4

350 g/12 oz/3 cups plain (all-purpose)
    flour

175 g/6 oz/¾ cup butter

120 ml/4 fl oz/½ cup water

225 g/8 oz ham, chopped

100 g/4 oz bamboo shoots, chopped

2 spring onions (scallions), chopped

15 ml/1 tbsp soy sauce

30 ml/2 tbsp sesame seeds

Place the flour in a bowl and rub in the butter. Mix in the water to form a dough. Roll out the dough and cut into 5 cm/2in circles. Mix together all the remaining ingredients except the sesame seeds and place a spoonful on each circle. Brush the edges of the pastry with water and seal together. Brush the outsides with water and sprinkle with sesame seeds. Bake in a preheated oven at 180° C/350° F/gas mark 4 for 30 minutes.

Pseudo Smoked Fish

Serves 4

1 sea bass
3 slices ginger root, sliced
1 clove garlic, crushed
1 spring onion (scallion), thickly sliced
75 ml/5 tbsp soy sauce
30 ml/2 tbsp rice wine or dry sherry
2.5 ml/½ tsp ground anise
2.5 ml/½ tsp sesame oil
10 ml/2 tsp sugar
120 ml/4 fl oz/½ cup stock
oil for deep-frying
5 ml/1 tsp cornflour (cornstarch)

Trim the fish and cut it into 5 mm (¼ in) slices against the grain. Mix together the ginger, garlic, spring onion, 60ml/ 4tbsp of soy sauce, the sherry, anise and sesame oil. Pour over the fish and toss gently. Leave to stand for 2 hours, turning occasionally.

Drain the marinade into a pan and pat the fish dry on kitchen paper. Add the sugar, stock and remaining soy sauce to the marinade, bring to the boil and simmer for 1 minute. If the sauce needs to be thickened, mix the cornflour with a little cold water, stir it into the sauce and simmer, stirring, until the sauce thickens.

Meanwhile, heat the oil and deepfry the fish until golden brown. Drain well. Dip the pieces of fish in the marinade then arrange them on a warmed serving plate. Serve hot or cold.

Stuffed Mushrooms

Serves 4

12 large dried mushroom caps
225 g/8 oz crab meat
3 water chestnuts, minced
2 spring onions (scallions), finely chopped
1 egg white
15 ml/1 tbsp cornflour (cornstarch)
15 ml/1 tbsp soy sauce
15 ml/1 tbsp rice wine or dry sherry

Soak the mushrooms in warm water overnight. Squeeze dry. Mix together the remaining ingredients and use to fill the mushroom caps. Arrange on a steamer rack and steam for 40 minutes. Serve hot.

Oyster Sauce Mushrooms

Serves 4

| 10 dried Chinese mushrooms |
| 250 ml/8 fl oz/1 cup beef stock |
| 15 ml/1 tbsp cornflour (cornstarch) |
| 30 ml/2 tbsp oyster sauce |
| 5 ml/1 tsp rice wine or dry sherry |

Soak the mushrooms in warm water for 30 minutes then drain, reserving 250 ml/8 fl oz/1 cup of soaking liquid. Discard the stalks. Mix 60 ml/4 tbsp of the beef stock with the cornflour to a paste. Bring the remaining beef stock to the boil with the mushrooms and mushroom liquid, cover and simmer for 20 minutes. Remove the mushrooms from the liquid with a slotted spoon and arrange on a warm serving plate. Add the oyster sauce and sherry to the pan and simmer, stirring for 2 minutes. Stir in the cornflour paste and simmer, stir until the sauce thickens. Pour over the mushrooms and serve at once.

Pork and Lettuce Rolls

Serves 4

| 4 dried Chinese mushrooms |
| 15 ml/1 tbsp groundnut (peanut) oil |
| 225 g/8 oz lean pork, chopped |
| 100 g/4 oz bamboo shoots, chopped |
| 100 g/4 oz water chestnuts, chopped |
| 4 spring onions (scallions), chopped |
| 175 g/6 oz crab meat, flaked |
| 30 ml/2 tbsp rice wine or dry sherry |
| 15 ml/1 tbsp soy sauce |
| 10 ml/2 tsp oyster sauce |
| 10 ml/2 tsp sesame oil |
| 9 Chinese leaves |

Soak the mushrooms in warm water for 30 minutes then drain. Discard the stalks and chop the caps. Heat the oil and stir-fry the pork for 5 minutes. Add the mushrooms, bamboo shoots, water chestnuts, spring onions and crab meat and stir-fry for 2 minutes. Mix the wine or sherry, soy sauce, oyster sauce and sesame oil and stir it into the pan. Remove from the heat. Meanwhile, blanch the Chinese leaves in boiling water for 1 minute then drain. Place spoonfuls of the pork mixture on the centre of each leaf, fold over the sides then roll up to serve.

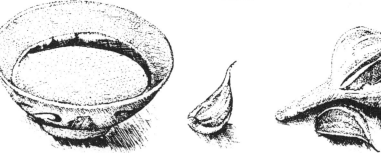

Pork and Chestnut Meatballs

Serves 4

450 g/1 lb minced (ground) pork

50 g/2 oz mushrooms, finely chopped

50 g/2 oz water chestnuts, finely
    chopped

1 clove garlic, crushed

1 egg, beaten

30 ml/2 tbsp soy sauce

15 ml/1 tbsp rice wine or dry sherry

5 ml/1 tsp minced ginger root

5 ml/1 tsp sugar

salt

30 ml/2 tbsp cornflour (cornstarch)

oil for deep-frying

Mix together all the ingredients except the cornflour and shape the mixture into small balls. Roll in the cornflour. Heat the oil and deep-fry the meatballs for about 10 minutes until golden brown. Drain well before serving.

Pork Dumplings

Serves 4–6

450 g/1 lb plain (all-purpose) flour

500 ml/17 fl oz/2 cups water

450 g/1 lb cooked pork, minced

225 g/8 oz peeled prawns, chopped

4 stalks celery, chopped

15 ml/1 tbsp soy sauce

15 ml/1 tbsp rice wine or dry sherry

15 ml/1 tbsp sesame oil

5 ml/1 tsp salt

2 spring onions (scallions), finely
    chopped

2 cloves garlic, crushed

1 slice ginger root, minced

Mix together the flour and water to a soft dough and knead well. Cover and leave to stand for 10 minutes. Roll out the dough as thinly as possible and cut into 5 cm/2 in circles. Mix together all the remaining ingredients. Place spoonfuls of the mixture on each circle, dampen the edges and seal into a semi-circle. Bring a saucepan of water to the boil then gently place the dumplings in the water. When the dumplings rise to the top add 150 ml/¼ pt/⅔ cup cold water then return the water to the boil. When the dumplings rise again, they are cooked.

Pork and Veal Rissoles

Serves 4

100 g/4 oz minced (ground) pork

100 g/4 oz minced (ground) veal

1 slice streaky bacon, minced (ground)

15 ml/1 tbsp soy sauce

salt and pepper

1 egg, beaten

30 ml/2 tbsp cornflour (cornstarch)

oil for deep-frying

Mix together the minced meats and bacon and season with salt and pepper. Bind together with the egg, shape into walnut sized balls and dust with cornflour. Heat the oil and deep-fry until golden brown. Drain well before serving.

Butterfly Prawns

Serves 4

450 g/1 lb large peeled prawns
15 ml/1 tbsp soy sauce
5 ml/1 tsp rice wine or dry sherry
5 ml/1 tsp minced ginger root
2.5 ml/½ tsp salt
2 eggs, beaten
30 ml/2 tbsp cornflour (cornstarch)
15 ml/1 tbsp plain (all-purpose) flour
oil for deep-frying

Slice the prawns halfway through the back and spread them out to form a butterfly shape. Mix together the soy sauce, wine or sherry, ginger and salt. Pour over the prawns and leave to marinate for 30 minutes. Remove from the marinade and pat dry. Beat the egg with the cornflour and flour to a batter and dip the prawns in the batter. Heat the oil and deepfry the prawns until golden brown. Drain well before serving.

Chinese Prawns

Serves 4

450 g/1 lb unpeeled prawns
30 ml/2 tbsp Worcestershire sauce
15 ml/1 tbsp soy sauce
15 ml/1 tbsp rice wine or dry sherry
15 ml/1 tbsp brown sugar

Place the prawns in a bowl. Mix together the remaining ingredients, pour over the prawns and leave to marinate for 30 minutes. Transfer to a baking tin and bake in a pre-heated oven at 150° C/300° F/ gas mark 2 for 25 minutes. Serve hot or cold in the shells for the guests to shell their own.

Prawn Crackers

Serves 4

100 g/4 oz prawn crackers
oil for deep-frying

Heat the oil until very hot. Add a handful of prawn crackers at a time and fry for a few seconds until they have puffed up. Remove from the oil and drain on kitchen paper while you continue to fry the crackers.

Crispy Prawns

Serves 4

450 g/1 lb peeled tiger prawns
15 ml/1 tbsp rice wine or dry sherry
10 ml/2 tsp soy sauce
5 ml/1 tsp five-spice powder
salt and pepper
90 ml/6 tbsp cornflour (cornstarch)
2 eggs, beaten
100g/4oz breadcrumbs
groundnut oil for deep-frying

Mix the prawns with the wine or sherry, soy sauce and five-spice powder and season with salt and pepper. Toss them in the cornflour then coat in beaten egg and breadcrumbs. Deep-fry in hot oil for a few minutes until lightly browned then drain and serve at once.

Prawns with Ginger Sauce

Serves 4

15 ml/1 tbsp soy sauce
5 ml/1 tsp rice wine or dry sherry
5 ml/1 tsp sesame oil
450 g/1 lb peeled prawns
30 ml/2 tbsp chopped fresh parsley
15 ml/1 tbsp wine vinegar
5 ml/1 tsp chopped ginger root

Mix together the soy sauce, wine or sherry and sesame oil. Pour over the prawns, cover and leave to marinate for 30 minutes. Grill the prawns for a few minutes until just cooked, basting with the marinade. Meanwhile, mix together the parsley, wine vinegar and ginger to serve with the prawns.

Prawn and Noodle Rolls

Serves 4

50 g/2 oz egg noodles, broken into pieces
15 ml/1 tbsp groundnut (peanut) oil
50 g/2 oz lean pork, finely chopped
100 g/4 oz mushrooms, chopped
3 spring onions (scallions), chopped
100 g/4 oz peeled prawns, chopped
15 ml/1 tbsp rice wine or dry sherry
salt and pepper
24 wonton skins (page 282)
1 egg, beaten
oil for deep-frying

Cook the noodles in boiling water for 5 minutes then drain and chop. Heat the oil and stir-fry the pork for 4 minutes. Add the mushrooms and onions and stir-fry for 2 minutes then remove from the heat. Mix in the prawns, wine or sherry and noodles and season to taste with salt and pepper. Place spoonfuls of the mixture on the centre of each wonton skin and brush the edges with beaten egg. Fold over the edges then roll up the wrappers, sealing the edges together. Heat the oil and deep-fry the rolls a few at a time for about 5 minutes until golden. Drain on kitchen paper before serving.

Prawn Toasts

Serves 4

2 eggs 450 g/1 lb peeled prawns, minced

15 ml/1 tbsp cornflour (cornstarch)

1 onion, finely chopped

30 ml/2 tbsp soy sauce

15 ml/1 tbsp rice wine or dry sherry

5 ml/1 tsp salt

5 ml/1 tsp minced ginger root

8 slices bread, cut into triangles

oil for deep-frying

Mix together 1 egg with all the remaining ingredients except the bread and oil. Spoon the mixture on to the bread triangles and press into a dome. Brush with the remaining egg. Heat about 5cm/2 in of oil and deep-fry the bread triangles until golden brown. Drain well before serving.

Pork and Prawn Wontons with Sweet and Sour Sauce

Serves 4

120 ml/4 fl oz/½ cup water

60 ml/4 tbsp wine vinegar

60 ml/4 tbsp brown sugar

30 ml/2 tbsp tomato purée (paste)

10 ml/2 tsp cornflour (cornstarch)

25 g/1 oz mushrooms, chopped

25 g/1 oz peeled prawns, chopped

50 g/2 oz lean pork, chopped

2 spring onions (scallions), chopped

5 ml/1 tsp soy sauce

2.5 ml/½ tsp grated ginger root

1 clove garlic, crushed

24 wonton skins (page 282)

oil for deep-frying

Mix together the water, wine vinegar, sugar, tomato purée and cornflour in a small saucepan. Bring to the boil, stirring continuously, then simmer for 1 minute. Remove from the heat and keep warm.

Mix the mushrooms, prawns, pork, spring onions, soy sauce, ginger and garlic. Place spoonfuls of the filling on each skin, brush the edges with water and press together to seal. Heat the oil and deep-fry the wontons a few at a time until golden brown. Drain on kitchen paper and serve hot with sweet and sour sauce.

Stock and Soups

Chicken stock is a basic in the Chinese kitchen, and if you make your own stock, you will get the finest results. It is very simple to do, but it does take a little time, so make stock in large quantities then freeze it in smaller portions to thaw and use as you need it.

If you do not have your own stock, you can use a good quality stock cube, although this will not have quite the same delicate flavour of a Chinese stock. Also you must be careful when seasoning the dish, as the resulting stock will be more salty than a home-made stock.

The wok is the perfect utensil in which to make your soups, but you can use any large saucepan.

Chicken Stock

Makes 2 litres/3½ pts/8½ cups

1 kg/2 lb cooked or raw bones of chicken
450 g/1 lb pork bones
1 cm/½ in piece ginger root
3 spring onions (scallions), sliced
1 clove garlic, crushed
5 ml/1 tsp salt
2.25 litres/4 pts/10 cups

Bring all the ingredients to the boil, cover and simmer for 15 minutes. Skim off any fat. Cover and simmer for 1½ hours. Strain, cool and skim. Freeze in small quantities or keep refrigerated and use within 2 days.

Bean Sprout and Pork Soup

Serves 4

450 g/1 lb pork, cubed
1.5 1/2½ pts/6 cups chicken stock
5 slices ginger root
350 g/12 oz bean sprouts
15 ml/1 tbsp salt

Blanch the pork in boiling water for 10 minutes then drain. Bring the stock to the boil and add the pork and ginger. Cover and simmer for 50 minutes. Add the bean sprouts and salt and simmer for 20 minutes.

Abalone and Mushroom Soup

Serves 4

60 ml/4 tbsp groundnut (peanut) oil
100 g/4 oz lean pork, cut into strips
225 g/8 oz canned abalone, cut into strips
100 g/4 oz mushrooms, sliced
2 stalks celery, sliced
50 g/2 oz ham, cut into strips
2 onions, sliced
1.5 l/2½ pts/6 cups water
30 ml/2 tbsp wine vinegar
45 ml/3 tbsp soy sauce
2 slices ginger root, chopped
salt and freshly ground pepper
15 ml/1 tbsp cornflour (cornstarch)
45 ml/3 tbsp water

Heat the oil and fry the pork, abalone, mushrooms, celery, ham and onions for 8 minutes. Add the water and wine vinegar, bring to the boil, cover and simmer for 20 minutes. Add the soy sauce, ginger, salt and pepper. Blend the cornflour to a paste with the water, stir it into the soup and simmer, stirring, for 5 minutes until the soup clears and thickens.

Chicken and Asparagus Soup

Serves 4

100 g/4 oz chicken, shredded
2 egg whites
2.5 ml/½ tsp salt
30 ml/2 tbsp cornflour (cornstarch)
225 g/8 oz asparagus, cut into 5 cm/2 in chunks
100 g/4 oz bean sprouts
1.5 l/2½ pts/6 cups chicken stock
100 g/4 oz button mushrooms

Mix the chicken with the egg whites, salt and cornflour and leave to stand for 30 minutes. Cook the chicken in boiling water for about 10 minutes until cooked through then drain well. Blanch the asparagus in boiling water for 2 minutes then drain. Blanch the bean sprouts in boiling water for 3 minutes then drain. Pour the stock into a large pan and add the chicken, asparagus, mushrooms and bean sprouts. Bring to the boil and season to taste with salt. Simmer for a few minutes to allow the flavours to develop and until the vegetables are tender but still crisp.

Beef Soup

Serves 4

225 g/8 oz minced (ground) beef
15 ml/1 tbsp soy sauce
15 ml/1 tbsp rice wine or dry sherry
15 ml/1 tbsp cornflour (cornstarch)
1.2 l/2 pts/5 cups chicken stock
5 ml/1 tsp chilli bean sauce
salt and pepper
2 eggs, beaten
6 spring onions (scallions), chopped

Mix the beef with the soy sauce, wine or sherry and cornflour. Add to the stock and gradually bring to the boil, stirring. Add the chilli bean sauce and season to taste with salt and pepper, cover and simmer for about 10 minutes, stirring occasionally. Stir in the eggs and serve sprinkled with the spring onions.

Beef and Chinese Leaves Soup

Serves 4

200 g/7 oz lean beef, cut into strips
15 ml/1 tbsp soy sauce
15 ml/1 tbsp groundnut (peanut) oil
1.5 l/2½ pts/6 cups beef stock
5 ml/1 tsp salt
2.5 ml/½ tsp sugar
½ head Chinese leaves, cut into chunks

Mix the beef with the soy sauce and oil and leave to marinate for 30 minutes, stirring occasionally. Bring the stock to the boil with the salt and sugar, add the Chinese leaves and simmer for about 10 minutes until almost cooked. Add the beef and simmer for a further 5 minutes.

Cabbage Soup

Serves 4

60 ml/4 tbsp groundnut (peanut) oil
2 onions, chopped
100 g/4 oz lean pork, cut into strips
225 g/8 oz Chinese cabbage, shredded
10 ml/2 tsp sugar
1.2 l/2 pts/5 cups chicken stock
45 ml/3 tbsp soy sauce
salt and pepper
15 ml/1 tbsp cornflour (cornstarch)

Heat the oil and fry the onions and pork until lightly browned. Add the cabbage and sugar and stir-fry for 5 minutes. Add the stock and soy sauce and season to taste with salt and pepper. Bring to the boil, cover and simmer gently for 20 minutes. Mix the cornflour with a little water, stir it into the soup and simmer, stirring, until the soup thickens and clears.

Piquant Beef Soup

Serves 4

45 ml/3 tbsp groundnut (peanut) oil
1 clove garlic, crushed
5 ml/1 tsp salt
225 g/8 oz minced (ground) beef
6 spring onions (scallions), cut into strips
1 red pepper, cut into strips
1 green pepper, cut into strips
225 g/8 oz cabbage, shredded
1 l/1¾ pts/4¼ cups beef stock
30 ml/2 tbsp plum sauce
30 ml/2 tbsp hoisin sauce
45 ml/3 tbsp soy sauce
2 pieces stem ginger, chopped
2 eggs
5 ml/1 tsp sesame oil
225 g/8 oz transparent noodles, soaked

Heat the oil and fry the garlic and salt until lightly browned. Add the beef and brown quickly. Add the vegetables and stir-fry until translucent. Add the stock, plum sauce, hoisin sauce, 30ml/2 tbsp of soy sauce and the ginger, bring to the boil simmer for 10 minutes. Beat the eggs with the sesame oil and remaining soy sauce. Add to the soup with the noodles and cook, stir, until the eggs form strands and the noodles are tender.

Celestial Soup

Serves 4

2 spring onions (scallions), minced
1 clove garlic, crushed
30 ml/2 tbsp chopped fresh parsley
5 ml/1 tsp salt
15 ml/1 tbsp groundnut (peanut) oil
30 ml/2 tbsp soy sauce
1.5 l/2½ pts/6 cups water

Mix together the spring onions, garlic, parsley, salt, oil and soy sauce. Bring to the water to the boil, pour over the spring onion mixture and leave to stand for 3 minutes.

Chicken and Bamboo Shoot Soup

Serves 4

2 chicken legs
30 ml/2 tbsp groundnut (peanut) oil
5 ml/1 tsp rice wine or dry sherry
1.5 l/2½ pts/6 cups chicken stock
3 spring onions, sliced
100 g/4 oz bamboo shoots, cut into chunks
5 ml/1 tsp minced ginger root
salt

Bone the chicken and cut the flesh into chunks. Heat the oil and fry the chicken until sealed on all sides. Add the stock, spring onions, bamboo shoots and ginger, bring to the boil and simmer for about 20 minutes until the chicken is tender. Season to taste with salt before serving.

Chicken and Corn Soup

Serves 4

1 litres/1¾ pts/4¼ cups chicken stock
100 g/4 oz chicken, minced
200 g/7 oz creamed sweetcorn
1 slice ham, chopped
2 eggs, beaten
15 ml/1 tbsp rice wine or dry sherry

Bring the stock and chicken to the boil, cover and simmer for 15 minutes. Add the sweetcorn and ham, cover and simmer for 5 minutes. Add the eggs and sherry, stirring slowly with a chop-stick so that the eggs form into threads. Remove from the heat, cover and leave to stand for 3 minutes before serving.

Chicken and Ginger Soup

Serves 4

4 dried Chinese mushrooms
1.5 l/2½ pts/6 cups water or chicken stock
225 g/8 oz chicken meat, cubed
10 slices ginger root
5 ml/1 tsp rice wine or dry sherry
salt

Soak the mushrooms in warm water for 30 minutes then drain. Discard the stalks. Bring the water or stock to the boil with the remaining ingredients and simmer gently for about 20 minutes until the chicken is cooked.

Chicken Soup with Chinese Mushrooms

Serves 4

25 g/1 oz Chinese dried mushrooms
100 g/4 oz chicken, shredded
50 g/2 oz bamboo shoots, shredded
30 ml/2 tbsp soy sauce
30 ml/2 tbsp rice wine or dry sherry
1.2 1/2 pts/5 cups chicken stock

Soak the mushrooms in warm water for 30 minutes then drain. Discard the stems and slice the caps. Blanch the mushrooms, chicken and bamboo shoots in boiling water for 30 seconds then drain. Place them in a bowl and stir in the soy sauce and wine or sherry. Leave to marinate for 1 hour. Bring the stock to the boil add the chicken mixture and the marinade. Stir well and simmer for a few minutes until the chicken is thoroughly cooked.

Chicken and Rice Soup

Serves 4

1 litre/1¾ pts/4¾ cups chicken
    stock (page 21)
225 g/8 oz/1 cup cooked long-grain rice
100 g/4 oz cooked chicken, cut into
    strips
1 onion, cut into wedges
5 ml/1 tsp soy sauce

Heat all the ingredients together gently until hot without allowing the soup to boil.

Chicken and Coconut Soup

Serves 4

350 g/12 oz chicken breast
salt
10 ml/2 tsp cornflour (cornstarch)
30 ml/2 tbsp groundnut (peanut) oil
1 green chilli pepper, chopped
1 l/1¾ pts/4¾ cups coconut milk
5 ml/1 tsp grated lemon rind
12 lychees
pinch of grated nutmeg
salt and freshly ground pepper
2 lemon balm leaves

Cut the chicken breast diagonally across the grain into strips. Sprinkle with salt and coat with cornflour. Heat 10 ml/2 tsp of oil in a wok, swirl round and pour it out. Repeat once more. Heat the remaining oil and stir-fry the chicken and chilli pepper for 1 minute. Add the coconut milk and bring to the boil. Add the lemon rind and simmer for 5 minutes. Add the lychees, season with nutmeg, salt and pepper and serve garnished with lemon balm.

Clam Soup

Serves 4

2 dried Chinese mushrooms
12 clams, soaked and scrubbed
1.5 l/2¼ pts/6 cups chicken stock
50g/2oz bamboo shoots, shredded
50 g/2 oz mangetout (snow peas), halved
2 spring onions (scallions), cut into rings
15 ml/1 tbsp rice wine or dry sherry
pinch of freshly ground pepper

Soak the mushrooms in warm water for 30 minutes then drain. Discard the stalks and halve the caps. Steam the clams for about 5 minutes until they open; discard any that remain closed. Remove the clams from their shells. Bring the stock to the boil and add the mushrooms, bamboo shoots, mangetout and spring onions. Simmer, uncovered, for 2 minutes. Add the clams, wine or sherry and pepper and simmer until heated through.

Egg Soup

Serves 4

1.2 l/2 pts/5 cups chicken stock
3 eggs, beaten
45 ml/3 tbsp soy sauce
salt and freshly ground pepper
4 spring onions (scallions), sliced

Bring the stock to the boil. Gradually whisk in the beaten eggs so that they separate into strands. Stir in the soy sauce and season to taste with salt and pepper. Serve garnished with spring onions.

Crab and Scallop Soup

Serves 4

4 dried Chinese mushrooms
15 ml/1 tbsp groundnut (peanut) oil
1 egg, beaten
1.5 l/2¼ pts/6 cups chicken stock
175 g/6 oz crab meat, flaked
100 g/4 oz shelled scallops, sliced
100 g/4 oz bamboo shoots, sliced
2 spring onions (scallions), chopped
1 slice ginger root, minced
a few cooked, peeled prawns (optional)
45 ml/3 tbsp cornflour (cornstarch)
90 ml/6 tbsp water
30 ml/2 tbsp rice wine or dry sherry
20 ml/4 tsp soy sauce
2 egg whites

Soak the mushrooms in warm water for 30 minutes then drain. Discard the stalks and slice the caps thinly. Heat the oil, add the egg and tilt the pan so that the egg covers the bottom. Cook until set then turn and cook the other side. Remove from the pan, roll up and cut into thin strips.

Bring the stock to the boil, add the mushrooms, egg strips, crab meat, scallops, bamboo shoots, spring onions, ginger and prawns, if using. Bring back to the boil. Mix the cornflour with 60 ml/4 tbsp of water, the wine or sherry and soy sauce and stir into soup. Simmer, stirring until the soup thickens. Beat the egg whites with the remaining water and drizzle the mixture slowly into the soup, stirring vigorously.

Crab Soup

Serves 4

90 ml/6 tbsp groundnut (peanut) oil
3 onions, chopped
225 g/8 oz white and brown crab meat
1 slice ginger root, minced
1.2 1/2 pts/5 cups chicken stock
150 ml/¼ pt/ cup rice wine or dry sherry
45 ml/3 tbsp soy sauce
salt and freshly ground pepper

Heat the oil and fry the onions until soft but not browned. Add the crab meat and ginger and stir-fry for 5 minutes. Add the stock, wine or sherry and soy sauce, season with salt and pepper. Bring to the boil then simmer for 5 minutes.

Fish Soup

Serves 4

225 g/8 oz fish fillets
1 slice ginger root, minced
15 ml/1 tbsp rice wine or dry sherry
30 ml/2 tbsp groundnut (peanut) oil
1.5 1/2¾ pts/6 cups fish stock

Cut the fish into thin strips against the grain. Mix the ginger, wine or sherry and oil, add the fish and toss gently. Leave to marinate for 30 minutes, turning occasionally. Bring the stock to the boil, add the fish and simmer gently for 3 minutes.

Fish and Lettuce Soup

Serves 4

225 g/8 oz white fish fillets
30 ml/2 tbsp plain (all-purpose) flour
salt and freshly ground pepper
90 ml/6 tbsp groundnut (peanut) oil
6 spring onions (scallions), sliced
100 g/4 oz lettuce, shredded
1.2 1/2 pts/5 cups water
10 ml/2 tsp finely chopped ginger root
150 ml/¼ pt/⅔ cup rice wine or dry sherry
30 ml/2 tbsp cornflour (cornstarch)
30 ml/2 tbsp chopped fresh parsley
10 ml/2 tsp lemon juice
30 ml/2 tbsp soy sauce

Cut the fish into thin strips then toss in seasoned flour. Heat the oil and fry the spring onions until soft. Add the lettuce and fry for 2 minutes. Add the fish and cook for 4 minutes. Add the water, ginger and wine or sherry, bring to the boil, cover and simmer for 5 minutes. Mix the cornflour with a little water then stir it into the soup. Simmer, stirring for a further 4 minutes until the soup clears then season with salt and pepper. Serve sprinkled with parsley, lemon juice and soy sauce.

Ginger Soup with Dumplings

Serves 4

5 cm/2 in piece ginger root, grated
350 g/12 oz brown sugar
1.5 l/2½ pts/7 cups water
225 g/8 oz/2 cups rice flour
2.5 ml/½ tsp salt
60 ml/4 tbsp water

Place the ginger, sugar and water in a pan and bring to the boil, stirring. Cover and simmer for about 20 minutes. Strain the soup and return it to the pan.

Meanwhile, place the flour and salt in a bowl and gradually knead in just enough water to make a thick dough. Roll it into small balls and drop the dumplings into the soup. Return the soup to the boil, cover and simmer for a further 6 minutes until the dumplings are cooked.

Hot and Sour Soup

Serves 4

8 Chinese dried mushrooms
1 litre/1¾ pts/4¼ cups chicken stock
100 g/4 oz chicken, cut into strips
100 g/4 oz bamboo shoots, cut into strips
100 g/4 oz tofu, cut into strips
15 ml/1 tbsp soy sauce
30 ml/2 tbsp wine vinegar
30 ml/2 tbsp cornflour (cornstarch)
2 eggs, beaten
a few drops sesame oil

Soak the mushrooms in warm water for 30 minutes then drain. Discard the stems and cut the caps into strips.

Bring the mushrooms, stock, chicken, bamboo shoots and tofu to the boil, cover and simmer for 10 minutes. Mix the soy sauce, wine vinegar and cornflour to a smooth paste, stir it into the soup and simmer for 2 minutes until the soup is translucent. Slowly add the eggs and sesame oil, stirring with a chopstick. Cover and leave to stand for 2 minutes before serving.

Mushroom Soup

Serves 4

15 dried Chinese mushrooms
1.5 l/2½ pts/6 cups chicken stock
5 ml/1 tsp salt

Soak the mushrooms in warm water for 30 minutes then drain, reserving the liquid. Discard the stalks and cut the caps in half if large and place in a large heatproof bowl. Stand the bowl on a rack in a steamer. Bring the stock to the boil, pour over the mushrooms then cover and steam for 1 hour over gently simmering water. Season to taste with salt and serve.

Mushroom and Cabbage Soup

Serves 4

25 g/1 oz Chinese dried mushrooms
15 ml/1 tbsp groundnut (peanut) oil
50 g/2 oz Chinese leaves, shredded
15 ml/1 tbsp rice wine or dry sherry
15 ml/1 tbsp soy sauce
1.2 l/2 pts/5 cups chicken or vegetable stock
salt and freshly ground pepper
5 ml/1 tsp sesame oil

Soak the mushrooms in warm water for 30 minutes then drain. Discard the stems and slice the caps. Heat the oil and stir-fry the mushrooms and Chinese leaves for 2 minutes until well coated. Stir in the wine or sherry and soy sauce then add the stock. Bring to the boil, season to taste with salt and pepper then simmer for 5 minutes. Sprinkle with sesame oil before serving.

Mushroom Egg Drop Soup

Serves 4

1 litre/1¾/ pts/4¾ cups chicken
   stock (page 21)
30 ml/2 tbsp cornflour (cornstarch)
100 g/4 oz mushrooms, sliced
1 slice onion, finely chopped
pinch of salt
3 drops sesame oil
2.5 ml/½ tsp soy sauce
1 egg, beaten

Mix a little stock with the cornflour then blend together all the ingredients except the egg. Bring to the boil, cover and simmer for 5 minutes. Add the egg, stirring with a chopstick so that the egg forms into threads. Remove from the heat and leave to stand for 2 minutes before serving.

Mushroom and Water Chestnut Soup

Serves 4

1 litre/1¾pts/4¾ cups vegetable
   stock or water
2 onions, finely chopped
5 ml/1 tsp rice wine or dry sherry
30 ml/2 tbsp soy sauce
225 g/8 oz button mushrooms
100 g/4 oz water chestnuts, sliced
100 g/4 oz bamboo shoots, sliced
few drops of sesame oil
2 lettuce leaves, cut into pieces
2 spring onions (scallions), cut into
   pieces

Bring the water, onions, wine or sherry and soy sauce to the boil, cover and simmer for 10 minutes. Add the mushrooms, water chestnuts and bamboo shoots, cover and simmer for 5 minutes. Stir in the sesame oil, lettuce leaves and spring onions, remove from the heat, cover and leave to stand for 1 minute before serving.

Pork and Mushroom Soup

Serves 4

60 ml/4 tbsp groundnut (peanut) oil
1 clove garlic, crushed
2 onions, sliced
225 g/8 oz lean pork, cut into strips
1 stick celery, chopped
50 g/2 oz mushrooms, sliced
2 carrots, sliced
1.2 l/2 pts/5 cups beef stock
15 ml/1 tbsp soy sauce
salt and freshly ground pepper
15 ml/1 tbsp cornflour (cornstarch)

Heat the oil and fry the garlic, onions and pork until the onions are soft and lightly browned. Add the celery, mushrooms and carrots, cover and simmer gently for 10 minutes. Bring the stock to the boil then add it to the pan with the soy sauce and season to taste with salt and pepper. Mix the cornflour with a little water then stir it into the pan and simmer, stirring, for about 5 minutes.

Pork and Watercress Soup

Serves 4

1.5 l/2½ pts/6 cups chicken stock
100 g/4 oz lean pork, cut into strips
3 stalks celery, diagonally sliced
2 spring onions (scallions), sliced
1 bunch watercress
5 ml/1 tsp salt

Bring the stock to the boil, add the pork and celery, cover and simmer for 15 minutes. Add the spring onions, watercress and salt and simmer, uncovered, for about 4 minutes.

Pork and Cucumber Soup

Serves 4

100 g/4 oz lean pork, thinly sliced
5 ml/1 tsp cornflour (cornstarch)
15 ml/1 tbsp soy sauce
15 ml/1 tbsp rice wine or dry sherry
1 cucumber
1.5 l/2½ pts/6 cups chicken stock
5 ml/1 tsp salt

Mix together the pork, cornflour, soy sauce and wine or sherry. Toss to coat the pork. Peel the cucumber and cut it in half lengthways then scoop out the seeds. Slice thickly. Bring the stock to the boil, add the pork, cover and simmer for 10 minutes. Stir in the cucumber and simmer for a few minutes until translucent. Stir in the salt and add a little more soy sauce, if liked.

Soup with Porkballs and Noodles

Serves 4

50 g/2 oz rice noodles
225 g/8 oz minced (ground) pork
5 ml/1 tsp cornflour (cornstarch)
2.5 ml/½ tsp salt
30 ml/2 tbsp water
1.5 l/2½ pts/6 cups chicken stock
1 spring onion (scallion), finely chopped
5 ml/1 tsp soy sauce

Place the noodles in cold water to soak while you prepare the meatballs. Mix together the pork, cornflour, a little salt and the water and shape into walnut sized balls. Bring a saucepan of water to a rolling boil, drop in the pork balls, cover and simmer for 5 minutes. Drain well and drain the noodles. Bring the stock to the boil, add the pork balls and noodles, cover and simmer for 5 minutes. Add the spring onion, soy sauce and remaining salt and simmer for a further 2 minutes.

Spinach and Tofu Soup

Serves 4

1.2 l/2 pts/5 cups chicken stock
200 g/7 oz canned tomatoes, drained and chopped
225 g/8 oz tofu, cubed
225 g/8 oz spinach, chopped
30 ml/2 tbsp soy sauce
5 ml/1 tsp brown sugar
salt and freshly ground pepper

Bring the stock to the boil then add the tomatoes, tofu and spinach and stir gently. Return to the boil and simmer for 5 minutes. Add the soy sauce and sugar and season to taste with salt and pepper. Simmer for 1 minute before serving.

Sweetcorn and Crab Soup

Serves 4

1.2 l/2 pts/5 cups chicken stock
200 g/7 oz sweetcorn
salt and freshly ground pepper
1 egg, beaten
200 g/7 oz crab meat, flaked
3 shallots, chopped

Bring the stock to the boil, add the sweetcorn season with salt and pepper. Simmer for 5 minutes. Just before serving, pour the eggs through a fork and swirl on top of the soup.

Serve sprinkled with crab meat and chopped shallots.

Szechuan Soup

Serves 4

4 dried Chinese mushrooms
1.5 l/2½ pts/6 cups chicken stock
75 ml/5 tbsp dry white wine
15 ml/1 tbsp soy sauce
2.5 ml/½ tsp chilli sauce
30 ml/2 tbsp cornflour (cornstarch)
60 ml/4 tbsp water
100 g/4 oz lean pork, cut into strips
50 g/2 oz cooked ham, cut into strips
1 red pepper, cut into strips
50 g/2 oz water chestnuts, sliced
10 ml/2 tsp wine vinegar
5 ml/1 tsp sesame oil
1 egg, beaten
100 g/4 oz peeled prawns
6 spring onions (scallions), chopped
175 g/6 oz tofu, cubed

Soak the mushrooms in warm water for 30 minutes then drain. Discard the stalks and slice the caps. Bring the stock, wine, soy sauce and chilli sauce to the boil, cover and simmer for 5 minutes. Blend the cornflour with half the water and stir it into the soup, stirring until the soup thickens. Add the mushrooms, pork, ham, pepper and water chestnuts and simmer for 5 minutes. Stir in the wine vinegar and sesame oil. Beat the egg with the remaining water and drizzle this into the soup, stirring vigorously. Add the prawns, spring onions and tofu and simmer for a few minutes to heat through.

Tofu Soup

Serves 4

1.5 1/2½ pts/6 cups chicken stock
225 g/8 oz tofu, cubed
5 ml/1 tsp salt
5 ml/1 tsp soy sauce

Bring the stock to the boil and add the tofu, salt and soy sauce. Simmer for a few minutes until the tofu is heated through.

Tofu and Fish Soup

Serves 4

225 g/8 oz white fish fillets, cut into strips
150 ml/¼ pt/⅔ cup rice wine or dry sherry
10 ml/2 tsp finely minced ginger root
45 ml/3 tbsp soy sauce
2.5 ml/½ tsp salt
60 ml/4 tbsp groundnut (peanut) oil
2 onions, chopped
100 g/4 oz mushrooms, sliced
1.2 1/2 pts/5 cups chicken stock
100 g/4 oz tofu, cubed
salt and freshly ground pepper

Place the fish in a bowl. Mix together the wine or sherry, ginger, soy sauce and salt and pour over the fish. Leave to marinate for 30 minutes. Heat the oil and fry the onion for 2 minutes. Add the mushrooms and continue to fry until the onions are soft but not browned. Add the fish and marinade, bring to the boil, cover and simmer for 5 minutes. Add the stock, bring back to the boil, cover and simmer for 15 minutes. Add the tofu and season to taste with salt and pep-per. Simmer until the tofu is cooked.

Tomato Soup

Serves 4

400 g/14 oz canned tomatoes, drained and chopped
1.2 1/2 pts/5 cups chicken stock
1 slice ginger root, minced
15 ml/1 tbsp soy sauce
15 ml/1 tbsp chilli bean sauce
10 ml/2 tsp sugar

Place all the ingredients in a pan and bring slowly to the boil, stirring occasionally. Simmer for about 10 minutes before serving.

Tomato and Spinach Soup

Serves 4

1.2 1/2 pts/5 cups chicken stock
225 g/8 oz canned chopped tomatoes
225 g/8 oz tofu, cubed
225 g/8 oz spinach
30 ml/2 tbsp soy sauce
salt and freshly ground pepper
2.5 ml/½ tsp sugar
2.5 ml/½ tsp rice wine or dry sherry

Bring the stock to the boil then add the tomatoes, tofu and spinach and simmer for 2 minutes. Add the remaining ingredients and simmer for 2 minutes then stir well and serve.

Turnip Soup

Serves 4

1 l/1¾pts/4¾ cups chicken stock

1 large turnip, thinly sliced

200 g/7 oz lean pork, thinly sliced

15 ml/1 tbsp soy sauce

60 ml/4 tbsp brandy

salt and freshly ground pepper

4 shallots, finely chopped

Bring the stock to the boil, add the turnip and pork, cover and simmer for 20 minutes until the turnip is tender and the meat cooked. Stir in the soy sauce and brandy season to taste. Simmer until hot serve sprinkled with shallots.

Vegetable Soup

Serves 4

6 Chinese dried mushrooms

1 litre/1¾ pts/4¾ cups vegetable stock

50 g/2 oz bamboo shoots, cut into strips

50 g/2 oz water chestnuts, sliced

8 mangetout (snow peas), sliced

5 ml/1 tsp soy sauce

Soak the mushrooms in warm water for 30 minutes then drain. Discard the stems and cut the caps into strips. Add them to the stock with the bamboo shoots and water chestnuts and bring to the boil, cover and simmer for 10 minutes. Add the mangetout and soy sauce, cover and simmer for 2 minutes. Leave to stand for 2 minutes before serving.

Vegetarian Soup

Serves 4

¼ white cabbage

2 carrots

3 stalks celery

2 spring onions (scallions)

30 ml/2 tbsp groundnut (peanut) oil

1.5 l/2¾ pts/6 cups water

15 ml/1 tbsp soy sauce

15 ml/1 tbsp rice wine or dry sherry

5 ml/1 tsp salt

freshly ground pepper

Cut the vegetables into strips. Heat the oil and fry the vegetables for 2 minutes until they begin to soften. Add the remaining ingredients, bring to the boil, cover and simmer for 15 minutes.

Watercress Soup

Serves 4

1 litre/1¾ pts/4¾ cups chicken stock (page 21)

1 onion, finely chopped

1 stick celery, finely chopped

225 g/8 oz watercress, roughly chopped

salt and freshly ground pepper

Bring the stock, onion and celery to the boil, cover and simmer for 15 minutes. Add the watercress, cover and simmer for 5 minutes. Season with salt and pepper.

Seafood

Fish and all kinds of seafood are popular in Chinese cooking and lend themselves particularly well to the quick cooking in a wok which is so popular and simple to do. Many of the recipes are interchangeable so you can use your favourite type of fish with any number of different sauces. The Chinese also use fish which are not available in the West, so we have suggested easily obtainable fish which suit the recipes.

Prawns are a particular favourite and can be used in all kinds of dishes. They are usually available cooked and peeled, in which case they only need heating through. If you can buy them uncooked, you will notice the difference in flavour. Simply blanch them briefly in boiling water or hot oil until they turn pink then continue with the recipe, or remove them from the pan and return them to heat through at the end of cooking.

Deep-Fried Fish with Vegetables

Serves 4

4 dried Chinese mushrooms

4 whole fish, cleaned and scaled

oil for deep-frying

30 ml/2 tbsp cornflour (cornstarch)

45 ml/3 tbsp groundnut (peanut) oil

100 g/4 oz bamboo shoots, cut into strips

50 g/2 oz water chestnuts, cut into strips

50 g/2 oz Chinese cabbage, shredded

2 slices ginger root, minced

30 ml/2 tbsp rice wine or dry sherry

30 ml/2 tbsp water

15 ml/1 tbsp soy sauce

5 ml/1 tsp sugar

120 ml/4 fl oz/½ cup fish stock

salt and freshly ground pepper

¼ head lettuce, shredded

15 ml/1 tbsp chopped flat-leaved parsley

Soak the mushrooms in warm water for 30 minutes then drain. Discard the stalks and slice the caps. Dust the fish in half cornflour and shake off any excess. Heat the oil and deep-fry the fish for about 12 minutes until cooked. Drain on kitchen paper and keep warm.

Heat the oil and stir-fry the mushrooms, bamboo shoots, water-chestnuts and cabbage for 3 minutes. Add the ginger, wine or sherry, 15 ml/1 tbsp of water, the soy sauce and sugar and stir-fry for 1 minute. Add the stock, salt and pepper, bring to the boil, cover and simmer for 3 minutes. Mix the cornflour with the remaining water, stir it into the pan and simmer, stirring, until the sauce thickens. Arrange the lettuce on a serving plate and place the fish on top. Pour over the vegetables and sauce and serve garnished with parsley.

Baked Whole Fish

Serves 4-6

1 large bass or similar fish
45 ml/3 tbsp cornflour (cornstarch)
45 ml/3 tbsp groundnut (peanut) oil
1 onion, chopped
2 cloves garlic, crushed
50 g/2 oz ham, cut into strips
100 g/4 oz peeled prawns
15 ml/1 tbsp soy sauce
15 ml/1 tbsp rice wine or dry sherry
5 ml/1 tsp sugar
5 ml/1 tsp salt

Coat the fish with cornflour. Heat the oil and fry the onion and garlic until lightly browned. Add the fish and fry until golden brown on both sides. Transfer the fish to a sheet of foil in a roasting tin and top with ham and prawns. Add the soy sauce, wine or sherry, sugar and salt to the pan and stir together well. Pour over the fish, close the foil over the top and bake in a preheated oven at 150°C/300°F/gas mark 2 for 20 minutes.

Braised Soy Fish

Serves 4

1 large bass or similar fish
salt
50 g/2 oz/½ cup plain (all-purpose)
   flour
60 ml/4 tbsp groundnut (peanut) oil
3 slices ginger root, minced
3 spring onions (scallions), minced
250 ml/8 fl oz/1 cup water
45 ml/3 tbsp soy sauce
15 ml/1 tbsp rice wine or dry sherry
2.5 ml/½ tsp sugar

Clean and scale the fish and score it diagonally on both sides. Sprinkle with salt and leave to stand for 10 minutes. Heat the oil and fry the fish until browned on both sides, turning once and basting with oil as you cook. Add the ginger, spring onions, water, soy sauce, wine or sherry and sugar, bring to the boil, cover and simmer for 20 minutes until the fish is cooked. Serve hot or cold.

Soy Fish with Oyster Sauce

Serves 4

1 large bass or similar fish
salt
60 ml/4 tbsp groundnut (peanut) oil
3 spring onions (scallions), minced
2 slices ginger root, minced
1 clove garlic, crushed
45 ml/3 tbsp oyster sauce
30 ml/2 tbsp soy sauce
5 ml/1 tsp sugar
250 ml/8 fl oz/1 cup fish stock

Clean and scale the fish and score diagonally a few times on each side. Sprinkle with salt and leave to stand for 10 minutes. Heat most of the oil and fry the fish until browned on both sides, turning once. Meanwhile, heat the remaining oil in a separate pan and fry the spring onions, ginger and garlic until lightly browned. Add the oyster sauce, soy sauce and sugar and stir-fry for 1 minute. Add the stock and bring to the boil. Pour the mixture into the browned fish, return to the boil, cover and simmer for about 15 minutes until the fish is cooked, turning once or twice during cooking.

Steamed Bass

Serves 4

1 large bass or similar fish
2.25 l/4 1/4 pts/10 cups water
3 slices ginger root, minced
15 ml/1 tbsp salt
15 ml/1 tbsp rice wine or dry sherry
30 ml/2 tbsp groundnut (peanut) oil

Clean and scale the fish and score both sides diagonally several times. Bring the water to a rolling boil in a large pan and add the remaining ingredients. Lower the fish into the water, cover tightly, turn off the heat and leave to stand for 30 minutes until the fish is cooked.

Braised Fish with Mushrooms

Serves 4

4 dried Chinese mushrooms
1 large carp or similar fish
salt
45 ml/3 tbsp groundnut (peanut) oil
2 spring onions (scallions), minced
1 slice ginger root, minced
3 cloves garlic, crushed
100 g/4 oz bamboo shoots, cut into strips
250 ml/8 fl oz/1 cup fish stock
30 ml/2 tbsp soy sauce
15 ml/1 tbsp rice wine or dry sherry
2.5 ml/½ tsp sugar

Soak the mushrooms in warm water for 30 minutes then drain. Discard the stalks and slice the caps. Score the fish diagonally a few times on both sides, sprinkle with salt and leave to stand for 10 minutes. Heat the oil and fry the fish until lightly browned on both sides. Add the spring onions, ginger and garlic and fry for 2 minutes. Add the remaining ingredients, bring to the boil, cover and simmer for 15 minutes until the fish is cooked, turning once or twice and stirring occasionally.

Sweet and Sour Fish

Serves 4

1 large bass or similar fish
1 egg, beaten
50 g/2 oz cornflour (cornstarch)
oil for frying
For the sauce:
15 ml/1 tbsp groundnut (peanut) oil
1 green pepper, cut into strips
100 g/4 oz canned pineapple chunks in syrup
1 onion, cut into wedges
100 g/4 oz/½ cup brown sugar
60 ml/4 tbsp chicken stock
60 ml/4 tbsp wine vinegar
15 ml/1 tbsp tomato purée (paste)
15 ml/1 tbsp cornflour (cornstarch)
15 ml/1 tbsp soy sauce
3 spring onions (scallions), chopped

Clean the fish and remove the fins and head if you prefer. Coat it in beaten egg then in cornflour. Heat the oil and fry the fish until cooked through. Drain well and keep warm.

To make the sauce, heat the oil and fry the pepper, drained pineapple and onion for 4 minutes. Add 30 ml/2 tbsp of the pineapple syrup, the sugar, stock, wine vinegar, tomato purée, cornflour and soy sauce and bring to the boil, stirring. Simmer, stirring, until the sauce clears and thickens. Pour over the fish and serve sprinkled with spring onions.

Pork-Stuffed Fish

Serves 4

| 1 large carp or similar fish |
| salt |
| 100 g/4 oz minced (ground) pork |
| 1 spring onion (scallion), minced |
| 4 slices ginger root, minced |
| 15 ml/1 tbsp cornflour (cornstarch) |
| 60 ml/4 tbsp soy sauce |
| 15 ml/1 tbsp rice wine or dry sherry |
| 5 ml/1 tsp sugar |
| 75 ml/5 tbsp groundnut (peanut) oil |
| 2 cloves garlic, crushed |
| 1 onion, sliced |
| 300 ml/½ pt/1¼ cups water |

Clean and scale the fish and sprinkle with salt. Mix the pork, spring onion, a little of the ginger, the cornflour, 15 ml/1 tbsp of soy sauce, the wine or sherry and sugar and use to stuff the fish. Heat the oil and fry the fish until lightly browned on both sides then remove it from the pan and drain off most of the oil. Add the garlic and remaining ginger and stir-fry until lightly browned. Add the remaining soy sauce and the water, bring to the boil and simmer for 2 minutes. Return the fish to the pan, cover and simmer for about 30 minutes until the fish is cooked, turning once or twice.

Braised Spiced Carp

Serves 4

| 1 large carp or similar fish |
| 150 ml/¼ pt/⅔ cup groundnut (peanut) oil |
| 15 ml/1 tbsp sugar |
| 2 cloves garlic, finely chopped |
| 100 g/4 oz bamboo shoots, sliced |
| 150 ml/¼ pt/⅔ cup fish stock |
| 15 ml/1 tbsp rice wine or dry sherry |
| 15 ml/1 tbsp soy sauce |
| 2 spring onions (scallions), chopped |
| 1 slice ginger root, chopped |
| 15 ml/1 tbsp wine vinegar |
| salt |

Clean and scale the fish and soak it for several hours in cold water. Drain and pat dry then score each side several times. Heat the oil and fry the fish on both sides until firm. Remove from the pan and pour off and reserve all but 30 ml/2 tbsp of the oil. Add the sugar to the pan and stir until it darkens. Add the garlic and bamboo shoots and stir well. Add the remaining ingredients, bring to the boil, then return the fish to the pan, cover and simmer gently for about 15 minutes until the fish is cooked. Place the fish on a warmed serving plate and strain the sauce over the top.

Sweet and Sour Carp

Serves 4

1 large carp or similar fish

300 g/11 oz ¼ cup cornflour
    (cornstarch)

250 ml/8 fl oz/1 cup vegetable oil

30 ml/2 tbsp soy sauce

5 ml/1 tsp salt

150 g/5 oz/⅔ cup sugar

75 ml/5 tbsp wine vinegar

15 ml/1 tbsp rice wine or dry sherry

3 spring onions (scallions), finely
    chopped

1 slice ginger root, finely chopped

250 ml/8 fl oz/1 cup boiling water

Clean and scale the fish and soak it for several hours in cold water. Drain and pat dry then score each side several times. Reserve 30 ml/2 tbsp of cornflour then gradually mix enough water into the remaining cornflour to make a stiff batter. Coat the fish in the batter. Heat the oil until very hot and deep-fry the fish until crisp on the outside then turn down the heat and continue to fry until the fish is tender. Meanwhile, mix together the remaining cornflour, the soy sauce, salt, sugar, wine vinegar, wine or sherry, spring onions and ginger. When the fish is cooked, transfer it to a warm serving plate. Add the sauce mixture and the water to the oil and bring to the boil, stirring well until the sauce thickens. Pour over the fish and serve immediately.

Carp with Tofu

Serves 4

1 carp

60 ml/4 tbsp groundnut (peanut) oil

225 g/8 oz tofu, cubed

2 spring onions (scallions), finely
    chopped

1 clove garlic, finely chopped

2 slices ginger root, finely chopped

15 ml/1 tbsp chilli sauce

30 ml/2 tbsp soy sauce

500 ml/16 fl oz/2 cups stock

30 ml/2 tbsp rice wine or dry sherry

15 ml/1 tbsp cornflour (cornstarch)

30 ml/2 tbsp water

Trim, scale and clean the fish and score 3 lines diagonally on each side. Heat the oil and fry the tofu gently until golden brown. Remove from the pan and drain well. Add the fish to the pan and fry until golden brown then remove from the pan. Pour off all but 15 ml/1 tbsp of oil then stir-fry the spring onions, garlic and ginger for 30 seconds. Add the chilli sauce, soy sauce, stock and wine and bring to the boil. Carefully add the fish to the pan with the tofu and simmer, uncovered, for about 10 minutes until the fish is cooked and the sauce reduced. Transfer the fish to a warmed serving plate and spoon the tofu on top. Blend the cornflour and water to a paste, stir it into the sauce and simmer, stirring, until the sauce thickens slightly. Spoon over the fish and serve at once.

Almond Fish Rolls

Serves 4

100 g/4 oz/1 cup almonds
450 g/1 lb cod fillets
4 slices smoked ham
1 spring onion (scallion), minced
1 slice ginger root, minced
5 ml/1 tsp cornflour (cornstarch)
5 ml/1 tsp sugar
2.5 ml/½ tsp salt
15 ml/1 tbsp soy sauce
5 ml/1 tbsp rice wine or dry sherry
1 egg, lightly beaten
oil for deep-frying
1 lemon, cut into wedges

Blanch the almonds in boiling water for 5 minutes then drain and mince. Cut the fish into 9 cm/3½ in squares and the ham into 5cm/2 in squares. Mix the spring onion, ginger, cornflour, sugar, salt, soy sauce, wine or sherry and egg. Dip the fish in the mixture then lay the fish on a work surface. Coat the top with almonds then lay a slice of ham on top. Roll up the fish and tie with cook's string. Heat the oil and fry the fish rolls for a few minutes until golden brown. Drain on kitchen paper and serve with lemon.

Cod with Bamboo Shoots

Serves 4

4 dried Chinese mushrooms
900 g/2 lb cod fillets, cubed
30 ml/2 tbsp cornflour (cornstarch)
oil for deep-frying
30 ml/2 tbsp groundnut (peanut) oil
1 spring onion (scallion), sliced
1 slice ginger root, minced
salt
100 g/4 oz bamboo shoots, sliced
120 ml/4 fl oz/½ cup fish stock
15 ml/1 tbsp soy sauce
45 ml/3 tbsp water

Soak the mushrooms in warm water for 30 minutes then drain. Discard the stalks and slice the caps. Dust the fish with half the cornflour. Heat the oil and deep-fry the fish until golden brown. Drain on kitchen paper and keep warm.

Meanwhile, heat the oil and fry the spring onion, ginger and salt until lightly browned. Add the bamboo shoots and stir-fry for 3 minutes. Add the stock and soy sauce, bring to the boil and simmer for 3 minutes. Mix the remaining cornflour to a paste with the water, stir into the pan and simmer, stirring, until the sauce thickens. Pour over the fish and serve at once.

Fish with Bean Sprouts

Serves 4

450 g/1 lb bean sprouts
45 ml/3 tbsp groundnut (peanut) oil
5 ml/1 tsp salt
3 slices ginger root, minced
450 g/1 lb fish fillets, sliced
4 spring onions (scallions), sliced
15 ml/1 tbsp soy sauce
60 ml/4 tbsp fish stock
10 ml/2 tsp cornflour (cornstarch)
15 ml/1 tbsp water

Blanch the bean sprouts in boiling water for 4 minutes then drain well. Heat half the oil and fry the salt and ginger for 1 minute. Add the fish and fry until lightly browned then remove it from the pan. Heat the remaining oil and fry the spring onions for 1 minute. Add the soy sauce and stock and bring to the boil. Return the fish to the pan, cover and simmer for 2 minutes until the fish is cooked. Mix the cornflour and water to a paste, stir into the pan and simmer, stirring, until the sauce clears and thickens.

Fish Fillets in Brown Sauce

Serves 4

450 g/1 lb cod fillets, thickly sliced
30 ml/2 tbsp rice wine or dry sherry
30 ml/2 tbsp soy sauce
3 spring onions (scallions), finely
    chopped
1 slice ginger root, finely chopped
5 ml/1 tsp salt
5 ml/1 tsp sesame oil
30 ml/2 tbsp cornflour (cornstarch)
3 eggs, beaten
90 ml/6 tbsp groundnut (peanut) oil
90 ml/6 tbsp fish stock

Place the fish fillets in a bowl. Mix together the wine or sherry, soy sauce, spring onions, ginger, salt and sesame oil, pour over the fish, cover and leave to marinate for 30 minutes. Remove the fish from the marinade and toss in the cornflour then dip in the beaten egg. Heat the oil and fry the fish until golden brown on the outside. Pour off the oil and stir in the stock and any remaining marinade. Bring to the boil and simmer gently for about 5 minutes until the fish is cooked.

Chinese Fish Cakes

Serves 4

450 g/1 lb minced (ground) cod

2 spring onions (scallions), finely chopped

1 clove garlic, crushed

5 ml/1 tsp salt

5 ml/1 tsp sugar

5 ml/1 tsp soy sauce

45 ml/3 tbsp vegetable oil

15 ml/1 tbsp cornflour (cornstarch)

Mix together the cod, spring onions, garlic, salt, sugar, soy sauce and 10 ml/2 tsp of oil. Knead together thoroughly, sprinkling with a little cornflour from time to time until the mixture is soft and elastic. Shape into 4 fish cakes. Heat the oil and fry the fish cakes for about 10 minutes until golden, pressing them flat as they cook. Serve hot or cold.

Crispy-Fried Fish

Serves 4

450 g/1 lb fish fillets, cut into strips

30 ml/2 tbsp rice wine or dry sherry

salt and freshly ground pepper

45 ml/3 tbsp cornflour (cornstarch)

1 egg white, lightly beaten

oil for deep-frying

Toss the fish in the wine or sherry and season with salt and pepper. Dust lightly with cornflour. Beat the remaining cornflour into the egg white until stiff then dip the fish in the batter. Heat the oil and deep-fry the fish strips for a few minutes until golden brown.

Deep-Fried Cod

Serves 4

900 g/2 lb cod fillets, cubed

salt and freshly ground pepper

2 eggs, beaten

100 g/4 oz/1 cup plain (all-purpose) flour

oil for deep-frying

1 lemon, cut into wedges

Season the cod with salt and pepper. Beat the eggs and flour to a batter and season with salt. Dip the fish in the batter. Heat the oil and deep-fry the fish for a few minutes until golden brown and cooked through. Drain on kitchen paper and serve with lemon wedges.

Five-Spice Fish

Serves 4

4 cod fillets

5 ml/1 tsp five-spice powder

5 ml/1 tsp salt

30 ml/2 tbsp groundnut (peanut) oil

2 cloves garlic, crushed

2.5 ml/1 in root ginger, minced

30 ml/2 tbsp rice wine or dry sherry

15 ml/1 tbsp soy sauce

few drops of sesame oil

Rub the fish with the five-spice powder and salt. Heat the oil and fry the fish until lightly browned on both sides. Remove from the pan and add the remaining ingredients. Heat through, stirring, then return the fish to the pan and reheat gently before serving.

Fragrant Fish Sticks

Serves 4

30 ml/2 tbsp rice wine or dry sherry
1 spring onion (scallion), finely chopped
2 eggs, beaten
10 ml/2 tsp curry powder
5 ml/1 tsp salt
450 g/1 lb white fish fillets, cut into strips
100 g/4 oz breadcrumbs
oil for deep-frying

Mix together the wine or sherry, spring onion, eggs, curry powder and salt. Dip the fish into the mixture so that the pieces are evenly coated then press them into the breadcrumbs. Heat the oil and deep-fry the fish for a few minutes until crisp and golden brown. Drain well and serve immediately.

Fish with Gherkins

Serves 4

4 white fish fillets
75 g/3 oz small gherkins
2 spring onions (scallions)
2 slices ginger root
30 ml/2 tbsp water
5 ml/1 tsp groundnut (peanut) oil
2.5 ml/½ tsp salt
2.5 ml/½ tsp rice wine or dry sherry

Place the fish on a heatproof plate and sprinkle with the remaining ingredients. Place on a rack in a steamer, cover and steam for about 15 minutes over boiling water until the fish is tender. Transfer to a warmed serving plate, discard the ginger and spring onions and serve.

Ginger-Spiced Cod

Serves 4

225 g/8 oz tomato purée (paste)
30 ml/2 tbsp rice wine or dry sherry
15 ml/1 tbsp grated ginger root
15 ml/1 tbsp chilli sauce
15 ml/1 tbsp water
15 ml/1 tbsp soy sauce
10 ml/2 tsp sugar
3 cloves garlic, crushed
100 g/4 oz/1 cup plain (all-purpose) flour
75 ml/5 tbsp cornflour (cornstarch)
175 ml/6 fl oz/¾ cup water
1 egg white
2.5 ml/½ tsp salt
oil for deep-frying
450 g/1 lb cod fillets, skinned and cubed

To make the sauce, mix together the tomato purée, wine or sherry, ginger, chilli sauce, water, soy sauce, sugar and garlic. Bring to the boil then simmer, stirring, for 4 minutes.

Beat together the flour, cornflour, water, egg white and salt until smooth. Heat the oil. Dip the fish pieces in the batter and fry for about 5 minutes until cooked through and golden brown. Drain on kitchen paper. Drain off all the oil and return the fish and sauce to the pan. Reheat gently for about 3 minutes until the fish is completely coated in sauce.

Cod with Mandarin Sauce

Serves 4

| 675 g/1½ lb cod fillets, cut into strips |
| 30 ml/2 tbsp cornflour (cornstarch) |
| 60 ml/4 tbsp groundnut (peanut) oil |
| 1 spring onion (scallion), chopped |
| 2 cloves garlic, crushed |
| 1 slice ginger root, minced |
| 100 g/4 oz mushrooms, sliced |
| 50 g/2 oz bamboo shoots, cut into strips |
| 120 ml/4 fl oz/½ cup soy sauce |
| 30 ml/2 tbsp rice wine or dry sherry |
| 15 ml/1 tbsp brown sugar |
| 5 ml/1 tsp salt |
| 250 ml/8 fl oz/1 cup chicken stock |

Dip the fish in the cornflour until lightly coated. Heat the oil and fry the fish until golden brown on both sides. Remove it from the pan. Add the spring onion, garlic and ginger and stir-fry until lightly browned. Add the mushrooms and bamboo shoots and stir-fry for 2 minutes. Add the remaining ingredients and bring to the boil, stirring. Return the fish to the pan, cover and simmer for 20 minutes.

Fish with Pineapple

Serves 4

| 450 g/1 lb fish fillets |
| 2 spring onions (scallions), minced |
| 30 ml/2 tbsp soy sauce |
| 15 ml/1 tbsp rice wine or dry sherry |
| 2.5 ml/½ tsp salt |
| 2 eggs, lightly beaten |
| 15 ml/1 tbsp cornflour (cornstarch) |
| 45 ml/3 tbsp groundnut (peanut) oil |
| 225 g/8 oz canned pineapple chunks in juice |

Cut the fish into 2.5 cm/1 in strips against the grain and place in a bowl. Add the spring onions, soy sauce, wine or sherry and salt, toss well and leave to stand for 30 minutes. Drain the fish, discarding the marinade. Beat the eggs and cornflour to a batter and dip the fish in the batter to coat, draining off any excess. Heat the oil and fry the fish until lightly browned on both sides. Reduce the heat and continue to cook until tender. Meanwhile, mix 60 ml/4 tbsp of the pineapple juice with any remaining batter and the pineapple chunks. Place in a pan over a gentle heat and simmer until heated through, stirring continuously. Arrange the cooked fish on a warmed serving plate and pour over the sauce to serve.

Fish Rolls with Pork

Serves 4

450 g/1 lb fish fillets
100 g/4 oz cooked pork, minced (ground)
30 ml/2 tbsp rice wine or dry sherry
15 ml/1 tbsp sugar
oil for deep-frying
120 ml/4 fl oz/½ cup fish stock
3 spring onions (scallions), minced
1 slice ginger root, minced
15 ml/1 tbsp soy sauce
15 ml/1 tbsp cornflour (cornstarch)
45 ml/3 tbsp water

Cut the fish into 9 cm/3½ in squares. Mix the pork with the wine or sherry and half the sugar, spread over the fish squares, roll them up and secure with string. Heat the oil and deep-fry the fish until golden brown. Drain on kitchen paper. Meanwhile, heat the stock and add the spring onions, ginger, soy sauce and remaining sugar. Bring to the boil and simmer for 4 minutes. Mix the cornflour and water to a paste, stir into the pan and simmer, stirring, until the sauce clears and thickens. Pour over the fish and serve at once.

Quick-Fried Fish

Serves 4

450 g/1 lb cod fillets, cut into strips
salt
soy sauce
oil for deep-frying

Sprinkle the fish with salt and soy sauce and leave to stand for 10 minutes. Heat the oil and deep-fry the fish for a few minutes until lightly golden. Drain on kitchen paper and sprinkle generously with soy sauce before serving.

Fish in Rice Wine

Serves 4

400 ml/14 fl oz/1¾ cups rice wine or dry sherry
120 ml/4 fl oz/½ cup water
30 ml/2 tbsp soy sauce
5 ml/1 tsp sugar
salt and freshly ground pepper
10 ml/2 tsp cornflour (cornstarch)
15 ml/1 tbsp water
450 g/1 lb cod fillets
5 ml/1 tsp sesame oil
2 spring onions (scallions), chopped

Bring the wine, water, soy sauce, sugar, salt and pepper to the boil and boil until reduced by half. Mix the cornflour to a paste with the water, stir it into the pan and simmer, stirring, for 2 minutes. Season the fish with salt and sprinkle with sesame oil. Add to the pan and simmer very gently for about 8 minutes until cooked. Serve sprinkled with spring onions.

Sesame Seed Fish

Serves 4

450 g/1 lb fish fillets, cut into strips

1 onion, chopped

2 slices ginger root, minced

120 ml/4 fl oz/½ cup rice wine or
    dry sherry

10 ml/2 tsp brown sugar

2.5 ml/½ tsp salt

1 egg, lightly beaten

15 ml/1 tbsp cornflour (cornstarch)

45 ml/3 tbsp plain (all-purpose) flour

60 ml/6 tbsp sesame seeds

oil for deep-frying

Place the fish in a bowl. Mix together the onion, ginger, wine or sherry, sugar and salt, add to the fish and leave to marinate for 30 minutes, turning occasionally. Beat the egg, cornflour and flour to make a batter. Dip the fish in the batter then press into the sesame seeds. Heat the oil and deep-fry the fish strips for about 1 minute until golden and crispy.

Steamed Fish Balls

Serves 4

450 g/1 lb minced (ground) cod

1 egg, lightly beaten

1 slice ginger root, minced

2.5 ml/½ tsp salt

pinch of freshly ground pepper

15 ml/1 tbsp cornflour (cornstarch)

15 ml/1 tbsp rice wine or dry sherry

Mix all the ingredients together well and shape into walnut-sized balls. Dust with a little flour if necessary. Arrange in a shallow ovenproof dish.

Stand the dish on a rack in a steamer, cover and steam over gently simmering water for about 10 minutes until cooked.

Marinated Sweet and Sour Fish

Serves 4

450 g/1 lb fish fillets, cut into chunks

1 onion, chopped

3 slices ginger root, minced

5 ml/1 tsp soy sauce

salt and freshly ground pepper

30 ml/2 tbsp cornflour (cornstarch)

oil for deep-frying

sweet and sour sauce (page 327)

Place the fish in a bowl. Mix together the onion, ginger, soy sauce, salt and pepper, add to the fish, cover and leave to stand for 1 hour, turning occasionally. Remove the fish from the marinade and dust with cornflour. Heat the oil and deep-fry the fish until crisp and golden brown. Drain on kitchen paper and arrange on a warmed serving plate. Meanwhile, prepare the sauce and pour over the fish to serve.

Braised Fish with Tofu

Serves 4

60 ml/4 tbsp groundnut (peanut) oil
450 g/1 lb fish steaks
2 spring onions (scallions), minced
1 clove garlic, crushed
15 ml/1 tbsp soy sauce
15 ml/1 tbsp rice wine or dry sherry
5 ml/1 tsp salt
120 ml/4 fl oz/½ cup water
225 g/8 oz tofu, cubed

Heat the oil and fry the fish until lightly browned on both sides. Add the spring onions and garlic and fry for 30 seconds. Add the soy sauce, wine or sherry, salt and water, bring to the boil, cover and simmer for 10 minutes. Add the tofu, cover again and simmer for a further 10 minutes or until the fish is cooked.

Fish with Vinegar Sauce

Serves 4

450 g/1 lb fish fillets, cut into strips
salt and freshly ground pepper
1 egg white, lightly beaten
45 ml/3 tbsp cornflour (cornstarch)
15 ml/1 tbsp rice wine or dry sherry
oil for deep-frying
250 ml/8 fl oz/1 cup fish stock
15 ml/1 tbsp brown sugar
15 ml/1 tbsp wine vinegar
2 slices root ginger, minced
2 spring onions (scallions), minced

Season the fish with a little salt and pepper. Beat the egg white with 30 ml/2 tbsp of cornflour and the wine or sherry. Toss the fish in the batter until coated. Heat the oil and deep-fry the fish for a few minutes until golden brown. Drain on kitchen paper.

Meanwhile, bring the stock, sugar and wine vinegar to the boil. Add the ginger and spring onion and simmer for 3 minutes. Blend the remaining cornflour to a paste with a little water, stir it into the pan and simmer, stirring, until the sauce clears and thickens. Pour over the fish to serve.

Deep-Fried Eel

Serves 4

450 g/1 lb eel
250 ml/8 fl oz/1 cup groundnut (peanut) oil
30 ml/2 tbsp dark soy sauce
30 ml/2 tbsp rice wine or dry sherry
15 ml/1 tbsp brown sugar
dash of sesame oil

Skin the eel and cut it into chunks. Heat the oil and fry the eel until golden. Remove from the pan and drain. Pour off all but 30 ml/2 tbsp of oil. Reheat the oil and add the soy sauce, wine or sherry and sugar. Heat through then add the eel and stir-fry until the eel is well coated and almost all the liquid has evaporated. Sprinkle with sesame oil and serve.

Dry-Cooked Eel

Serves 4

5 dried Chinese mushrooms
3 spring onions (scallions)
30 ml/2 tbsp groundnut (peanut) oil
20 cloves garlic
6 slices ginger root
10 water chestnuts
900 g/2 lb eels
30 ml/2 tbsp soy sauce
15 ml/1 tbsp brown sugar
15 ml/1 tbsp rice wine or dry sherry
450 ml/¾ pt/2 cups water
15 ml/1 tbsp cornflour (cornstarch)
45 ml/3 tbsp water
5 ml/1 tsp sesame oil

Soak the mushrooms in warm water for 30 minutes then drain and discard the stalks. Cut 1 spring onion into chunks and chop the other. Heat the oil and fry the mushrooms, spring onion chunks, garlic, ginger and chestnuts for 30 seconds. Add the eels and stir-fry for 1 minute. Add the soy sauce, sugar, wine or sherry and water, bring to the boil, cover and simmer gently for 1½ hours, adding a little water during cooking if necessary. Blend the cornflour and water to a paste, stir into the pan and simmer, stirring, until the sauce thickens. Serve sprinkled with sesame oil and the chopped spring onions.

Eel with Celery

Serves 4

350 g/12 oz eel
6 stalks celery
30 ml/2 tbsp groundnut (peanut) oil
2 spring onions (scallions), chopped
1 slice ginger root, minced
30 ml/2 tbsp water
5 ml/1 tsp sugar
5 ml/1 tsp rice wine or dry sherry
5 ml/1 tsp soy sauce
freshly ground pepper
30 ml/2 tbsp chopped fresh parsley

Skin and cut the eel into strips. Cut the celery into strips. Heat the oil and fry the spring onions and ginger for 30 seconds. Add the eel and stir-fry for 30 seconds. Add the celery and stir-fry for 30 seconds. Add half the water, the sugar, wine or sherry, soy sauce and pepper. Bring to the boil and simmer for a few minutes until the celery is just tender but still crisp and the liquid has reduced. Serve sprinkled with parsley.

Haddock-Stuffed Peppers

Serves 4

225 g/8 oz haddock fillets, minced
    (ground)
100 g/4 oz peeled prawns, minced
    (ground)
1 spring onion (scallion), chopped
2.5 ml/½ tsp salt
pepper
4 green peppers
45 ml/3 tbsp groundnut (peanut) oil
120 ml/4 fl oz/½ cup chicken stock
10 ml/2 tsp cornflour (cornstarch)
5 ml/1 tsp soy sauce

Mix together the haddock, prawns, spring onion, salt and pepper. Cut off the stem of the peppers and lift out the centre. Stuff the peppers with the seafood mixture. Heat the oil and add the peppers and stock. Bring to the boil, cover and simmer for 15 minutes. Transfer the peppers to a warmed serving plate. Mix the cornflour, soy sauce and a little water and stir it into the pan. Bring to the boil and simmer, stirring, until the sauce clears and thickens.

Haddock in Black Bean Sauce

Serves 4

15 ml/1 tbsp groundnut (peanut) oil
2 cloves garlic, crushed
1 slice ginger root, minced
15 ml/1 tbsp black bean sauce
2 onions, cut into wedges
1 stick celery, sliced
450 g/1 lb haddock fillets
15 ml/1 tbsp soy sauce
15 ml/1 tbsp rice wine or dry sherry
250 ml/8 fl oz/½ cup chicken stock

Heat the oil and fry the garlic, ginger and black bean sauce until lightly browned. Add the onions and celery and stir-fry for 2 minutes. Add the haddock and fry for about 4 minutes each side or until the fish is cooked. Add the soy sauce, wine or sherry and chicken stock, bring to the boil, cover and simmer for 3 minutes.

Fish in Brown Sauce

Serves 4

4 haddock or similar fish
45 ml/3 tbsp groundnut (peanut) oil
2 spring onions (scallions), chopped
2 slices ginger root, chopped
5 ml/1 tsp soy sauce
2.5 ml/½ tsp wine vinegar
2.5 ml/½ tsp rice wine or dry sherry
2.5 ml/½ tsp sugar
freshly ground pepper
2.5 ml/½ tsp sesame oil

Trim the fish and cut into large chunks. Heat the oil and fry the spring onions and ginger for 30 seconds. Add the fish and fry until lightly browned on both sides. Add the soy sauce, wine vinegar, wine or sherry, sugar and pepper and simmer for 5 minutes until the sauce is thick. Serve sprinkled with sesame oil.

Five-Spice Fish

Serves 4

450 g/1 lb haddock fillets
5 ml/1 tsp five-spice powder
5 ml/1 tsp salt
30 ml/2 tbsp groundnut (peanut) oil
2 cloves garlic, crushed
2 slices ginger root, minced
30 ml/2 tbsp rice wine or dry sherry
15 ml/1 tbsp soy sauce
10 ml/2 tsp sesame oil

Rub the haddock fillets with the five-spice powder and salt. Heat the oil and fry the fish until lightly browned on both sides then remove it from the pan. Add the garlic, ginger, wine or sherry, soy sauce and sesame oil and fry for 1 minute. Return the fish to the pan and simmer gently until the fish is tender.

Haddock with Garlic

Serves 4

450 g/1 lb haddock fillets
5 ml/1 tsp salt
30 ml/2 tbsp cornflour (cornstarch)
60 ml/4 tbsp groundnut (peanut) oil
6 cloves garlic
2 slices ginger root, crushed
45 ml/3 tbsp water
30 ml/2 tbsp soy sauce
15 ml/1 tbsp yellow bean sauce
15 ml/1 tbsp rice wine or dry sherry
15 ml/1 tbsp brown sugar

Sprinkle the haddock with salt and dust with cornflour. Heat the oil and fry the fish until golden brown on both sides then remove it from the pan. Add the garlic and ginger and fry for 1 minute. Add the remaining ingredients, bring to the boil, cover and simmer for 5 minutes. Return the fish to the pan, cover and simmer until tender.

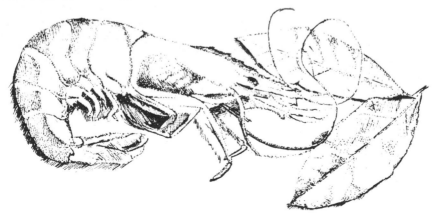

Hot-Spiced Fish

Serves 4

450 g/1 lb haddock fillets, diced
juice of 1 lemon
30 ml/2 tbsp soy sauce
30 ml/2 tbsp oyster sauce
15 ml/1 tbsp grated lemon rind
pinch of ground ginger
salt and pepper
2 egg whites
45 ml/3 tbsp cornflour (cornstarch)
6 dried Chinese mushrooms
oil for deep-frying
5 spring onions (scallions), cut into
    strips
1 stick celery, cut into strips
100 g/4 oz bamboo shoots, cut into
    strips
250 ml/8 fl oz/1 cup chicken stock
5 ml/1 tsp five-spice powder

Put the fish in a bowl and sprinkle with lemon juice. Mix together the soy sauce, oyster sauce, lemon rind, ginger, salt, pepper, egg whites and all but 5 ml/1 tsp of the cornflour. Leave to marinate for 2 hours, stirring occasionally. Soak the mushrooms in warm water for 30 minutes then drain. Discard the stalks and slice the caps. Heat the oil and fry the fish for a few minutes until golden. Remove from the pan. Add the vegetables and fry until tender but still crisp. Pour off the oil. Mix the chicken stock with the remaining cornflour, add it to the vegetables and bring to the boil. Return the fish to the pan, season with five-spice powder and heat through before serving.

Ginger Haddock with Pak Soi

Serves 4

450 g/1 lb haddock fillet
salt and pepper
225 g/8 oz pak soi
30 ml/2 tbsp groundnut (peanut) oil
1 slice ginger root, chopped
1 onion, chopped
2 dried red chilli peppers
5 ml/1 tsp honey
10 ml/2 tsp tomato ketchup (catsup)
10 ml/2 tsp malt vinegar
30 ml/2 tbsp dry white wine
10 ml/2 tsp soy sauce
10 ml/2 tsp fish sauce
10 ml/2 tsp oyster sauce
5 ml/1 tsp shrimp paste

Skin the haddock then cut into 2 cm/ ¾ in pieces. Sprinkle with salt and pepper. Cut the cabbage into small pieces. Heat the oil and fry the ginger and onion for 1 minute. Add the cabbage and chilli peppers and fry for 30 seconds. Add the honey, tomato ketchup, vinegar and wine. Add the haddock and simmer for 2 minutes. Stir in the soy, fish and oyster sauces and the shrimp paste and simmer gently until the haddock is cooked.

Haddock Plaits

Serves 4

450 g/1 lb haddock fillets, skinned	
salt	
5 ml/1 tsp five-spice powder	
juice of 2 lemons	
5 ml/1 tsp aniseed, ground	
5 ml/1 tsp freshly ground pepper	
30 ml/2 tbsp soy sauce	
30 ml/2 tbsp oyster sauce	
15 ml/1 tbsp honey	
60 ml/4 tbsp chopped chives	
8–10 spinach leaves	
45 ml/3 tbsp wine vinegar	

Cut the fish into long thin strips and shape into plaits. sprinkle with salt, five-spice powder and lemon juice and transfer to a bowl. Mix together the aniseed, pepper, soy sauce, oyster sauce, honey and chives, pour over the fish and leave to marinate for at least 30 minutes. Line the steam basket with the spinach leaves, place the plaits on top, cover and steam over gently boiling water with the vinegar for about 25 minutes.

Steamed Fish Roulades

Serves 4

450 g/1 lb haddock fillets, skinned and diced	
juice of 1 lemon	
30 ml/2 tbsp soy sauce	
30 ml/2 tbsp oyster sauce	
30 ml/2 tbsp plum sauce	
5 ml/1 tsp rice wine or dry sherry	
salt and pepper	
6 dried Chinese mushrooms	
100 g/4 oz bean sprouts	
100 g/4 oz green peas	
50 g/2 oz/½ cup walnuts, chopped	
1 egg, beaten	
30 ml/2 tbsp cornflour (cornstarch)	
225 g/8 oz Chinese cabbage, blanched	

Put the fish in a bowl. Mix together the lemon juice, soy, oyster and plum sauces, wine or sherry and salt and pepper. Pour over the fish and leave to marinate for 30 minutes. Add the vegetables, nuts, egg and corn-flour and mix together well. Lay 3 Chinese leaves on top of each other, spoon on some of the fish mixture and roll up. Continue until all the ingredients have been used up. Place the rolls in a steam basket, cover and cook over gently simmering water for 30 minutes.

Halibut with Tomato Sauce

Serves 4

450 g/1 lb halibut fillets

salt

15 ml/1 tbsp black bean sauce

1 clove garlic, crushed

2 spring onions (scallions), chopped

2 slices ginger root, minced

15 ml/1 tbsp rice wine or dry sherry

15 ml/1 tbsp soy sauce

200 g/7 oz canned tomatoes, drained

30 ml/2 tbsp groundnut (peanut) oil

Sprinkle the halibut generously with salt and leave to stand for 1 hour. Rinse off the salt and pat dry. Place the fish in an oven-proof bowl and sprinkle with the black bean sauce, garlic, spring onions, ginger, wine or sherry, soy sauce and tomatoes. Place the bowl on a rack in a steamer, cover and steam for 20 minutes over boiling water until the fish is cooked. Heat the oil until almost smoking and sprinkle over the fish before serving.

Monkfish with Broccoli

Serves 4

450 g/1 lb monkfish tail, cubed

salt and pepper

45 ml/3 tbsp groundnut (peanut) oil

50 g/2 oz mushrooms, sliced

1 small carrot, cut into strips

1 clove garlic, crushed

2 slices ginger root, minced

45 ml/3 tbsp water

275 g/10 oz broccoli florets

5 ml/1 tsp sugar

5 ml/1 tsp cornflour (cornstarch)

45 ml/3 tbsp water

Season the monkfish well with salt and pepper. Heat 30 ml/2 tbsp of oil and fry the monkfish, mushrooms, carrot, garlic and ginger until lightly browned. Add the water and continue to simmer, uncovered, over a low heat. Meanwhile, blanch the broccoli in boiling water until just tender then drain well. Heat the remaining oil and stir-fry the broccoli and sugar with a pinch of salt until the broccoli is well coated in the oil. Arrange round a warmed serving plate. Mix the cornflour and water to a paste, stir into the fish and simmer, stirring, until the sauce thickens. Pour over the broccoli and serving at once.

Mullet with Thick Soy Sauce

Serves 4

1 red mullet
oil for deep-frying
30 ml/2 tbsp groundnut (peanut) oil
2 spring onions (scallions), sliced
2 slices ginger root, shredded
1 red chilli pepper, shredded
250 ml/8 fl oz/1 cup fish stock
15 ml/1 tbsp thick soy sauce
15 ml/1 tbsp freshly ground white pepper
15 ml/1 tbsp rice wine or dry sherry

Trim the fish and score it diagonally on each side. Heat the oil and deep-fry the fish until half-cooked. Remove from the oil and drain well. Heat the oil and fry the spring onions, ginger and chilli pepper for 1 minute. Add the remaining ingredients, stir together well and bring to the boil. Add the fish and simmer gently, uncovered, until the fish is cooked and the liquid has almost evaporated.

West Lake Fish

Serves 4

1 mullet
30 ml/2 tbsp groundnut (peanut) oil
4 spring onions (scallions), shredded
1 red chilli pepper, chopped
4 slices ginger root, shredded
45 ml/3 tbsp brown sugar
30 ml/2 tbsp red wine vinegar
30 ml/2 tbsp water
30 ml/2 tbsp soy sauce
freshly ground pepper

Clean and trim the fish and make 2 or 3 diagonal cuts on each side. Heat the oil and stir-fry half the spring onions, the chilli pepper and ginger for 30 seconds. Add the fish and fry until lightly browned on both sides. Add the sugar, wine vinegar, water, soy sauce and pepper, bring to the boil, cover and simmer for about 20 minutes until the fish is cooked and the sauce has reduced. Serve garnished with the remaining spring onions.

Fried Plaice

Serves 4

4 plaice fillets
salt and freshly ground pepper
30 ml/2 tbsp groundnut (peanut) oil
1 slice ginger root, minced
1 clove garlic, crushed
lettuce leaves

Season the plaice generously with salt and pepper. Heat the oil and fry the ginger and garlic for 20 seconds. Add the fish and fry until cooked through and golden brown. Drain well and serve on a bed of lettuce.

Steamed Plaice with Chinese Mushrooms

Serves 4

4 Chinese dried mushrooms

450 g/1 lb plaice fillets, cubed

1 clove garlic, crushed

1 slice ginger root, minced

15 ml/1 tbsp soy sauce

15 ml/1 tbsp rice wine or dry sherry

5 ml/1 tsp brown sugar

350 g/12 oz cooked long-grain rice

Soak the mushrooms in warm water for 30 minutes then drain. Discard the stems and chop the caps. Mix with the plaice, garlic, ginger, soy sauce, wine or sherry and sugar, cover and leave to marinate for 1 hour. Place the rice in a steamer and arrange the fish on top. Steam for about 30 minutes until the fish is cooked.

Plaice with Garlic

Serves 4

350 g/12 oz plaice fillets

salt

45 ml/3 tbsp cornflour (cornstarch)

1 egg, beaten

60 ml/4 tsp groundnut (peanut) oil

3 cloves garlic, chopped

4 spring onions (scallions), chopped

15 ml/1 tbsp rice wine or dry sherry

5 ml/1 tsp sesame oil

Skin the plaice and cut it into strips. Sprinkle with salt and leave to stand for 20 minutes. Dust the fish with cornflour then dip in the egg. Heat the oil and fry the fish strips for about 4 minutes until golden brown. Remove from the pan and drain on kitchen paper. Pour off all but 5 ml/1 tsp of oil from the pan and add the remaining ingredients. Bring to the boil, stirring, then simmer for 3 minutes. Pour over the fish and serve immediately.

Plaice with Pineapple Sauce

Serves 4

450 g/1 lb plaice fillets

5 ml/1 tsp salt

30 ml/2 tbsp soy sauce

200 g/7 oz canned pineapple chunks

2 eggs, beaten

100 g/4 oz/½ cup cornflour (cornstarch)

oil for deep-frying

30 ml/2 tbsp water

5 ml/1 tsp sesame oil

Cut the plaice into strips and place in a bowl. Sprinkle with salt, soy sauce and 30 ml/2 tbsp of the pineapple juice and leave to stand for 10 minutes. Beat the eggs with 45 ml/3 tbsp of cornflour to a batter and dip the fish in the batter. Heat the oil and deep-fry the fish until golden brown. Drain on kitchen pepper. Put the remaining pineapple juice in a small saucepan. Blend 30 ml/2 tbsp of cornflour with the water and stir it into the pan. Bring to the boil and simmer, stirring, until thickened. Add half the pineapple pieces and heat through. Just before serving, stir in the sesame oil. Arrange the cooked fish on a warmed serving plate and garnish with the reserved pineapple. Pour over the hot sauce and serve at once.

Salmon with Tofu

Serves 4

120 ml/4 fl oz/½ cup groundnut
   (peanut) oil
450 g/1 lb tofu, cubed
2.5 ml/½ tsp sesame oil
100 g/4 oz salmon fillet, chopped
dash of chilli sauce
250 ml/8 fl oz/1 cup fish stock
15 ml/1 tbsp cornflour (cornstarch)
45 ml/3 tbsp water
2 spring onions (scallions), chopped

Heat the oil and fry the tofu until lightly browned. Remove from the pan. Reheat the oil and sesame oil and fry the salmon and chilli sauce for 1 minute. Add the stock, bring to the boil, then return the tofu to the pan. Simmer gently, uncovered, until the ingredients are cooked through and the liquid has reduced. Blend the cornflour and water to a paste. Stir in a little at a time and simmer, stirring, until the mixture thickens. You may not need all the cornflour paste if you have allowed the liquid to reduce. Transfer to a warmed serving plate and sprinkle with the spring onions.

Deep-Fried Marinated Fish

Serves 4

450 g/1 lb sprats or other small fish,
   cleaned
3 slices ginger root, minced
120 ml/4 fl oz/½ cup soy sauce
15 ml/1 tbsp rice wine or dry sherry
1 clove star anise
oil for deep-frying
15 ml/1 tbsp sesame oil

Place the fish in a bowl. Mix together the ginger, soy sauce, wine or sherry and anise, pour over the fish and leave to stand for 1 hour, turning occasionally. Drain the fish, discarding the marinade. Heat the oil and fry the fish in batches until crispy and golden brown. Drain on kitchen paper and serve sprinkled with sesame oil.

55

Sautéed Swordfish

Serves 4

450 g/1 lb swordfish steaks
salt
30 ml/2 tbsp groundnut (peanut) oil
2 slices ginger root, minced
1 clove garlic, crushed
2.5 ml/½ tsp freshly ground pepper
5 ml/1 tsp sugar
30 ml/2 tbsp soy sauce
1 spring onion, chopped

Sprinkle the swordfish steaks on both sides with salt and leave to stand for 30 minutes. Rinse and pat dry. Heat the oil and add the swordfish. Sprinkle with ginger, garlic, salt, pepper, sugar and soy sauce and sautè gently for about 10 minutes each side. Add the spring onions and fry for a further 1 minute before serving.

Trout with Carrots

Serves 4

15 ml/1 tbsp groundnut (peanut) oil
1 clove garlic, crushed
1 slice ginger root, minced
4 trout
2 carrots, cut into strips
25 g/1 oz bamboo shoots, cut into
    strips
25 g/1 oz water chestnuts, cut into
    strips
15 ml/1 tbsp soy sauce
15 ml/1 tbsp rice wine or dry sherry

Heat the oil and fry the garlic and ginger until lightly browned. Add the fish, cover and fry until the fish turns opaque. Add the carrots, bamboo shoots, chestnuts, soy sauce and wine or sherry, stir carefully, cover and simmer for about 5 minutes.

Deep-Fried Trout

Serves 4

4 trout, cleaned and scaled
2 eggs, beaten
50 g/2 oz/½ cup plain (all-purpose)
    flour
oil for deep-frying
1 lemon, cut into wedges

Slash the fish diagonally a few times on each side. Dip in the beaten eggs then toss in the flour to coat completely. Shake off any excess. Heat the oil and deep-fry the fish for about 10 to 15 minutes until cooked. Drain on kitchen paper and serve with lemon.

Trout with Lemon Sauce

Serves 4

450 ml/¾ pt/2 cups chicken stock
5 cm/2 in square piece lemon rind
150 ml/¼ pt/⅔ cup lemon juice
90 ml/6 tbsp brown sugar
2 slices ginger root, cut into strips
30 ml/2 tbsp cornflour (cornstarch)
4 trout
375 g/12 oz/3 cups plain (all-
    purpose) flour
175 ml/6 fl oz/¾ cup water
oil for deep-frying
2 egg whites
8 spring onions (scallions), thinly
    sliced

To make the sauce, mix together the stock, lemon rind and juice, sugar and ginger. Bring to the boil the simmer for 5 minutes. Remove from the heat, strain and return to the pan. Mix the cornflour with a little water then stir it into the pan. Simmer for 5 minutes, stirring frequently. Remove from the heat and keep the sauce warm.

Lightly coat the fish on both sides with a little of the flour. Beat the remaining flour with the water and 10 ml/2 tsp of oil until smooth. Beat the egg whites until stiff but not dry and fold them into the batter. Heat the remaining oil. Dip the fish in the batter to coat it completely. Cook the fish for about 10 minutes, turning once, until cooked through and golden. Drain on kitchen paper. Arrange the fish on a warmed serving plate. Stir the spring onions into the warm sauce, pour over the fish and serve immediately.

Chinese Tuna

Serves 4

30 ml/2 tbsp groundnut (peanut) oil
1 onion, chopped
200 g/7 oz canned tuna, drained and flaked
2 stalks celery, chopped
100 g/4 oz mushrooms, chopped
1 green pepper, chopped
250 ml/8 fl oz/1 cup stock
30 ml/2 tbsp soy sauce
100 g/4 oz fine egg noodles
salt
15 ml/1 tbsp cornflour (cornstarch)
45 ml/3 tbsp water

Heat the oil and fry the onion until softened. Add the tuna and stir until well coated with oil. Add the celery, mushrooms and pepper and stir-fry for 2 minutes. Add the stock and soy sauce, bring to the boil, cover and simmer for 15 minutes. Meanwhile, cook the noodles in boiling salt water for about 5 minutes until just tender then drain well and arrange on a warmed serving plate. Mix the cornflour and water, stir the mixture into the tuna sauce and simmer, stirring, until the sauce clears and thickens.

Marinated Fish Steaks

Serves 4

4 whiting or haddock steaks
2 cloves garlic, crushed
2 slices ginger root, crushed
3 spring onions (scallions), chopped
15 ml/1 tbsp rice wine or dry sherry
15 ml/1 tbsp wine vinegar
salt and freshly ground pepper
45 ml/3 tbsp groundnut (peanut) oil

Place the fish in a bowl. Mix the garlic, ginger, spring onions, wine or sherry, wine vinegar, salt and pepper, pour over the fish, cover and leave to marinate for several hours. Remove the fish from the marinade. Heat the oil and fry the fish until browned on both sides then remove from the pan. Add the marinade to the pan, bring to the boil then return the fish to the pan and simmer gently until cooked through.

Prawns with Almonds

Serves 4

100 g/4 oz almonds
225 g/8 oz large unpeeled prawns
2 slices ginger root, minced
15 ml/1 tbsp cornflour (cornstarch)
2.5 ml/½ tsp salt
30 ml/2 tbsp groundnut (peanut) oil
2 cloves garlic
2 stalks celery, chopped
5 ml/1 tsp soy sauce
5 ml/1 tsp rice wine or dry sherry
30 ml/2 tbsp water

Toast the almonds in a dry pan until lightly browned then put to one side. Peel the prawns, leaving on the tails, and cut in half lengthways to the tail. Mix with the ginger, cornflour and salt. Heat the oil and fry the garlic until lightly browned then discard the garlic. Add the celery, soy sauce, wine or sherry and water to the pan and bring to the boil. Add the prawns and stir-fry until heated through. Serve sprinkled with toasted almonds.

Anise Prawns

Serves 4

45 ml/3 tbsp groundnut (peanut) oil
15 ml/1 tbsp soy sauce
5 ml/1 tsp sugar
120 ml/4 fl oz/½ cup fish stock
pinch of ground anise
450 g/1 lb peeled prawns

Heat the oil, add the soy sauce, sugar, stock and anise and bring to the boil. Add the prawns and simmer for a few minutes until heated through and flavoured.

Prawns with Asparagus

Serves 4

450 g/1 lb asparagus, cut into chunks
45 ml/3 tbsp groundnut (peanut) oil
2 slices ginger root, minced
15 ml/1 tbsp soy sauce
15 ml/1 tbsp rice wine or dry sherry
5 ml/1 tsp sugar
2.5 ml/½ tsp salt
225 g/8 oz peeled prawns

Blanch the asparagus in boiling water for 2 minutes then drain well. Heat the oil and fry the ginger for a few seconds. Add the asparagus and stir until well coated with oil. Add the soy sauce, wine or sherry, sugar and salt and heat through. Add the prawns and stir over a low heat until the asparagus is tender.

Prawns with Bacon

Serves 4

450 g/1 lb large unpeeled prawns
100 g/4 oz bacon
1 egg, lightly beaten
2.5 ml/½ tsp salt
15 ml/1 tbsp soy sauce
50 g/2 oz/½ cup cornflour (cornstarch)
oil for deep-frying

Peel the prawns, leaving the tails intact. Cut in half lengthways to the tail. Cut the bacon into small squares. Press a piece of bacon in the centre of each prawn and press the two halves together. Beat the egg with the salt and soy sauce. Dip the prawns in the egg then dust with cornflour. Heat the oil and deep-fry the prawns until crispy and golden.

Prawn Balls

Serves 4

3 Chinese dried mushrooms
450 g/1 lb prawns, finely minced
6 water chestnuts, finely minced
1 spring onion (scallion), finely
    minced
1 slice ginger root, finely minced
salt and freshly ground pepper
2 eggs, beaten
15 ml/1 tbsp cornflour (cornstarch)
50 g/2 oz/½ cup plain (all-purpose)
    flour
groundnut (peanut) oil for deep-frying

Soak the mushrooms in warm water
for 30 minutes then drain. Discard
the stems and finely chop the caps.
Mix with the prawns, water
chestnuts, spring onion and ginger
and season with salt and pepper. Mix
in 1 egg and 5 ml/1 tsp cornflour roll
into balls about the size of a heaped
teaspoon.

Beat together the remaining egg,
cornflour and flour and add enough
water to make a thick, smooth batter.
Roll the balls in the batter. Heat the
oil and deep-fry for a few minutes
until light golden brown.

Barbecued Prawns

Serves 4

450 g/1 lb large peeled prawns
100 g/4 oz bacon
225 g/8 oz chicken livers, sliced
1 clove garlic, crushed
2 slices ginger root, minced
30 ml/2 tbsp sugar
120 ml/4 fl oz/½ cup soy sauce
salt and freshly ground pepper

Cut the prawns lengthways down the
back without cutting right through
and flatten them slightly. Cut the
bacon into chunks and place in a bowl
with the prawns and chicken livers.
Mix together the remaining
ingredients, pour over the prawns and
leave to stand for 30 minutes. Thread
the prawns, bacon and livers on to
skewers and grill or barbecue for
about 5 minutes, turning frequently,
until cooked through, basting
occasionally with the marinade.

Prawns with Bamboo Shoots

Serves 4

60 ml/4 tbsp groundnut (peanut) oil
1 clove garlic, minced
1 slice ginger root, minced
450 g/1 lb peeled prawns
30 ml/2 tbsp rice wine or dry sherry
225 g/8 oz bamboo shoots
30 ml/2 tbsp soy sauce
15 ml/1 tbsp cornflour (cornstarch)
45 ml/3 tbsp water

Heat the oil and fry the garlic and
ginger until lightly browned. Add the
prawns and stir-fry for 1 minute. Add
the wine or sherry and stir together
well. Add the bamboo shoots and stir-
fry for 5 minutes. Add the remaining
ingredients and stir-fry for 2 minutes.

Prawns with Bean Sprouts

Serves 4

4 Chinese dried mushrooms
30 ml/2 tbsp groundnut (peanut) oil
1 clove garlic, crushed
225 g/8 oz peeled prawns
15 ml/1 tbsp rice wine or dry sherry
450 g/1 lb bean sprouts
120 ml/4 fl oz/½ cup chicken stock
15 ml/1 tbsp soy sauce
15 ml/1 tbsp cornflour (cornstarch)
salt and freshly ground pepper
2 spring onion (scallions), chopped

Soak the mushrooms in warm water for 30 minutes then drain. Discard the stems and slice the caps. Heat the oil and fry the garlic until lightly browned. Add the prawns and stir-fry for 1 minute. Add the wine or sherry and fry for 1 minute. Stir in the mushrooms and bean sprouts. Mix together the stock, soy sauce and cornflour and stir it into the pan. Bring to the boil then simmer, stirring, until the sauce clears and thickens. Season to taste with salt and pepper. Serve sprinkled with spring onions.

Prawns with Black Bean Sauce

Serves 4

30 ml/2 tbsp groundnut (peanut) oil
5 ml/1 tsp salt
1 clove garlic, crushed
45 ml/3 tbsp black bean sauce
1 green pepper, chopped
1 onion, chopped
120 ml/4 fl oz/½ cup fish stock
5 ml/1 tsp sugar
15 ml/1 tbsp soy sauce
225 g/8 oz peeled prawns
15 ml/1 tbsp cornflour (cornstarch)
45 ml/3 tbsp water

Heat the oil and stir-fry the salt, garlic and black bean sauce for 2 minutes. Add the pepper and onion and stir-fry for 2 minutes. Add the stock, sugar and soy sauce and bring to the boil. Add the prawns and simmer for 2 minutes. Mix the cornflour and water to a paste, add it to the pan and simmer, stirring, until the sauce clears and thickens.

Prawns with Celery

Serves 4

45 ml/3 tbsp groundnut (peanut) oil
3 slices ginger root, minced
450 g/1 lb peeled prawns
5 ml/1 tsp salt
15 ml/1 tbsp sherry
4 stalks celery, chopped
100 g/4 oz almonds, chopped

Heat half the oil and fry the ginger until lightly browned. Add the prawns, salt and sherry and stir-fry until well coated in oil then remove from the pan. Heat the remaining oil and stir-fry the celery and almonds for a few minutes until the celery is just tender but still crisp. Return the prawns to the pan, mix well and heat through before serving.

Stir-Fried Prawns with Chicken

Serves 4

30 ml/2 tbsp groundnut (peanut) oil
2 cloves garlic, crushed
225 g/8 oz cooked chicken, thinly
   sliced
100 g/4 oz bamboo shoots, sliced
100 g/4 oz mushrooms, sliced
75 ml/5 tbsp fish stock
225 g/8 oz peeled prawns
225 g/8 oz mangetout (snow peas)
15 ml/1 tbsp cornflour (cornstarch)
45 ml/3 tbsp water

Heat the oil and fry the garlic until lightly browned. Add the chicken, bamboo shoots and mushrooms and stir-fry until well coated in oil. Add the stock and bring to the boil. Add the prawns and mangetout, cover and simmer for 5 minutes. Mix the cornflour and water to a paste, stir into the pan and simmer, stirring, until the sauce clears and thickens. Serve at once.

Chilli Prawns

Serves 4

450 g/1 lb peeled prawns
1 egg white
10 ml/2 tsp cornflour (cornstarch)
5 ml/1 tsp salt
60 ml/4 tbsp groundnut (peanut) oil
25 g/1 oz dried red chilli peppers,
   trimmed
1 clove garlic, crushed
5 ml/1 tsp freshly ground pepper
15 ml/1 tbsp soy sauce
5 ml/1 tsp rice wine or dry sherry
2.5 ml/½ tsp sugar
2.5 ml/½ tsp wine vinegar
2.5 ml/½ tsp sesame oil

Place the prawns in a bowl with the egg white, cornflour and salt and leave to marinate for 30 minutes. Heat the oil and fry the chilli peppers, garlic and pepper for 1 minute. Add the prawns and remaining ingredients and stir-fry for a few minutes until the prawns are heated through and the ingredients well mixed.

Prawn Chop Suey

Serves 4

60 ml/4 tbsp groundnut (peanut) oil

2 spring onions (scallions), chopped

2 cloves garlic, crushed

1 slice ginger root, chopped

225 g/8 oz peeled prawns

100 g/4 oz frozen peas

100 g/4 oz button mushrooms, halves

30 ml/2 tbsp soy sauce

15 ml/1 tbsp rice wine or dry sherry

5 ml/1 tsp sugar

5 ml/1 tsp salt

15 ml/1 tbsp cornflour (cornstarch)

Heat 45 ml/3 tbsp of oil and fry the spring onions, garlic and ginger until lightly browned. Add the prawns and stir-fry for 1 minute. Remove from the pan. Heat the remaining oil and stir-fry the peas and mushrooms for 3 minutes. Add the prawns, soy sauce, wine or sherry, sugar and salt and stir-fry for 2 minutes. Mix the cornflour with a little water, stir it into the pan and simmer, stirring, until the sauce clears and thickens.

Prawn Chow Mein

Serves 4

450 g/1 lb peeled prawns

15 ml/1 tbsp cornflour (cornstarch)

15 ml/1 tbsp soy sauce

15 ml/1 tbsp rice wine or dry sherry

4 dried Chinese mushrooms

30 ml/2 tbsp groundnut (peanut) oil

5 ml/1 tsp salt

1 slice ginger root, minced

100 g/4 oz Chinese cabbage, sliced

100 g/4 oz bamboo shoots, sliced

Soft Fried Noodles (page 276)

Mix the prawns with the cornflour, soy sauce and wine or sherry and leave to stand, stirring occasionally. Soak the mushrooms in warm water for 30 minutes then drain. Discard the stalks and slice the caps. Heat the oil and fry the salt and ginger for 1 minute. Add the cabbage and bamboo shoots and stir until coated with oil. Cover and simmer for 2 minutes. Stir in the prawns and marinade and stir-fry for 3 minutes. Stir in the drained noodles and heat through before serving.

Prawns with Courgettes and Lychees

Serves 4

12 king prawns

salt and pepper

10 ml/2 tsp soy sauce

10 ml/2 tsp cornflour (cornstarch)

15 ml/1 tbsp groundnut (peanut) oil

4 cloves garlic, crushed

2 red chilli peppers, chopped

225 g/8 oz courgettes (zucchini), diced

2 spring onions (scallions), chopped

12 lychees, stoned

120 ml/4 fl oz/½ cup coconut cream

10 ml/2 tsp mild curry powder

5 ml/1 tsp fish sauce

Peel the prawns, leaving on the tails. Sprinkle with salt, pepper and soy sauce then coat with cornflour. Heat the oil and fry the garlic, chilli peppers and prawns for 1 minute. Add the courgettes, spring onions and lychees and stir-fry for 1 minute. Remove from the pan. Pour the coconut cream into the pan, bring to the boil and simmer for 2 minutes until thick. Stir in the curry powder and fish sauce and season with salt and pepper. Return the prawns and vegetables to the sauce to heat through before serving.

Prawns with Crab

Serves 4

45 ml/3 tbsp groundnut (peanut) oil
3 spring onions (scallions), chopped
1 sliced ginger root, minced
225 g/8 oz crab meat
15 ml/1 tbsp rice wine or dry sherry
30 ml/2 tbsp chicken or fish stock
15 ml/1 tbsp soy sauce
5 ml/1 tsp brown sugar
5 ml/1 tsp wine vinegar
freshly ground pepper
10 ml/2 tsp cornflour (cornstarch)
225 g/8 oz peeled prawns

Heat 30 ml/2 tbsp of oil and fry the spring onions and ginger until lightly browned. Add the crab meat and stir-fry for 2 minutes. Add the wine or sherry, stock, soy sauce, sugar and vinegar and season to taste with pepper. Stir-fry for 3 minutes. Mix the corn-flour with a little water and stir it into the sauce. Simmer, stirring, until the sauce thickens. Meanwhile, heat the remaining oil in a separate pan and stir-fry the prawns for a few minutes until heated through. Arrange the crab mixture on a warmed serving plate and top with the prawns.

Prawns with Cucumber

Serves 4

225 g/8 oz peeled prawns
salt and freshly ground pepper
15 ml/1 tbsp cornflour (cornstarch)
1 cucumber
45 ml/3 tbsp groundnut (peanut) oil
2 cloves garlic, crushed
1 onion, finely chopped
15 ml/1 tbsp rice wine or dry sherry
2 slices ginger root, minced

Season the prawns with salt and pepper and toss with the cornflour. Peel and seed the cucumber and cut it into thick slices. Heat half the oil and fry the garlic and onion until lightly browned. Add the prawns and sherry and stir-fry for 2 minutes then remove the ingredients from the pan. Heat the remaining oil and fry the ginger for 1 minute. Add the cucumber and stir-fry for 2 minutes. Return the prawn mixture to the pan and stir-fry until well mixed and heated through.

Prawn Curry

Serves 4

| 45 ml/3 tbsp groundnut (peanut) oil |
| 4 spring onions (scallions), sliced |
| 30 ml/2 tbsp curry powder |
| 2.5 ml/½ tsp salt |
| 120 ml/4 fl oz/½ cup chicken stock |
| 450 g/1 lb peeled prawns |

Heat the oil and fry the spring onions for 30 seconds. Add the curry powder and salt and stir-fry for 1 minute. Add the stock, bring to the boil and simmer, stirring, for 2 minutes. Add the prawns and heat through gently.

Prawn and Mushroom Curry

Serves 4

| 5 ml/1 tsp soy sauce |
| 5 ml/1 tsp rice wine or dry sherry |
| 225 g/8 oz peeled prawns |
| 30 ml/2 tbsp groundnut (peanut) oil |
| 2 cloves garlic, crushed |
| 1 slice ginger root, finely chopped |
| 1 onion, cut into wedges |
| 100 g/4 oz button mushrooms |
| 100 g/4 oz fresh or frozen peas |
| 15 ml/1 tbsp curry powder |
| 15 ml/1 tbsp cornflour (cornstarch) |
| 150 ml/¼ pt/⅔ cup chicken stock |

Mix together the soy sauce, wine or sherry and prawns. Heat the oil with the garlic and ginger and fry until lightly browned. Add the onion, mushrooms and peas and stir-fry for 2 minutes. Add the curry powder and cornflour and stir-fry for 2 minutes. Gradually stir in the stock, bring to the boil, cover and simmer for 5 minutes, stirring occasionally. Add the prawns and marinade, cover and simmer for 2 minutes.

Deep-Fried Prawns

Serves 4

| 450 g/1 lb peeled prawns |
| 30 ml/2 tbsp rice wine or dry sherry |
| 5 ml/1 tsp salt |
| oil for deep-frying |
| soy sauce |

Toss the prawns in the wine or sherry and sprinkle with salt. Leave to stand for 15 minutes then drain and pat dry. Heat the oil and deep-fry the prawns for a few seconds until crisp. Serve sprinkled with soy sauce.

Deep-Fried Battered Prawns

Serves 4

| 50 g/2 oz/½ cup plain (all-purpose) flour |
| 2.5 ml/½ tsp salt |
| 1 egg, lightly beaten |
| 30 ml/2 tbsp water |
| 450 g/1 lb peeled prawns |
| oil for deep-frying |

Beat the flour, salt, egg and water to a batter, adding a little more water if necessary. Mix with the prawns until well coated. Heat the oil and deep-fry the prawns for a few minutes until crispy and golden.

Photograph opposite: Crispy Prawns (page 18)

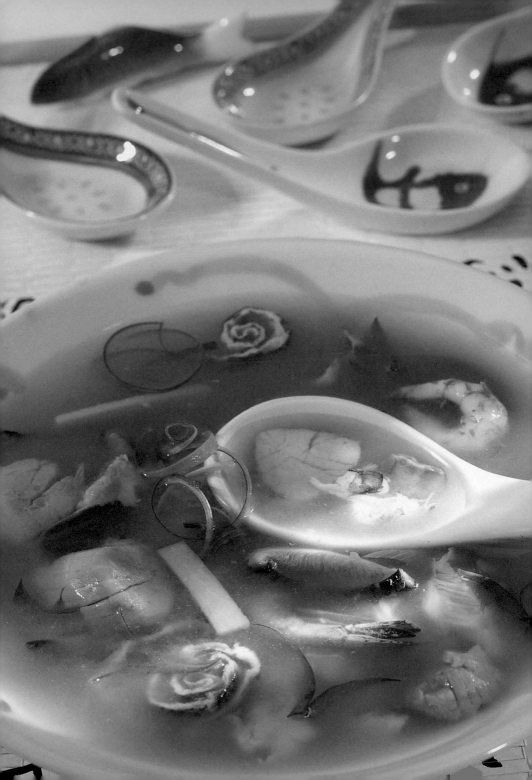

Prawn Dumplings with Tomato Sauce

Serves 4

900 g/2 lb peeled prawns
450 g/1 lb minced (ground) cod
4 eggs, beaten
50 g/2 oz/½ cup cornflour (cornstarch)
2 cloves garlic, crushed
30 ml/2 tbsp soy sauce
15 ml/1 tbsp sugar
15 ml/1 tbsp groundnut (peanut) oil
For the sauce:
30 ml/2 tbsp groundnut (peanut) oil
100 g/4 oz spring onions (scallions), chopped
100 g/4 oz mushrooms, chopped
100 g/4 oz ham, chopped
2 stalks celery, chopped
200 g/7 oz tomatoes, skinned and chopped
300 ml/½ pt/1¼ cups water
salt and freshly ground pepper
15 ml/1 tbsp cornflour (cornstarch)

Finely chop the prawns and mix with the cod. Stir in the eggs, cornflour, garlic, soy sauce, sugar and oil. Bring a large saucepan of water to the boil and drop spoonfuls of the mixture into the saucepan. Return to the boil and simmer for a few minutes until the dumplings float to the surface. Drain well. To make the sauce, heat the oil and fry the spring onions until soft but not browned. Add the mushrooms and fry for 1 minute then add the ham, celery and tomatoes and fry for 1 minute. Add the water, bring to the boil and season with salt and pepper. Cover and simmer for 10 minutes, stirring occasionally. Mix the cornflour with a little water and stir it into the sauce. Simmer for a few minutes, stirring, until the sauce clears and thickens. Serve with the dumplings.

Prawn and Egg Cups

Serves 4

15 ml/1 tbsp sesame oil
8 peeled king prawns
1 red chilli pepper, chopped
2 spring onions (scallions), chopped
30 ml/2 tbsp chopped abalone (optional)
8 eggs
15 ml/1 tbsp soy sauce
salt and freshly ground pepper
few sprigs of flat-leaved parsley

Use the sesame oil to grease 8 ramekin dishes. Place one prawn in each dish with a little of the chilli pepper, spring onions and abalone, if using. Break an egg into each bowl and season with soy sauce, salt and pepper. Stand the ramekins on a baking sheet and bake in a preheated oven at 200° C/400° F/gas mark 6 for about 15 minutes until the eggs are set and slightly crisp around the outside. Lift them carefully on to a warmed serving plate and garnish with parsley.

Photograph opposite: Crab and Scallop Soup (page 26)

Prawn Egg Rolls

Serves 4

225 g/8 oz bean sprouts
30 ml/2 tbsp groundnut (peanut) oil
4 stalks celery, chopped
100 g/4 oz mushrooms, chopped
225 g/8 oz peeled prawns, chopped
15 ml/1 tbsp rice wine or dry sherry
2.5 ml/½ tsp cornflour (cornstarch)
2.5 ml/½ tsp salt
2.5 ml/½ tsp sugar
12 egg roll skins (page 282)
1 egg, beaten
oil for deep-frying

Blanch the bean sprouts in boiling water for 2 minutes then drain. Heat the oil and stir-fry the celery for 1 minute. Add the mushrooms and stir-fry for 1 minute. Add the prawns, wine or sherry, cornflour, salt and sugar and stir-fry for 2 minutes. Leave to cool.

Place a little of the filling on the centre of each skin and brush the edges with beaten egg. Fold in the edges then roll the egg roll away from you, sealing the edges with egg. Heat the oil and deep-fry until golden brown.

Far Eastern Style Prawns

Serves 4

16–20 peeled king prawns
juice of 1 lemon
120 ml/4 fl oz/½ cup dry white wine
30 ml/2 tbsp soy sauce
30 ml/2 tbsp honey
15 ml/1 tbsp grated lemon rind
salt and pepper
45 ml/3 tbsp groundnut (peanut) oil
1 clove garlic, chopped
6 spring onions (scallions), cut into strips
2 carrots, cut into strips
5 ml/1 tsp five-spice powder
5 ml/1 tsp cornflour (cornstarch)

Mix the prawns with the lemon juice, wine, soy sauce, honey and lemon rind and season with salt and pepper. Cover and marinate for 1 hour. Heat the oil and fry the garlic until lightly browned. Add the vegetables and stir-fry until tender but still crisp. Drain the prawns, add them to the pan and stir-fry for 2 minutes. Strain the marinade and mix it with the five-spice powder and cornflour. Add to the wok, stir well and bring to the boil.

Prawn Foo Yung

Serves 4

6 eggs, beaten
45 ml/3 tbsp cornflour (cornstarch)
225 g/8 oz peeled prawns
100 g/4 oz mushrooms, sliced
5 ml/1 tsp salt
2 spring onions (scallions), chopped
45 ml/3 tbsp groundnut (peanut) oil

Beat the eggs then beat in the cornflour. Add all the remaining ingredients except the oil. Heat the oil and pour the mixture into the pan a little at a time to make pancakes about 7.5 cm/3in across. Fry until the bottom is golden brown then turn and brown the other side.

Prawn Fries

Serves 4

| 12 large uncooked prawns |
| 1 egg, beaten |
| 30 ml/2 tbsp cornflour (cornstarch) |
| pinch of salt |
| pinch of pepper |
| 3 slices bread |
| 1 hardboiled (hard-cooked) egg yolk, chopped |
| 25 g/1 oz cooked ham, chopped |
| 1 spring onion (scallion), chopped |
| oil for deep-frying |

Remove the shells and back veins from the prawns, leaving the tails intact. Cut down the back of the prawns with a sharp knife and gently press them flat. Beat the egg, cornflour, salt and pepper. Toss the prawns in the mixture until completely coated. Remove the crusts from the bread and cut it into quarters. Place one prawn, cut side down, on each piece and press down. Brush a little egg mixture over each prawn then sprinkle with the egg yolk, ham and spring onion. Heat the oil and fry the prawn bread pieces in batches until golden. Drain on kitchen paper and serve hot.

Fried Prawns in Sauce

Serves 4

| 75 g/3 oz/⅓ cup cornflour (cornstarch) |
| ½ egg, beaten |
| 5 ml/1 tsp rice wine or dry sherry |
| salt |
| 450 g/1 lb peeled prawns |
| 45 ml/3 tbsp groundnut (peanut) oil |
| 5 ml/1 tsp sesame oil |
| 1 clove garlic, crushed |
| 1 slice ginger root, minced |
| 3 spring onions (scallions), sliced |
| 15 ml/1 tbsp fish stock |
| 5 ml/1 tsp wine vinegar |
| 5 ml/1 tsp sugar |

Mix together the cornflour, egg, wine or sherry and a pinch of salt to make a batter. Dip the prawns in the batter so that they are lightly coated. Heat the oil and fry the prawns until they are crisp outside. Remove them from the pan and drain off the oil. Heat the sesame oil in the pan, add the prawns, garlic, ginger and spring onions and stir-fry for 3 minutes. Stir in the stock, wine vinegar and sugar, stir well and heat through before serving.

Poached Prawns with Ham and Tofu

Serves 4

30 ml/2 tbsp groundnut (peanut) oil
225 g/8 oz tofu, cubed
600 ml/1 pt/2½ cups chicken stock
100 g/4 oz smoked ham, cubed
225 g/8 oz peeled prawns

Heat the oil and fry the tofu until lightly browned. Remove from the pan and drain. Heat the stock, add the tofu and ham and simmer gently for about 10 minutes until the tofu is cooked. Add the prawns and simmer for a further 5 minutes until heated through. Serve in deep bowls.

Hot-Fried Prawns with Croûtons

Serves 4

oil for deep-frying
8 slices stale bread, cubed
2 cloves garlic, crushed
1 slice ginger root, chopped
225 g/8 oz peeled prawns, chopped
15 ml/1 tbsp soy sauce
15 ml/1 tbsp rice wine or dry sherry
5 ml/1 tsp salt
5 ml/1 tsp cornflour (cornstarch)
15 l/1 tbsp water

Heat the oil and fry the bread until golden brown. Remove from the pan and drain well. Pour off and reserve all but 30 ml/2tbsp of oil. Reheat the oil and fry the garlic and ginger until lightly browned. Add the prawns and all the remaining ingredients and stir-fry for 2 minutes. Return the bread to the pan and stir together well before serving.

Prawns in Lobster Sauce

Serves 4

45 ml/3 tbsp groundnut (peanut) oil
2 cloves garlic, crushed
5 ml/1 tsp minced black beans
100 g/4 oz minced (ground) pork
450 g/1 lb peeled prawns
15 ml/1 tbsp rice wine or dry sherry
300 ml/½ pt/1¼ cups chicken stock
30 ml/2 tbsp cornflour (cornstarch)
2 eggs, beaten
15 ml/1 tbsp soy sauce
2.5 ml/½ tsp salt
2.5 ml/½ tsp sugar
2 spring onions (scallions), chopped

Heat the oil and fry the garlic and black beans until the garlic is until lightly browned. Add the pork and fry until browned. Add the prawns and stir-fry for 1 minute. Add the sherry, cover and simmer for 1 minute. Add the stock and cornflour, bring to the boil, stirring, cover and simmer for 5 minutes. Add the eggs, stirring all the time so that they form into threads. Add the soy sauce, salt, sugar and spring onions and simmer for a few minutes before serving.

Prawns with Lychee Sauce

Serves 4

50 g/2 oz/½ cup plain (all-purpose) flour
2.5 ml/½ tsp salt
1 egg, lightly beaten
30 ml/2 tbsp water
450 g/1 lb peeled prawns
oil for deep-frying
30 ml/2 tbsp groundnut (peanut) oil
2 slices ginger root, minced
30 ml/2 tbsp wine vinegar
5 ml/1 tsp sugar
2.5 ml/½ tsp salt
15 ml/1 tbsp soy sauce
200 g/7 oz canned lychees, drained

Beat together the flour, salt, egg and water to make a batter, adding a little more water if necessary. Mix with the prawns until they are well coated. Heat the oil and deep-fry the prawns for a few minutes until crispy and golden. Drain on kitchen paper and arrange on a warmed serving plate. Meanwhile, heat the oil and fry the ginger for 1 minute. Add the wine vinegar, sugar, salt and soy sauce. Add the lychees and stir until warm and coated with sauce. Pour over the prawns and serve at once.

Mandarin Fried Prawns

Serves 4

60 ml/4 tbsp groundnut (peanut) oil
1 clove garlic, crushed
1 slice ginger root, minced
450 g/1 lb peeled prawns
30 ml/2 tbsp rice wine or dry sherry
30 ml/2 tbsp soy sauce
15 ml/1 tbsp cornflour (cornstarch)
45 ml/3 tbsp water

Heat the oil and fry the garlic and ginger until lightly browned. Add the prawns and stir-fry for 1 minute. Add the wine or sherry and stir together well. Add the soy sauce, cornflour and water and stir-fry for 2 minutes.

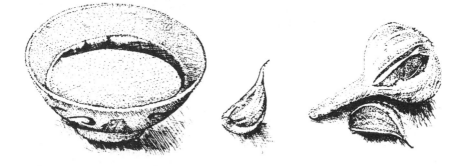

Prawns with Mangetout

Serves 4

5 dried Chinese mushrooms
225 g/8 oz bean sprouts
60 ml/4 tbsp groundnut (peanut) oil
5 ml/1 tsp salt
2 stalks celery, chopped
4 spring onions (scallions), chopped
2 cloves garlic, crushed
2 slices ginger root, minced
60 ml/4 tbsp water
15 ml/1 tbsp soy sauce
15 ml/1 tbsp rice wine or dry sherry
225 g/8 oz mangetout (snow peas)
225 g/8 oz peeled prawns
15 ml/1 tbsp cornflour (cornstarch)

Soak the mushrooms in warm water for 30 minutes then drain. Discard the stalks and slice the caps. Blanch the bean sprouts in boiling water for 5 minutes then drain well. Heat half the oil and fry the salt, celery, spring onions and bean sprouts for 1 minute then remove them from the pan. Heat the remaining oil and fry the garlic and ginger until lightly browned. Add half the water, the soy sauce, wine or sherry, mangetout and prawns, bring to the boil and simmer for 3 minutes. Mix the cornflour and remaining water to a paste, stir into the pan and simmer, stirring, until the sauce thickens. Return the vegetables to the pan, simmer until heated through. Serve at once.

Prawns with Chinese Mushrooms

Serves 4

8 dried Chinese mushrooms
45 ml/3 tbsp groundnut (peanut) oil
3 slices ginger root, minced
450 g/1 lb peeled prawns
15 ml/1 tbsp soy sauce
5 ml/1 tsp salt
60 ml/4 tbsp fish stock

Soak the mushrooms in warm water for 30 minutes then drain. Discard the stalks and slice the caps. Heat half the oil and fry the ginger until lightly browned. Add the prawns, soy sauce and salt and stir-fry until coated in oil then remove from the pan. Heat the remaining oil and stir-fry the mushrooms until coated with oil. Add the stock, bring to the boil, cover and simmer for 3 minutes. Return the prawns to the pan and stir until heated through.

Prawn and Pea Stir-Fry

Serves 4

450 g/1 lb peeled prawns
5 ml/1 tsp sesame oil
5 ml/1 tsp salt
30 ml/2 tbsp groundnut (peanut) oil
1 clove garlic, crushed
1 slice ginger root, minced
225 g/8 oz blanched or frozen peas, thawed
4 spring onions (scallions), chopped
30 ml/2 tbsp water
salt and pepper

Mix the prawns with the sesame oil and salt. Heat the oil and stir-fry the garlic and ginger for 1 minute. Add the prawns and stir-fry for 2 minutes. Add the peas and stir-fry for 1 minute. Add the spring onions and water and season with salt and pepper and a little more sesame oil, if liked. Heat through, stirring carefully, before serving.

Prawns with Mango Chutney

Serves 4

12 king prawns
salt and pepper
juice of 1 lemon
30 ml/2 tbsp cornflour (cornstarch)
1 mango
5 ml/1 tsp mustard powder
5 ml/1 tsp honey
30 ml/2 tbsp coconut cream
30 ml/2 tbsp mild curry powder
120 ml/4 fl oz/½ cup chicken stock
45 ml/3 tbsp groundnut (peanut) oil
2 cloves garlic, chopped
2 spring onions (scallions), chopped
1 fennel bulb, chopped
100 g/4 oz mango chutney

Peel the prawns, leaving the tails intact. Sprinkle with salt, pepper and lemon juice then coat with half the cornflour. Peel the mango, cut the flesh away from the stone then dice the flesh. Mix the mustard, honey, coconut cream, curry powder, the remaining cornflour and the stock. Heat half the oil and fry the garlic, spring onions and fennel for 2 minutes. Add the stock mixture, bring to the boil and simmer for 1 minute. Add the mango cubes and chutney and heat through gently then transfer to a warmed serving plate. Heat the remaining oil and stir-fry the prawns for 2 minutes. Arrange them on the vegetables and serve at once.

Fried Prawn Balls with Onion Sauce

Serves 4

3 eggs, lightly beaten
45 ml/3 tbsp plain (all-purpose) flour
salt and freshly ground pepper
450 g/1 lb peeled prawns
oil for deep-frying
15 ml/1 tbsp groundnut (peanut) oil
2 onions, chopped
15 ml/1 tbsp cornflour (cornstarch)
30 ml/2 tbsp soy sauce
175 ml/6 fl oz/¾ water

Mix the eggs, flour, salt and pepper. Toss the prawns in the batter. Heat the oil and deep-fry the prawns until golden brown. Meanwhile, heat the oil and fry the onions for 1 minute. Blend the remaining ingredients to a paste, stir into the onions and cook, stirring, until the sauce thickens. Drain the prawns and arrange on a warmed serving plate. Pour over the sauce and serve at once.

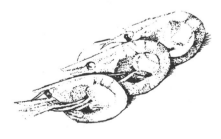

Mandarin Prawns with Peas

Serves 4

60 ml/4 tbsp groundnut (peanut) oil
1 clove garlic, minced
1 slice ginger root, minced
450 g/1 lb peeled prawns
30 ml/2 tbsp rice wine or dry sherry
225 g/8 oz frozen peas, thawed
30 ml/2 tbsp soy sauce
15 ml/1 tbsp cornflour (cornstarch)
45 ml/3 tbsp water

Heat the oil and fry the garlic and ginger until lightly browned. Add the prawns and stir-fry for 1 minute. Add the wine or sherry and stir together well. Add the peas and stir-fry for 5 minutes. Add the remaining ingredients and stir-fry for 2 minutes.

Peking Prawns

Serves 4

30 ml/2 tbsp groundnut (peanut) oil
2 cloves garlic, crushed
1 slice ginger root, finely chopped
225 g/8 oz peeled prawns
4 spring onions (scallions), thickly sliced
120 ml/4 fl oz/½ cup chicken stock
5 ml/1 tsp brown sugar
5 ml/1 tsp soy sauce
5 ml/1 tsp hoisin sauce
5 ml/1 tsp tabasco sauce

Heat the oil with the garlic and ginger and fry until the garlic is lightly browned. Add the prawns and stir-fry for 1 minute. Add the spring onions and stir-fry for 1 minute. Add the remaining ingredients, bring to the boil, cover and simmer for 4 minutes, stirring occasionally. Check the seasoning and add a little more tabasco sauce if you prefer.

Prawns with Peppers

Serves 4

30 ml/2 tbsp groundnut (peanut) oil
1 green pepper, cut into chunks
450 g/1 lb peeled prawns
10 ml/2 tsp cornflour (cornstarch)
60 ml/4 tbsp water
5 ml/1 tsp rice wine or dry sherry
2.5 ml/½ tsp salt
45 ml/2 tbsp tomato purée (paste)

Heat the oil and stir-fry the pepper for 2 minutes. Add the prawns and tomato purée and stir well. Blend the cornflour water, wine or sherry and salt to a paste, stir it into the pan and simmer, stirring, until the sauce clears and thickens.

Stir-Fried Prawns with Pork

Serves 4

225 g/8 oz peeled prawns
100 g/4 oz lean pork, shredded
60 ml/4 tbsp rice wine or dry sherry
1 egg white
45 ml/3 tbsp cornflour (cornstarch)
5 ml/1 tsp salt
15 ml/1 tbsp water (optional)
90 ml/6 tbsp groundnut (peanut) oil
45 ml/3 tbsp fish stock
5 ml/1 tsp sesame oil

Place the prawns and pork in

separate bowls. Mix together 45ml/ 3 tbsp of wine or sherry, the egg white, 30 ml/2 tbsp of cornflour and the salt to make a loose batter, adding the water if necessary. Divide the mixture between the pork and prawns and stir well to coat them evenly. Heat the oil and fry the pork and prawns for a few minutes until golden brown. Remove from the pan and pour off all but 15 ml/1 tbsp of oil. Add the stock to the pan with the remaining wine or sherry and cornflour. Bring to the boil and simmer, stirring, until the sauce thickens. Pour over the prawns and pork and serve sprinkled with sesame oil.

Deep-Fried Prawns with Sherry Sauce

Serves 4

50 g/2 oz/½ cup plain (all-purpose) flour
2.5 ml/½ tsp salt
1 egg, lightly beaten
30 ml/2 tbsp water
450 g/1 lb peeled prawns
oil for deep-frying
15 ml/1 tbsp groundnut (peanut) oil
1 onion, finely chopped
45 ml/3 tbsp rice wine or dry sherry
15 ml/1 tbsp soy sauce
120 ml/4 fl oz/½ cup fish stock
10 ml/2 tsp cornflour (cornstarch)
30 ml/2 tbsp water

Beat together the flour, salt, egg and water to make a batter, adding a little more water if necessary. Mix with the prawns until they are well coated. Heat the oil and deep-fry the prawns for a few minutes until crispy and gol-

den. Drain on kitchen paper and arrange on a warmed serving dish. Meanwhile, heat the oil and fry the onion until softened. Add the wine or sherry, soy sauce and stock, bring to the boil and simmer for 4 minutes. Mix the cornflour and water to a paste, stir into the pan and simmer, stirring, until the sauce clears and thickens. Pour the sauce over the prawns and serve.

Sautéed Prawns

Serves 4

450 g/1 lb uncooked prawns
90 ml/6 tbsp groundnut (peanut) oil
4 spring onions (scallions), chopped
1 slice ginger root, minced
30 ml/2 tbsp rice wine or dry sherry
15 ml/1 tbsp sugar
15 ml/1 tbsp fish stock or water
5 ml/1 tsp salt
5 ml/1 tsp sesame oil

Clean the prawns and cut away the tentacles and feet. Heat the oil and fry the prawns until pink. Remove from the pan and pour off all but 30 ml/2 tbsp of oil. Add the spring onions and ginger and stir-fry for 30 seconds. Add all the remaining ingredients except the sesame oil and bring to the boil. Simmer, uncovered, for 2 minutes then return the prawns to the pan and simmer, stirring, for 5 minutes. Serve sprinkled with sesame oil.

Deep-Fried Sesame Prawns

Serves 4

450 g/1 lb peeled prawns
½ egg white
5 ml/1 tsp soy sauce
5 ml/1 tsp sesame oil
50 g/2 oz/½ cup cornflour (cornstarch)
salt and freshly ground white pepper
oil for deep-frying
60 ml/4 tbsp sesame seeds
lettuce leaves

Mix the prawns with the egg white, soy sauce, sesame oil, cornflour, salt and pepper. Add a little water if the mixture is too thick. Heat the oil and deep-fry the prawns for a few minutes until lightly golden. Meanwhile, toast the sesame seeds briefly in a dry pan until golden. Drain the prawns and mix with the sesame seeds. Serve on a bed of lettuce.

Stir-Fried Prawns in their Shells

Serves 4

60 ml/4 tbsp groundnut (peanut) oil
750 g/1½ lb unpeeled prawns
3 spring onions (scallions), chopped
3 slices ginger root, minced
2.5 ml/½ tsp salt
15 ml/1 tbsp rice wine or dry sherry
120 ml/4 fl oz/½ cup tomato
    ketchup (catsup)
15 ml/1 tbsp soy sauce
15 ml/1 tbsp sugar
15 ml/1 tbsp cornflour (cornstarch)
60 ml/4 tbsp water

Heat the oil and fry the prawns for 1 minute if cooked or until they turn pink if they are uncooked. Add the spring onions, ginger, salt and wine or sherry and stir-fry for 1 minute. Add the tomato ketchup, soy sauce and sugar and stir-fry for 1 minute. Mix together the cornflour and water, stir it into the pan and simmer, stirring, until the sauce clears and thickens.

Soft-Fried Prawns

Serves 4

75 g/3 oz/⅓ cup cornflour (cornstarch)
1 egg white
5 ml/1 tsp rice wine or dry sherry
salt
350 g/12 oz peeled prawns
oil for deep-frying

Beat together the cornflour, egg white, wine or sherry and a pinch of salt to make a thick batter. Dip the prawns in the batter until they are well coated. Heat the oil until moderately hot and fry the prawns for a few minutes until golden brown. Remove from the oil, reheat it until hot then fry the prawns again until crisp and brown.

Prawn Tempura

Serves 4

450 g/1 lb peeled prawns
30 ml/2 tbsp plain (all-purpose) flour
30 ml/2 tbsp cornflour (cornstarch)
30 ml/2 tbsp water
2 eggs, beaten
oil for deep-frying

Cut the prawns half way through on

the inner curve and spread open to make a butterfly. Mix the flour, cornflour and water to a batter then stir in the eggs. Heat the oil and deep-fry the prawns until golden brown.

Sub Gum

Serves 4

30 ml/2 tbsp groundnut (peanut) oil

2 spring onions (scallions), chopped

1 clove garlic, crushed

1 slice ginger root, chopped

100 g/4 oz chicken breast, cut into strips

100 g/4 oz ham, cut into strips

100 g/4 oz bamboo shoots, cut into strips

100 g/4 oz water chestnuts, cut into strips

225 g/8 oz peeled prawns

30 ml/2 tbsp soy sauce

30 ml/2 tbsp rice wine or dry sherry

5 ml/1 tsp salt

5 ml/1 tsp sugar

5 ml/1 tsp cornflour (cornstarch)

Heat the oil and fry the spring onions, garlic and ginger until lightly browned. Add the chicken and stir-fry for 1 minute. Add the ham, bamboo shoots and water chestnuts and stir-fry for 3 minutes. Add the prawns and stir-fry for 1 minute. Add the soy sauce, wine or sherry, salt and sugar and stir-fry for 2 minutes. Mix the cornflour with a little water, stir it into the pan and simmer, stirring for 2 minutes.

Sweet and Sour Prawns with Croûtons

Serves 4

oil for deep-frying

8 slices stale bread, cubed

1 spring onion (scallion), chopped

1 clove garlic, crushed

1 slice ginger root, chopped

350 g/12 oz peeled prawns

75 ml/5 tbsp brown sugar

75 ml/5 tbsp wine vinegar

15 ml/1 tbsp cornflour (cornstarch)

30 ml/2 tbsp water

10 ml/2 tsp soy sauce

5 ml/1 tsp rice wine or dry sherry

Heat the oil and fry the bread cubes until golden brown. Remove from the pan and drain well. Pour off all but 30 ml/2 tbsp of the oil. Reheat the oil and fry the onion, garlic and ginger until lightly browned. Add the prawns, sugar and wine vinegar and stir-fry for 2 minutes. Add the cornflour, water, soy sauce and wine or sherry and stir-fry for 3 minutes. Return the croûtons to the pan and stir together well before serving.

Prawns with Tofu

Serves 4

45 ml/3 tbsp groundnut (peanut) oil
225 g/8 oz tofu, cubed
1 spring onion (scallion), minced
1 clove garlic, crushed
15 ml/1 tbsp soy sauce
5 ml/1 tsp sugar
90 ml/6 tbsp fish stock
225 g/8 oz peeled prawns
15 ml/1 tbsp cornflour (cornstarch)
45 ml/3 tbsp water

Heat half the oil and fry the tofu until lightly browned then remove it from the pan. Heat the remaining oil and stir-fry the spring onions and garlic until lightly browned. Add the soy sauce, sugar and stock and bring to the boil. Add the prawns and stir over a low heat for 3 minutes. Blend the cornflour and water to a paste, stir into the pan and simmer, stirring, until the sauce thickens. Return the tofu to the pan and simmer gently until heated through.

Prawns with Tomatoes

Serves 4

2 egg whites
30 ml/2 tbsp cornflour (cornstarch)
5 ml/1 tsp salt
450 g/1 lb peeled prawns
oil for deep-frying
30 ml/2 tbsp rice wine or dry sherry
225 g/8 oz tomatoes, skinned, seeded and chopped

Mix together the egg whites, cornflour and salt. Stir in the prawns until they are well coated. Heat the oil and deep-fry the prawns until cooked. Pour off all but 15 ml/1 tbsp of the oil and reheat. Add the wine or sherry and tomatoes and bring to the boil. Stir in the prawns and heat through quickly before serving.

Prawns with Tomato Sauce

Serves 4

30 ml/2 tbsp groundnut (peanut) oil
1 clove garlic, crushed
2 slices ginger root, minced
2.5 ml/½ tsp salt
15 ml/1 tbsp rice wine or dry sherry
15 ml/1 tbsp soy sauce
6 ml/4 tbsp tomato ketchup (catsup)
120 ml/4 fl oz/½ cup fish stock
350 g/12 oz peeled prawns
10 ml/2 tsp cornflour (cornstarch)
30 ml/2 tbsp water

Heat the oil and stir-fry the garlic, ginger and salt for 2 minutes. Add the wine or sherry, soy sauce, tomato ketchup and stock and bring to the boil. Add the prawns, cover and simmer for 2 minutes. Mix the cornflour and water to a paste, stir it into the pan and simmer, stirring, until the sauce clears and thickens.

Prawns with Tomato and Chilli Sauce

Serves 4

60 ml/4 tbsp groundnut (peanut) oil
15 ml/1 tbsp minced ginger
15 ml/1 tbsp minced garlic
15 l/1 tbsp minced spring onion
60 ml/4 tbsp tomato purée (paste)
15 ml/1 tbsp chilli sauce
450 g/1 lb peeled prawns
5 ml/1 tbsp cornflour (cornstarch)
15 ml/1 tbsp water

Heat the oil and stir-fry the ginger, garlic and spring onion for 1 minute. Add the tomato purée and chilli sauce and mix well. Add the prawns and stir-fry for 2 minutes. Blend the cornflour and water to a paste, stir it into the pan and simmer until the sauce thickens. Serve at once.

Deep-Fried Prawns with Tomato Sauce

Serves 4

50 g/2 oz/½ cup plain (all-purpose) flour
2.5 ml/½ tsp salt
1 egg, lightly beaten
30 ml/2 tbsp water
450 g/1 lb peeled prawns
oil for deep-frying
30 ml/2 tbsp groundnut (peanut) oil
1 onion, finely chopped
2 slices ginger root, minced
75 ml/5 tbsp tomato ketchup (catsup)
10 ml/2 tsp cornflour (cornstarch)
30 ml/2 tbsp water

Beat together the flour, salt, egg and water to make a batter, adding a little more water if necessary. Mix with the prawns until they are well coated. Heat the oil and deep-fry the prawns for a few minutes until crispy and golden. Drain on kitchen paper.

Meanwhile heat the oil and fry the onion and ginger until softened. Add the tomato ketchup and simmer for 3 minutes. Mix the cornflour and water to a paste, stir into the pan and simmer, stirring, until the sauce thickens. Add the prawns to the pan and simmer until heated through. Serve at once.

Prawns with Vegetables

Serves 4

15 ml/1 tbsp groundnut (peanut) oil
225 g/8 oz broccoli florets
225 g/8 oz button mushrooms
225 g/8 oz bamboo shoots, sliced
450 g/1 lb peeled prawns
120 ml/4 fl oz/½ cup chicken stock
5 ml/1 tsp cornflour (cornstarch)
5 ml/1 tsp oyster sauce
2.5 ml/½ tsp sugar
2.5 ml/½ tsp grated ginger root
pinch of freshly ground pepper

Heat the oil and stir-fry the broccoli for 1 minute. Add the mushrooms and bamboo shoots and stir-fry for 2 minutes. Add the prawns and stir-fry for 2 minutes. Mix together the remaining ingredients and stir into the prawn mixture. Bring to the boil, stirring, then simmer for 1 minute, stirring continuously.

Prawns with Water Chestnuts

Serves 4

60 ml/4 tbsp groundnut (peanut) oil
1 clove garlic, minced
1 slice ginger root, minced
450 g/1 lb peeled prawns
30 ml/2 tbsp rice wine or dry sherry
225 g/8 oz water chestnuts, sliced
30 ml/2 tbsp soy sauce
15 ml/1 tbsp cornflour (cornstarch)
45 ml/3 tbsp water

Heat the oil and fry the garlic and ginger until lightly browned. Add the prawns and stir-fry for 1 minute. Add the wine or sherry and stir together well. Add the water chestnuts and stir-fry for 5 minutes. Add the remaining ingredients and stir-fry for 2 minutes.

Prawn Wontons

Serves 4

450 g/1 lb peeled prawns, chopped
225 g/8 oz mixed vegetables, chopped
15 ml/1 tbsp soy sauce
2.5 ml/½ tsp salt
few drops of sesame oil
40 wonton skins (page 282)
oil for deep-frying

Mix together the prawns, vegetables, soy sauce, salt and sesame oil.

To fold the wontons, hold the skin in the palm of your left hand and spoon a little filling into the centre. Moisten the edges with egg and fold the skin into a triangle, sealing the edges. Moisten the corners with egg and twist them together.

Heat the oil and fry the wontons a few at a time until golden brown. Drain well before serving.

Abalone with Chicken

Serves 4

400 g/14 oz canned abalone
30 ml/2 tbsp groundnut (peanut) oil
100 g/4 oz chicken breast, diced
100 g/4 oz bamboo shoots, sliced
250 ml/8 fl oz/1 cup fish stock
15 ml/1 tbsp rice wine or dry sherry
5 ml/1 tsp sugar
2.5 ml/½ tsp salt
15 ml/1 tbsp cornflour (cornstarch)
45 ml/3 tbsp water

Drain and slice the abalone, reserving the juice. Heat the oil and stir-fry the chicken until lightly coloured. Add the abalone and bamboo shoots and stir-fry for 1 minute. Add the abalone liquid, stock, wine or sherry, sugar and salt, bring to the boil and simmer for 2 minutes. Mix the cornflour and water to a paste and simmer, stirring, until the sauce clears and thickens. Serve at once.

Abalone with Asparagus

Serves 4

10 dried Chinese mushrooms
30 ml/2 tbsp groundnut (peanut) oil
15 ml/1 tbsp water
225 g/8 oz asparagus
2.5 ml/½ tsp fish sauce
15 ml/1 tbsp cornflour (cornstarch)
225 g/8 oz canned abalone, sliced
60 ml/4 tbsp stock
½ small carrot, sliced
5 ml/1 tsp soy sauce
5 ml/1 tsp oyster sauce
5 ml/1 tsp rice wine or dry sherry

Soak the mushrooms in warm water for 30 minutes then drain. Discard the stalks. Heat 15 ml/1 tbsp of oil with the water and fry the mushroom caps for 10 minutes. Meanwhile, cook the asparagus in boiling water with the fish sauce and 5 ml/1 tsp cornflour until tender. Drain well and arrange on a warmed serving plate with the mushrooms. Keep them warm. Heat the remaining oil and fry the abalone for a few seconds then add the stock, carrot, soy sauce, oyster sauce, wine or sherry and remaining cornflour. Cook for about 5 minutes until well done then spoon over the asparagus and serve.

Abalone with Mushrooms

Serves 4

6 dried Chinese mushrooms
400 g/14 oz canned abalone
45 ml/3 tbsp groundnut (peanut) oil
2.5 ml/½ tsp salt
15 ml/1 tbsp rice wine or dry sherry
3 spring onions (scallions), thickly sliced

Soak the mushrooms in warm water for 30 minutes then drain. Discard the stalks and slice the caps. Drain and slice the abalone, reserving the juice. Heat the oil and stir-fry the salt and mushrooms for 2 minutes. Add the abalone liquid and sherry, bring to the boil, cover and simmer for 3 minutes. Add the abalone and spring onions and simmer until heated through. Serve at once.

Abalone with Oyster Sauce

Serves 4

400 g/14 oz canned abalone
15 ml/1 tbsp cornflour (cornstarch)
15 ml/1 tsp soy sauce
45 ml/3 tbsp oyster sauce
30 ml/2 tbsp groundnut (peanut) oil
50 g/2 oz smoked ham, minced

Drain the can of abalone and reserve 90 ml/6 tbsp of the liquid. Mix this with the cornflour, soy sauce and oyster sauce. Heat the oil and stir-fry the drained abalone for 1 minute. Stir in the sauce mixture and simmer, stirring, for about 1 minute until heated through. Transfer to a warmed serving plate and serve garnished with ham.

Steamed Clams

Serves 4

24 clams

Scrub the clams thoroughly then soak them in salted water for a few hours. Rinse under running water and arrange on a shallow ovenproof plate. Place on a rack in a steamer, cover and steam over gently simmering water for about 10 minutes until all the clams have opened. Discard any that remain closed. Serve with dips (pages 333-336).

Clams with Bean Sprouts

Serves 4

24 clams
15 ml/1 tbsp groundnut (peanut) oil
150 g/5 oz bean sprouts
1 green pepper, cut into strips
2 spring onions (scallions), chopped
15 ml/1 tbsp rice wine or dry sherry
salt and freshly ground pepper
2.5 ml/½ tsp sesame oil
50 g/2 oz smoked ham, chopped

Scrub the clams thoroughly then soak them in salted water for a few hours. Rinse under running water. Bring a pan of water to the boil, add the clams and simmer for a few minutes until they open. Drain and discard any that remain closed. Remove the clams from the shells.

Heat the oil and fry the bean sprouts for 1 minute. Add the pepper and spring onions and stir-fry for 2 minutes. Add the wine or sherry and season with salt and pepper. Heat through then stir in the clams and stir until well mixed and heated through. Transfer to a warmed serving plate and serve sprinkled with sesame oil and ham.

Clams with Ginger and Garlic

Serves 4

24 clams
15 ml/1 tbsp groundnut (peanut) oil
2 slices ginger root, minced
2 cloves garlic, crushed
15 ml/1 tbsp water
5 ml/1 tsp sesame oil
salt and freshly ground pepper

Scrub the clams thoroughly then soak them in salted water for a few hours. Rinse under running water. Heat the oil and fry the ginger and garlic for 30 seconds. Add the clams, water and sesame oil, cover and cook for about 5 minutes until the clams open. Discard any that remain closed. Season lightly with salt and pepper and serve at once.

Pork-Stuffed Clams

Serves 4

24 clams
175 g/6 oz lean minced (ground) pork
2 slices ginger root, minced
1 spring onion (scallion), minced
15 ml/1 tbsp soy sauce
15 ml/1 tbsp rice wine or dry sherry
2.5 ml/½ tsp salt
2.5 ml/½ tsp sugar

Scrub the clams thoroughly then soak them in salted water for a few hours. Rinse under running water and arrange on a shallow ovenproof plate. Place on a rack in a steamer, cover and steam over gently simmering water for about 10 minutes until all the clams have opened. Discard any that remain closed. Remove the clams from their shells and mix the clams with the remaining ingredients. Stuff the mixture back into the half shells and arrange on an oven proof plate. Stand the plate on a rack in a steamer, cover and steam over simmering water for about 15 minutes until the pork mixture is cooked.

Stir-Fried Clams

Serves 4

24 clams
60 ml/4 tbsp groundnut (peanut) oil
4 cloves garlic, minced
1 onion, minced
2.5 ml/½ tsp salt

Scrub the clams thoroughly then soak them in salted water for a few hours. Rinse under running water then pat dry. Heat the oil and fry the garlic, onion and salt until softened. Add the clams, cover and cook over a low heat for about 5 minutes until all the shells have opened. Discard any that remain closed. Stir-fry gently for a further 1 minute, basting with oil.

Crab Cakes

Serves 4

225 g/8 oz bean sprouts
60 ml/4 tbsp groundnut (peanut) oil
100 g/4 oz bamboo shoots, cut into
    strips
1 onion, chopped
225 g/8 oz crab meat, flaked
4 eggs, lightly beaten
15 ml/1 tbsp cornflour (cornstarch)
30 ml/2 tbsp soy sauce
salt and freshly ground pepper

Blanch the bean sprouts in boiling water for 4 minutes then drain. Heat half the oil and stir-fry the bean sprouts, bamboo shoots and onion until softened. Remove from the heat and mix in the remaining ingredients, except the oil. Heat the remaining oil in a clean pan and fry spoonfuls of the crab meat mixture to make small cakes. Fry until lightly browned on both sides then serve at once.

Crab Custard

Serves 4

225 g/8 oz crab meat
5 eggs, beaten
1 spring onion (scallion) finely chopped
250 ml/8 fl oz/1 cup water
5 ml/1 tsp salt
5 ml/1 tsp sesame oil

Mix all the ingredients together well. Place in a bowl, cover and stand in the top of the double boiler over hot water or on a steamer rack. Steam for about 35 minutes until the consistency of custard, stirring occasionally. Serve with rice.

Crab Meat with Chinese Leaves

Serves 4

450 g/1 lb Chinese leaves, shredded
45 ml/3 tbsp vegetable oil
2 spring onions (scallions), chopped
225 g/8 oz crab meat
15 ml/1 tbsp soy sauce
15 ml/1 tbsp rice wine or dry sherry
5 ml/1 tsp salt

Blanch the Chinese leaves in boiling water for 2 minutes then drain thoroughly and rinse in cold water. Heat the oil and fry the spring onions until lightly browned. Add the crab meat and stir-fry for 2 minutes. Add the Chinese leaves and stir-fry for 4 minutes. Add the soy sauce, wine or sherry and salt and mix well. Add the stock and cornflour, bring to the boil and simmer, stirring, for 2 minutes until the sauce clears and thickens.

Crab Foo Yung with Bean Sprouts

Serves 4

6 eggs, beaten
45 ml/3 tbsp cornflour (cornstarch)
225 g/8 oz crab meat
100 g/4 oz bean sprouts
2 spring onions (scallions), finely
    chopped
2.5 ml/½ tsp salt
45 ml/3 tbsp groundnut (peanut) oil

Beat the eggs then beat in the cornflour. Mix in the remaining ingredients except the oil. Heat the oil and pour the mixture into the pan a little at a time to make small pan-cakes about 7.5cm/3 in across. Fry until browned on the bottom then turn and brown the other side.

Crab with Ginger

Serves 4

15 ml/1 tbsp groundnut (peanut) oil
2 slices ginger root, chopped
4 spring onions (scallions), chopped
3 cloves garlic, crushed
1 red chilli pepper, chopped
350 g/12 oz crab meat, flaked
2.5 ml/½ tsp fish paste
2.5 ml/½ tsp sesame oil
15 ml/1 tbsp rice wine or dry sherry
5 ml/1 tsp cornflour (cornstarch)
15 ml/1 tbsp water

Heat the oil and fry the ginger, spring onions, garlic and chilli for 2 minutes. Add the crab meat and stir until well coated with the spices. Stir in the fish paste. Mix the remaining ingredients to a paste then stir them into the pan and stir-fry for 1 minutes. Serve at once.

Crab Lo Mein

Serves 4

100 g/4 oz bean sprouts
30 ml/2 tbsp groundnut (peanut) oil
5 ml/1 tsp salt
1 onion, sliced
100 g/4 oz mushrooms, sliced
225 g/8 oz crab meat, flaked
100 g/4 oz bamboo shoots, sliced
Tossed Noodles (page 275)
30 ml/2 tbsp soy sauce
5 ml/1 tsp sugar
5 ml/1 tsp sesame oil
salt and freshly ground pepper

Blanch the bean sprouts in boiling water for 5 minutes then drain. Heat the oil and fry the salt and onion until softened. Add the mushrooms and stir-fry until softened. Add the crab meat and stir-fry for 2 minutes. Add the bean sprouts and bamboo shoots and stir-fry for 1 minute. Add the drained noodles to the pan and stir gently. Mix the soy sauce, sugar and sesame oil and season with salt and pepper. Stir into the pan until heated through.

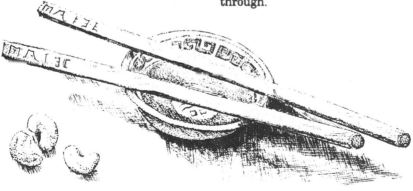

Stir-Fried Crab with Pork

Serves 4

30 ml/2 tbsp groundnut (peanut) oil
100 g/4 oz minced (ground) pork
350 g/12 oz crab meat, flaked
2 slices ginger root, minced
2 eggs, lightly beaten
15 ml/1 tbsp soy sauce
15 ml/1 tbsp rice wine or dry sherry
30 ml/2 tbsp water
salt and freshly ground pepper
4 spring onions (scallions), cut into strips

Heat the oil and stir-fry the pork until lightly coloured. Add the crab meat and ginger and stir-fry for 1 minute. Stir in the eggs. Add the soy sauce, wine or sherry, water, salt and pepper and simmer for about 4 minutes, stirring. Serve garnished with spring onions.

Sautéed Crab Meat

Serves 4

45 ml/3 tbsp groundnut (peanut) oil
1 clove garlic, crushed
4 spring onions (scallions), finely chopped
1 slice ginger root, minced
225 g/8 oz crab meat
45 ml/3 tbsp soy sauce
15 ml/1 tbsp rice wine or dry sherry
15 ml/1 tbsp wine vinegar
10 ml/2 tsp cornflour (cornstarch)

Heat the oil and fry the garlic, spring onions and ginger until lightly browned. Add the crab meat and stir-fry for 1 minute. Mix the remaining ingredients and stir them into the pan. Simmer, stirring, until the sauce clears and thickens.

Stir-Fried Crab Meat

Serves 4

30 ml/2 tbsp groundnut (peanut) oil
450 g/1 lb crab meat, flaked
2 spring onions (scallions), minced
2 slices ginger root, minced
30 ml/2 tbsp soy sauce
30 ml/2 tbsp rice wine or dry sherry
2.5 ml/½ tsp salt
15 ml/1 tbsp cornflour (cornstarch)
60 ml/4 tbsp water

Heat the oil and stir-fry the crab meat, spring onions and ginger for 1 minute. Add the soy sauce, wine or sherry and salt, cover and simmer for 3 minutes. Mix the cornflour and water to a paste, stir into the pan and simmer, stirring, until the sauce clears and thickens.

Deep-Fried Cuttlefish Balls

Serves 4

450 g/1 lb cuttlefish
50 g/2 oz lard, mashed
1 egg white
2.5 ml/½ tsp sugar
2.5 ml/½ tsp cornflour (cornstarch)
salt and freshly ground pepper
oil for deep-frying

Trim the cuttlefish and mash or purée it to a pulp. Mix with the lard, egg white, sugar and cornflour and season with salt and pepper. Press the mixture into small balls. Heat the oil and fry the cuttlefish balls, in batches if necessary, until they float to the top of the oil and turn golden brown. Drain well and serve at once.

Lobster Cantonese

Serves 4

2 lobsters
30 ml/2 tbsp oil
15 ml/1 tbsp black bean sauce
1 clove garlic, crushed
1 onion, chopped
225 g/8 oz minced (ground) pork
45 ml/3 tbsp soy sauce
5 ml/1 tsp sugar
salt and freshly ground pepper
15 ml/1 tbsp cornflour (cornstarch)
75 ml/5 tbsp water
1 egg, beaten

Break open the lobsters, take out the meat and cut it into 2.5cm/1 in cubes. Heat the oil and fry the black bean sauce, garlic and onion until lightly browned. Add the pork and fry until browned. Add the soy sauce, sugar, salt, pepper and lobster, cover and simmer for about 10 minutes. Blend the cornflour and water to a paste, stir it into the pan and simmer, stirring, until the sauce clears and thickens. Turn off the heat and stir in the egg before serving.

Deep-Fried Lobster

Serves 4

450 g/1 lb lobster meat
30 ml/2 tbsp soy sauce
5 ml/1 tsp sugar
1 egg, beaten
30 ml/3 tbsp plain (all-purpose) flour
oil for deep-frying

Cut the lobster meat into 2.5 cm/1 in cubes and toss with the soy sauce and sugar. Leave to stand for 15 minutes then drain. Beat the egg and flour then add the lobster and toss well to coat. Heat the oil and deep-fry the lobster until golden brown. Drain on kitchen paper before serving.

Steamed Lobster with Ham

Serves 4

4 eggs, lightly beaten
60 ml/4 tbsp water
5 ml/1 tsp salt
15 ml/1 tbsp soy sauce
450 g/1 lb lobster meat, flaked
15 ml/1 tbsp chopped smoked ham
15 ml/1 tbsp chopped fresh parsley

Beat the eggs with the water, salt and soy sauce. Pour into an ovenproof bowl and sprinkle with lobster meat. Place the bowl on a rack in a steamer, cover and steam for 20 minutes until the eggs are set. Serve garnished with ham and parsley.

Lobster with Mushrooms

Serves 4

| 450 g/1 lb lobster meat |
| 15 ml/1 tbsp cornflour (cornstarch) |
| 60 ml/4 tbsp water |
| 30 ml/2 tbsp groundnut (peanut) oil |
| 4 spring onions (scallions), thickly sliced |
| 100 g/4 oz mushrooms, sliced |
| 2.5 ml/½ tsp salt |
| 1 clove garlic, crushed |
| 30 ml/2 tbsp soy sauce |
| 15 ml/1 tbsp rice wine or dry sherry |

Cut the lobster meat into 2.5 cm/1 in cubes. Mix the cornflour and water to a paste and toss the lobster cubes in the mixture to coat. Heat half the oil and fry the lobster cubes until lightly browned them remove them from the pan. Heat the remaining oil and fry the spring onions until lightly browned. Add the mushrooms and stir-fry for 3 minutes. Add the salt, garlic, soy sauce and wine or sherry and stir-fry for 2 minutes. Return the lobster to the pan and stir-fry until heated through.

Lobster Tails with Pork

Serves 4

| 3 dried Chinese mushrooms |
| 4 lobster tails |
| 60 ml/4 tbsp groundnut (peanut) oil |
| 100 g/4 oz minced (ground) pork |
| 50 g/2 oz water chestnuts, finely chopped |
| salt and freshly ground pepper |
| 2 cloves garlic, crushed |
| 45 ml/3 tbsp soy sauce |
| 30 ml/2 tbsp rice wine or dry sherry |
| 30 ml/2 tbsp black bean sauce |
| 10 ml/2 tbsp cornflour (cornstarch) |
| 120 ml/4 fl oz/½ cup water |

Soak the mushrooms in warm water for 30 minutes then drain. Discard the stalks and chop the caps. Cut the lobster tails in half lengthways. Remove the meat from the lobster tails, reserving the shells. Heat half the oil and fry the pork until lightly coloured. Remove from the heat and mix in the mushrooms, lobster meat, water chestnuts, salt and pepper. Press the meat back into the lobster shells and arrange on an ovenproof plate. Place on a rack in a steamer, cover and steam for about 20 minutes until cooked. Meanwhile, heat the remaining oil and fry the garlic, soy sauce, wine or sherry and black bean sauce for 2 minutes. Mix the cornflour and water to a paste, stir it into the pan and simmer, stirring, until the sauce thickens. Arrange the lobster on a warmed serving plate, pour over the sauce and serve at once.

Stir-Fried Lobster

Serves 4

450 g/1 lb lobster tails
30 ml/2 tbsp groundnut (peanut) oil
1 clove garlic, crushed
2.5 ml/½ tsp salt
350 g/12 oz bean sprouts
50 g/2 oz button mushrooms
4 spring onions (scallions), thickly
    sliced
150 ml/¼ pt/⅔ cup chicken stock
15 ml/1 tbsp cornflour (cornstarch)

Bring a pan of water to the boil, add the lobster tails and boil for 1 minute. Drain, cool, remove the shell and cut into thick slices. Heat the oil with the garlic and salt and fry until the garlic is lightly browned. Add the lobster and stir-fry for 1 minute. Add the bean sprouts and mushrooms and stir-fry for 1 minute. Stir in the spring onions. Add most of the stock, bring to the boil, cover and simmer for 3 minutes. Mix the cornflour with the remaining stock, stir it into the pan and simmer, stirring, until the sauce clears and thickens.

Lobster Nests

Serves 4

30 ml/2 tbsp groundnut (peanut) oil
5 ml/1 tsp salt
1 onion, thinly sliced
100 g/4 oz mushrooms, sliced
100 g/4 oz bamboo shoots, sliced
225 g/8 oz cooked lobster meat
15 ml/1 tbsp rice wine or dry sherry
120 ml/4 fl oz/½ cup chicken stock
pinch of freshly ground pepper
10 ml/2 tsp cornflour (cornstarch)
15 ml/1 tbsp water
4 noodle baskets (page 276)

Heat the oil and fry the salt and onion until softened. Add the mushrooms and bamboo shoots and stir-fry for 2 minutes. Add the lobster meat, wine or sherry and stock, bring to the boil, cover and simmer for 2 minutes. Season with pepper. Mix the cornflour and water to a paste, stir into the pan and simmer, stirring, until the sauce thickens. Arrange the noodle nests on a warmed serving plate and top with the lobster stir-fry.

Mussels in Black Bean Sauce

Serves 4

45 ml/3 tbsp groundnut (peanut) oil
2 cloves garlic, crushed
2 slices ginger root, minced
30 ml/2 tbsp black bean sauce
15 ml/1 tbsp soy sauce
1.5 kg/3 lb mussels, scrubbed and bearded
2 spring onions (scallions), chopped

Heat the oil and fry the garlic and ginger for 30 seconds. Add the black bean sauce and soy sauce and fry for 10 seconds. Add the mussels, cover and cook for about 6 minutes until the mussels have opened. Discard any that remain closed. Transfer to a warmed serving dish and serve sprinkled with spring onions.

Mussels with Ginger

Serves 4

45 ml/3 tbsp groundnut (peanut) oil
2 cloves garlic, crushed
4 slices ginger root, minced
1.5 kg/3 lb mussels, scrubbed and bearded
45 ml/3 tbsp
15 ml/1 tbsp oyster sauce

Heat the oil and fry the garlic and ginger for 30 seconds. Add the mussels and water, cover and cook for about 6 minutes until the mussels have opened. Discard any that remain closed. Transfer to a warmed serving dish and serve sprinkled with oyster sauce.

Steamed Mussels

Serves 4

1.5 kg/3 lb mussels, scrubbed and bearded
45 ml/3 tbsp soy sauce
3 spring onions (scallions), finely chopped

Arrange the mussels on a rack in a steamer, cover and steam over boiling water for about 10 minutes until all the mussels have opened. Discard any that remain closed. Transfer to a warmed serving dish and serve sprinkled with soy sauce and spring onions.

Deep-Fried Oysters

Serves 4

24 oysters, shelled
salt and freshly ground pepper
1 egg, beaten
50 g/2 oz/½ cup plain (all-purpose) flour
250 ml/8 fl oz/1 cup water
oil for deep-frying
4 spring onions (scallions), chopped

Sprinkle the oysters with salt and pepper. Beat the egg with the flour and water to a batter and use to coat the oysters. Heat the oil and deep-fry the oysters until golden brown. Drain on kitchen paper and serve garnished with spring onions.

Oysters with Bacon

Serves 4

175 g/6 oz bacon
24 oysters, shelled
1 egg, lightly beaten
15 ml/1 tbsp water
45 ml/3 tbsp groundnut (peanut) oil
2 onions, chopped
15 ml/1 tbsp cornflour (cornstarch)
15 ml/1 tbsp soy sauce
90 ml/6 tbsp chicken stock

Cut the bacon into pieces and wrap one piece around each oyster. Beat the egg with the water then dip in the oysters to coat. Heat half the oil and fry the oysters until lightly browned on both sides then remove them from the pan and drain off the fat. Heat the remaining oil and fry the onions until softened. Mix the cornflour, soy sauce and stock to a paste, pour into the pan and simmer, stirring, until the sauce clears and thickens. Pour over the oysters and serve at once.

Deep-Fried Oysters with Ginger

Serves 4

24 oysters, shelled
2 slices ginger root, minced
30 ml/2 tbsp soy sauce
15 ml/1 tbsp rice wine or dry sherry
4 spring onions (scallions), cut into strips
100 g/4 oz bacon
1 egg
50 g/2 oz/½ cup plain (all-purpose) flour
salt and freshly ground pepper
oil for deep-frying
1 lemon, cut into wedges

Place the oysters in a bowl with the ginger, soy sauce and wine or sherry and toss well to coat. Leave to stand for 30 minutes. Place a few strips of spring onion on top of each oyster. Cut the bacon into pieces and wrap a piece around each oyster. Beat the egg and flour to a batter and season with salt and pepper. Dip the oysters in the batter until well coated. Heat the oil and deep-fry the oysters until golden brown. Serve garnished with lemon wedges.

Oysters with Black Bean Sauce

Serves 4

350 g/12 oz shelled oysters
120 ml/4 fl oz/½ cup groundnut (peanut) oil
2 cloves garlic, crushed
3 spring onions (scallions), sliced
15 ml/1 tbsp black bean sauce
30 ml/2 tbsp dark soy sauce
15 ml/1 tbsp sesame oil
pinch chilli powder

Blanch the oysters in boiling water for 30 seconds then drain. Heat the oil and stir-fry the garlic and spring onions for 30 seconds. Add the black bean sauce, soy sauce, sesame oil and oysters and season to taste with chilli powder. Stir-fry until heated through and serve at once.

Scallops with Bamboo Shoots

Serves 4

60 ml/4 tbsp groundnut (peanut) oil
6 spring onions (scallions), chopped
225 g/8 oz mushrooms, quartered
15 ml/1 tbsp sugar
450 g/1 lb shelled scallops
2 slices ginger root, chopped
225 g/8 oz bamboo shoots, sliced
salt and freshly ground pepper
300 ml/½ pt/1¼ cups water
30 ml/2 tbsp wine vinegar
30 ml/2 tbsp cornflour (cornstarch)
150 ml/¼ pt/⅔cup water
45ml/3 tbsp soy sauce

Heat the oiland fry the spring onions and mushrooms for 2 minutes. Add the sugar, scallops, ginger, bamboo shoots, salt and pepper, cover and cook for 5 minutes. Add the water and wine vinegar, bring to the boil, cover and simmer for 5 minutes. Blend the cornflour and water to a paste, stir into the pan and simmer, stirring, until the sauce thickens. Season with soy sauce and serve

Scallops with Egg

Serves 4

45 ml/3 tbsp groundnut (peanut) oil
350 g/12 oz shelled scallops
25 g/1 oz smoked ham, chopped
30 ml/2 tbsp rice wine or dry sherry
5 ml/1 tsp sugar
2.5 ml/½ tsp salt
pinch of freshly ground pepper
2 eggs, lightly beaten
15 ml/1 tbsp soy sauce

Heat the oil and stir-fry the scallops for 30 seconds. Add the ham and stir-fry for 1 minute. Add the wine or sherry, sugar, salt and pepper and stir-fry for 1 minute. Add the eggs and stir gently over a high heat until the ingredients are well coated in egg. Serve sprinkled with soy sauce.

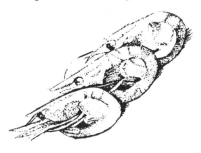

Scallops with Broccoli

Serves 4

350 g/12 oz scallops, sliced
3 slices ginger root, minced
½ small carrot, sliced
1 clove garlic, crushed
45 ml/3 tbsp plain (all-purpose) flour
2.5 ml/½ tsp bicarbonate of soda (baking soda)
30 ml/2 tbsp groundnut (peanut) oil
15 ml/1 tbsp water
1 banana, sliced
oil for deep-frying
275 g/10 oz broccoli
salt
5 ml/1 tsp sesame oil
2.5 ml/½ tsp chilli sauce
2.5 ml/½ tsp wine vinegar
2.5 ml/½ tsp tomato purée (paste)

Mix the scallops with the ginger, carrot and garlic and leave to stand. Mix the flour, bicarbonate of soda, 15 ml/1 tbsp of oil and the water to a paste and use to coat the banana slices. Heat the oil and deep fry the banana until golden brown then drain and arrange around a warmed serving plate. Meanwhile, cook the broccoli in boiling, salted water until just tender then drain. Heat the remaining oil with the sesame oil and stir-fry the broccoli briefly then arrange it round the plate with the bananas. Add the chilli sauce, wine vinegar and tomato purée to the pan and stir-fry the scallops until just cooked. Spoon on to the serving plate and serve at once.

Scallops with Ginger

Serves 4

45 ml/3 tbsp groundnut (peanut) oil
2.5 ml/½ tsp salt
3 slices ginger root, minced
2 spring onions (scallions), thickly sliced
450 g/1 lb shelled scallops, halved
15 ml/1 tbsp cornflour (cornstarch)
60 ml/4 tbsp water

Heat the oil and fry the salt and ginger for 30 seconds. Add the spring onions and stir-fry until lightly browned. Add the scallops and stir-fry for 3 minutes. Mix the cornflour and water to a paste, add to the pan and simmer, stirring, until thickened. Serve at once.

Scallops with Ham

Serves 4

450 g/1 lb shelled scallops, halved
250 ml/8 fl oz/1 cup rice wine or dry sherry
1 onion, finely chopped
2 slices ginger root, minced
2.5 ml/½ tsp salt
100 g/4 oz smoked ham, chopped

Place the scallops in a bowl and add the wine or sherry. Cover and leave to marinate for 30 minutes, turning occasionally, then drain the scallops and discard the marinade. Place the scallops in an ovenproof dish with the remaining ingredients. Place the dish on a rack in a steamer, cover and steam over boiling water for about 6 minutes until the scallops are tender.

Scallop Scramble with Herbs

Serves 4

225 g/8 oz shelled scallops

30 ml/2 tbsp chopped fresh coriander

4 eggs, beaten

15 ml/1 tbsp rice wine or dry sherry

salt and freshly ground pepper

15 ml/1 tbsp groundnut (peanut) oil

Place the scallops in a steamer and steam for about 3 minutes until cooked, depending on the size. Remove from the steamer and sprinkle with coriander. Beat the eggs with the wine or sherry and season to taste with salt and pepper. Mix in the scallops and coriander. Heat the oil and fry the egg and scallop mixture, stirring constantly, until the eggs are just set. Serve immediately.

Scallop and Onion Stir-Fry

Serves 4

45 ml/3 tbsp groundnut (peanut) oil

1 onion, sliced

450 g/l lb shelled scallops, quartered

salt and freshly ground pepper

15 ml/1 tbsp rice wine or dry sherry

Heat the oil and fry the onion until softened. Add the scallops and stir-fry until lightly browned. Season with salt and pepper, sprinkle with wine or sherry and serve at once.

Scallops with Vegetables

Serves 4 –6

4 dried Chinese mushrooms

2 onions

30 ml/2 tbsp groundnut (peanut) oil

3 stalks celery, diagonally sliced

225 g/8 oz green beans, diagonally sliced

10 ml/2 tsp grated ginger root

1 clove garlic, crushed

20 ml/4 tsp cornflour (cornstarch)

250 ml/8 fl oz/1 cup chicken stock

30 ml/2 tbsp rice wine or dry sherry

30 ml/2 tbsp soy sauce

450 g/1 lb shelled scallops, quartered

6 spring onions (scallions), sliced

425 g/15 oz canned baby corn cobs

Soak the mushrooms in warm water for 30 minutes then drain. Discard the stalks and slice the caps. Cut the onions into wedges and separate the layers. Heat the oil and stir-fry the onions, celery, beans, ginger and garlic for 3 minutes. Blend the cornflour with a little of the stock then mix in the remaining stock, wine or sherry and soy sauce. Add to the wok and bring to the boil, stirring. Add the mushrooms, scallops, spring onions and corn and stir-fry for about 5 minutes until the scallops are tender.

Scallops with Peppers

Serves 4

30 ml/2 tbsp groundnut (peanut) oil
3 spring onions (scallions), chopped
1 clove garlic, crushed
2 slices ginger root, chopped
2 red peppers, diced
450 g/1 lb shelled scallops
30 ml/2 tbsp rice wine or dry sherry
15 ml/1 tbsp soy sauce
15 ml/1 tbsp yellow bean sauce
5 ml/1 tsp sugar
5 ml/1 tsp sesame oil

Heat the oil and stir-fry the spring onions, garlic and ginger for 30 seconds. Add the peppers and stir-fry for 1 minute. Add the scallops and stir-fry for 30 seconds then add the remaining ingredients and cook for about 3 minutes until the scallops are tender.

Squid with Bean Sprouts

Serves 4

450 g/1 lb squid
30 ml/2 tbsp groundnut (peanut) oil
15 ml/1 tbsp rice wine or dry sherry
100 g/4 oz bean sprouts
15 ml/1 tbsp soy sauce
salt
1 red chilli pepper, shredded
2 slices ginger root, shredded
2 spring onions (scallions), shredded

Remove the head, guts and membrane from the squid and cut into large pieces. Cut a criss-cross pattern on each piece. Bring a pan of water to the boil, add the squid and simmer until the pieces roll up then remove and drain. Heat half the oil and stir-fry the squid quickly. Sprinkle with wine or sherry. Meanwhile, heat the remaining oil and stir-fry the bean sprouts until just tender. Season with soy sauce and salt. Arrange the chilli pepper, ginger and spring onions around a serving plate. Pile the bean sprouts in the centre and top with the squid. Serve at once.

Deep-Fried Squid

Serves 4

50 g/2 oz plain (all-purpose) flour
25 g/1 oz/¼ cup cornflour (cornstarch)
2.5 ml/½ tsp baking powder
2.5 ml/½ tsp salt
1 egg
75 ml/5 tbsp water
15 ml/1 tbsp groundnut (peanut) oil
450 g/1 lb squid, cut into rings
oil for deep-frying

Beat the flour, cornflour, baking powder, salt, egg, water and oil together to make a batter. Dip the squid in the batter until well coated. Heat the oil and deep-fry the squid a few pieces at a time until golden brown. Drain on kitchen paper before serving.

Squid Parcels

Serves 4

8 dried Chinese mushrooms
450 g/1 lb squid
100 g/4 oz smoked ham
100 g/4 oz tofu
1 egg, beaten
15 ml/1 tbsp plain (all-purpose) flour
2.5 ml/½ tsp sugar
2.5 ml/½ tsp sesame oil
salt and freshly ground pepper
8 wonton skins
oil for deep-frying

Soak the mushrooms in warm water for 30 minutes then drain. Discard the stalks. Trim the squid and cut into 8 pieces. Cut the ham and tofu into 8 pieces. Place them all in a bowl. Mix the egg with the flour, sugar, sesame oil, salt and pepper. Pour over the ingredients in the bowl and mix together gently. Arrange a mushroom cap and a piece each of squid, ham and tofu just below the centre of each wonton skin. Fold up the bottom corner, fold in the sides then roll up, moistening the edges with water to seal. Heat the oil and deep-fry the parcels for about 8 minutes until golden brown. Drain well before serving.

Fried Squid Rolls

Serves 4

45 ml/3 tbsp groundnut (peanut) oil
225 g/8 oz squid rings
1 large green pepper, cut into chunks
100 g/4 oz bamboo shoots, sliced
2 spring onions (scallions), finely chopped
1 slice ginger root, finely chopped
45 ml/2 tbsp soy sauce
30 ml/2 tbsp rice wine or dry sherry
15 ml/1 tbsp cornflour (cornstarch)
15 ml/1 tbsp fish stock or water
5 ml/1 tsp sugar
5 ml/1 tsp wine vinegar
5 ml/1 tsp sesame oil
salt and freshly ground pepper

Heat 15 ml/1 tbsp oil and fry the squid rings quickly until just sealed. Meanwhile, heat the remaining oil in a separate pan and stir-fry the pepper, bamboo shoots, spring onions and ginger for 2 minutes. Add the squid and stir-fry for 1 minute. Stir in the soy sauce, wine or sherry, corn-flour, stock, sugar, wine vinegar and sesame oil and season with salt and pepper. Stir-fry until the sauce clears and thickens.

Squid Stir-Fry

Serves 4

45 ml/3 tbsp groundnut (peanut) oil
3 spring onions (scallions), thickly sliced
2 slices ginger root, minced
450 g/1 lb squid, cut into chunks
15 ml/1 tbsp soy sauce
15 ml/1 tbsp rice wine or dry sherry
5 ml/1 tsp cornflour (cornstarch)
15 ml/1 tbsp water

Heat the oil and fry the spring onions and ginger until softened. Add the squid and stir-fry until coated in oil. Add the soy sauce and wine or sherry, cover and simmer for 2 minutes. Mix the corn-flour and water to a paste, add it to the pan and simmer, stirring, until the sauce thickens and the squid is tender.

Squid with Dried Mushrooms

Serves 4

50 g/2 oz Chinese dried mushrooms
450 g/1 lb squid rings
45 ml/3 tbsp groundnut (peanut) oil
45 ml/3 tbsp soy sauce
2 spring onions (scallions), finely chopped
1 slice ginger root, minced
225 g/8 oz bamboo shoots, cut into strips
30 ml/2 tbsp cornflour (cornstarch)
150 ml/¼ pt/⅔ cup fish stock

Soak the mushrooms in warm water for 30 minutes then drain. Discard the stems and slice the caps. Blanch the squid rings fora few seconds in boiling water. Heat the oil then stir in the mushrooms, soy sauce, spring onions and ginger and stir-fry for 2 minutes. Add the squid and bamboo shoots and stir-fry for 2 minutes. Mix together the cornflour and stock and stir it into the pan. Simmer, stirring, until the sauce clears and thickens.

Squid with Vegetables

Serves 4

45 ml/3 tbsp groundnut (peanut) oil
1 onion, sliced
5 ml/1 tsp salt
450 g/1 lb squid, cut into chunks
100 g/4 oz bamboo shoots, sliced
2 stalks celery, diagonally sliced
60 ml/4 tbsp chicken stock
5 ml/1 tsp sugar
100 g/4 oz mangetout (snow peas)
5 ml/1 tsp cornflour (cornstarch)
15 ml/1 tbsp water

Heat the oil and fry the onion and salt until lightly browned. Add the squid and fry until coated in oil. Add the bamboo shoots and celery and stir-fry for 3 minutes. Add the stock and sugar, bring to the boil, cover and simmer for 3 minutes until the vegetables are just tender. Stir in the mange tout. Mix the cornflour and water to a paste, stir into the pan and simmer, stirring, until the sauce thickens.

Beef

Good quality meat is very important for quick cooked Chinese dishes otherwise the meat will not be sufficiently tender. Although this means that you need to use the more expensive cuts of meat, you can combine smaller quantities of beef with many different vegetables to make interesting dishes which are tasty but less costly.

Braised Anise Beef

Serves 4

30 ml/2 tbsp groundnut (peanut) oil
450 g/1 lb chuck steak
1 clove garlic, crushed
45 ml/3 tbsp soy sauce
15 ml/1 tbsp water
15 ml/1 tbsp rice wine or dry sherry
5 ml/1 tsp salt
5 ml/1 tsp sugar
2 cloves star anise

Heat the oil and fry the beef until browned on all sides. Add the remaining ingredients, bring to a simmer, cover and simmer gently for about 45 minutes then turn the meat over, adding a little more water and soy sauce if the meat is drying. Simmer for a further 45 minutes until the meat is tender. Discard the star anise before serving.

Beef with Asparagus

Serves 4

450 g/1 lb rump steak, cubed
30 ml/2 tbsp soy sauce
30 ml/2 tbsp rice wine or dry sherry
45 ml/3 tbsp cornflour (cornstarch)
45 ml/3 tbsp groundnut (peanut) oil
5 ml/1 tsp salt
1 clove garlic, crushed
350 g/12 oz asparagus tips
120 ml/4 fl oz/½ cup chicken stock
15 ml/1 tbsp soy sauce

Place the steak in a bowl. Mix together the soy sauce, wine or sherry and 30 ml/2 tbsp of cornflour, pour over the steak and stir well. Leave to marinate for 30 minutes. Heat the oil with the salt and garlic and fry until the garlic is lightly browned. Add the meat and marinade and stir-fry for 4 minutes. Add the asparagus and stir-fry gently for 2 minutes. Add the stock and soy sauce, bring to the boil and simmer, stirring for 3 minutes until the meat is cooked. Mix the remaining cornflour with a little more water or stock and stir it into the sauce. Simmer, stirring, for a few minutes until the sauce clears and thickens.

Photograph opposite: Braised Soy Fish (page 35)

Beef with Bamboo Shoots

Serves 4

45 ml/3 tbsp groundnut (peanut) oil
1 clove garlic, crushed
1 spring onion (scallion), chopped
1 slice ginger root, minced
225 g/8 oz lean beef, cut into strips
100 g/4 oz bamboo shoots
45 ml/3 tbsp soy sauce
15 ml/1 tbsp rice wine or dry sherry
5 ml/1 tsp cornflour (cornstarch)

Heat the oil and fry the garlic, spring onion and ginger until lightly browned. Add the beef and stir-fry for 4 minutes until lightly browned. Add the bamboo shoots and stir-fry for 3 minutes. Add the soy sauce, wine or sherry and cornflour and stir-fry for 4 minutes.

Beef with Bamboo Shoots and Mushrooms

Serves 4

225 g/8 oz lean beef
45 ml/3 tbsp groundnut (peanut) oil
1 slice ginger root, minced
100 g/4 oz bamboo shoots, sliced
100 g/4 oz mushrooms, sliced
45 ml/3 tbsp rice wine or dry sherry
5 ml/1 tsp sugar
10 ml/2 tsp soy sauce
salt and pepper
120 ml/4 fl oz/½ cup beef stock
15 ml/1 tbsp cornflour (cornstarch)
30 ml/2 tbsp water

Slice the beef thinly against the grain. Heat the oil and stir-fry the ginger for a few seconds. Add the beef and stir-fry until just browned. Add the bamboo shoots and mushrooms and stir-fry for 1 minute. Add the wine or sherry, sugar and soy sauce and season with salt and pepper. Stir in the stock, bring to the boil, cover and simmer for 3 minutes. Mix the cornflour and water, stir it into the pan and simmer, stirring, until the sauce thickens.

Chinese Braised Beef

Serves 4

45 ml/3 tbsp groundnut (peanut) oil
900 g/2 lb chuck steak
1 spring onion (scallion), sliced
1 clove garlic, minced
1 slice ginger root, minced
60 ml/4 tbsp soy sauce
30 ml/2 tbsp rice wine or dry sherry
5 ml/1 tsp sugar
5 ml/1 tsp salt
pinch of pepper
750 ml/1¼ pts/3 cups boiling water

Heat the oil and brown the beef quickly on all sides. Add the spring onion, garlic, ginger, soy sauce, wine or sherry, sugar, salt and pepper. Bring to the boil, stirring. Add the boiling water, bring back to the boil, stirring, then cover and simmer for about 2 hours until the beef is tender.

Photograph opposite: Stir-fried Prawns with Chicken (page 61)

Beef with Bean Sprouts

Serves 4

450 g/1 lb lean beef, sliced
1 egg white
30 ml/2 tbsp groundnut (peanut) oil
15 ml/1 tbsp cornflour (cornstarch)
15 ml/1 tbsp soy sauce
100 g/4 oz bean sprouts
25 g/1 oz pickled cabbage, shredded
1 red chilli pepper, shredded
2 spring onions (scallions), shredded
2 slices ginger root, shredded
salt
5 ml/1 tsp oyster sauce
5 ml/1 tsp sesame oil

Mix the beef with the egg white, half the oil, the cornflour and soy sauce and leave to stand for 30 minutes. Blanch the bean sprouts in boiling water for about 8 minutes until almost tender then drain. Heat the remaining oil and stir-fry the beef until lightly browned then remove from the pan. Add the pickled cabbage, chilli pepper, ginger, salt, oyster sauce and sesame oil and stir-fry for 2 minutes. Add the bean sprouts and stir-fry for 2 minutes. Return the beef to the pan and stir-fry until well mixed and heated through. Serve at once.

Beef with Broccoli

Serves 4

450 g/1 lb rump steak, thinly sliced
30 ml/2 tbsp cornflour (cornstarch)
15 ml/1 tbsp rice wine or dry sherry
15 ml/1 tbsp soy sauce
30 ml/2 tbsp groundnut (peanut) oil
5 ml/1 tsp salt
1 clove garlic, crushed
225 g/8 oz broccoli florets
150 ml/¼ pt/⅔ cup beef stock

Place the steak in a bowl. Mix together 15 ml/1 tbsp of cornflour with the wine or sherry and soy sauce, stir into the meat and leave to marinate for 30 minutes. Heat the oil with the salt and garlic and fry until the garlic is lightly browned. Add the steak and marinade and stir-fry for 4 minutes. Add the broccoli and stir-fry for 3 minutes. Add the stock, bring to the boil, cover and simmer for 5 minutes until the broccoli is just tender but still crisp. Mix the remaining cornflour with a little water and stir it into the sauce. Simmer, stirring until the sauce clears and thickens.

Sesame Beef with Broccoli

Serves 4

150 g/5 oz lean beef, thinly sliced
2.5 ml/½ tsp oyster sauce
5 ml/1 tsp cornflour (cornstarch)
5 ml/1 tsp white wine vinegar
60 ml/4 tbsp groundnut (peanut) oil
100 g/4 oz broccoli florets
5 ml/1 tsp fish sauce
2.5 ml/½ tsp soy sauce
250 ml/8 fl oz/1 cup beef stock
30 ml/2 tbsp sesame seeds

Marinate the beef with the oyster sauce, 2.5 ml/½ tsp of cornflour, 2.5 ml/ tsp of wine vinegar and 15 ml/ 1 tbsp of oil for 1 hour.

Meanwhile, heat 15 ml/1 tbsp of oil, add the broccoli, 2.5 ml/½ tsp of fish sauce, the soy sauce and remaining wine vinegar and just cover with boiling water. Simmer for about 10 minutes until just tender.

Heat 30 ml/2 tbsp of oil in a separate pan and stir-fry the beef briefly until sealed. Add the stock, the remaining cornflour and fish sauce, bring to the boil, cover and simmer for about 10 minutes until the meat is tender. Drain the broccoli and arrange on a warmed serving plate. Top with the meat and sprinkle generously with sesame seeds.

Barbecued Beef

Serves 4

450 g/1 lb lean steak, sliced
60 ml/4 tbsp soy sauce
2 cloves garlic, crushed
5 ml/1 tsp salt
2.5 ml/½ tsp freshly ground pepper
10 ml/2 tsp sugar

Mix together all the ingredients and leave to marinate for 3 hours. Barbecue or grill (broil) over a hot grill for about 5 minutes each side.

Cantonese Beef

Serves 4

30 ml/2 tbsp cornflour (cornstarch)
2 egg whites, beaten
450 g/1 lb steak, cut into strips
oil for deep-frying
4 stalks celery, sliced
2 onions, sliced
60 ml/4 tbsp water
20 ml/4 tsp salt
75 ml/5 tbsp soy sauce
60 ml/4 tbsp rice wine or dry sherry
30 ml/2 tbsp sugar
freshly ground pepper

Mix half the cornflour with the egg whites. Add the steak and mix to coat the beef in the batter. Heat the oil and deep-fry the steak until browned. Remove from the pan and drain on kitchen paper. Heat 15 ml/1 tbsp of oil and stir-fry the celery and onions for 3 minutes. Add the meat, water, salt, soy sauce, wine or sherry and sugar and season with pepper. Bring to the boil and simmer, stirring, until the sauce thickens.

Beef with Carrots

Serves 4

30 ml/2 tbsp groundnut (peanut) oil
450 g/1 lb lean beef, cubed
2 spring onions (scallions), sliced
2 cloves garlic, crushed
1 slice ginger root, minced
250 ml/8 fl oz/1 cup soy sauce
30 ml/2 tbsp rice wine or dry sherry
30 ml/2 tbsp brown sugar
5 ml/1 tsp salt
600 ml/1 pt/2½ cups water
4 carrots, diagonally sliced

Heat the oil and fry the beef until lightly browned. Drain off the excess oil and add the spring onions, garlic, ginger and anise fry for 2 minutes. Add the soy sauce, wine or sherry, sugar and salt and mix together well. Add the water, bring to the boil, cover and simmer for 1 hour. Add the carrots, cover and simmer for a further 30 minutes. Remove the lid and simmer until the sauce has reduced.

Beef with Cashews

Serves 4

60 ml/4 tbsp groundnut (peanut) oil
450 g/1 lb rump steak, thinly sliced
8 spring onions (scallions), cut into chunks
2 cloves garlic, crushed
1 slice ginger root, chopped
75 g/3 oz/¾ cup roasted cashews
120 ml/4 fl oz/½ cup water
20 ml/4 tsp cornflour (cornstarch)
20 ml/4 tsp soy sauce
5 ml/1 tsp sesame oil
5 ml/1 tsp oyster sauce
5 ml/1 tsp chilli sauce

Heat half the oil and stir-fry the meat until lightly browned. Remove from the pan. Heat the remaining oil and stir-fry the spring onions (scallions), garlic, ginger and cashews for 1 minute. Return the meat to the pan. Mix together the remaining ingredients and stir the mixture into the pan. Bring to the boil and simmer, stirring, until the mixture thickens.

Slow Beef Casserole

Serves 4

30 ml/2 tbsp groundnut (peanut) oil
450 g/1 lb stewing beef, cubed
3 slices ginger root, minced
3 carrots, sliced
1 turnip, cubed
15 ml/1 tbsp black dates, stoned
15 ml/1 tbsp lotus seeds
30 ml/2 tbsp tomato purée (paste)
10 ml/2 tbsp salt
900 ml/1½ pts/3¾ cups beef stock
250 ml/8 fl oz/1 cup rice wine or dry sherry

Heat the oil in a large flameproof casserole or pan and fry the beef until sealed on all sides. Add the remaining ingredients, bring to the boil, cover tightly and simmer on the lowest heat for about 5 hours. Serve from the pot.

Beef with Cauliflower

Serves 4

225 g/8 oz cauliflower florets
oil for deep-frying
225 g/8 oz beef, cut into strips
50 g/2 oz bamboo shoots, cut into strips
10 water chestnuts, cut into strips
120 ml/4 fl oz/½ cup chicken stock
15 ml/1 tbsp soy sauce
15 ml/1 tbsp oyster sauce
15 ml/1 tbsp tomato purée (paste)
15 ml/1 tbsp cornflour (cornstarch)
2.5 ml/½ tsp sesame oil

Parboil the cauliflower for 2 minutes in boiling water then drain. Heat the oil and deep-fry the cauliflower until lightly browned. Remove and drain on kitchen paper. Reheat the oil and deep-fry the beef until lightly browned then remove and drain. Pour off all but 15 ml/1 tbsp of oil and stir-fry the bamboo shoots and water chestnuts for 2 minutes. Add the remaining ingredients, bring to the boil and simmer, stirring, until the sauce thickens. Return the beef and cauliflower to the pan and reheat gently. Serve at once.

Beef with Celery

Serves 4

100 g/4 oz celery, cut into strips
45 ml/3 tbsp groundnut (peanut) oil
2 spring onions (scallions), chopped
1 slice ginger root, minced
225 g/8 oz lean beef, cut into strips
30 ml/2 tbsp soy sauce
30 ml/2 tbsp rice wine or dry sherry
2.5 ml/½ tsp sugar
2.5 ml/½ tsp salt

Blanch the celery in boiling water for 1 minute then drain thoroughly. Heat the oil and fry the spring onions and ginger until lightly browned. Add the beef and stir-fry for 4 minutes. Add the celery and stir-fry for 2 minutes. Add the soy sauce, wine or sherry, sugar and salt and stir-fry for 3 minutes.

Deep-Fried Beef Slivers with Celery

Serves 4

30 ml/2 tbsp groundnut (peanut) oil
450 g/1 lb lean beef, cut into slivers
3 stalks celery, shredded
1 onion, shredded
1 spring onion (scallion), sliced
1 slice ginger root, minced
30 ml/2 tbsp soy sauce
15 ml/1 tbsp rice wine or dry sherry
2.5 ml/½ tsp sugar
2.5 ml/½ tsp salt
10 ml/2 tsp cornflour (cornstarch)
30 ml/2 tbsp water

Heat half the oil until very hot and fry the beef for 1 minute until just browned. Remove from the pan. Heat the remaining oil and fry the celery, onion, spring onion and ginger until slightly softened. Return the beef to the pan with the soy sauce, wine or sherry, sugar and salt, bring to the boil and stir-fry to heat through. Mix together the cornflour and water, stir into the pan and simmer until the sauce is thickened. Serve at once.

Shredded Beef with Chicken and Celery

Serves 4

4 dried Chinese mushrooms
45 ml/3 tbsp groundnut (peanut) oil
2 cloves garlic, crushed
1 sliced ginger root, minced
5 ml/1 tsp salt
100 g/4 oz lean beef, cut into strips
100 g/4 oz chicken, cut into strips
2 carrots, cut into strips
2 stalks celery, cut into strips
4 spring onions (scallions), cut into strips
5 ml/1 tsp sugar
5 ml/1 tsp soy sauce
5 ml/1 tsp rice wine or dry sherry
45 ml/3 tbsp water
5 ml/1 tsp cornflour (cornstarch)

Soak the mushrooms in warm water for 30 minutes then drain. Discard the stalks and chop the caps. Heat the oil and fry the garlic, ginger and salt until lightly browned. Add the beef and chicken and fry until just beginning to brown. Add the celery, spring onions, sugar, soy sauce, wine or sherry and water and bring to the boil. Cover and simmer for about 15 minutes until the meat is tender. Mix the cornflour with a little water, stir it into the sauce and simmer, stirring, until the sauce thickens.

Chilli Beef

Serves 4

450 g/1 lb rump steak, cut into strips
45 ml/3 tbsp soy sauce
15 ml/1 tbsp rice wine or dry sherry
15 ml/1 tbsp brown sugar
15 ml/1 tbsp finely chopped ginger root
30 ml/2 tbsp groundnut (peanut) oil
50 g/2 oz bamboo shoots, cut into
    matchsticks
1 onion, cut into strips
1 stick celery, cut into matchsticks
2 red chilli peppers, seeded and cut into
    strips
120 ml/4 fl oz/½ cup chicken stock
15 ml/1 tbsp cornflour (cornstarch)

Place the steak in a bowl. Mix together the soy sauce, wine or sherry, sugar and ginger and stir it into the steak. Leave to marinate for 1 hour. Remove the steak from the marinade. Heat half the oil and stir-fry the bamboo shoots, onion, celery and chilli for 3 minutes then remove them from the pan. Heat the remaining oil and stir-fry the steak for 3 minutes. Stir in the marinade, bring to the boil and add the fried vegetables. Simmer, stirring, for 2 minutes. Mix together the stock and cornflour and add it to the pan. Bring to the boil and simmer, stirring, until the sauce clears and thickens.

Beef with Chinese Cabbage

Serves 4

225 g/8 oz lean beef
30 ml/2 tbsp groundnut (peanut) oil
350 g/12 oz Chinese cabbage, shredded
120 ml/4 fl oz/½ cup beef stock
salt and freshly ground pepper
10 ml/2 tsp cornflour (cornstarch)
30 ml/1 tbsp water

Slice the beef thinly against the grain. Heat the oil and stir-fry the beef until just browned. Add the Chinese cabbage and stir-fry until slightly softened. Add the stock, bring to the boil and season with salt and pepper. Cover and simmer for 4 minutes until the beef is tender. Mix the cornflour and water, stir it into the pan and simmer, stirring, until the sauce thickens.

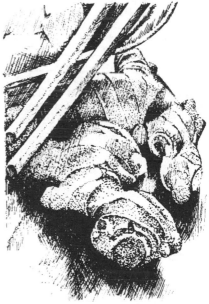

Beef Chop Suey

Serves 4

3 stalks celery, sliced
100 g/4 oz bean sprouts
100 g/4 oz broccoli florets
60 ml/4 tbsp groundnut (peanut) oil
3 spring onions (scallions), chopped
2 cloves garlic, crushed
1 slice ginger root, chopped
225 g/8 oz lean beef, cut into strips
45 ml/3 tbsp soy sauce
15 ml/1 tbsp rice wine or dry sherry
5 ml/1 tsp salt
2.5 ml/½ tsp sugar
freshly ground pepper
15 ml/1 tbsp cornflour (cornstarch)

Blanch the celery, bean sprouts and broccoli in boiling water for 2 minutes then drain and pat dry. Heat 45 ml/ 3 tbsp of oil and fry the spring onions, garlic and ginger until lightly browned. Add the beef and stir-fry for 4 minutes. Remove from the pan. Heat the remaining oil and stir-fry the vegetables for 3 minutes. Add the beef, soy sauce, wine or sherry, salt, sugar and a pinch of pepper and stir-fry for 2 minutes. Mix the cornflour with a little water, stir it into the pan and simmer, stirring, until the sauce clears and thickens.

Beef with Cucumber

Serves 4

450 g/1 lb rump steak, thinly sliced
45 ml/3 tbsp soy sauce
30 ml/2 tbsp cornflour (cornstarch)
60 ml/4 tbsp groundnut (peanut) oil
2 cucumbers, peeled, seeded and sliced
60 ml/4 tbsp chicken stock
30 ml/2 tbsp rice wine or dry sherry
salt and freshly ground pepper

Place the steak in a bowl. Mix together the soy sauce and cornflour and stir into the steak. Leave to marinate for 30 minutes. Heat half the oil and stir-fry the cucumbers for 3 minutes until opaque then remove them from the pan. Heat the remaining oil and stir-fry the steak until browned. Add the cucumbers and stir-fry for 2 minutes. Add the stock, wine or sherry and season with salt and pepper. Bring to the boil, cover and simmer for 3 minutes

Beef Chow Mein

Serves 4

750 g/1½ lb rump steak
2 onions
45 ml/3 tbsp soy sauce
45 ml/3 tbsp rice wine or dry sherry
15 ml/1 tbsp peanut butter
5 ml/1 tsp lemon juice
350 g/12 oz egg noodles
60 ml/4 tbsp groundnut (peanut) oil
175 ml/6 fl oz/¾ cup chicken stock
15 ml/1 tbsp cornflour (cornstarch)
30 ml/2 tbsp oyster sauce
4 spring onions (scallions), chopped
3 stalks celery, sliced
100 g/4 oz mushrooms, sliced
1 green pepper, cut into strips
100 g/4 oz bean sprouts

Remove and discard the fat from the meat. Cut across the grain into thin slices. Cut the onions into wedges and separate the layers. Mix together 15 ml/1 tbsp of soy sauce with 15 ml/1 tbsp of wine or sherry, the peanut butter and lemon juice. Stir in the meat, cover and leave to stand for 1 hour. Cook the noodles in boiling water for about 5 minutes or until tender. Drain well. Heat 15 ml/1 tbsp of oil, add 15 ml/1 tbsp of soy sauce and the noodles and fry for 2 minutes until lightly browned. Transfer to a warmed serving plate. Mix together the remaining soy sauce and wine or sherry with the stock, cornflour and oyster sauce. Heat 15 ml/1 tbsp of oil and stir-fry the onions for 1 minute. Add the celery, mushrooms, pepper and bean sprouts and stir-fry for 2 minutes. Remove from the wok. Heat the remaining oil and stir-fry the beef until browned. Add the stock mixture, bring to the boil, cover and simmer for 3 minutes. Return the vegetables to the wok and simmer, stirring, for about 4 minutes until hot. Spoon the mixture over the noodles and serve.

Cucumber Steak

Serves 4

450 g/1 lb rump steak
10 ml/2 tsp cornflour (cornstarch)
10 ml/2 tsp salt
2.5 ml/½ tsp freshly ground pepper
90 ml/6 tbsp groundnut (peanut) oil
1 onion, finely chopped
1 cucumber, peeled and sliced
120 ml/4 fl oz/½ cup beef stock

Cut the steak into strips then into thin slices against the grain. Place in a bowl and stir in the cornflour, salt, pepper and half the oil. Leave to marinate for 30 minutes. Heat the remaining oil and fry the beef and onion until lightly browned. Add the cucumbers and stock, bring to the boil, cover and simmer for 5 minutes.

Baked Beef Curry

Serves 4

45 ml/3 tbsp butter
15 ml/1 tbsp curry powder
45 ml/3 tbsp plain (all-purpose) flour
375 ml/13 fl oz/1½ cups milk
15 ml/1 tbsp soy sauce
salt and freshly ground pepper
450 g/1 lb cooked beef, chopped
100 g/4 oz peas
2 carrots, chopped
2 onions, chopped
225 g/8 oz cooked long-grain rice, hot
1 hard-boiled (hard-cooked) egg, sliced

Melt the butter, stir in the curry powder and flour and cook for 1 minute. Stir in the milk and soy sauce, bring to the boil and simmer, stirring, for 2 minutes. Season with salt and pepper. Add the beef, peas, carrots and onions and stir well to coat with the sauce. Stir in the rice then transfer the mixture to an ovenproof dish and bake in a preheated over at 200°C/400°F/gas mark 6 for 20 minutes until the vegetables are tender. Serve garnished with slices of hard-boiled egg.

Crispy Beef with Curry Sauce

Serves 4

1 egg, beaten
15 ml/1 tbsp cornflour (cornstarch)
5 ml/1 tsp bicarbonate of soda (baking soda)
15 ml/1 tbsp rice wine or dry sherry
15 ml/1 tbsp soy sauce
225 g/8 oz lean beef, sliced
90 ml/6 tbsp oil
100 g/4 oz curry paste

Mix the egg, cornflour, bicarbonate of soda, wine or sherry and soy sauce. Stir in the beef and 15 ml/1 tbsp of oil. Heat the remaining oil and stir-fry the beef and egg mixture for 2 minutes. Remove the beef and drain off the oil. Add the curry paste to the pan and bring to the boil then return the beef to the pan, stir well and serve.

Braised Curried Beef

Serves 4

45 ml/3 tbsp groundnut (peanut) oil
5 ml/1 tsp salt
1 clove garlic, crushed
450 g/1 lb chuck steak, cubed
4 spring onions (scallions), sliced
1 slice ginger root, minced
30 ml/2 tbsp curry powder
15 ml/1 tbsp rice wine or dry sherry
15 ml/1 tbsp sugar
400 ml/14 fl oz/1¾ cups beef stock
15 ml/1 tbsp cornflour (cornstarch)
45 ml/3 tbsp water

Heat the oil and fry the salt and garlic until lightly browned. Add the steak and toss in the oil then add the spring onions and ginger and fry until the meat is browned on all sides. Add the curry powder and stir-fry for 1 minute. Stir in the wine or sherry and sugar then add the stock, bring to the boil, cover and simmer for about 35 minutes until the beef is tender. Blend the cornflour and water to a paste, stir into the sauce and simmer, stirring, until the sauce thickens.

Stir-Fried Curried Beef

Serves 4

225 g/8 oz lean beef
30 ml/2 tbsp groundnut (peanut) oil
1 large onion, sliced
30 ml/2 tbsp curry powder
1 slice ginger root, minced
15 ml/1 tbsp rice wine or dry sherry
120 ml/4 fl oz/½ cup beef stock
5 ml/1 tsp sugar
15 ml/1 tbsp cornflour (cornstarch)
45 ml/3 tbsp water

Slice the beef thinly against the grain. Heat the oil and fry the onion until translucent. Add the curry and ginger and stir-fry for a few seconds. Add the beef and stir-fry until just browned. Add the wine or sherry and stock, bring to the boil, cover and simmer for about 5 minutes until the beef is cooked. Mix the sugar, cornflour and water, stir into the pan and simmer, stirring, until the sauce thickens.

Beef with Garlic

Serves 4

350 g/12 oz lean beef, sliced
4 cloves garlic, sliced
1 red chilli pepper, sliced
45 ml/3 tbsp soy sauce
45 ml/3 tbsp groundnut (peanut) oil
5 ml/1 tsp cornflour (cornstarch)
15 ml/1 tbsp water

Mix the beef with the garlic, chilli pepper and 30 ml/2 tbsp of soy sauce and leave to stand for 30 minutes, stirring occasionally. Heat the oil and fry the beef mixture for a few minutes until almost cooked. Mix the remaining ingredients to a paste, stir in to the pan and continue to stir-fry until the beef is cooked.

Beef with Ginger

Serves 4

15 ml/1 tbsp groundnut (peanut) oil
450 g/1 lb lean beef, sliced
1 onion, thinly sliced
2 cloves garlic, crushed
2 pieces crystallised ginger, thinly sliced
15 ml/1 tbsp soy sauce
150 ml/¼ pt/⅔ cup water
2 stalks celery, diagonally sliced
5 ml/1 tsp salt

Heat the oil and fry the beef, onion and garlic until lightly browned. Add the ginger, soy sauce and water, bring to the boil, cover and simmer for 25 minutes. Add the celery, cover and simmer for a further 5 minutes. Sprinkle with salt before serving.

Red-Cooked Beef with Ginger

Serves 4

450 g/1 lb lean beef

2 slices ginger root, minced

4 spring onions (scallions) chopped

120 ml/4 fl oz/½ cup soy sauce

60 ml/4 tbsp rice wine or dry sherry

400 ml/14 fl oz/1¾ cups water

15 ml/1 tbsp brown sugar

Place all the ingredients in a heavy pan, bring to the boil, cover and simmer, turning occasionally, for about 1 hour until the beef is tender.

Beef with Green Beans

Serves 4

225 g/8 oz rump steak, thinly sliced

30 ml/2 tbsp cornflour (cornstarch)

15 ml/1 tbsp rice wine or dry sherry

15 ml/1 tbsp soy sauce

30 ml/2 tbsp groundnut (peanut) oil

2.5 ml/½ tsp salt

2 cloves garlic, crushed

225 g/8 oz green beans

225 g/8 oz bamboo shoots, sliced

50 g/2 oz mushrooms, sliced

50 g/2 oz water chestnuts, sliced

150 ml/¼ pt/⅔ cup chicken stock

Place the steak in a bowl. Mix together 15 ml/1 tbsp of the cornflour, the wine or sherry and soy sauce, stir into the meat and marinate for 30 minutes. Heat the oil with the salt and garlic and fry until the garlic is lightly browned. Add the meat and marinade and stir-fry for 4 minutes. Add the beans and stir-fry for 2 minutes. Add the remaining ingredients, bring to the boil and simmer for 4 minutes. Mix the remaining cornflour with a little water and stir it into the sauce. Simmer, stirring, until the sauce clears and thickens.

Hot Beef

Serves 4

450 g/1 lb lean beef

6 spring onions (scallions), sliced

4 slices ginger root

15 ml/1 tbsp rice wine or dry sherry

15 ml/1 tbsp soy sauce

4 dried red chilli peppers, chopped

10 peppercorns

1 clove star anise

300 ml/½ pt/1¼ cups water

2.5 ml/½ tsp chilli oil

Place the beef in a bowl with 2 spring onions, 1 slice of ginger and half the wine and leave to marinate for 30 minutes. Bring a large pan of water to the boil, add the beef and boil until sealed on all sides then remove and drain. Place the remaining spring onions, ginger and wine or sherry in a pan with the chilli peppers, peppercorns and star anise and add the water. Bring to the boil, add the beef, cover and simmer for about 40 minutes until the beef is tender. Remove the beef from the liquid and drain well. Slice it thinly and arrange on a warmed serving plate. Serve sprinkled with chilli oil.

Hot Beef Shreds

Serves 4

150 ml/¼ pt/⅔ cup groundnut (peanut) oil

450 g/1 lb lean beef, sliced against the grain

45 ml/3 tbsp soy sauce

15 ml/1 tbsp rice wine or dry sherry

1 slice ginger root, minced

1 dried red chilli pepper, chopped

2 carrots, shredded

2 stalks celery, diagonally sliced

10 ml/2 tsp salt

225 g/8 oz/1 cup long-grain rice

Heat two-thirds of the oil and stir-fry the beef, soy sauce and wine or sherry for 10 minutes. Remove the beef and reserve the sauce. Heat the remaining oil and stir-fry the ginger, pepper and carrots for 1 minute. Add the celery and stir-fry for 1 minute. Add the beef and salt and stir-fry for 1 minute.

Meanwhile, cook the rice in boiling water for about 20 minutes until just tender. Drain well and arrange on a serving dish. Pour over the beef mixture and the hot sauce.

Beef with Mangetout

Serves 4

225 g/8 oz lean beef

30 ml/2 tbsp cornflour (cornstarch)

5 ml/1 tsp sugar

5 ml/1 tsp soy sauce

10 ml/2 tsp rice wine or dry sherry

30 ml/2 tbsp groundnut (peanut) oil

2.5 ml/¼ tsp salt

2 slices ginger root, minced

225 g/8 oz mangetout (snow peas)

60 ml/4 tbsp beef stock

10 ml/2 tsp water

freshly ground pepper

Slice the beef thinly against the grain. Mix half the cornflour, the sugar, soy sauce and wine or sherry, add to the beef and stir well to coat. Heat half the oil and stir-fry the salt and ginger and a few seconds. Add mangetout and stir to coat with oil. Add the stock, bring to the boil and stir well then remove the mangetout and liquid from the pan. Heat the remaining oil and stir-fry the beef until lightly browned. Return the mangetout to the pan. Mix the remaining cornflour with the water, stir into the pan and season with pepper. Simmer, stirring, until the sauce thickens.

Marinated Braised Beef

Serves 4

450 g/1 lb chuck steak
75 ml/5 tbsp soy sauce
60 ml/4 tbsp rice wine or dry sherry
5 ml/1 tsp salt
15 ml/1 tbsp cornflour (cornstarch)
45 ml/3 tbsp groundnut (peanut) oil
15 ml/1 tbsp brown sugar
15 ml/1 tbsp wine vinegar

Pierce the steak in several places and place in a bowl. Mix the soy sauce, wine or sherry and salt, pour over the meat and leave to stand for 3 hours, turning occasionally. Drain the beef and discard the marinade. Pat the beef dry and dust with cornflour. Heat the oil and fry the beef until browned on all sides. Add the sugar and wine vinegar and enough water just to cover the beef. Bring to the boil, cover and simmer for about 1 hour until the meat is tender.

Marinated Stir-Fried Beef

Serves 4

450 g/1 lb lean beef, sliced
2 cloves garlic, crushed
60 ml/4 tbsp soy sauce
15 ml/1 tbsp brown sugar
5 ml/1 tsp salt
30 ml/2 tbsp groundnut (peanut) oil

Place the beef in a bowl and add the garlic, soy sauce, sugar and salt. Mix together well, cover and leave to marinate for about 2 hours, turning occasionally. Drain, discarding the marinade. Heat the oil and stir-fry the beef until browned on all sides then serve at once.

Stir-Fried Beef and Mushrooms

Serves 4

225 g/8 oz lean beef
15 ml/1 tbsp cornflour (cornstarch)
15 ml/1 tbsp rice wine or dry sherry
15 ml/1 tbsp soy sauce
2.5 ml/½ tsp sugar
45 ml/3 tbsp groundnut (peanut) oil
1 slice ginger root, minced
2.5 ml/½ tsp salt
225 g/8 oz mushrooms, sliced
120 ml/4 fl oz/½ cup beef stock

Slice the beef thinly against the grain. Mix the cornflour, wine or sherry, soy sauce and sugar, stir into the beef and toss well to coat. Heat the oil and stirfry the ginger for 1 minute. Add the beef and stir-fry until just browned. Add the salt and mushrooms and stir well. Add the stock, bring to the boil and simmer, stirring, until the sauce thickens.

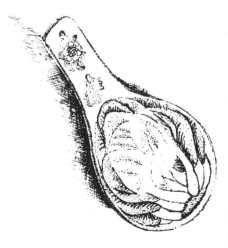

Braised Beef with Mushrooms

Serves 4

1 kg/2 lb topside of beef
salt and freshly ground pepper
60 ml/4 tbsp soy sauce
30 ml/2 tbsp hoisin sauce
30 ml/2 tbsp honey
30 ml/2 tbsp wine vinegar
5 ml/1 tsp freshly ground pepper
5 ml/1 tsp aniseed, ground
5 ml/1 tsp ground coriander
6 dried Chinese mushrooms
60 ml/4 tbsp groundnut (peanut) oil
5 ml/2 tsp cornflour (cornstarch)
15 ml/1 tbsp water
400 g/14 oz canned tomatoes
6 spring onions (scallions), cut into strips
2 carrots, grated
30 ml/2 tbsp plum sauce
60 ml/4 tbsp chopped chives

Pierce the beef several times with a fork. Season with salt and pepper and place in a bowl. Mix the sauces, honey, wine vinegar, pepper and spices, pour over the meat, cover and leave to marinate in the refrigerator overnight.

Soak the mushrooms in warm water for 30 minutes then drain. Discard the stalks and slice the caps. Heat the oil and fry the meat until well browned, turning frequently. Mix the cornflour and water and add it to the pan with the tomatoes. Bring to the boil, cover and simmer gently for about 1½ hours until tender. Add the spring onions and carrots and continue to simmer for 10 minutes until the carrots are tender. Stir in the plum sauce and simmer for 2 minutes. Remove the meat from the sauce and cut it into thick slices. Return it to the sauce to heat through then serve sprinkled with chives.

Stir-Fried Beef with Noodles

Serves 4

100 g/4 oz thin egg noodles
30 ml/2 tbsp groundnut (peanut) oil
225 g/8 oz lean beef, shredded
30 ml/2 tbsp soy sauce
15 ml/1 tbsp rice wine or dry sherry
2.5 ml/½ tsp salt
2.5 ml/½ tsp sugar
120 ml/4 fl oz/½ cup water

Soak the noodles until slightly softened then drain and cut them into 7.5 cm/3 in lengths. Heat half the oil and stir-fry the beef until just browned. Add the soy sauce, wine or sherry, salt and sugar and stir-fry for 2 minutes then remove from the pan. Heat the remaining oil and stir-fry the noodles until coated with oil. Return the beef mixture to the pan, add the water and bring to the boil. Cook and simmer for about 5 minutes until the liquid is absorbed.

Beef with Rice Noodles

Serves 4

4 dried Chinese mushrooms
30 ml/2 tbsp groundnut (peanut) oil
2.5 ml/½ tsp salt
225 g/8 oz lean beef, sliced
100 g/4 oz bamboo shoots, sliced
100 g/4 oz celery, sliced
1 onion, sliced
120 ml/4 fl oz/½ cup beef stock
2.5 ml/½ tsp sugar
10 ml/2 tsp cornflour (cornstarch)
5 ml/1 tsp soy sauce
15 ml/1 tbsp water
100 g/4 oz rice noodles
oil for deep-frying

Soak the mushrooms in warm water for 30 minutes then drain. Discard the stalks and slice the caps. Heat half the oil and fry the salt and beef until lightly browned then remove from the pan. Heat the remaining oil and stir-fry the vegetables until softened. Stir in the stock and sugar and bring to the boil. Return the beef to the pan, cover and simmer for 3 minutes. Mix together the cornflour, soy sauce and water, stir into the pan and simmer, stirring, until the mixture thickens. Meanwhile, deep-fry the rice noodles in hot oil for a few seconds until puffed and crisp and serve on top of the beef.

Beef with Onions

Serves 4

60 ml/4 tbsp groundnut (peanut) oil
300 g/11 oz lean beef, cut into strips
100 g/4 oz onions, cut into strips
15 ml/1 tbsp chicken stock
5 ml/1 tsp rice wine or dry sherry
5 ml/1 tsp sugar
5 ml/1 tsp soy sauce
salt
sesame oil

Heat the oil and fry the beef and onions over a high heat until lightly browned. Stir in the stock, wine or sherry, sugar and soy sauce and stir-fry quickly until well mixed. Season to taste with salt and sesame oil before serving.

Beef and Peas

Serves 4

30 ml/2 tbsp groundnut (peanut) oil
450 g/1 lb lean beef, cubed
2 onions, sliced
2 stalks celery, sliced
100 g/4 oz fresh or frozen peas, thawed
250 ml/8 fl oz/1 cup chicken stock
15 ml/1 tbsp soy sauce
15 ml/1 tbsp cornflour (cornstarch)

Heat the oil and stir-fry the beef until lightly browned. Add the onions, celery and peas and stir-fry for 2 minutes. Add the stock and soy sauce, bring to the boil, cover and simmer for 10 minutes. Mix the cornflour with a little water and stir it into the sauce. Simmer, stirring, until the sauce clears and thickens.

Stir-Fried Onion Crackle Beef

Serves 4

225 g/8 oz lean beef

2 spring onions (scallions), minced

30 ml/2 tbsp soy sauce

30 ml/2 tbsp rice wine or dry sherry

30 ml/2 tbsp groundnut (peanut) oil

1 clove garlic, crushed

5 ml/1 tsp wine vinegar

few drops of sesame oil

Cut the beef into thin slices against the grain. Mix the spring onions, soy sauce and wine or sherry, stir into the beef and leave to stand for 30 minutes. Drain, discarding the marinade. Heat the oil and fry the garlic until lightly browned. Add the beef and stir-fry until just browned. Add the vinegar and sesame oil, cover and simmer for 2 minutes.

Beef with Dried Orange Rind

Serves 4

450 g/1 lb lean beef, thinly sliced

5 ml/1 tsp salt

oil for deep-frying

30 ml/2 tbsp groundnut (peanut) oil

100 g/4 oz dried orange rind

2 dried chilli peppers, finely chopped

5 ml/1 tsp freshly ground pepper

45 ml/3 tbsp beef stock

2.5 ml/½ tsp sugar

15 ml/1 tbsp rice wine or dry sherry

5 ml/1 tsp wine vinegar

2.5 ml/½ tsp sesame oil

Sprinkle the beef with salt and leave to stand for 30 minutes. Heat the oil and deep-fry the beef until half cooked. Remove and drain well. Heat the oil and stir-fry the orange rind, chilli peppers and pepper for 1 minute. Add the beef and stock and bring to the boil. Add the sugar and wine vinegar and simmer until there is not much liquid left. Stir in the wine vinegar and sesame oil and mix well. Serve on a bed of lettuce leaves.

Beef with Oyster Sauce

Serves 4

15 ml/1 tbsp groundnut (peanut) oil

2 cloves garlic, crushed

450 g/1 lb rump steak, sliced

100 g/4 oz button mushrooms

15 ml/1 tbsp rice wine or dry sherry

150 ml/¼ pt/⅔ cup chicken stock

30 ml/2 tbsp oyster sauce

5 ml/1 tsp brown sugar

salt and freshly ground pepper

4 spring onions (scallions), sliced

15 ml/1 tbsp cornflour (cornstarch)

Heat the oil and fry the garlic until lightly browned. Add the steak and mushrooms and stir-fry until lightly browned. Add the wine or sherry and stir-fry for 2 minutes. Add the stock, oyster sauce and sugar and season with salt and pepper. Bring to the boil and simmer, stirring occasionally, for 4 minutes. Add the spring onions. Mix the cornflour with a little water and stir it into the pan. Simmer, stirring, until the sauce clears and thickens.

Beef with Pepper

Serves 4

350 g/12 oz lean beef, cut into strips
75 ml/5 tbsp soy sauce
75 ml/5 tbsp groundnut (peanut) oil
5 ml/1 tsp cornflour (cornstarch)
75 ml/5 tbsp water
2 onions, sliced
5 ml/1 tsp oyster sauce
freshly ground pepper
noodles baskets (page 276)

Marinate the beef with the soy sauce, 15 ml/1 tbsp of oil, the cornflour and water for 1 hour. Remove the meat from the marinade and drain well. Heat the remaining oil stir-fry the beef and onions until lightly browned. Add the marinade and the oyster sauce and season generously with pepper. Bring to the boil, cover and simmer for 5 minutes, stirring occasionally. Serve with noodle baskets.

Pepper Steak

Serves 4

45 ml/3 tbsp groundnut (peanut) oil
5 ml/1 tsp salt
2 cloves garlic, crushed
450 g/1 lb sirloin steak, thinly sliced
1 onion, cut into wedges
2 green peppers, roughly chopped
120 ml/4 fl oz/½ cup beef stock
5 ml/1 tsp brown sugar
5 ml/1 tsp rice wine or dry sherry
salt and freshly ground pepper
30 ml/2 tbsp cornflour (cornstarch)
30 ml/2 tbsp soy sauce

Heat the oil with the salt and garlic until the garlic is lightly browned then add the steak and stir-fry until just browned on all sides. Add the onion and peppers and stir-fry for 2 minutes. Add the stock, sugar, wine or sherry and season with salt and pepper. Bring to the boil, cover and simmer for 5 minutes. Mix together the cornflour and soy sauce and stir then into the sauce. Simmer, stirring, until the sauce clears and thickens, adding a little extra water if necessary to make the sauce the consistency you prefer.

Beef with Peppers

Serves 4

350 g/12 oz lean beef, thinly sliced
3 red chilli peppers, seeded and
  chopped
3 spring onions (scallions), cut into
  chunks
2 cloves garlic, crushed
15 ml/1 tbsp black bean sauce
1 carrot, sliced
3 green peppers, cut into chunks
salt
15 ml/1 tbsp groundnut (peanut) oil
5 ml/1 tsp soy sauce
45 ml/3 tbsp water
5 ml/1 tsp rice wine or dry sherry
5 ml/1 tsp cornflour (cornstarch)

Marinate the beef with the chilli peppers, spring onions, garlic, black bean sauce and carrot for 1 hour. Blanch the peppers in boiling salted water for 3 minutes then drain well. Heat the oil and stir-fry the beef mixture for 2 minutes. Add the peppers and stir-fry for 3 minutes. Add the soy sauce, water and wine or sherry. Mix the cornflour with a little water, stir it into the pan and simmer, stirring, until the sauce thickens.

Stir-Fried Beef Shreds with Green Peppers

Serves 4

225 g/8 oz lean beef, shredded
1 egg white
15 ml/1 tbsp cornflour (cornstarch)
2.5 ml/½ tsp salt
5 ml/1 tsp rice wine or dry sherry
2.5 ml/½ tsp sugar
oil for deep-frying
30 ml/2 tbsp groundnut (peanut) oil
2 red chilli peppers, diced
2 slices ginger root, shredded
15 ml/1 tbsp soy sauce
2 large green peppers, diced

Place the beef in a bowl with the egg white, cornflour, salt, wine or sherry and sugar and leave to marinate for 30 minutes. Heat the oil and deep-fry the beef until lightly browned. Remove from the pan and drain well. Heat the oil and stir-fry the chilli peppers and ginger for a few seconds. Add the beef and soy sauce and stir-fry until just tender. Add the green peppers, mix well and stir-fry for 2 minutes. Serve at once.

Beef with Chinese Pickles

Serves 4

100 g/4 oz Chinese pickles, shredded
450 g/1 lb lean steak, sliced against the grain
30 ml/2 tbsp soy sauce
5 ml/1 tsp salt
2.5 ml/½ tsp freshly ground pepper
60 ml/4 tbsp groundnut (peanut) oil
15 ml/1 tbsp cornflour (cornstarch)

Mix all the ingredients thoroughly and place in an ovenproof bowl. Stand the bowl on a rack in a steamer, cover and steam over boiling water for 40 minutes until the beef is cooked.

Steak with Potatoes

Serves 4

450 g/1 lb steak

60 ml/4 tbsp groundnut (peanut) oil

5 ml/1 tsp salt

2.5 ml/½ tsp freshly ground pepper

1 onion, chopped

1 clove garlic, crushed

225 g/8 oz potatoes, cubed

175 ml/6 fl oz/¾ cup beef stock

250 ml/8 fl oz/1 cup chopped celery
leaves

30 ml/2 tbsp cornflour (cornstarch)

15 ml/1 tbsp soy sauce

60 ml/4 tbsp water

Cut the steak into strips then into thin slivers against the grain. Heat the oil and fry the steak, salt, pepper, onion and garlic until lightly browned. Add the potatoes and stock, bring to the boil, cover and simmer for 10 minutes. Add the celery leaves and simmer for about 4 minutes until just tender. Blend the cornflour, soy sauce and water to a paste, add to the pan and simmer, stirring, until the sauce clears and thickens.

Red-Cooked Beef

Serves 4

450 g/1 lb lean beef

120 ml/4 fl oz/½ cup soy sauce

60 ml/4 tbsp rice wine or dry sherry

15 ml/1 tbsp brown sugar

375 ml/13 fl oz/1½ cups water

Place the beef, soy sauce, wine or sherry and sugar in a heavy-based pan and bring to a simmer. Cover and simmer for 10 minutes, turning once or twice. Stir in the water and bring to the boil. Cover and simmer for about 1 hour until the meat is tender, adding a little boiling water if necessary during cooking if the meat becomes too dry. Serve hot or cold.

Savoury Beef

Serves 4

30 ml/2 tbsp groundnut (peanut) oil

450 g/1 lb lean beef, cubed

2 spring onions (scallions), sliced

2 cloves garlic, crushed

1 slice ginger root, minced

2 cloves star anise, crushed

250 ml/8 fl oz/1 cup soy sauce

30 ml/2 tbsp rice wine or dry sherry

30 ml/2 tbsp brown sugar

5 ml/1 tsp salt

600 ml/1 pt/2½ cups water

Heat the oil and fry the beef until lightly browned. Drain off the excess oil and add the spring onions, garlic, ginger and anise and fry for 2 minutes. Add the soy sauce, wine or sherry, sugar and salt and mix together well. Add the water, bring to the boil, cover and simmer for 1 hour. Remove the lid and simmer until the sauce has reduced.

Shredded Beef

Serves 4

750 g/1½ lb lean beef, cubed
250 ml/8 fl oz/1 cup beef stock
120 ml/4 fl oz/½ cup soy sauce
60 ml/4 tbsp rice wine or dry sherry
45 ml/3 tbsp groundnut (peanut) oil

Place the beef, stock, soy sauce and wine or sherry in a heavy-based pan. Bring to the boil and boil, stirring, until the liquid evaporated. Leave to cool then chill. Shred the beef with two forks. Heat the oil then add the beef and stir-fry quickly until coated with oil. Continue to cook over a medium heat until the beef dries out completely. Leave to cool and serve with noodles or rice.

Family-Style Shredded Beef

Serves 4

225 g/8 oz beef, shredded
15 ml/1 tbsp soy sauce
15 ml/1 tbsp oyster sauce
45 ml/3 tbsp groundnut (peanut) oil
1 slice ginger root, minced
1 red chilli pepper, chopped
4 stalks celery, diagonally sliced
15 ml/1 tbsp hot bean sauce
5 ml/1 tsp salt
15 ml/1 tbsp rice wine or dry sherry
5 ml/1 tsp sesame oil
5 ml/1 tsp wine vinegar
freshly ground pepper

Place the beef in a bowl with the soy sauce and oyster sauce and leave to marinate for 30 minutes. Heat the oil and fry the beef until lightly browned then remove them from the pan. Add the ginger and chilli pepper and stir-fry for a few seconds. Add the celery and stir-fry until half cooked. Add the beef, hot bean sauce and salt and mix well. Add the wine or sherry, sesame oil and vinegar and stir-fry until the beef is tender and the ingredients well mixed. Serve sprinkled with pepper.

Shredded Spiced Beef

Serves 4

90 ml/6 tbsp groundnut (peanut) oil
450 g/1 lb lean beef, cut into strips
50 g/2 oz chilli bean paste
freshly ground pepper
15 ml/1 tbsp minced ginger root
30 ml/2 tbsp rice wine or dry sherry
225 g/8 oz celery, cut into chunks
30 ml/2 tbsp soy sauce
5 ml/1 tsp sugar
5 ml/1 tsp wine vinegar

Heat the oil and fry the beef until browned. Add the chilli bean paste and pepper and stir-fry for 3 minutes. Add the ginger, wine or sherry and celery and stir well together. Add the soy sauce, sugar and vinegar and stir-fry for 2 minutes.

Marinated Beef with Spinach

Serves 4

450 g/1 lb lean beef, thinly sliced
45 ml/3 tbsp rice wine or dry sherry
15 ml/1 tbsp soy sauce
5 ml/1 tsp sugar
2.5 ml/½ tsp sesame oil
450 g/1 lb spinach
45 ml/3 tbsp groundnut (peanut) oil
2 slices ginger root, minced
30 ml/2 tbsp beef stock
5 ml/1 tsp cornflour (cornstarch)

Flatten the meat slightly by pressing with the fingers. Mix together the wine or sherry, soy sauce, sherry and sesame oil. Add the meat, cover and refrigerate for 2 hours, stirring occasionally. Cut the spinach leaves into large pieces and the stems into thick slices. Heat 30 ml/2 tbsp of oil and stir-fry the spinach stems and ginger for 2 minutes. Remove from the pan. Heat the remaining oil. Drain the meat, reserving the marinade. Add half the meat to the pan, spreading out the slices so they do not overlap. Cook for about 3 minutes until lightly browned on both sides. Remove from the pan and fry the remaining meat, then remove it from the pan. Blend the stock and cornflour into the marinade. Add the mixture to the pan and bring to the boil. Add the spinach leaves, stems and ginger. Simmer for about 3 minutes until the spinach wilts then mix in the meat. Cook for a further 1 minute then serve at once.

Black Bean Beef with Spring Onions

Serves 4

225 g/8 oz lean beef, thinly sliced
1 egg, lightly beaten
5 ml/1 tsp light soy sauce
2.5 ml/½ tsp rice wine or dry sherry
2.5 ml/½ tsp cornflour (cornstarch)
250 ml/8 fl oz/1 cup groundnut (peanut) oil
2 cloves garlic, crushed
30 ml/2 tbsp black bean sauce
15 ml/1 tbsp water
6 spring onions (scallions), diagonally sliced
2 slices ginger root, shredded

Mix the beef with the egg, soy sauce, wine or sherry and cornflour. Leave to stand for 10 minutes. Heat the oil and fry the beef until almost cooked. Remove from the pan and drain well. Pour off all but 15 ml/1 tbsp of oil, reheat then fry the garlic and black bean sauce for 30 seconds. Add the beef, and water and fry for about 4 minutes until the beef is tender. Meanwhile, heat a further 15 ml/1 tbsp of the oil and briefly stir-fry the spring onions and ginger. Spoon the beef on to a warmed serving plate, top with the spring onions and serve.

Stir-Fried Beef with Spring Onions

Serves 4

45 ml/3 tbsp groundnut (peanut) oil
225 g/8 oz lean beef, thinly sliced
8 spring onions (scallions), sliced
75 ml/5 tbsp soy sauce
15 ml/1 tbsp rice wine or dry sherry
30 ml/2 tbsp sesame oil

Heat the oil and stir-fry the beef and onions until lightly browned. Add the soy sauce and wine or sherry and stir-fry until the meat is cooked to your liking. Stir in the sesame oil before serving.

Beef and Spring Onions with Fish Sauce

Serves 4

350 g/12 oz lean beef, thinly sliced
15 ml/1 tbsp cornflour (cornstarch)
15 ml/1 tbsp water
2.5 ml/½ tsp rice wine or dry sherry
pinch of bicarbonate of soda (baking soda)
pinch of salt
45 ml/3 tbsp groundnut (peanut) oil
6 spring onions (scallions), cut into 5 cm/2 in pieces
2 cloves garlic, crushed
2 slices ginger, minced
5 ml/1 tsp fish sauce
2.5 ml/½ tsp oyster sauce

Marinate the beef with the cornflour, water, wine or sherry, bicarbonate of soda and salt for 1 hour. Heat 30 ml/2 tbsp of oil and stir-fry the beef with half the spring onions, half the garlic and the ginger until well browned. Meanwhile, heat the remaining oil and fry the remaining spring onions, garlic and ginger with the fish sauce and oyster sauce until softened. Mix the two together and heat through before serving.

Steamed Beef

Serves 4

450 g/1 lb lean beef, sliced
5 ml/1 tsp cornflour (cornstarch)
2 slices ginger root, minced
15 ml/1 tbsp soy sauce
15 ml/1 tbsp rice wine or dry sherry
2.5 ml/½ tsp salt
2.5 ml/½ tsp sugar
15 ml/1 tbsp groundnut (peanut) oil
2 spring onions (scallions), minced
15 ml/1 tbsp chopped flat-leaved parsley

Place the beef in a bowl. Mix together the cornflour, ginger, soy sauce, wine or sherry, salt and sugar then stir into the beef. Leave to stand for 30 minutes, stirring occasionally. Arrange the beef slices in a shallow heatproof dish and sprinkle with the oil and spring onions. Steam on a rack over boiling water for about 40 minutes until the beef is cooked. Serve sprinkled with parsley.

Beef Stew

Serves 4

15 ml/1 tbsp groundnut (peanut) oil
1 clove garlic, crushed
1 slice ginger root, chopped
450 g/1 lb braising steak, cubed
45 ml/3 tbsp soy sauce
30 ml/2 tbsp rice wine or dry sherry
15 ml/1 tbsp brown sugar
300 ml/½ pt/1¼ cups chicken stock
2 onions, cut into wedges
2 carrots, thickly sliced
100 g/4 oz cabbage, shredded

Heat the oil with the garlic and ginger and fry until the garlic is lightly browned. Add the steak and fry for 5 minutes until browned. Add the soy sauce, wine or sherry and sugar, cover and simmer for 10 minutes. Add the stock, bring to the boil, cover and simmer for about 30 minutes. Add the onions, carrots and cabbage, cover and simmer for a further 15 minutes.

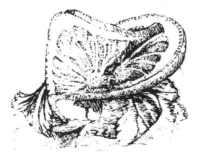

Stewed Beef Brisket

Serves 4

450 g/1 lb beef brisket
45 ml/3 tbsp groundnut (peanut) oil
3 spring onions (scallions), sliced
2 slices ginger root, chopped
1 clove garlic, crushed
120 ml/4 fl oz/½ cup soy sauce
5 ml/1 tsp sugar
45 ml/3 tbsp rice wine or dry sherry
3 cloves star anise
4 carrots, cubed
225 g/8 oz Chinese cabbage
15 ml/1 tbsp cornflour (cornstarch)
45 ml/3 tbsp water

Place the beef in a pan and just cover with water. Bring to the boil, cover and simmer gently for about 1½ hours until the meat is tender. Remove from the pan and drain well. Cut into 2.5cm/1 in cubes and reserve 250 ml/ 8 fl oz/1 cup of stock.

Heat the oil and fry the spring onions, ginger and garlic for a few seconds. Add the soy sauce, sugar, wine or sherry and star anise and stir well. Add the beef and reserved stock. Bring to the boil, cover and simmer for 20 minutes. Meanwhile, cook the Chinese cabbage in boiling water until tender. Transfer the meat and vegetables to a warmed serving plate. Blend the cornflour and water to a paste, stir it into the sauce and simmer, stirring, until the sauce clears and thickens. Pour over the beef and serve with the Chinese cabbage.

Beef Stir-Fry

Serves 4

225 g/8 oz lean beef
45 ml/3 tbsp groundnut (peanut) oil
1 slice ginger root, chopped
2 cloves garlic, crushed
2 spring onions (scallions), chopped
50 g/2 oz mushrooms, sliced
1 red pepper, sliced
225 g/8 oz cauliflower florets
50 g/2 oz mangetout (snow peas)
30 ml/2 tbsp soy sauce
15 ml/1 tbsp cornflour (cornstarch)
15 ml/1 tbsp rice wine or dry sherry
120 ml/4 fl oz/½ cup beef stock

Slice the beef thinly against the grain.
Heat half the oil and stir-fry the
ginger, garlic and spring onions until
lightly browned. Add the beef and
stir-fry until just browned then
remove from the pan. Heat the
remaining oil and stir-fry the
vegetables until coated with oil. Stir
in the stock, bring to the boil, cover
and simmer until the vegetables are
tender but still crisp. Mix the soy
sauce, cornflour and wine or sherry
and stir it into the pan. Simmer, stirring, until the sauce thickens.

Steak Strips

Serves 4

450 g/1 lb rump steak
120 ml/4 fl oz/½ cup soy sauce
120 ml/4 fl oz/½ cup chicken stock
1 cm/½ in slice ginger root
2 cloves garlic, crushed
30 ml/2 tbsp rice wine or dry sherry
15 ml/1 tbsp brown sugar
15 ml/1 tbsp groundnut (peanut) oil

Firm the steak in the freezer then cut
it into long thin slices. Mix together
all the remaining ingredients and
marinate the steak in the mixture for
about 6 hours. Weave the steak on to
soaked wooden skewers and grill for a
few minutes until cooked to your
liking, brushing occasionally with the
marinade.

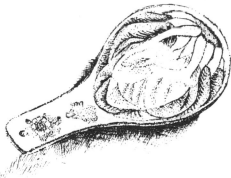

Steamed Beef with Sweet Potatoes

Serves 4

450 g/1 lb lean beef, thinly sliced

15 ml/1 tbsp black bean sauce

15 ml/1 tbsp sweet bean sauce

15 ml/1 tbsp soy sauce

5 ml/1 tsp sugar

2 slices ginger root, minced

2 sweet potatoes, cubed

30 ml/2 tbsp groundnut (peanut) oil

100 g/4 oz breadcrumbs

15 ml/1 tbsp sesame oil

3 spring onions (scallions), finely
    chopped

Place the beef in a bowl with the bean sauces, soy sauce, sugar and ginger and leave to marinate for 30 minutes. Remove the beef from the marinade and add the sweet potatoes. Leave to stand for 20 minutes. Arrange the potatoes on the base of a small bamboo steamer. Coat the beef in the breadcrumbs and arrange on top of the potatoes. Cover and steam over boiling water for 40 minutes.

Heat the sesame oil and stir-fry the spring onions for a few seconds. Spoon over the beef and serve.

Beef Tenderloin

Serves 4

450 g/1 lb lean beef

45 ml/3 tbsp rice wine or dry sherry

15 ml/1 tbsp soy sauce

10 ml/2 tsp oyster sauce

5 ml/1 tsp sugar

5 ml/1 tsp cornflour (cornstarch)

2.5 ml/½ tsp bicarbonate of soda
    (baking soda)

pinch of salt

1 clove garlic, crushed

30 ml/2 tbsp groundnut (peanut) oil

2 onions, thinly sliced

Cut the meat across the grain into thin slices. Mix together the wine or sherry, soy sauce, oyster sauce, sugar, cornflour, bicarbonate of soda, salt and garlic. Stir in the meat, cover and refrigerate for at least 3 hours. Heat the oil and stir-fry the onions for about 5 minutes until golden brown. Transfer to a warmed serving plate and keep warm. Add some of the meat to the wok, spreading the slices so they do not overlap. Fry for about 3 minutes on each side until browned then arrange on top of the onions and continue to fry the remaining meat.

Beef Toasts

Serves 4

4 slices lean beef
1 egg, beaten
50 g/2 oz/½ cup walnuts, chopped
4 slices bread
oil for deep-frying

Flatten the beef slices then brush them well with egg. Sprinkle with walnuts and top with a slice of bread. Heat the oil and fry the beef and bread slices for about 2 minutes. Remove from the oil and leave to cool. Reheat the oil and fry again until well browned.

Shredded Tofu-Chill Beef

Serves 4

225 g/8 oz lean beef, chopped
1 egg white
2.5 ml/½ tsp sesame oil
5 ml/1 tsp cornflour (cornstarch)
pinch of salt
250 ml/8 fl oz/1 cup groundnut (peanut) oil
100 g/4 oz dried tofu, cut into strips
5 red chilli peppers, cut into strips
15 ml/1 tbsp water
1 slice ginger root, chopped
10 ml/2 tsp soy sauce

Mix the beef with the egg white, half the sesame oil, the cornflour and salt. Heat the oil and stir-fry the beef until almost cooked. Remove from the pan. Add the tofu to the pan and stir-fry for 2 minutes then remove from the pan. Add the chilli peppers and stir-fry for 1 minute. Return the tofu to the pan with the water, ginger and soy sauce and stir well. Add the beef and stir-fry until well blended. Serve sprinkled with the remaining sesame oil.

Beef with Tomatoes

Serves 4

30 ml/2 tbsp groundnut (peanut) oil
3 spring onions (scallions), cut into chunks
225 g/8 oz lean beef, cut into strips
60 ml/4 tbsp beef stock
15 ml/1 tbsp cornflour (cornstarch)
45 ml/3 tbsp water
4 tomatoes, skinned and quartered

Heat the oil and stir-fry the spring onions until softened. Add the beef and stir-fry until just browned. Stir in the stock, bring to the boil, cover and simmer for 2 minutes. Mix the cornflour and water, stir into the pan and simmer, stirring, until the sauce thickens. Stir in the tomatoes and simmer just until they are heated through.

Red-Cooked Beef with Turnips

Serves 4

450 g/1 lb lean beef
1 slice ginger root, minced
1 spring onion (scallion), chopped
120 ml/4 fl oz/½ cup rice wine or dry
  sherry
250 ml/8 fl oz/1 cup water
2 cloves star anise
1 small turnip, diced
120 ml/4 fl oz/½ cup soy sauce
15 ml/1 tbsp sugar

Place the beef, ginger, spring onion, wine or sherry, water and anise in a heavy based pan, bring to the boil, cover and simmer for 45 minutes. Add the turnip, soy sauce and sugar and a little more water if necessary, bring back to the boil, cover and simmer for a further 45 minutes until the beef is tender. Leave to cool. Remove the beef and turnip from the sauce. Slice the beef and arrange on a serving plate with the turnip. Strain over the sauce and serve cold.

Beef with Vegetables

Serves 4

225 g/8 oz lean beef
15 ml/1 tbsp cornflour (cornstarch)
15 ml/1 tbsp soy sauce
15 ml/1 tbsp rice wine or dry sherry
2.5 ml/½ tsp sugar
45 ml/3 tbsp groundnut (peanut) oil
1 slice ginger root, chopped
2.5 ml/½ tsp salt
100 g/4 oz onion, sliced
2 stalks celery, sliced
1 red pepper, sliced
100 g/4 oz bamboo shoots, sliced
100 g/4 oz carrots, sliced
120 ml/4 fl oz/½ cup beef stock

Slice the beef thinly against the grain and place it in a bowl. Mix together the cornflour, soy sauce, wine or sherry and sugar, pour over the beef and toss to coat. Leave to stand for 30 minutes, turning occasionally. Heat half the oil and stir-fry the beef until just browned then remove it from the pan. Heat the remaining oil, stir in the ginger and salt then add the vegetables and stir-fry until coated with oil. Stir in the stock, bring to the boil, cover and simmer until the vegetables are tender but still crisp. Return the beef to the pan and stir over a gentle heat for about 1 minute to heat through.

Stewed Beef

Serves 4

350 g/12 oz rolled joint of beef
30 ml/2 tbsp sugar
30 ml/2 tbsp rice wine or dry sherry
30 ml/2 tbsp soy sauce
5 ml/1 tsp cinnamon
2 spring onions (scallions), chopped
1 slice ginger root, chopped
45 ml/3 tbsp sesame oil

Bring a saucepan of water to a rolling boil, add the meat, return the water to the boil and boil rapidly to seal the meat. Remove from the pan. Place the meat in a clean pan and add all the remaining ingredients, reserving 15 ml/1 tbsp of sesame oil. Fill the pan with just enough water to cover the meat, bring to the boil, cover and simmer gently for about 1 hour until the meat is tender. Sprinkle with the remaining sesame oil before serving.

Stuffed Steak

Serves 4–6

675 g/1½ lb rump steak in one piece
60 ml/4 tbsp wine vinegar
30 ml/2 tbsp sugar
10 ml/2 tsp soy sauce
2.5 ml/½ tsp freshly ground pepper
2.5 ml/½ tsp whole cloves
5 ml/1 tsp ground cinnamon
1 bay leaf, crushed
225 g/8 oz cooked long-grain rice
5 ml/1 tsp chopped fresh parsley
pinch of salt
30 ml/2 tbsp groundnut (peanut) oil
30 ml/2 tbsp lard
1 onion, sliced

Put the steak into a large bowl. Bring the wine vinegar, sugar, soy sauce, pepper, cloves, cinnamon and bay leaf to the boil in a pan then leave to cool. Pour over the steak, cover and leave to marinate in the refrigerator overnight, turning occasionally.

Mix the rice, parsley, salt and oil. Drain the beef and spread the mixture over the steak, roll up and tie securely with string. Melt the lard, add the onion and steak and fry until browned on all sides. Pour in enough water almost to cover the steak, cover and simmer for 1½ hours or until the meat is tender.

Beef Dumplings

Serves 4

450 g/1 lb plain (all-purpose) flour

1 sachet easy-mix yeast

10 ml/2 tsp caster sugar

5 ml/1 tsp salt

300 ml/½ pt/1¼ cup warm milk or
  water

30 ml/2 tbsp groundnut (peanut) oil

225 g/8 oz minced (ground) beef

1 onion, chopped

2 pieces stem ginger, chopped

50 g/2 oz cashews, chopped

2.5 ml/½ tsp five-spice powder

15 ml/1 tbsp soy sauce

30 ml/2 tbsp hoisin sauce

2.5 ml/½ tsp wine vinegar

15 ml/1 tbsp cornflour (cornstarch)

45 ml/3 tbsp water

Mix the flour, yeast, sugar, salt and warm milk or water and knead to a smooth dough. Cover and leave to rise in a warm place for 45 minutes. Heat the oil and fry the beef until lightly browned. Add the onion, ginger, cashews, five-spice powder, soy sauce, hoisin sauce and wine vinegar and bring to the boil. Mix the cornflour and water, stir into the sauce and simmer for 2 minutes. Leave to cool. Shape the dough into 16 balls. Press flat, spoon some filling into each and close the dough around the filling. Put in a steam basket in a wok or pan, cover and steam over salted water for about 30 minutes.

Crispy Meatballs

Serves 4

225 g/8 oz minced (ground) beef

100 g/4 oz water chestnuts, minced

2 eggs, beaten

5 ml/1 tsp grated orange rind

5 ml/1 tsp minced ginger root

5 ml/1 tsp salt

15 ml/1 tbsp cornflour (cornstarch)

225 g/8 oz/2 cups plain (all-purpose)
  flour

5 ml/1 tsp baking powder

300 ml/½ pt/1¼ cups water

15 ml/1 tbsp groundnut (peanut) oil

oil for deep-frying

Mix together the beef, water chestnuts, 1 egg, orange rind, ginger, salt and cornflour. Form into small balls. Arrange in a bowl in a steamer over boiling water and steam for about 20 minutes until cooked. Leave to cool.

Mix the flour, baking powder, remaining egg, water and groundnut (peanut) oil to a thick batter. Dip the meatballs in the batter. Heat the oil and fry the meatballs until golden brown.

Minced Beef with Cashew Nuts

Serves 4

450 g/1 lb minced (ground) beef
½ egg white
5 ml/1 tsp oyster sauce
5 ml/1 tsp light soy sauce
few drops of sesame oil
25 g/1 oz fresh parsley, chopped
45 ml/3 tbsp groundnut (peanut) oil
25 g/1 oz/¼ cup cashew nuts, chopped
15 ml/1 tbsp beef stock
4 large lettuce leaves

Mix the beef with the egg white, oyster sauce, soy sauce, sesame oil and parsley and leave to stand. Heat half the oil and fry the cashew nuts until lightly browned then remove them from the pan. Heat the remaining oil and stir-fry the meat mixture until browned. Add the stock and continue to fry until almost all the liquid has evaporated. Arrange the lettuce leaves on a warmed serving plate and spoon in the meat. Serve sprinkled with the fried cashew nuts.

Beef in Red Sauce

Serves 4

60 ml/4 tbsp groundnut (peanut) oil
450 g/1 lb minced (ground) beef
1 onion, chopped
1 red pepper, chopped
1 green pepper, chopped
2 slices pineapple, chopped
45 ml/3 tbsp soy sauce
45 ml/3 tbsp dry white wine
30 ml/2 tbsp wine vinegar
30 ml/2 tbsp honey
300 ml/½ pt/1¼ cups beef stock
salt and freshly ground pepper
few drops of chilli oil

Heat the oil and fry the beef until lightly browned. Add the vegetables and pineapple and stir-fry for 3 minutes. Add the soy sauce, wine, wine vinegar, honey and stock. Bring to the boil, cover and simmer for 30 minutes until cooked. Season to taste with salt, pepper and chilli oil.

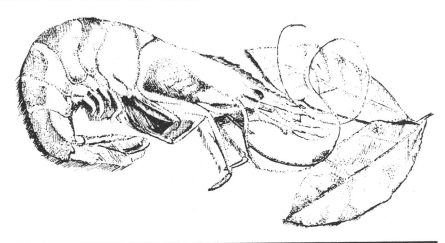

Beef Balls with Glutinous Rice

Serves 4

225 g/8 oz glutinous rice

450 g/1 lb lean beef, minced (ground)

1 slice ginger root, minced

1 small onion, minced

1 egg, lightly beaten

15 ml/1 tbsp soy sauce

2.5 ml/½ tsp cornflour (cornstarch)

2.5 ml/½ tsp sugar

2.5 ml/½ tsp salt

5 ml/1 tsp rice wine or dry sherry

Soak the rice for 30 minutes then drain and spread on a plate. Mix together the beef, ginger, onion, egg, soy sauce, cornflour, sugar, salt and wine or sherry. Form into walnut-sized balls. Roll the meatballs in the rice to coat them completely then arrange them on a shallow ovenproof dish with spaces between. Steam on a rack above gently simmering water for 30 minutes. Serve with dips of soy sauce and Chinese mustard.

Photograph opposite: Shredded Spiced Beef (page 117)

Meatballs with Sweet and Sour Sauce

Serves 4

450 g/1 lb minced (ground) beef

1 onion, finely chopped

25 g/1 oz water chestnuts, finely chopped

15 ml/1 tbsp soy sauce

15 ml/1 tbsp rice wine or dry sherry

1 egg, beaten

100 g/4 oz/½ cup cornflour (cornstarch)

oil for deep-frying

For the sauce:

15 ml/1 tbsp groundnut (peanut) oil

1 green pepper, cubed

100 g/4 oz pineapple chunks in syrup

100 g/4 oz mixed Chinese sweet pickles

100 g/4 oz/½ cup brown sugar

120 ml/4 fl oz/½ cup chicken stock

60 ml/4 tbsp wine vinegar

15 ml/1 tbsp tomato purée (paste)

15 ml/1 tbsp cornflour (cornstarch)

15 ml/1 tbsp soy sauce

salt and freshly ground pepper

45 ml/3 tbsp shredded coconut

Mix together the beef, onion, water chestnuts, soy sauce and wine or sherry. Shape into small balls and roll in beaten egg then in cornflour. Deep-fry in hot oil for a few minutes until browned. Transfer to a warmed serving plate and keep them warm.

Meanwhile, heat the oil and stir-fry the pepper for 2 minutes. Add 30 ml/2 tbsp of the pineapple syrup, 15 ml/1 tbsp of the pickle vinegar, the sugar, stock, wine vinegar, tomato purèe, cornflour and soy sauce. Stir well, bring to the boil and simmer, stirring, until the mixture clears and thickens. Drain the remaining

pineapple and pickles and add them to the pan. Simmer, stirring, for 2 minutes. Pour over the meatballs and serve sprinkled with coconut.

Steamed Meat Pudding

Serves 4

6 dried Chinese mushrooms
225 g/8 oz minced (ground) beef
225 g/8 oz minced (ground) pork
1 onion, diced
20 ml/2 tbsp mango chutney
30 ml/2 tbsp hoisin sauce
30 ml/2 tbsp soy sauce
5 ml/1 tsp five-spice powder
1 clove garlic, crushed
5 ml/1 tsp salt
1 egg, beaten
45 ml/3 tbsp cornflour (cornstarch)
60 ml/4 tbsp chopped chives
10 cabbage leaves
300 ml/½ pt/1¼ cups beef stock

Soak the mushrooms in warm water for 30 minutes then drain. Discard the caps and chop the caps. Mix with the minced meats, onion, chutney, hoisin sauce, soy sauce, five-spice powder and garlic and season with salt. Add the egg and cornflour and mix in the chives. Line the steam basket with the cabbage leaves. Shape the mince into a cake shape and place on the leaves. Cover and steam over gently simmering meat stock for 30 minutes.

Steamed Minced Beef

Serves 4

450 g/1 lb minced (ground) beef
2 onions, finely chopped
100 g/4 oz water chestnuts, finely chopped
60 ml/4 tbsp soy sauce
60 ml/4 tbsp rice wine or dry sherry
salt and freshly ground pepper

Mix together all the ingredients, seasoning to taste with salt and pepper. Press into a small heatproof bowl and stand in a steamer over simmering water. Cover and steam for about 20 minutes until the meat is cooked and the dish has created its own tasty sauce.

Photograph opposite: Willow Lamb (page 142)

Stir-Fried Mince with Oyster Sauce

Serves 4

30 ml/2 tbsp groundnut (peanut) oil

2 cloves garlic, crushed

225 g/8 oz minced (ground) beef

1 onion, chopped

50 g/2 oz water chestnuts, chopped

50 g/2 oz bamboo shoots, chopped

15 ml/1 tbsp soy sauce

30 ml/2 tbsp rice wine or dry sherry

15 ml/1 tbsp oyster sauce

Heat the oil and fry the garlic until lightly browned. Add the meat and stir until browned on all sides. Add the onion, water chestnuts and bamboo shoots and stir-fry for 2 minutes. Stir in the soy sauce and wine or sherry, cover and simmer for 4 minutes.

Beef Rolls

Serves 4

350 g/12 oz minced (ground) beef

1 egg, beaten

5 ml/1 tsp cornflour (cornstarch)

5 ml/1 tsp groundnut (peanut) oil

salt and freshly ground pepper

4 spring onions (scallions), chopped

8 spring roll wrappers

oil for deep-frying

Mix the beef, egg, cornflour, oil, salt, pepper and spring onions. Leave to stand for 1 hour. Place spoonfuls of the mixture in each spring roll wrapper, fold up the base, fold in the sides then roll up the wrappers, sealing the edges with a little water. Heat the oil and deep-fry the rolls until golden brown and cooked through. Drain well before serving.

Beef and Spinach Balls

Serves 4

450 g/1 lb minced (ground) beef
1 egg
100 g/4 oz breadcrumbs
60 ml/4 tbsp water
15 ml/1 tbsp cornflour (cornstarch)
2.5 ml/½ tsp salt
15 ml/1 tbsp rice wine or dry sherry
30 ml/2 tbsp groundnut (peanut) oil
45 ml/3 tbsp soy sauce
120 ml/4 fl oz/½ cup beef stock
350 g/12 oz spinach, shredded

Mix the beef, egg, breadcrumbs, water, cornflour, salt and wine or sherry. Shape into walnut-sized balls. Heat the oil and fry the meatballs until browned on all sides. Remove from the pan and drain off any excess oil. Add the soy sauce and stock to the pan and return the meatballs. Bring to the boil, cover and simmer for 30 minutes, turning occasionally. Steam the spinach in a separate pan until just softened then stir into the beef and heat through.

Stir-Fried Beef with Tofu

Serves 4

20 ml/4 tsp cornflour (cornstarch)
10 ml/2 tsp soy sauce
10 ml/2 tsp rice wine or dry sherry
225 g/8 oz minced (ground) beef
2.5 ml/½ tsp sugar
30 ml/2 tbsp groundnut (peanut) oil
2.5 ml/½ tsp salt
1 clove garlic, crushed
120 ml/4 fl oz/½ cup beef stock
225 g/8 oz tofu, cubed
2 spring onions (scallions), chopped
pinch of freshly ground pepper

Mix half the cornflour, half the soy sauce and half the wine or sherry. Add to the beef and mix well. Heat the oil and stir-fry the salt and garlic for a few seconds. Add the beef and stir-fry until just browned. Stir in the stock and bring to the boil. Add the tofu, cover and simmer for 2 minutes. Mix the remaining cornflour, soy sauce and wine or sherry, add them to the pan and simmer, stirring, until the sauce thickens.

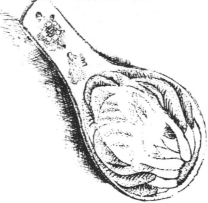

Lamb

Lamb is less popular than chicken or beef in Chinese cooking, but there are still a number of interesting ways of preparing lamb dishes Chinese style.

Lamb with Asparagus

Serves 4

350 g/12 oz asparagus
450 g/1 lb lean lamb
45 ml/3 tbsp groundnut (peanut) oil
salt and freshly ground pepper
2 cloves garlic, crushed
250 ml/8 fl oz/1 cup stock
1 tomato, skinned and cut into wedges
15 ml/1 tbsp cornflour (cornstarch)
45 ml/3 tbsp water
15 ml/1 tbsp soy sauce

Cut the asparagus into diagonal chunks and place in a bowl. Pour over boiling water and leave to stand for 2 minutes then drain. Slice the lamb thinly against the grain. Heat the oil and stir-fry the lamb until lightly coloured. Add the salt, pepper and garlic and stir-fry for 5 minutes. Add the asparagus, stock and tomato, bring to the boil, cover and simmer for 2 minutes. Mix the cornflour, water and soy sauce to a paste, stir it into the pan and simmer, stirring, until the sauce clears and thickens.

Barbecued Lamb

Serves 4

450 g/1 lb lean lamb, cut into strips
120 ml/4 fl oz/½ cup soy sauce
120 ml/4 fl oz/½ cup rice wine or dry sherry
1 clove garlic, crushed
3 spring onions (scallions), chopped
5 ml/1 tsp sesame oil
salt and freshly ground pepper

Place the lamb in a bowl. Mix together the remaining ingredients, pour over the lamb and leave to marinate for 1 hour. Grill (broil) over hot coals until the lamb is cooked, basting with the sauce, as required.

Lamb with Green Beans

Serves 4

450 g/1 lb green beans, cut into julienne strips
45 ml/3 tbsp groundnut (peanut) oil
450 g/1 lb lean lamb, thinly sliced
250 ml/8 fl oz/1 cup stock
5 ml/1 tsp salt
2.5 ml/½ tsp freshly ground pepper
15 ml/1 tbsp cornflour (cornstarch)
5 ml/1 tsp soy sauce
75 ml/5 tbsp water

Blanch the beans in boiling water for 3 minutes then drain well. Heat the oil and fry the meat until lightly browned on all sides. Add the stock, bring to the boil, cover and simmer for 5 minutes. Add the beans, salt and pepper, cover and simmer for 4 minutes until the meat is cooked. Blend the cornflour, soy sauce and water to a paste, stir into the pan and simmer, stirring, until the sauce clears and thickens.

Braised Lamb

Serves 4

450 g/1 lb boned shoulder of lamb, cubed

15 ml/1 tbsp groundnut (peanut) oil

4 spring onions (scallions), sliced

10 ml/2 tsp grated ginger root

200 ml/⅓ pt/1¼ cups chicken stock

30 ml/2 tbsp sugar

30 ml/2 tbsp soy sauce

15 ml/1 tbsp hoisin sauce

15 ml/1 tbsp rice wine or dry sherry

5 ml/1 tsp sesame oil

Blanch the lamb in boiling water for 5 minutes then drain. Heat the oil and stir-fry the lamb for about 5 minutes until browned. Remove from the pan and drain on kitchen paper. Remove all but 15 ml/1 tbsp of oil from the pan. Reheat the oil and stir-fry the spring onions and ginger for 2 minutes. Return the meat to the pan with the remaining ingredients. Bring to the boil, cover and simmer gently for 1¼ hours until the meat is tender.

Lamb with Broccoli

Serves 4

75 ml/5 tbsp groundnut (peanut) oil

1 clove garlic, crushed

450 g/1 lb lamb, cut into strips

450 g/1 lb broccoli florets

250 ml/8 fl oz/1 cup stock

5 ml/1 tsp salt

2.5 ml/½ tsp freshly ground pepper

30 ml/2 tbsp cornflour (cornstarch)

75 ml/5 tbsp water

5 ml/1 tsp soy sauce

Heat the oil and fry the garlic and lamb until cooked through. Add the broccoli and stock, bring to the boil, cover and simmer for about 15 minutes until the broccoli is tender. Season with salt and pepper. Mix the cornflour, water and soy sauce to a paste, stir it into the pan and simmer, stirring, until the sauce clears and thickens.

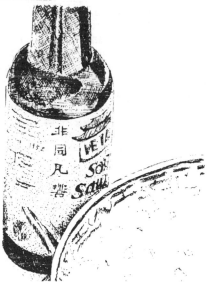

Lamb with Water Chestnuts

Serves 4

350 g/12 oz lean lamb, cut into chunks

15 ml/1 tbsp groundnut (peanut) oil

2 spring onions (scallions), sliced

2 slices ginger root, chopped

2 red chilli peppers, chopped

600 ml/1 pt/2½ cups water

100 g/4 oz turnip, cubed

1 carrot, diced

1 stick cinnamon

2 cloves star anise

2.5 ml/½ tsp sugar

15 ml/1 tbsp soy sauce

15 ml/1 tbsp rice wine or dry sherry

100 g/4 oz water chestnuts

15 ml/1 tbsp cornflour (cornstarch)

45 ml/3 tbsp water

Blanch the lamb in boiling water for 2 minutes then drain. Heat the oil and fry the spring onions, ginger and chilli peppers for 30 seconds. Add the lamb and stir-fry until well coated in the spices. Add the remaining ingredients except the water chestnuts, cornflour and water, bring to the boil, partially cover and simmer for about 1 hour until the lamb is tender. Check occasionally and top up with boiling water if necessary. Remove the cinnamon and anise, add the water chestnuts and simmer, uncovered for about 5 minutes. Blend the cornflour and water to a paste and stir a little into the sauce. Simmer, stirring, until the sauce thickens. You may not need all the cornflour paste if you have let the sauce reduce while cooking.

Lamb with Cabbage

Serves 4

45 ml/3 tbsp groundnut (peanut) oil

450 g/1 lb lamb, thinly sliced

salt and freshly ground black pepper

1 clove garlic, crushed

450 g/1 lb Chinese cabbage, shredded

120 ml/4 fl oz/½ cup stock

15 ml/1 tbsp cornflour (cornstarch)

15 ml/1 tbsp soy sauce

60 ml/4 tbsp water

Heat the oil and fry the lamb, salt, pepper and garlic until lightly browned. Add the cabbage and stir until coated with oil. Add the stock, bring to the boil, cover and simmer for 10 minutes. Mix the cornflour, soy sauce and water to a paste, stir into the pan and simmer, stirring, until the sauce clears and thickens.

Lamb Chow Mein

Serves 4

450 g/1 lb egg noodles

45 ml/3 tbsp groundnut (peanut) oil

450 g/1 lb lamb, sliced

1 onion, sliced

1 celery heart, sliced

100 g/4 oz mushrooms

100 g/4 oz bean sprouts

20 ml/2 tsp cornflour (cornstarch)

175 ml/6 fl oz/¾ cup water

salt and freshly ground pepper

Cook the noodles in boiling water for about 8 minutes then drain. Heat the oil and stir-fry the lamb until lightly browned. Add the onion, celery, mushrooms and bean sprouts and stir-fry for 5 minutes. Mix together the cornflour and water, pour into the pan and bring to the boil. Simmer, stirring, until the sauce thickens. Pour over the noodles and serve at once.

Lamb Curry

Serves 4

30 ml/2 tbsp groundnut (peanut) oil
2 cloves garlic, crushed
1 slice ginger root, minced
450 g/1 lb lean lamb, cubed
100 g/4 oz potato, cubed
2 carrots, cubed
15 ml/1 tbsp curry powder
250 ml/8 fl oz/1 cup chicken stock
100 g/4 oz mushrooms, sliced
1 green pepper, diced
50 g/2 oz water chestnuts, sliced

Heat the oil and fry the garlic and ginger until lightly browned. Add the lamb and stir-fry for 5 minutes. Add the potato and carrots and stir-fry for 3 minutes. Add the curry powder and stir-fry for 1 minute. Stir in the stock, bring to the boil, cover and simmer for about 25 minutes. Add the mushrooms, pepper and water chestnuts and simmer for 5 minutes. If you prefer a thicker sauce, boil for a few minutes to reduce the sauce or thicken it with 15 ml/1 tbsp cornflour mixed with a little water.

Fragrant Lamb

Serves 4

30 ml/2 tbsp groundnut (peanut) oil
450 g/1 lb lean lamb, cubed
2 spring onions (scallions), chopped
1 clove garlic, crushed
1 slice ginger root, minced
120 ml/4 fl oz/½ cup soy sauce
15 ml/1 tbsp rice wine or dry sherry
15 ml/1 tbsp brown sugar
2.5 ml/½ tsp salt
freshly ground pepper
300 ml/½ pt/1¼ cups water

Heat the oil and fry the lamb until lightly browned. Add the spring onions (scallions), garlic and ginger and fry for 2 minutes. Add the soy sauce, wine or sherry, sugar and salt and season to taste with pepper. Stir the ingredients together well. Add the water, bring to the boil, cover and simmer for 2 hours.

Grilled Lamb Cubes

Serves 4

120 ml/4 fl oz/½ cup groundnut
   (peanut) oil
60 ml/4 tbsp wine vinegar
2 cloves garlic, crushed
15 ml/1 tbsp soy sauce
5 ml/1 tsp salt
2.5 ml/½ tsp freshly ground pepper
2.5 ml/½ tsp oregano
450 g/1 lb lean lamb, cubed

Mix together all the ingredients, cover
and leave to marinate overnight.
Drain. Arrange the meat on a grill
(broiler) rack and grill (broil) for
about 15 minutes, turning several
times, until the lamb is tender and
lightly browned.

Lamb with Mangetout

Serves 4

2 cloves garlic, crushed
2.5 ml/½ tsp salt
450 g/1 lb lamb, diced
30 ml/ 2 tbsp cornflour (cornstarch)
30 ml/2 tbsp groundnut (peanut) oil
450 g/1 lb mangetout (snow peas), cut
   into 4
250 ml/8 fl oz/1 cup chicken stock
10 ml/2 tsp grated lemon rind
30 ml/2 tbsp honey
30 ml/2 tbsp soy sauce
5 ml/1 tsp ground coriander
5 ml/1 tsp caraway seeds, ground
30 ml/2 tbsp tomato purée (paste)
30 ml/2 tbsp wine vinegar

Mix the garlic and salt and toss with
the lamb. Coat the lamb in cornflour.
Heat the oil and stir-fry the lamb
until cooked. Add the mangetout and
stir-fry for 2 minutes. Mix the
remaining cornflour with the stock
and pour into the pan with the
remaining ingredients. Bring to the
boil, stirring, then simmer for 3
minutes.

Marinated Lamb

Serves 4

450 g/1 lb lean lamb
2 cloves garlic, crushed
5 ml/1 tsp salt
120 ml/4 fl oz/½ cup soy sauce
5 ml/1 tsp celery salt
oil for deep-frying

Place the lamb in a pot and just cover with cold water. Add the garlic and salt, bring to the boil, cover and simmer for 1 hour until the lamb is cooked. Remove from the pan and drain. Place the lamb in a bowl, add the soy sauce and sprinkle with celery salt. Cover and leave to marinate for 2 hours or overnight. Chop the lamb into small pieces. Heat the oil and deep-fry the lamb until brittle. Drain well before serving.

Lamb with Mushrooms

Serves 4

45 ml/3 tbsp groundnut (peanut) oil
350 g/12 oz mushrooms, sliced
100 g/4 oz bamboo shoots, sliced
3 slices ginger root, chopped
450 g/1 lb lamb, thinly sliced
250 ml/8 fl oz/1 cup stock
15 ml/1 tbsp cornflour (cornstarch)
15 ml/1 tbsp soy sauce
60 ml/4 tbsp water

Heat the oil and fry the mushrooms, bamboo shoots and ginger for 3 minutes. Add the lamb and stir-fry until lightly browned. Add the stock, bring to the boil, cover and simmer for about 30 minutes until the lamb is cooked and the sauce has reduced by half. Mix together the cornflour, soy sauce and water, stir into the pan and simmer, stirring, until the sauce clears and thickens.

Lamb with Oyster Sauce

Serves 4

30 ml/2 tbsp groundnut (peanut) oil
1 clove garlic, crushed
1 slice ginger, finely chopped
450 g/1 lb lean lamb, sliced
250 ml/8 fl oz/1 cup stock
30 ml/2 tbsp oyster sauce
15 ml/1 tbsp rice wine or sherry
5 ml/1 tsp sugar

Heat the oil with the garlic and ginger and fry until lightly browned. Add the lamb and stir-fry for about 3 minutes until lightly browned. Add the stock, oyster sauce, wine or sherry and sugar, bring to the boil, stirring, then cover and simmer for about 30 minutes, stirring occasionally, until the lamb is cooked through. Remove the lid and continue to cook, stirring, for about 4 minutes until the sauce has reduced and thickened.

Red-Cooked Lamb

Serves 4

30 ml/2 tbsp groundnut (peanut) oil
450 g/1 lb lamb chops
250 ml/8 fl oz/1 cup chicken stock
1 onion, cut into wedges
120 ml/4 fl oz/½ cup soy sauce
5 ml/1 tsp salt
1 slice ginger root, chopped

Heat the oil and fry the chops until browned on both sides. Add the remaining ingredients, bring to the boil, cover and simmer for about 1½ hours until the lamb is tender and the sauce has reduced.

Lamb with Spring Onions

Serves 4

350 g/12 oz lean lamb, cubed
30 ml/2 tbsp soy sauce
30 ml/2 tbsp rice wine or dry sherry
30 ml/2 tbsp groundnut (peanut) oil
2 cloves garlic, crushed
8 spring onions (scallions), thickly
    sliced

Place the lamb in a bowl. Mix 15 ml/ 1 tbsp of soy sauce, 15 ml/1 tbsp of wine or sherry and 15 ml/1 tbsp of oil and stir into the lamb. Leave to marinate for 30 minutes. Heat the remaining oil and fry the garlic until lightly browned. Drain the meat, add it to the pan and stir-fry for 3 minutes. Add the spring onions and stir-fry for 2 minutes. Add the marinade and remaining soy sauce and wine or sherry and stir-fry for 3 minutes.

Tender Lamb Steaks

Serves 4

450 g/1 lb lean lamb
15 ml/1 tbsp soy sauce
10 ml/2 tsp rice wine or dry sherry
2.5 ml/½ tsp salt
1 small onion, chopped
45 ml/3 tbsp groundnut (peanut) oil

Slice the lamb thinly against the grain and arrange in a dish. Mix together the soy sauce, wine or sherry, salt and oil, pour over the lamb, cover and marinate for 1 hour. Drain well. Heat the oil and fry the lamb for about 2 minutes until just tender.

Lamb Stew

Serves 4

45 ml/3 tbsp groundnut (peanut) oil
2 cloves garlic, crushed
5 ml/1 tsp soy sauce
450 g/1 lb lean lamb, cubed
freshly ground pepper
30 ml/2 tbsp plain (all-purpose) flour
300 ml/½ pt/1¼ cups water
15 ml/1 tbsp tomato purée (paste)
1 bay leaf
100 g/4 oz mushrooms, halved
3 carrots, quartered
6 small onions, quartered
15 ml/1 tbsp sugar
1 stalk celery, sliced
3 potatoes, cubed
15 ml/1 tbsp rice wine or dry sherry
50 g/2 oz peas
15 ml/1 tbsp chopped fresh parsley

Heat half the oil. Toss the garlic and soy sauce with the lamb and season with pepper. Fry the meat until lightly browned. Sprinkle with flour and cook, stirring, until the flour is absorbed. Add the water, tomato purée and bay leaf, bring to the boil, cover and simmer for 30 minutes. Heat the remaining oil and fry the mushrooms for 3 minutes then remove them from the pan. Add the carrots and onions to the pan and fry for 2 minutes. Sprinkle with sugar and heat until the vegetables glisten. Add the mushrooms, carrots, onions, celery and potatoes to the stew, cover again and simmer for a further 1 hour. Add the wine or sherry, peas and parsley, cover and simmer for a further 30 minutes.

Stir-Fried Lamb

Serves 4

350 g/12 oz lean lamb, cut into strips
1 slice ginger root, finely chopped
3 eggs, beaten
45 ml/3 tbsp groundnut (peanut) oil
2.5 ml/½ tsp salt
5 ml/1 tsp rice wine or dry sherry

Mix together the lamb, ginger and eggs. Heat the oil and stir-fry the lamb mixture for 2 minutes. Stir in the salt and wine or sherry and stir-fry for 2 minutes.

Lamb and Vegetables

Serves 4

225 g/8 oz lean lamb, sliced
100 g/4 oz bamboo shoots, sliced
100 g/4 oz water chestnuts, sliced
100 g/4 oz mushrooms, sliced
30 ml/2 tbsp groundnut (peanut) oil
30 ml/2 tbsp soy sauce
30 ml/2 tbsp rice wine or dry sherry
2 cloves garlic, crushed
4 spring onions (scallions), sliced
150 ml/¼ pt/⅔ cup chicken stock
5 ml/1 tbsp sesame oil
15 ml/1 tbsp cornflour (cornstarch)

Mix together the lamb, bamboo shoots, water chestnuts and mushrooms. Mix 15 ml/1 tbsp of oil, 15 ml/1 tbsp of soy sauce and 15 ml/1 tbsp of wine or sherry and pour over the lamb mixture. Leave to marinate for 1 hour. Heat the remaining oil and fry the garlic until lightly browned. Add the meat mixture and stir-fry until browned. Stir in the spring onions then add the remaining soy sauce and wine or sherry, most of the stock and the sesame oil. Bring to the boil, stirring, cover and simmer for 10 minutes. Mix the cornflour with the remaining stock, stir it into the sauce and simmer, stirring, until the sauce clears and thickens.

Lamb with Tofu

Serves 4

60 ml/4 tbsp groundnut (peanut) oil
450 g/1 lb lean lamb, coarsely chopped
3 cloves garlic, crushed
2 spring onions (scallions), chopped
4 water chestnuts, diced
5 ml/1 tsp grated orange rind
15 ml/1 tbsp soy sauce
pinch of salt
100 g/4 oz tofu, cubed
2.5 ml/½ tsp oyster sauce
2.5 ml/½ tsp sesame oil

Heat half the oil and stir-fry the lamb, garlic and onions until lightly browned. Add the water chestnuts, orange rind and soy sauce and enough boiling water just to cover the meat. Bring back to the boil, cover and simmer for about 30 minutes until the lamb is very tender. Meanwhile, heat the remaining oil and stir-fry the tofu until lightly browned. Add it to the lamb with the oyster sauce and sesame oil and simmer, uncovered for 5 minutes.

Roast Lamb

Serves 4 –6

2 kg/4 lb leg of lamb
120 ml/4 fl oz/½ cup soy sauce
1 onion, finely chopped
2 cloves garlic, crushed
1 slice ginger root, chopped
50 g/2 oz/¼ cup brown sugar
30 ml/2 tbsp rice wine or dry sherry
30 ml/2 tbsp tomato purée (paste)
15 ml/1 tbsp wine vinegar
15 ml/1 tbsp lemon juice

Place the lamb in a dish. Purée the remaining ingredients then pour them over the lamb, cover and refrigerate overnight, turning and basting occasionally.

Roast the lamb in a preheated oven at 220°C/425°F/gas mark 7 for 10 minutes then reduce the heat to 190°C/375°F/gas mark 5 and continue to cook for 20 minutes per 450 g/1 lb plus 20 minutes, basting occasionally with the marinade.

Mustard-Roast Lamb

Serves 8

75 ml/5 tbsp prepared mustard
15 ml/1 tbsp soy sauce
1 clove garlic, crushed
5 ml/1 tsp chopped fresh thyme
1 slice ginger root, minced
15 ml/1 tbsp groundnut (peanut) oil
1.25 kg/3 lb leg of lamb

Mix together all the seasoning ingredients until creamy. Spread over the lamb and leave to stand for a few hours. Roast in a preheated oven at 180°C/350°F/gas mark 4 for about 1½ hours.

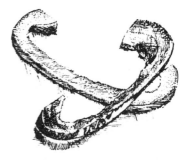

Stuffed Breast of Lamb

Serves 6 – 8

1 breast of lamb
225 g/8 oz cooked long-grain rice
1 small green pepper, chopped
2 spring onions (scallions), chopped
90 ml/6 tbsp groundnut (peanut) oil
salt and freshly ground pepper
375 ml/13 fl oz/1½ cups water
15 ml/1 tbsp cornflour (cornstarch)
15 ml/1 tbsp soy sauce

Cut a pock in the wide end of the breast of lamb. Mix together the rice, pepper, spring onions, 30 ml/2 tbsp of oil, salt and pepper and stuff the cavity with the mixture. Secure the end with string. Heat the remaining oil and fry the lamb until lightly browned on all sides. Season with salt and pepper, add 250 ml/8 fl oz/1 cup of water, bring to the boil, cover and simmer for 2 hours or until the meat is tender. Blend the cornflour, soy sauce and remaining water to a paste, stir into the pan and simmer, stirring, until the sauce clears and thickens.

Baked Lamb

Serves 4

100 g/4 oz breadcrumbs
4 hard-boiled (hard-cooked) eggs, chopped
225 g/8 oz cooked lamb, chopped
300 ml/½ pt/1¼ cups stock
15 ml/1 tbsp soy sauce
15 ml/1 tbsp cornflour (cornstarch)
30 ml/2 tbsp water

Arrange the breadcrumbs, hard-boiled eggs and lamb in layers in an ovenproof dish. Bring the stock and soy sauce to the boil in a saucepan. Mix the cornflour and water to a paste, stir into the stock and simmer, stirring, until the sauce thickens. Pour over the lamb mixture, cover and bake in a preheated oven at 180°C/350°C/gas mark 4 for about 25 minutes until golden brown.

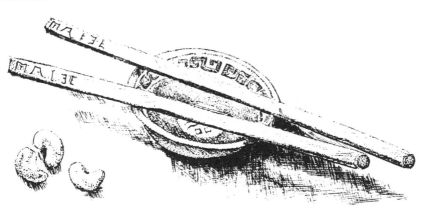

Lamb and Rice

Serves 4

30 ml/2 tbsp groundnut (peanut) oil
350 g/12 oz cooked lamb, cubed
600 ml/1 pt/2½ cups stock
10 ml/2 tsp salt
10 ml/2 tsp soy sauce
4 onions, quartered
2 carrots, sliced
50 g/2 oz peas
15 ml/1 tbsp cornflour (cornstarch)
30 ml/2 tbsp water
350 g/12 oz cooked long-grain rice, hot

Heat the oil and fry the lamb until lightly browned. Add the stock, salt and soy sauce, bring to the boil, cover and simmer for 10 minutes. Add the onions, carrots and peas, cover and simmer for 20 minutes until the vegetables are tender. Pour off the liquid into a saucepan. Blend the cornflour and water to a paste, stir into the sauce and simmer, stirring, until the sauce clears and thickens. Arrange the rice on a warmed serving plate and pile the lamb mixture on top. Pour over the sauce and serve at once.

Willow Lamb

Serves 3

450 g/1 lb lean lamb
1 egg, lightly beaten
30 ml/2 tbsp soy sauce
5 ml/1 tsp cornflour (cornstarch)
pinch of salt
oil for deep-frying
1 small carrot, shredded
1 clove garlic, crushed
2.5 ml/½ tsp sugar
2.5 ml/½ tsp wine vinegar
2.5 ml/½ tsp rice wine or dry sherry
freshly ground pepper

Slice the lamb into thin strips about 5 cm/2 in long. Mix together the egg, 15 ml/1 tbsp of soy sauce, the cornflour and salt, mix with the lamb and leave to marinate for a further 30 minutes. Heat the oil and deep-fry the lamb until half-cooked. Remove from the pan and drain. Pour off all but 30 ml/2 tbsp of oil and fry the carrot and garlic for 1 minute. Add the lamb and the remaining ingredients and stir-fry for 3 minutes.

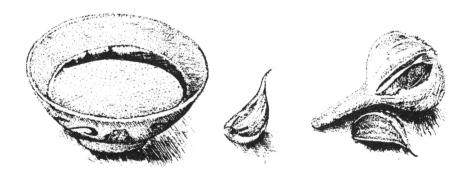

Pork and Ham

Pork is most famous for the delicious sweet and sour Chinese dishes which are so popular, but it is far more versatile and can be used in any number of flavour combinations. Pork fillet, or tenderloin, is a particularly good cut of pork to buy as it is very tender and has almost no fat.

Pork with Almonds

Serves 4

60 ml/4 tbsp groundnut (peanut) oil
50 g/2 oz/½ cup flaked almonds
350 g/12 oz pork, diced
100 g/4 oz bamboo shoots, diced
3 stalks celery, diced
50 g/2 oz peas
4 water chestnuts, diced
100 g/4 oz mushrooms, diced
250 ml/8 fl oz/1 cup stock
45 ml/3 tbsp soy sauce
salt and freshly ground pepper

Heat the oil and fry the almonds until lightly browned. Pour off most of the oil, add the pork and stir-fry for 1 minute. Add the bamboo shoots, celery, peas, water chestnuts and mushrooms and stir-fry for 1 minute. Add the stock, soy sauce, salt and pepper, bring to the boil, cover and simmer for 10 minutes.

Pork with Bamboo Shoots

Serves 4

30 ml/2 tbsp groundnut (peanut) oil
450 g/1 lb lean pork, cubed
3 spring onions (scallions), sliced
2 cloves garlic, crushed
1 slice ginger root, minced
250 ml/8 fl oz/1 cup soy sauce
30 ml/2 tbsp rice wine or dry sherry
30 ml/2 tbsp brown sugar
5 ml/1 tsp salt
600 ml/1 pt/2½ cups water
100 g/4 oz bamboo shoots, sliced

Heat the oil and fry the pork until golden brown. Drain off any excess oil, add the spring onions, garlic and ginger and fry for 2 minutes. Add the soy sauce, wine or sherry, sugar and salt and stir well. Add the water, bring to the boil, cover and simmer for 45 minutes. Add the bamboo shoots, cover and simmer for a further 20 minutes.

Barbecued Pork

Serves 4

2 pork fillets
30 ml/2 tbsp red wine
15 ml/1 tbsp brown sugar
15 ml/1 tbsp honey
60 ml/4 tbsp soy sauce
2.5 ml/½ tsp cinnamon
10 ml/2 tsp red food colour (optional)
1 clove garlic, crushed
1 spring onion (scallion), cut into chunks

Place the meat in a bowl. Mix together all the remaining ingredients, pour over the pork and leave to marinate for 2 hours, turning occasionally. Drain the meat and place it on a wire rack in a roasting tin. Cook in a preheated oven at 180°C/350°F/gas mark 4 for about 45 minutes, turning and basting with the marinade during cooking. Serve cut into thin slices.

Pork and Bean Sprouts

Serves 4

225 g/8 oz lean pork, cut into strips
1 slice ginger root, minced
30 ml/2 tbsp soy sauce
15 ml/1 tbsp rice wine or dry sherry
2.5 ml/½ tsp sugar
450 g/1 lb bean sprouts
45 ml/3 tbsp groundnut (peanut) oil
2.5 ml/½ tsp salt

Mix together the pork, ginger, 15 ml/ 1 tbsp of soy sauce, the wine or sherry and sugar. Blanch the bean sprouts in boiling water for 2 minutes then drain. Heat half the oil and stir-fry the pork for 3 minutes until lightly browned. Remove from the pan. Heat the remaining oil and stir-fry the bean sprouts with the salt for 1 minute. Sprinkle with the remaining soy sauce and stir-fry for a further 1 minute. Return the pork to the pan and stir-fry until heated through.

Spicy Braised Pork

Serves 4

450 g/1 lb pork, diced
salt and pepper
30 ml/2 tbsp soy sauce
30 ml/2 tbsp hoisin sauce
45 ml/3 tbsp groundnut (peanut) oil
120 ml/4 fl oz/½ cup rice wine or dry sherry
300 ml/½ pt/1¼ cups chicken stock
5 ml/1 tsp five-spice powder
6 spring onions (scallions), chopped
225 g/8 oz oyster mushrooms, sliced
15 ml/1 tbsp cornflour (cornstarch)

Season the meat with salt and pepper. Place in a dish and mix in the soy sauce and hoisin sauce. Cover and leave to marinate for 1 hour. Heat the oil and stir-fry the meat until golden brown. Add the wine or sherry, stock and five-spice powder, bring to the boil, cover and simmer for 1 hour. Add the spring onions and mushrooms, remove the lid and simmer for a further 4 minutes. Blend the cornflour with a little water, bring back to the boil and simmer, stirring, for 3 minutes until the sauce thickens.

Steamed Pork Buns

Makes 12

| 30 ml/2 tbsp hoisin sauce |
| 15 ml/1 tbsp oyster sauce |
| 15 ml/1 tbsp soy sauce |
| 2.5 ml/½ tsp sesame oil |
| 30 ml/2 tbsp groundnut (peanut) oil |
| 10 ml/2 tsp grated ginger root |
| 1 clove garlic, crushed |
| 300 ml/½ pt/1¼ cups water |
| 15 ml/1 tbsp cornflour (cornstarch) |
| 225 g/8 oz cooked pork, finely chopped |
| 4 spring onions (scallions), finely chopped |
| 350 g/12 oz/3 cups plain (all-purpose) flour |
| 15 ml/1 tbsp baking powder |
| 2.5 ml/½ tsp salt |
| 50 g/2 oz/¼ cup lard |
| 5 ml/1 tsp wine vinegar |
| 12 x 13 cm/5 in greaseproof paper squares |

Mix together the hoisin, oyster and soy sauces and the sesame oil. Heat the oil and fry the ginger and garlic until lightly browned. Add the sauce mixture and fry for 2 minutes. Blend 120ml/4 fl oz/½ cup of the water with the cornflour and stir it into the pan. Bring to the boil, stirring, then simmer until the mixture thickens. Stir in the pork and onions then leave to cool.

Mix together the flour, baking powder and salt. Rub in the lard until the mixture resembles fine breadcrumbs. Mix the wine vinegar and remaining water then mix this into the flour to form a firm dough. Knead lightly on a floured surface then cover and leave to stand for 20 minutes.

Knead the dough again then divide it into 12 and shape each one into a ball. Roll out to 15 cm/6 in circles on a floured surface. Place spoonfuls of the filling in the centre of each circle, brush the edges with water and pinch the edges together to seal around the filling. Brush one side of each greaseproof paper square with oil. Place each bun on a square of paper, seam side down. Place the buns in a single layer on a steamer rack over boiling water. Cover and steam the buns for about 20 minutes until cooked.

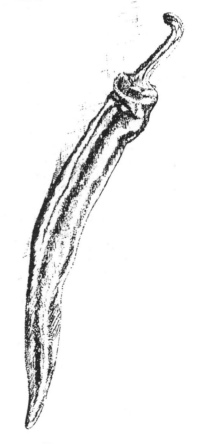

Pork with Cabbage

Serves 4

6 dried Chinese mushrooms
30 ml/2 tbsp groundnut (peanut) oil
450 g/1 lb pork, cut into strips
2 onions, sliced
2 red peppers, cut into strips
350 g/12 oz white cabbage, shredded
2 cloves garlic, chopped
2 pieces stem ginger, chopped
30 ml/2 tbsp honey
45 ml/3 tbsp soy sauce
120 ml/4 fl oz/½ cup dry white wine
salt and pepper
10 ml/2 tsp cornflour (cornstarch)
15 ml/1 tbsp water

Soak the mushrooms in warm water for 30 minutes then drain. Discard the stalks and slice the caps. Heat the oil and fry the pork until lightly browned. Add the vegetables, garlic and ginger and stir-fry for 1 minute. Add the honey, soy sauce and wine, bring to the boil, cover and simmer for 40 minutes until the meat is cooked. Season with salt and pepper. Mix together the cornflour and water and stir it into the pan. Bring just up to the boil, stirring continuously, then simmer for 1 minute.

Pork with Cabbage and Tomatoes

Serves 4

30 ml/2 tbsp groundnut (peanut) oil
450 g/1 lb lean pork, cut into slivers
salt and freshly ground pepper
1 clove garlic, crushed
1 onion, finely chopped
½ cabbage, shredded
450 g/1 lb tomatoes, skinned and quartered
250 ml/8 fl oz/1 cup stock
30 ml/2 tbsp cornflour (cornstarch)
15 ml/1 tbsp soy sauce
60 ml/4 tbsp water

Heat the oil and fry the pork, salt, pepper, garlic and onion until lightly browned. Add the cabbage, tomatoes and stock, bring to the boil, cover and simmer for 10 minutes until the cabbage is just tender. Blend the cornflour, soy sauce and water to a paste, stir into the pan and simmer, stirring, until the sauce clears and thickens.

Marinated Pork with Cabbage

Serves 4

350 g/12 oz belly pork
2 spring onions (scallions), chopped
1 slice ginger root, minced
1 stick cinnamon
3 cloves star anise
45 ml/3 tbsp brown sugar
600 ml/1 pt/2½ cups water
15 ml/1 tbsp groundnut (peanut) oil
15 ml/1 tbsp soy sauce
5 ml/1 tsp tomato purée (paste)
5 ml/1 tsp oyster sauce
100 g/4 oz Chinese cabbage hearts
100 g/4 oz pak choi

Cut the pork into 10 cm/4 in chunks and place in a bowl. Add the spring onions, ginger, cinnamon, star anise, sugar and water and leave to stand for 10 minutes. Heat the oil, lift the pork from the marinade and add it to the pan. Fry until lightly browned then add the soy sauce, tomato purée and oyster sauce. Bring to the boil and simmer for about 30 minutes until the pork is tender and the liquid has reduced, adding a little more water during cooking, if necessary.

Meanwhile, steam the cabbage hearts and pak choi over boiling water for about 10 minutes until tender. Arrange them on a warmed serving plate, top with the pork and spoon over the sauce.

Pork with Celery

Serves 4

45 ml/3 tbsp groundnut (peanut) oil
1 clove garlic, crushed
1 spring onion (scallion), chopped
1 slice ginger root, minced
225 g/8 oz lean pork, cut into strips
100 g/4 oz celery, thinly sliced
45 ml/3 tbsp soy sauce
15 ml/1 tbsp rice wine or dry sherry
5 ml/1 tsp cornflour (cornstarch)

Heat the oil and fry the garlic, spring onion and ginger until lightly browned. Add the pork and stir-fry for 10 minutes until golden brown. Add the celery and stir-fry for 3 minutes. Add the remaining ingredients and stir-fry for 3 minutes.

Pork with Chestnuts and Mushrooms

Serves 4

4 Chinese dried mushrooms
100 g/4 oz/1 cup chestnuts
30 ml/2 tbsp groundnut (peanut) oil
2.5 ml/½ tsp salt
450 g/1 lb lean pork, cubed
15 ml/1 tbsp soy sauce
375 ml/13 fl oz/1½ cups chicken stock
100 g/4 oz water chestnuts, sliced

Soak the mushrooms in warm water for 30 minutes then drain. Discard the stalks and halve the caps. Blanch the chestnuts in boiling water for 1 minute then drain. Heat the oil and salt then fry the pork until lightly browned. Add the soy sauce and stir-fry for 1 minute. Add the stock and bring to the boil. Add the chestnuts and water chestnuts, bring back to the boil, cover and simmer for about 1½ hours until the meat is tender.

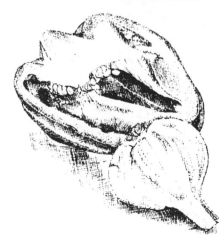

Pork Chop Suey

Serves 4

100 g/4 oz bamboo shoots, cut into strips
100 g/4 oz water chestnuts, thinly sliced
60 ml/4 tbsp groundnut (peanut) oil
3 spring onions (scallions), chopped
2 cloves garlic, crushed
1 slice ginger root, chopped
225 g/8 oz lean pork, cut into strips
45 ml/3 tbsp soy sauce
15 ml/1 tbsp rice wine or dry sherry
5 ml/1 tsp salt
5 ml/1 tsp sugar
freshly ground pepper
15 ml/1 tbsp cornflour (cornstarch)

Blanch the bamboo shoots and water chestnuts in boiling water for 2 minutes then drain and pat dry. Heat 45 ml/3 tbsp of oil and fry the spring onions, garlic and ginger until lightly browned. Add the pork and stir-fry for 4 minutes. Remove from the pan. Heat the remaining oil and stir-fry the vegetables for 3 minutes. Add the pork, soy sauce, wine or sherry, salt, sugar and a pinch of pepper and stir-fry for 4 minutes. Mix the cornflour with a little water, stir it into the pan and simmer, stirring, until the sauce clears and thickens.

Pork Chow Mein

Serves 4

4 dried Chinese mushrooms
30 ml/2 tbsp groundnut (peanut) oil
2.5 ml/½ tsp salt
4 spring onions (scallions), chopped
225 g/8 oz lean pork, cut into strips
15 ml/1 tbsp soy sauce
5 ml/1 tsp sugar
3 stalks celery, chopped
1 onion, cut into wedges
100 g/4 oz mushrooms, halved
120 ml/4 fl oz/½ cup chicken stock
soft-fried noodles (page 276)

Soak the mushrooms in warm water for 30 minutes then drain. Discard the stalks and slice the caps. Heat the oil and salt and fry the spring onions until softened. Add the pork and fry until lightly browned. Mix in the soy sauce, sugar, celery, onion and both fresh and dried mushrooms and stir-fry for about 4 minutes until the ingredients are well blended. Add the stock and simmer for 3 minutes. Add half the noodles to the pan and stir gently,then add the remaining noodles and stir until heated through.

Roast Pork Chow Mein

Serves 4

100 g/4 oz bean sprouts
45 ml/3 tbsp groundnut (peanut) oil
100 g/4 oz Chinese cabbage, shredded
225 g/8 oz roast pork, sliced
5 ml/1 tsp salt
15 ml/1 tbsp rice wine or dry sherry

Blanch the bean sprouts in boiling water for 4 minutes then drain. Heat the oil and stir-fry the bean sprouts and cabbage until just softened. Add the pork, salt and sherry and stir-fry until heated through. Add half the drained noodles to the pan and stir gently until heated through. Add the remaining noodles and stir until heated through.

Pork with Chutney

Serves 4

5 ml/1 tsp five-spice powder
5 ml/1 tsp curry powder
450 g/1 lb pork, cut into strips
30 ml/2 tbsp groundnut (peanut) oil
6 spring onions (scallions), cut into strips
1 stick celery, cut into strips
100 g/4 oz bean sprouts
1 x 200 g/7 oz jar Chinese sweet pickles, diced
45 ml/3 tbsp mango chutney
30 ml/2 tbsp soy sauce
30 ml/2 tbsp tomato purée (paste)
150 ml/¼ pt/⅔ cup chicken stock
10 ml/2 tsp cornflour (cornstarch)

Rub the spices well into the pork. Heat the oil and stir-fry the meat for 8 minutes or until cooked. Remove from the pan. Add the vegetables to the pan and stir-fry for 5 minutes. Return the pork to the pan with all the remaining ingredients except the cornflour. Stir until heated through. Mix the cornflour with a little water, stir it into the pan and simmer, stirring, until the sauce thickens.

Pork with Cucumber

Serves 4

225 g/8 oz lean pork, cut into strips
30 ml/2 tbsp plain (all-purpose) flour
salt and freshly ground pepper
60 ml/4 tbsp groundnut (peanut) oil
225 g/8 oz cucumber, peeled and sliced
30 ml/2 tbsp soy sauce

Toss the pork in the flour and season with salt and pepper. Heat the oil and stir-fry the pork for about 5 minutes until cooked. Add the cucumber and soy sauce and stir-fry for a further 4 minutes. Check and adjust the seasoning and serve with fried-rice.

Crispy Pork Parcels

Serves 4

4 dried Chinese mushrooms
30 ml/2 tbsp groundnut (peanut) oil
225 g/8 oz pork fillet, minced (ground)
50 g/2 oz peeled prawns, chopped
15 ml/1 tbsp soy sauce
15 ml/1 tbsp cornflour (cornstarch)
30 ml/2 tbsp water
8 spring roll wrappers
100 g/4 oz/1 cup cornflour (cornstarch)
oil for deep-frying

Soak the mushrooms in warm water for 30 minutes then drain. Discard the stalks and finely chop the caps. Heat the oil and fry the mushrooms, pork, prawns and soy sauce for 2 minutes. Blend the cornflour and water to a paste and stir into the mixture to make the filling.
    Cut the wrappers into strips, place a little filling on the end of each one and roll up into triangles, sealing with a little flour and water mixture. Dust generously with cornflour. Heat the oil and deep-fry the triangles until crisp and golden brown. Drain well before serving.

Pork Egg Rolls

Serves 4

225 g/8 oz lean pork, shredded
1 slice ginger root, minced
1 spring onion, chopped
15 ml/1 tbsp soy sauce
15 ml/1 tbsp water
12 egg roll skins (page 282)
1 egg, beaten
oil for deep-frying

Mix together the pork, ginger, onion, soy sauce and water. Place a little of the filling on the centre of each skin and brush the edges with beaten egg. Fold in the sides then roll the egg roll away from you, sealing the edges with egg. Steam on a rack in a steamer for 30 minutes until the pork is cooked. Heat the oil and deep-fry for a few minutes until crisp and golden.

Pork and Prawn Egg Rolls

Serves 4

30 ml/2 tbsp groundnut (peanut) oil
225 g/8 oz lean pork, shredded
6 spring onions (scallions), chopped
225 g/8 oz bean sprouts
100 g/4 oz peeled prawns, chopped
15 ml/1 tbsp soy sauce
2.5 ml/½ tsp salt
12 egg roll skins (page 282)
1 egg, beaten
oil for deep-frying

Heat the oil and fry the pork and spring onions until lightly browned. Meanwhile blanch the bean sprouts in boiling water for 2 minutes then drain. Add the bean sprouts to the pan and stir-fry for 1 minute. Add the prawns, soy sauce and salt and stir-fry for 2 minutes. Leave to cool.

Place a little filling on the centre of each skin and brush the edges with beaten egg. Fold in the sides then roll up the egg rolls, sealing the edges with egg. Heat the oil and deep-fry the egg rolls until crisp and golden.

Braised Pork with Eggs

Serves 4

450 g/1 lb lean pork
30 ml/2 tbsp groundnut (peanut) oil
1 onion, chopped
90 ml/6 tbsp soy sauce
45 ml/3 tbsp rice wine or dry sherry
15 ml/1 tbsp brown sugar
3 hard-boiled (hard-cooked) eggs

Bring a saucepan of water to the boil, add the pork, return to the boil and boil until sealed. Remove from the pan, drain well then cut into cubes. Heat the oil and fry the onion until softened. Add the pork and stir-fry until lightly browned. Stir in the soy sauce, wine or sherry and sugar, cover and simmer for 30 minutes, stirring occasionally. Score the outside of the eggs slightly then add them to the pan, cover and simmer for a further 30 minutes.

Fiery Pork

Serves 4

450 g/1 lb pork fillet, cut into strips
30 ml/2 tbsp soy sauce
30 ml/2 tbsp hoisin sauce
5 ml/1 tsp five-spice powder
15 ml/1 tbsp pepper
15 ml/1 tbsp brown sugar
15 ml/1 tbsp sesame oil
30 ml/2 tbsp groundnut (peanut) oil
6 spring onions (scallions), chopped
1 green pepper, cut into chunks
200 g/7 oz bean sprouts
2 slices pineapple, diced
45 ml/3 tbsp tomato ketchup (catsup)
150 ml/½ pt/⅔ cup chicken stock

Place the meat in a bowl. Mix the soy sauce, hoisin sauce, five-spice powder, pepper and sugar, pour over the meat and leave to marinate for 1 hour. Heat the oils and stir-fry the meat until golden brown. Remove from the pan. Add the vegetables and fry for 2 minutes. Add the pineapple, tomato ketchup and stock and bring to the boil. Return the meat to the pan and heat through before serving.

Deep-Fried Pork Fillet

Serves 4

350 g/12 oz pork fillet, cubed
15 ml/1 tbsp rice wine or dry sherry
15 ml/1 tbsp soy sauce
5 ml/1 tsp sesame oil
30 ml/2 tbsp cornflour (cornstarch)
oil for deep-frying

Mix together the pork, wine or sherry, soy sauce, sesame oil and cornflour so that the pork is coated with a thick batter. Heat the oil and deep-fry the pork for about 3 minutes until crisp. Remove the pork from the pan, reheat the oil and deep-fry again for about 3 minutes.

Five-Spice Pork

Serves 4

225 g/8 oz lean pork
5 ml/1 tsp cornflour (cornstarch)
2.5 ml/½ tsp five-spice powder
2.5 ml/½ tsp salt
15 ml/1 tbsp rice wine or dry sherry
20 ml/2 tbsp groundnut (peanut) oil
120 ml/4 fl oz/½ cup chicken stock

Slice the pork thinly against the grain. Mix the pork with the cornflour, five-spice powder, salt and wine or sherry and stir well to coat the pork. Leave to stand for 30 minutes, stirring occasionally. Heat the oil, add the pork and stir-fry for about 3 minutes. Add the stock, bring to the boil, cover and simmer for 3 minutes. Serve immediately.

Braised Fragrant Pork

Serves 6–8

1 piece tangerine peel
45 ml/3 tbsp groundnut (peanut) oil
900 g/2 lb lean pork, cubed
250 ml/8 fl oz/1 cup rice wine or dry
    sherry
120 ml/4 fl oz/½ cup soy sauce
2.5 ml/½ tsp anise powder
½ cinnamon stick
4 cloves
5 ml/1 tsp salt
250 ml/8 fl oz/1 cup water
2 spring onions (scallions), sliced
1 slice ginger root, chopped

Soak the tangerine peel in water while you prepare the dish. Heat the oil and fry the pork until lightly browned. Add the wine or sherry, soy sauce, anise powder, cinnamon, cloves, salt and water. Bring to the boil, add the tangerine peel, spring onion and ginger. Cover and simmer for about 1½ hours until tender, stirring occasionally and adding a little extra boiling water if necessary. Remove the spices before serving.

Pork with Minced Garlic

Serves 4

450 g/1 lb belly of pork, skinned
3 slices ginger root
2 spring onions (scallions), chopped
30 ml/2 tbsp minced garlic
30 ml/2 tbsp soy sauce
5 ml/1 tsp salt
15 ml/1 tbsp chicken stock
2.5 ml/½ tsp chilli oil
4 sprigs coriander

Place the pork in a pan with the ginger and spring onions, cover with water, bring to the boil and simmer for 30 minutes until cooked through. Remove and drain well, then cut into thin slices about 5 cm/2 in square. Arrange the slices in a metal strainer. Bring a pan of water to the boil, add the pork slices and cook for 3 minutes until heated through. Arrange on a warmed serving plate. Mix together the garlic, soy sauce, salt, stock and chilli oil and spoon over the pork. Serve garnished with coriander.

Stir-Fried Pork with Ginger

Serves 4

225 g/8 oz lean pork
5 ml/1 tsp cornflour (cornstarch)
30 ml/2 tbsp soy sauce
30 ml/2 tbsp groundnut (peanut) oil
1 slice ginger root, minced
1 spring onion (scallion), sliced
45 ml/3 tbsp water
5 ml/1 tsp brown sugar

Slice the pork thinly against the grain. Toss in cornflour then sprinkle with soy sauce and toss again. Heat the oil and stir-fry the pork for 2 minutes until sealed. Add the ginger and spring onion and stir-fry for 1 minute. Add the water and sugar, cover and simmer for about 5 minutes until cooked through.

Pork with Green Beans

Serves 4

450 g/1 lb green beans, cut into chunks
30 ml/2 tbsp groundnut (peanut) oil
2.5 ml/½ tsp salt
1 slice ginger root, minced
225 g/8 oz lean pork, minced (ground)
120 ml/4 fl oz/½ cup chicken stock
75 ml/5 tbsp water
2 eggs
15 ml/1 tbsp cornflour (cornstarch)

Parboil the beans for about 2 minutes then drain. Heat the oil and stir-fry the salt and ginger for a few seconds. Add the pork and stir-fry until lightly browned. Add the beans and stir-fry for 30 seconds, coating with the oil. Stir in the stock, bring to the boil, cover and simmer for 2 minutes. Beat 30 ml/2 tbsp of water with the eggs and stir them into the pan. Mix the remaining water with the cornflour. When the eggs begin to set, stir in the cornflour and cook until the mixture thickens. Serve immediately.

Pork with Ham and Tofu

Serves 4

4 Chinese dried mushrooms
5 ml/1 tsp groundnut (peanut) oil
100 g/4 oz smoked ham, sliced
225 g/8 oz tofu, sliced
225 g/8 oz lean pork, sliced
15 ml/1 tbsp rice wine or dry sherry
salt and freshly ground pepper
1 slice ginger root, chopped
1 spring onion (scallion), chopped
10 ml/2 tsp cornflour (cornstarch)
30 ml/2 tbsp water

Soak the mushrooms in warm water for 30 minutes then drain. Discard the stalks and halve the caps. Rub a heatproof bowl with the groundnut (peanut) oil. Arrange the mushrooms, ham, tofu and pork in layers in the dish, with pork on top. Sprinkle with wine or sherry, salt and pepper, ginger and spring onion. Cover and steam on a rack over boiling water for about 45 minutes until cooked. Drain the gravy from the bowl without disturbing the ingredients. Add enough water to make up 250 ml/8 fl oz/1 cup. Mix together the cornflour and water and stir it into the sauce. Bring to the bowl and simmer, stirring, until the sauce clears and thickens. Turn the pork mixture on to a warmed serving plate, pour over the sauce and serve.

Fried Pork Kebabs

Serves 4

450 g/1 lb pork fillet, thinly sliced
100 g/4 oz cooked ham, thinly sliced
6 water chestnuts, thinly sliced
30 ml/2 tbsp soy sauce
30 ml/2 tbsp wine vinegar
15 ml/1 tbsp brown sugar
15 ml/1 tbsp oyster sauce
few drops of chilli oil
45 ml/3 tbsp cornflour (cornstarch)
30 ml/2 tbsp rice wine or dry sherry
2 eggs, beaten
oil for deep-frying

Thread the pork, ham and water chestnuts alternately on to small skewers. Mix together the soy sauce, wine vinegar, sugar, oyster sauce and chilli oil. Pour over the kebabs, cover and leave to marinate in the refrigerator for 3 hours. Mix the cornflour, wine or sherry and eggs to a smooth, thickish batter. Twist the kebabs in the batter to coat them. Heat the oil and deep-fry the kebabs until light golden brown.

Braised Pork Knuckle in Red Sauce

Serves 4

1 large knuckle of pork
1 1/1¾ pts/4¾ cups boiling water
5 ml/1 tsp salt
120 ml/4 fl oz/½ cup wine vinegar
120 ml/4 fl oz/½ cup soy sauce
45 ml/3 tbsp honey
5 ml/1 tsp juniper berries
5 ml/1 tsp aniseed
5 ml/1 tsp coriander
60 ml/4 tbsp groundnut (peanut) oil
6 spring onions (scallions), sliced
2 carrots, thinly sliced
1 stick celery, sliced
45 ml/3 tbsp hoisin sauce
30 ml/2 tbsp mango chutney
75 ml/5 tbsp tomato purée (paste)
1 clove garlic, crushed
60 ml/4 tbsp chopped chives

Bring the knuckle of pork to the boil with the water, salt, wine vinegar, 45 ml/3 tbsp of soy sauce, the honey and spices. Add the vegetables, bring back to the boil, cover and simmer for about 1¾ hours until the meat is tender. Remove the meat and vegetables from the pan, cut the meat off the bone and dice it. Heat the oil and fry the meat until golden brown. Add the vegetables and stir-fry for 5 minutes. Add the remaining soy sauce, the hoisin sauce, chutney, tomato purée and garlic. Bring to the boil, stirring, then simmer for 3 minutes. Serve sprinkled with chives.

Marinated Pork

Serves 4

450 g/1 lb lean pork
1 slice ginger root, minced
1 clove garlic, crushed
90 ml/6 tbsp soy sauce
15 ml/1 tbsp rice wine or dry sherry
45 ml/3 tbsp groundnut (peanut) oil
1 spring onion (scallion), sliced
15 ml/1 tbsp brown sugar
freshly ground pepper

Mix the pork with the ginger, garlic, 30 ml/2 tbsp soy sauce and wine or sherry. Leave to stand for 30 minutes, stirring occasionally, then lift the meat from the marinade. Heat the oil and fry the pork until lightly browned. Add the spring onion, sugar, remaining soy sauce and a pinch of pepper, cover and simmer for about 45 minutes until the pork is cooked. Cut the pork into cubes then serve.

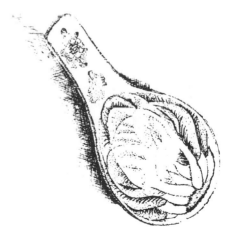

Marinated Pork Chops

Serves 6

6 pork chops
1 slice ginger root, minced
1 clove garlic, crushed
90 ml/6 tbsp soy sauce
30 ml/2 tbsp rice wine or dry sherry
45 ml/3 tbsp groundnut (peanut) oil
2 spring onions (scallions), chopped
15 ml/1 tbsp brown sugar
freshly ground pepper

Cut the bone from the pork chops and cut the meat into cubes. Mix the ginger, garlic, 30 ml/2 tbsp of soy sauce and the wine or sherry, pour over the pork and leave to marinate for 30 minutes, stirring occasionally. Remove the meat from the marinade. Heat the oil and fry the pork until lightly browned. Add the spring onions and stir-fry for 1 minute. Mix the remaining soy sauce with the sugar and a pinch of pepper. Stir into the sauce, bring to the boil, cover and simmer for about 30 minutes until the pork is tender.

Pork with Mushrooms

Serves 4

25 g/1 oz Chinese dried mushrooms
30 ml/2 tbsp groundnut (peanut) oil
1 clove garlic, chopped
225 g/8 oz lean pork, cut into slivers
4 spring onions (scallions), chopped
15 ml/1 tbsp soy sauce
15 ml/1 tbsp rice wine or dry sherry
5 ml/1 tsp sesame oil

Soak the mushrooms in warm water for 30 minutes then drain. Discard the stems and slice the caps. Heat the oil and fry the garlic until lightly browned. Add the pork and stir-fry until browned. Stir in the spring onions, mushrooms, soy sauce and wine or sherry and stir-fry for 3 minutes. Stir in the sesame oil and serve immediately.

Steamed Meat Cake

Serves 4

450 g/1 lb minced (ground) pork
4 water chestnuts, finely chopped
225 g/8 oz mushrooms, finely chopped
5 ml/1 tsp soy sauce
salt and freshly ground pepper
1 egg, lightly beaten

Mix all the ingredients together well and shape the mixture into a flat pie on an ovenproof plate. Place the plate on a rack in a steamer, cover and steam for 1 ½ hours.

Red-Cooked Pork with Mushrooms

Serves 4

450 g/1 lb lean pork, cubed
250 ml/8 fl oz/1 cup water
15 ml/1 tbsp soy sauce
15 ml/1 tbsp rice wine or dry sherry
5 ml/1 tsp sugar
5 ml/1 tsp salt
225 g/8 oz button mushrooms

Place the pork and water in a pan and bring the water to the boil. Cover and simmer for 30 minutes then drain, reserving the stock. Return the pork to the pan and add the soy sauce. Simmer over a low heat, stirring, until the soy sauce is absorbed. Stir in the wine or sherry, sugar and salt. Pour in the reserved stock, bring to the boil, cover and simmer for about 30 minutes, turning the meat occasionally. Add the mushrooms and simmer for a further 20 minutes.

Pork with Noodle Pancake

Serves 4

30 ml/2 tbsp groundnut (peanut) oil
5 ml/2 tsp salt
225 g/8 oz lean pork, cut into strips
225 g/8 oz Chinese cabbage, shredded
100 g/4 oz bamboo shoots, shredded
100 g/4 oz mushrooms, thinly sliced
150 ml/¼ pt/⅔ cup chicken stock
10 ml/2 tsp cornflour (cornstarch)
15 ml/1 tbsp rice wine or dry sherry
15 ml/1 tbsp water
noodle pancake (page 277)

Heat the oil and fry the salt and pork until lightly coloured. Add the cabbage, bamboo shoots and mushrooms and stir-fry for 1 minute. Add the stock, bring to the boil, cover and simmer for 4 minutes until the pork is cooked. Mix the cornflour to a paste with the wine or sherry and water, stir it into the pan and simmer, stirring, until the sauce clears and thickens. Pour over the noodle pancake to serve.

Pork and Prawns with Noodle Pancake

Serves 4

30 ml/2 tbsp groundnut (peanut) oil
5 ml/1 tsp salt
4 spring onions (scallions), chopped
1 clove garlic, crushed
225 g/8 oz lean pork, cut into strips
100 g/4 oz mushrooms, sliced
4 stalks celery, sliced
225 g/8 oz peeled prawns
30 ml/2 tbsp soy sauce
10 ml/1 tsp cornflour (cornstarch)
45 ml/3 tbsp water
noodle pancake (page 277)

Heat the oil and salt and fry the spring onions and garlic until softened. Add the pork and stir-fry until lightly browned. Add the mushrooms and celery and stir-fry for 2 minutes. Add the prawns, sprinkle with soy sauce and stir until heated through. Mix the cornflour and water to a paste, stir into the pan and simmer, stirring, until hot. Pour over the noodle pancake to serve.

Pork with Oyster Sauce

Serves 4–6

450 g/1 lb lean pork
15 ml/1 tbsp cornflour (cornstarch)
10 ml/2 tsp rice wine or dry sherry
pinch of sugar
45 ml/3 tbsp groundnut (peanut) oil
10 ml/2 tsp water
30 ml/2 tbsp oyster sauce
freshly ground pepper
1 slice ginger root, minced
60 ml/4 tbsp chicken stock

Slice the pork thinly against the grain. Mix 5 ml/1 tsp of cornflour with the wine or sherry, sugar and 5 ml/1 tsp of oil, add to the pork and stir well to coat. Blend the remaining cornflour with the water, oyster sauce and a pinch of pepper. Heat the remaining oil and fry the ginger for 1 minute. Add the pork and stir-fry until lightly browned. Add the stock and the water and oyster sauce mixture, bring to the boil, cover and simmer for 3 minutes.

Pork with Peanuts

Serves 4

450 g/1 lb lean pork, cubed
15 ml/1 tbsp cornflour (cornstarch)
5 ml/1 tsp salt
1 egg white
3 spring onions (scallions), chopped
1 clove garlic, chopped
1 slice ginger root, chopped
45 ml/3 tbsp chicken stock
15 ml/1 tbsp rice wine or dry sherry
15 ml/1 tbsp soy sauce
10 ml/2 tbsp black treacle
45 ml/3 tbsp groundnut (peanut) oil
¼ cucumber, cubed
25 g/1 oz/¼ cup shelled peanuts
5 ml/1 tsp chilli oil

Mix the pork with half the cornflour, the salt and egg white and stir well to coat the pork. Mix the remaining cornflour with the spring onions, garlic, ginger, stock, wine or sherry, soy sauce and treacle. Heat the oil and stir-fry the pork until lightly browned then remove it from the pan. Add the cucumber to the pan and stir-fry for a few minutes. Return the pork to the pan and stir lightly. Stir in the seasoning mixture, bring to the boil and simmer, stirring, until the sauce clears and thickens. Stir in the peanuts and chilli oil and heat through before serving.

Pork with Peppers

Serves 4

45 ml/3 tbsp groundnut (peanut) oil
225 g/8 oz lean pork, cubed
1 onion, diced
2 green peppers, diced
½ head Chinese leaves, diced
1 slice ginger root, minced
15 ml/1 tbsp soy sauce
15 ml/1 tbsp sugar
2.5 ml/½ tsp salt

Heat the oil and stir-fry the pork for about 4 minutes until golden brown. Add the onion and stir-fry for about 1 minute. Add the peppers and stir-fry for 1 minute. Add the Chinese leaves and stir-fry for 1 minute. Mix together the remaining ingredients, stir them into the pan and stir-fry for a further 2 minutes.

Spicy Pork with Pickles

Serves 4

900 g/2 lb pork chops
30 ml/2 tbsp cornflour (cornstarch)
45 ml/3 tbsp soy sauce
30 ml/2 tbsp sweet sherry
5 ml/1 tsp grated ginger root
2.5 ml/½ tsp five-spice powder
pinch of freshly ground pepper
oil for deep-frying
60 ml/4 tbsp chicken stock
Chinese pickled vegetables (page 358)

Trim the chops, discarding all the fat and bones. Mix together the cornflour, 30 ml/2 tbsp of soy sauce, the sherry, ginger, five-spice powder and pepper. Pour over the pork and stir to coat it completely. Cover and leave to marinate for 2 hours, turning occasionally. Heat the oil and deep-fry the pork until golden brown and cooked through. Drain on kitchen paper. Cut the pork into thick slices, transfer to a warmed serving dish and keep warm. Mix together the stock and remaining soy sauce in a small pan. Bring to the boil and pour over the sliced pork. Serve garnished with mixed pickles.

Pork with Plum Sauce

Serves 4

450 g/1 lb stewing pork, diced
2 cloves garlic, crushed
salt
60 ml/4 tbsp tomato ketchup (catsup)
30 ml/2 tbsp soy sauce
45 ml/3 tbsp plum sauce
5 ml/1 tsp curry powder
5 ml/1 tsp paprika
2.5 ml/½ tsp freshly ground pepper
45 ml/3 tbsp groundnut (peanut) oil
6 spring onions (scallions), cut into strips
4 carrots, cut into strips

Marinate the meat with the garlic, salt, tomato ketchup, soy sauce, plum sauce, curry powder, paprika and pepper for 30 minutes. Heat the oil and fry the meat until lightly browned. Remove from the wok. Add the vegetables to the oil and fry until just tender. Return the meat to the pan and reheat gently before serving.

Pork with Prawns

Serves 6–8

900 g/2 lb lean pork
30 ml/2 tbsp groundnut (peanut) oil
1 onion, sliced
1 spring onion (scallion), chopped
2 cloves garlic, crushed
30 ml/2 tbsp soy sauce
50 g/2 oz peeled prawns, minced (ground)
600 ml/1 pt/2½ cups boiling water
15 ml/1 tbsp sugar

Bring a saucepan of water to the boil, add the pork, cover and simmer for 10 minutes. Remove from the pan and drain well then cut into cubes. Heat the oil and fry the onion, spring onion and garlic until lightly browned. Add the pork and fry until lightly browned. Add the soy sauce and prawns and stir-fry for 1 minute. Add the boiling water and sugar, cover and simmer for about 40 minutes until the pork is tender.

Red-Cooked Pork

Serves 4

675 g/1½ lb lean pork, cubed
250 ml/8 fl oz/1 cup water
1 slice ginger root, crushed
60 ml/4 tbsp soy sauce
15 ml/1 tbsp rice wine or dry sherry
5 ml/1 tsp salt
10 ml/2 tsp brown sugar

Place the pork and water in a pan and bring the water to the boil. Add the ginger, soy sauce, sherry and salt, cover and simmer for 45 minutes.

Add the sugar, turn the meat over, cover and simmer for a further 45 minutes until the pork is tender.

Pork in Red Sauce

Serves 4

30 ml/2 tbsp groundnut (peanut) oil
225 g/8 oz pork kidneys, cut into strips
450 g/1 lb pork, cut into strips
1 onion, sliced
4 spring onions (scallions), cut into strips
2 carrots, cut into strips
1 stick celery, cut into strips
1 red pepper, cut into strips
45 ml/3 tbsp soy sauce
45 ml/3 tbsp dry white wine
300 ml/½ pt/1¼ cups chicken stock
30 ml/2 tbsp plum sauce
30 ml/2 tbsp wine vinegar
5 ml/1 tsp five-spice powder
5 ml/1 tsp brown sugar
15 ml/1 tbsp cornflour (cornstarch)
15 ml/1 tbsp water

Heat the oil and fry the kidneys for 2 minutes then remove them from the pan. Reheat the oil and fry the pork until lightly browned. Add the vegetables and stir-fry for 3 minutes. Add the soy sauce, wine, stock, plum sauce, wine vinegar, five-spice powder and sugar, bring to the boil, cover and simmer for 30 minutes until cooked. Add the kidneys. Mix together the cornflour and water and stir into the pan. Bring to the boil then simmer, stirring, until the sauce thickens.

Photograph opposite: Marinated Pork with Cabbage (page 147)

Pork with Rice Noodles

Serves 4

4 Chinese dried mushrooms
100 g/4 oz rice noodles
225 g/8 oz lean pork, cut into strips
15 ml/1 tbsp cornflour (cornstarch)
15 l/1 tbsp soy sauce
15 ml/1 tbsp rice wine or dry sherry
45 ml/3 tbsp groundnut (peanut) oil
2.5 ml/½ tsp salt
1 slice ginger root, minced
2 stalks celery, chopped
120 ml/4 fl oz/½ cup chicken stock
2 spring onions (scallions), sliced

Soak the mushrooms in warm water for 30 minutes then drain. Discard and stalks and slice the caps. Soak the noodles in warm water for 30 minutes then drain and cut into 5 cm/2 in pieces. Place the pork in a bowl. Mix together the cornflour, soy sauce and wine or sherry, pour over the pork and toss to coat. Heat the oil and fry the salt and ginger for a few seconds. Add the pork and stir-fry until lightly browned. Add the mushrooms and celery and stir-fry for 1 minute. Add the stock, bring to the boil, cover and simmer for 2 minutes. Add and noodles and heat through for 2 minutes. Stir in the spring onions and serve at once.

Rich Pork Balls

Serves 4

450 g/1 lb minced (ground) pork
100 g/4 oz tofu, mashed
4 water chestnuts, finely chopped
salt and freshly ground pepper
120 ml/4 fl oz/½ cup groundnut
   (peanut) oil
1 slice ginger root, minced
600 ml/1 pt/2½ cups chicken stock
15 ml/1 tbsp soy sauce
5 ml/1 tsp brown sugar
5 ml/1 tsp rice wine or dry sherry

Mix the pork, tofu and chestnuts and season with salt and pepper. Shape into large balls. Heat the oil and fry the pork balls until golden brown on all sides then remove from the pan. Drain off all but 15 ml/1 tbsp of the oil and add the ginger, stock, soy sauce, sugar and wine or sherry. Return the pork balls to the pan, bring to the boil and simmer gently for 20 minutes until cooked through.

Photograph opposite: Pork with Noodle Pancake (page 157)

Roast Pork Chops

Serves 4

4 pork chops
75 ml/5 tbsp soy sauce
oil for deep-frying
100 g/4 oz celery sticks
3 spring onions (scallions), chopped
1 slice ginger root, chopped
15 ml/1 tbsp rice wine or dry sherry
120 ml/4 fl oz/½ cup chicken stock
salt and freshly ground pepper
5 ml/1 tsp sesame oil

Dip the pork chops in the soy sauce until they are well coated. Heat the oil and deep-fry the chops until golden brown. Remove and drain well. Arrange the celery in the base of a shallow ovenproof dish. Sprinkle with the spring onions and ginger and arrange the pork chops on top. Pour over the wine or sherry and stock and season with salt and pepper. Sprinkle with sesame oil. Roast in a preheated oven at 200°C/400°C/gas mark 6 for 15 minutes.

Spiced Pork

Serves 4

1 cucumber, cubed
salt
450 g/1 lb lean pork, cubed
5 ml/1 tsp salt
45 ml/3 tbsp soy sauce
30 ml/2 tbsp rice wine or dry sherry
30 ml/2 tbsp cornflour (cornstarch)
15 ml/1 tbsp brown sugar
60 ml/4 tbsp groundnut (peanut) oil
1 slice ginger root, chopped
1 clove garlic, chopped
1 red chilli pepper, seeded and chopped
60 ml/4 tbsp chicken stock

Sprinkle the cucumber with salt and leave to one side. Mix together the pork, salt, 15 ml/1 tbsp of soy sauce, 15 ml/1 tbsp of wine or sherry, 15 ml/1 tbsp of cornflour, the brown sugar and 15 ml/1 tbsp of oil. Leave to stand for 30 minutes then lift the meat from the marinade. Heat the remaining oil and stir-fry the pork until lightly browned. Add the ginger, garlic and chilli and stir-fry for 2 minutes. Add the cucumber and stir-fry for 2 minutes. Mix the stock and remaining soy sauce, wine or sherry and cornflour into the marinade. Stir this into the pan and bring to the boil, stirring. Simmer, stirring, until the sauce clears and thickens and continue to simmer until the meat is cooked through.

Slippery Pork Slices

Serves 4

225 g/8 oz lean pork, sliced
2 egg whites
15 ml/1 tbsp cornflour (cornstarch)
45 ml/3 tbsp groundnut (peanut) oil
50 g/2 oz bamboo shoots, sliced
6 spring onions (scallions), chopped
2.5 ml/⅟ tsp salt
15 ml/1 tbsp rice wine or dry sherry
150 ml/⅟ pt/⅔ cup chicken stock

Toss the pork with the egg whites and cornflour until well coated. Heat the oil and stir-fry the pork until lightly browned then remove it from the pan. Add the bamboo shoots and spring onions and stir-fry for 2 minutes. Return the pork to the pan with the salt, wine or sherry and chicken stock. Bring to the boil and simmer, stirring for 4 minutes until the pork is cooked.

Pork with Spinach and Carrots

Serves 4

225 g/8 oz lean pork
2 carrots, cut into strips
225 g/8 oz spinach
45 ml/3 tbsp groundnut (peanut) oil
1 spring onion (scallion), finely chopped
15 ml/1 tbsp soy sauce
2.5 ml/⅟ tsp salt
10 ml/2 tsp cornflour (cornstarch)
30 ml/2 tbsp water

Slice the pork thinly against the grain then cut it into strips. Parboil the carrots for about 3 minutes then drain. Halve the spinach leaves. Heat the oil and fry the spring onion until translucent. Add the pork and stir-fry until lightly browned. Add the carrots and soy sauce and stir-fry for 1 minute. Add the salt and spinach and stir-fry for about 30 seconds until it begins to soften. Mix the cornflour and water to a paste, stir it into the sauce and stir-fry until it clears then serve at once.

Steamed Pork

Serves 4

450 g/1 lb lean pork, cubed
120 ml/4 fl oz/⅟ cup soy sauce
120 ml/4 fl oz/⅟ cup rice wine or dry sherry
15 ml/1 tbsp brown sugar

Mix together all the ingredients and place in a heatproof bowl. Steam on a rack over boiling water for about 1⅟ hours until cooked through.

Stir-Fried Pork

Serves 4

25 g/1 oz Chinese dried mushrooms
15 ml/1 tbsp groundnut (peanut) oil
450 g/1 lb lean pork, sliced
1 green pepper, diced
15 ml/1 tbsp soy sauce
15 ml/1 tbsp rice wine or dry sherry
5 ml/1 tsp salt
5 ml/1 tsp sesame oil

Soak the mushrooms in warm water for 30 minutes then drain. Discard the stems and slice the caps. Heat the oil and stir-fry the pork until lightly browned. Add the pepper and stir-fry for 1 minute. Add the mushrooms, soy sauce, wine or sherry and salt and stir-fry for a few minutes until the meat is cooked. Stir in the sesame oil before serving.

Pork with Sweet Potatoes

Serves 4

oil for deep-frying
2 large sweet potatoes, sliced
30 ml/2 tbsp groundnut (peanut) oil
1 slice ginger root, sliced
1 onion, sliced
450 g/1 lb lean pork, cubed
15 ml/1 tbsp soy sauce
2.5 ml/½ tsp salt
freshly ground pepper
250 ml/8 fl oz/1 cup chicken stock
30 ml/2 tbsp curry powder

Heat the oil and deep-fry the sweet potatoes until golden. Remove from the pan and drain well. Heat the groundnut (peanut) oil and fry the ginger and onion until lightly browned. Add the pork and stir-fry until lightly browned. Add the soy sauce, salt and a pinch of pepper then stir in the stock and curry powder, bring to the boil and simmer, stirring for 1 minute. Add the fried potatoes, cover and simmer for 30 minutes until the pork is cooked.

Sweet and Sour Pork

Serves 4

450 g/1 lb lean pork, cubed
15 ml/1 tbsp rice wine or dry sherry
15 ml/1 tbsp groundnut (peanut) oil
5 ml/1 tsp curry powder
1 egg, beaten
salt
100 g/4 oz cornflour (cornstarch)
oil for deep-frying
1 clove garlic, crushed
75 g/3 oz/⅓ cup sugar
50 g/2 oz tomato ketchup (catsup)
5 ml/1 tsp wine vinegar
5 ml/1 tsp sesame oil

Mix the pork with the wine or sherry, oil, curry powder, egg and a little salt. Mix in the cornflour until the pork is covered with the batter. Heat the oil until smoking then add the pork cubes a few a time. Fry for about 3 minutes then drain and set aside. Reheat the oil and fry the cubes again for about 2 minutes. Remove and drain. Heat the garlic, sugar, tomato ketchup and wine vinegar, stirring until the sugar dissolves. Bring to the boil then add the pork cubes and stir well. Stir in the sesame oil and serve.

Savoury Pork

Serves 4

30 ml/2 tbsp groundnut (peanut) oil
450 g/1 lb lean pork, cubed
3 spring onions (scallions), sliced
2 cloves garlic, crushed
1 slice ginger root, minced
250 ml/8 fl oz/1 cup soy sauce
30 ml/2 tbsp rice wine or dry sherry
30 ml/2 tbsp brown sugar
5 ml/1 tsp salt
600 ml/1 pt/2½ cups water

Heat the oil and fry the pork until golden brown. Drain off any excess oil,
add the spring onions, garlic and
ginger and fry for 2 minutes. Add the
soy sauce, wine or sherry, sugar and
salt and stir well. Add the water,
bring to the boil, cover and simmer for
1 hour.

Soft-Fried Pork

Serves 4

225 g/8 oz pork fillet, cubed
1 egg white
30 ml/2 tbsp rice wine or dry sherry
salt
225 g/8 oz cornflour (cornstarch)
oil for deep-frying

Mix the pork with the egg white, wine
or sherry and a little salt. Gradually
work in enough cornflour to make a
thick batter. Heat the oil and fry the
pork until golden brown and crisp outside and tender inside.

Pork with Tofu

Serves 4

450 g/1 lb lean pork
45 ml/3 tbsp groundnut (peanut) oil
1 onion, sliced
1 clove garlic, crushed
225 g/8 oz tofu, cubed
375 ml/13 fl oz/1½ cups chicken stock
15 ml/1 tbsp brown sugar
60 ml/4 tbsp soy sauce
2.5 ml/½ tsp salt

Place the pork in a saucepan and
cover with water. Bring to the boil
then simmer for 5 minutes. Drain
and leave to cool then cut into cubes.

Heat the oil and fry the onion and
garlic until lightly browned. Add the
pork and fry until lightly browned.
Add the tofu and stir gently until
coated with oil. Add the stock, sugar,
soy sauce and salt, bring to the boil,
cover and simmer for about 40
minutes until the pork is tender.

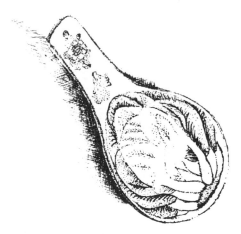

Twice-Cooked Pork

Serves 4

225 g/8 oz lean pork
45 ml/3 tbsp groundnut (peanut) oil
2 green peppers, cut into chunks
2 cloves garlic, chopped
2 spring onions (scallions), sliced
15 ml/1 tbsp hot bean sauce
15 ml/1 tbsp chicken stock
5 ml/1 tsp sugar

Place the piece of pork in a pan, cover with water, bring to the boil and simmer for 20 minutes until cooked through. Remove and drain then leave to cool. Slice thinly.

Heat the oil and stir-fry the pork until lightly browned. Add the peppers, garlic and spring onions and stir-fry for 2 minutes. Remove from the pan. Add the bean sauce, stock and sugar to the pan and simmer, stirring, for 2 minutes. Return the beef and peppers and stir-fry until heated through. Serve at once.

Pork with Vegetables

Serves 4

2 cloves garlic, crushed
5 ml/1 tsp salt
2.5 ml/½ tsp freshly ground pepper
30 ml/2 tbsp groundnut (peanut) oil
30 ml/2 tbsp soy sauce
225 g/8 oz broccoli florets
200 g/7 oz cauliflower florets
1 red pepper, diced
1 onion, chopped
2 oranges, peeled and diced
1 piece stem ginger, chopped
30 ml/2 tbsp cornflour (cornstarch)
300 ml/½ pt/1¼ cups water
20 ml/2 tbsp wine vinegar
15 ml/1 tbsp honey
pinch of ground ginger
2.5 ml/½ tsp cumin

Crush the garlic, salt and pepper into the meat. Heat the oil and stir-fry for meat until lightly browned. Remove from the pan. Add the soy sauce and vegetables to the pan and stir-fry until tender but still crisp. Add the oranges and ginger. Mix the cornflour and water and stir it into the pan with the wine vinegar, honey, ginger and cumin. Bring to the boil and simmer, stirring, for 2 minutes. Return the pork to the pan and heat through before serving.

Pork with Walnuts

Serves 4

50 g/2 oz/½ cup walnuts

225 g/8 oz lean pork, cut into strips

30 ml/2 tbsp plain (all-purpose) flour

30 ml/2 tbsp brown sugar

30 ml/2 tbsp soy sauce

oil for deep-frying

15 ml/1 tbsp groundnut (peanut) oil

Blanch the walnuts in boiling water for 2 minutes then drain. Mix the pork with the flour, sugar and 15 ml/ 1 tbsp of soy sauce until well coated. Heat the oil and deep-fry the pork until crispy and golden. Drain on kitchen paper. Heat the groundnut (peanut) oil and stir-fry the walnuts until golden. Add the pork to the pan, sprinkle with the remaining soy sauce and stir-fry until heated through.

Pork Wontons

Serves 4

450 g/1 lb minced (ground) pork

1 spring onion (scallion), chopped

225 g/8 oz mixed vegetables, chopped

30 ml/2 tbsp soy sauce

5 ml/1 tsp salt

40 wonton skins (page 282)

oil for deep-frying

Heat a pan and fry the pork and spring onion until lightly browned. Remove from the heat and stir in the vegetables, soy sauce and salt.

To fold the wontons, hold the skin in the palm of your left hand and spoon a little filling into the centre. Moisten the edges with egg and fold the skin into a triangle, sealing the edges. Moisten the corners with egg and twist them together.

Heat the oil and fry the wontons a few at a time until golden brown. Drain well before serving.

Pork with Water Chestnuts

Serves 4

45 ml/3 tbsp groundnut (peanut) oil

1 clove garlic, crushed

1 spring onion (scallion), chopped

1 slice ginger root, minced

225 g/8 oz lean pork, cut into strips

100 g/4 oz water chestnuts, thinly sliced

45 ml/3 tbsp soy sauce

15 ml/1 tbsp rice wine or dry sherry

5 ml/1 tsp cornflour (cornstarch)

Heat the oil and fry the garlic, spring onion and ginger until lightly browned. Add the pork and stir fry for 10 minutes until golden brown. Add the water chestnuts and stir-fry for 3 minutes. Add the remaining ingredients and stir-fry for 3 minutes.

Pork and Prawn Wontons

Serves 4

225 g/8 oz minced (ground) pork
2 spring onions (scallions), chopped
100 g/4 oz mixed vegetables, chopped
100 g/4 oz mushrooms, chopped
225 g/8 oz peeled prawns, chopped
15 ml/1 tbsp soy sauce
2.5 ml/½ tsp salt
40 wonton skins (page 282)
oil for deep-frying

Heat a pan and fry the pork and spring onions until lightly browned. Stir in the remaining ingredients.

To fold the wontons, hold the skin in the palm of your left hand and spoon a little filling into the centre. Moisten the edges with egg and fold the skin into a triangle, sealing the edges. Moisten the corners with egg and twist them together.

Heat the oil and fry the wontons a few at a time until golden brown. Drain well before serving.

Steamed Minced Meatballs

Serves 4

2 cloves garlic, crushed
2.5 ml/½ tsp salt
450 g/1 lb minced (ground) pork
1 onion, chopped
1 red pepper, chopped
1 green pepper, chopped
2 pieces stem ginger, chopped
5 ml/1 tsp curry powder
5 ml/1 tsp paprika
1 egg, beaten
45 ml/3 tbsp cornflour (cornstarch)
50 g/2 oz short-grain rice
salt and freshly ground pepper
60 ml/4 tbsp chopped chives

Mix together the garlic, salt, pork, onion, peppers, ginger, curry powder and paprika. Work the egg into the mixture with the cornflour and rice. Season with salt and pepper then mix in the chives. With wet hands, shape the mixture into small balls. Place these in a steam basket, cover and cook over gently boiling water for 20 minutes until cooked.

Spare Ribs with Black Bean Sauce

Serves 4

900 g/2 lb pork spare ribs
2 cloves garlic, crushed
2 spring onions (scallions), chopped
30 ml/2 tbsp black bean sauce
30 ml/2 tbsp rice wine or dry sherry
15 ml/1 tbsp water
30 ml/2 tbsp soy sauce
15 ml/1 tbsp cornflour (cornstarch)
5 ml/1 tsp sugar
120 ml/4 fl oz/½ cup water
30 ml/2 tbsp oil
2.5 ml/½ tsp salt
120 ml/4 fl oz/½ cup chicken stock

Cut the spare ribs into 2.5 cm/1 in pieces. Mix the garlic, spring onions, black bean sauce, wine or sherry, water and 15ml/1 tbsp of soy sauce. Mix the remaining soy sauce with the cornflour, sugar and water. Heat the oil and salt and fry the spare ribs until golden brown. Drain off the oil. Add the garlic mixture and stir-fry for 2 minutes. Add the stock, bring to the boil, cover and simmer for 4 minutes. Stir in the cornflour mixture and simmer, stirring, until the sauce clears and thickens.

Barbecued Spare Ribs

Serves 4

3 cloves garlic, crushed
75 ml/5 tbsp soy sauce
60 ml/4 tbsp hoisin sauce
60 ml/4 tbsp rice wine or dry sherry
45 ml/3 tbsp brown sugar
30 ml/2 tbsp tomato purée (paste)
900 g/2 lb pork spare ribs
15 ml/1 tbsp honey

Mix the garlic, soy sauce, hoisin sauce, wine or sherry, brown sugar and tomato purée, pour over the ribs, cover and leave to marinate overnight.

Drain the ribs and arrange them on a rack in a roasting tin with a little water underneath. Roast in a preheated oven at 180°C/350°F/gas mark 4 for 45 minutes, basting occasionally with the marinade, reserving 30 ml/2 tbsp of the marinade. Mix the reserved marinade with the honey and brush over the ribs. Barbecue or grill (broil) under a hot grill for about 10 minutes.

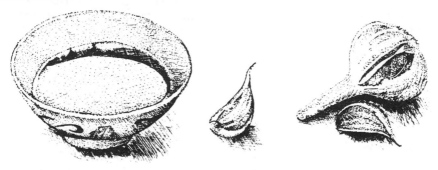

Barbecued Maple Spare Ribs

Serves 4

900 g/2 lb pork spare ribs
60 ml/4 tbsp maple syrup
5 ml/1 tsp salt
5 ml/1 tsp sugar
45 ml/3 tbsp soy sauce
15 ml/1 tbsp rice wine or dry sherry
1 clove garlic, crushed

Chop the spare ribs into 5 cm/2 in pieces and place in a bowl. Mix together all the ingredients, add the spare ribs and stir well. Cover and leave to marinate overnight. Grill (broil) or barbecue over a medium heat for about 30 minutes.

Deep-Fried Spare Ribs

Serves 4

900 g/2 lb pork spare ribs
120 ml/4 fl oz/½ cup tomato ketchup (catsup)
120 ml/4 fl oz/½ cup wine vinegar
60 ml/4 tbsp mango chutney
45 ml/3 tbsp rice wine or dry sherry
2 cloves garlic, chopped
5 ml/1 tsp salt
45 ml/3 tbsp soy sauce
30 ml/2 tbsp honey
15 ml/1 tbsp mild curry powder
15 ml/1 tbsp paprika
oil for deep-frying
60 ml/4 tbsp chopped chives

Place the spare ribs in a bowl. Mix together all the ingredients except the oil and chives, pour over the ribs, cover and leave to marinate for at least 1 hour. Heat the oil and deep-fry the ribs until crisp. Serve sprinkled with chives.

Spare Ribs with Leeks

Serves 4

450 g/1 lb pork spare ribs
oil for deep-frying
250 ml/8 fl oz/1 cup stock
30 ml/2 tbsp tomato ketchup (catsup)
2.5 ml/½ tsp salt
2.5 ml/½ tsp sugar
2 leeks, cut into chunks
6 spring onions (scallions), cut into chunks
50 g/2 oz broccoli florets
5 ml/1 tsp sesame oil

Chop the spare ribs into 5 cm/2 in chunks. Heat the oil and deep-fry the spare ribs until just beginning to brown. Remove them from the pan and pour off all but 30 ml/2 tbsp of oil. Add the stock, tomato ketchup, salt and sugar, bring to the boil and simmer for 1 minute. Return the spare ribs to the pan and simmer for about 20 minutes until tender.

Meanwhile, heat a further 30 ml/ 2 tbsp of oil and fry the leeks, spring onions and broccoli for about 5 minutes. Sprinkle with sesame oil and arrange round a warmed serving plate. Spoon the spare ribs and sauce into the centre and serve.

Spare Ribs with Mushrooms

Serves 4 –6

6 Chinese dried mushrooms
900 g/2 lb pork spare ribs
2 cloves star anise
45 ml/3 tbsp soy sauce
5 ml/1 tsp salt
15 ml/1 tbsp cornflour (cornstarch)

Soak the mushrooms in warm water for 30 minutes then drain. Discard and stalks and slice the caps. Chop the spare ribs into 5 cm/2 in pieces. Bring a pan of water to the boil, add the spare ribs and simmer for 15 minutes. Drain well. Return the ribs to the pan and cover with cold water. Add the mushrooms, star anise, soy sauce and salt. Bring to the boil, cover and simmer for about 45 minutes until the meat is tender. Mix the cornflour with a little cold water, stir it into the pan and simmer, stirring, until the sauce clears and thickens.

Spare Ribs with Orange

Serves 4

900 g/2 lb pork spare ribs
5 ml/1 tsp grated cheese
5 ml/1 tsp cornflour (cornstarch)
45 ml/3 tbsp rice wine or dry sherry
salt
oil for deep-frying
15 ml/1 tbsp water
2.5 ml/½ tsp sugar
15 ml/1 tbsp tomato purée (paste)
2.5 ml/½ tsp chilli sauce
grated rind of 1 orange
1 orange, sliced

Chop the spare ribs into chunks and mix with the cheese, cornflour, 5 ml/1 tsp wine or sherry and a pinch of salt. Leave to marinate for 30 minutes. Heat the oil and deep-fry the ribs for about 3 minutes until golden brown. Heat 15 ml/1 tbsp of oil in a wok, add the water, sugar, tomato purée, chilli sauce, orange rind and remaining wine or sherry and stir over a gently heat for 2 minutes. Add the pork and stir together until well coated. Transfer to a warmed serving plate and serve garnished with orange slices.

Pineapple Spare Ribs

Serves 4

900 g/2 lb pork spare ribs
600 ml/1 pt/2½ cups water
30 ml/2 tbsp groundnut (peanut) oil
2 cloves garlic, finely chopped
200 g/7 oz canned pineapple chunks in fruit juice
120 ml/4 fl oz/½ cup chicken stock
60 ml/4 tbsp wine vinegar
50 g/2 oz/¼ cup brown sugar
15 ml/1 tbsp soy sauce
15 ml/1 tbsp cornflour (cornstarch)
3 spring onions (scallions), chopped

Place the pork and water in a pan, bring to the boil, cover and simmer for 20 minutes. Drain well.

Heat the oil and fry the garlic until lightly browned. Add the ribs and stir-fry until well coated in the oil. Drain the pineapple chunks and add 120 ml/4 fl oz/½ cup of juice to the pan with the stock, wine vinegar, sugar and soy sauce. Bring to the boil, cover and simmer for 10 minutes. Add the drained pineapple. Mix the cornflour with a little water, stir it into the sauce and simmer, stirring, until the sauce clears and thickens. Serve sprinkled with spring onions.

Crispy Prawn Spare Ribs

Serves 4

900 g/2 lb pork spare ribs
450 g/1 lb peeled prawns
5 ml/1 tsp sugar
salt and freshly ground pepper
30 ml/2 tbsp plain (all-purpose) flour
1 egg, lightly beaten
100 g/4 oz breadcrumbs
oil for deep-frying

Cut the spare ribs into 5 cm/2 in chunks. Trim off a little of the meat and mince it with the prawns, sugar, salt and pepper. Stir in the flour and enough egg to make the mixture sticky. Press round the pieces of spare rib then sprinkle them with breadcrumbs. Heat the oil and deep-fry the spare ribs until they come to the surface. Drain well and serve hot.

Spare Ribs with Rice Wine

Serves 4

900 g/2 lb pork spare ribs
450 ml/¾ pt/2 cups water
60 ml/4 tbsp soy sauce
5 ml/1 tsp salt
30 ml/2 tbsp rice wine
5 ml/1 tsp sugar

Cut the ribs into 2.5 cm/1 in pieces. Place in a pan with the water, soy sauce and salt, bring to the boil, cover and simmer for 1 hour. Drain well. Heat a pan and add the spare ribs, rice wine and sugar. Stir-fry over a high heat until the liquid evaporates.

Spare Ribs with Sesame Seeds

Serves 4

900 g/2 lb pork spare ribs
1 egg
30 ml/2 tbsp plain (all-purpose) flour
5 ml/1 tsp potato flour
45 ml/3 tbsp water
oil for deep-frying
30 ml/2 tbsp groundnut (peanut) oil
30 ml/2 tbsp tomato ketchup (catsup)
30 ml/2 tbsp brown sugar
10 ml/2 tsp wine vinegar
45 ml/3 tbsp sesame seeds
4 lettuce leaves

Chop the spare ribs into 10 cm/4 in pieces and place in a bowl. Mix the egg with the flour, potato flour and water, stir into the spare ribs and leave to stand for 4 hours.

Heat the oil and deep-fry the spare ribs until golden then remove and drain. Heat the oil and fry the tomato ketchup, brown sugar, wine vinegar for a few minutes. Add the spare ribs and stir-fry until thoroughly coated. Sprinkle with sesame seeds and stir-fry for 1 minutes. Arrange the lettuce leaves on a warmed serving plate, top with the spare ribs and serve.

Sweet and Sour Spare Ribs

900 g/2 lb pork spare ribs
600 ml/1 pt/2½ cups water
30 ml/2 tbsp groundnut (peanut) oil
2 cloves garlic, crushed
5 ml/1 tsp salt
100 g/4 oz/½ cup brown sugar
75 ml/5 tbsp chicken stock
60 ml/4 tbsp wine vinegar
100 g/4 oz canned pineapple chunks in syrup
15 ml/1 tbsp tomato purée (paste)
15 ml/1 tbsp soy sauce
15 ml/1 tbsp cornflour (cornstarch)
30 ml/2 tbsp desiccated coconut

Place the pork and water in a pan, bring to the boil, cover and simmer for 20 minutes. Drain well.

Heat the oil and fry the ribs with the garlic and salt until browned. Add the sugar, stock and wine vinegar and bring to the boil. Drain the pineapple and add 30 ml/2 tbsp of the syrup to the pan with the tomato purée, soy sauce and cornflour. Stir well and simmer, stirring, until the sauce clears and thickens. Add the pineapple, simmer for 3 minutes and serve sprinkled with coconut.

Sautéed Spare Ribs

Serves 4

900 g/2 lb pork spare ribs
1 egg, beaten
5 ml/1 tsp soy sauce
5 ml/1 tsp salt
10 ml/2 tsp cornflour (cornstarch)
10 ml/2 tsp sugar
60 ml/4 tbsp groundnut (peanut) oil
250 ml/8 fl oz/1 cup wine vinegar
250 ml/8 fl oz/1 cup water
250 ml/8 fl oz/1 cup rice wine or dry
    sherry

Place the spare ribs in a bowl. Mix the egg with the soy sauce, salt, half the cornflour and half the sugar, add to the spare ribs and stir well. Heat the oil and fry the spare ribs until browned. Add the remaining ingredients, bring to the boil and simmer until the liquid has almost evaporated.

Spare Ribs with Tomato

Serves 4

900 g/2 lb pork spare ribs
75 ml/5 tbsp soy sauce
30 ml/2 tbsp rice wine or dry sherry
2 eggs, beaten
45 ml/3 tbsp cornflour (cornstarch)
oil for deep-frying
45 ml/3 tbsp groundnut (peanut) oil
1 onion, thinly sliced
250 ml/8 fl oz/1 cup chicken stock
60 ml/4 tbsp tomato ketchup (catsup)
10 ml/2 tsp brown sugar

Cut the spare ribs into 2.5 cm/1 in pieces. Mix with 60 ml/4tbsp of soy sauce and the wine or sherry and leave to marinate for 1 hour, stirring occasionally. Drain, discarding marinade. Coat the spare ribs in egg then in cornflour. Heat the oil and deep-fry the ribs, a few at a time, until golden. Drain well. Heat the groundnut (peanut) oil and fry the onion until translucent. Add the stock, remaining soy sauce, ketchup and brown sugar and simmer for 1 minute, stirring. Add the ribs and simmer for 10 minutes.

Barbecue-Roast Pork

Serves 4–6

1.25 kg/3 lb boned pork shoulder
2 cloves garlic, crushed
2 spring onions (scallions), chopped
250 ml/8 fl oz/1 cup soy sauce
120 ml/4 fl oz/½ cup rice wine or dry
    sherry
100 g/4 oz/½ cup brown sugar
5 ml/1 tsp salt

Place the pork in a bowl. Mix together the remaining ingredients, pour over the pork, cover and leave to marinate for 3 hours. Transfer the pork and marinade to a roasting tin and roast in a preheated oven at 200°C/400°F/gas mark 6 for 10 minutes. Reduce the temperature to 160°C/325°F/gas mark 3 for 1¼ hours until the pork is cooked.

Cold Pork with Mustard

Serves 4

1 kg/2 lb boned roasting pork
250 ml/8 fl oz/1 cup soy sauce
120 ml/4 fl oz/½ cup rice wine or dry sherry
100 g/4 oz/½ cup brown sugar
3 spring onions (scallions), chopped
5 ml/1 tsp salt
30 ml/2 tbsp mustard powder

Place the pork in a bowl Mix all the remaining ingredients except the mustard and pour over the pork. Leave to marinate for at least 2 hours, basting frequently. Line a roasting tin with foil and stand the pork on a rack in the tin. Roast in a preheated oven at 200°C/400°F/gas mark 6 for 10 minutes then reduce the temperature to 160°C/325°F/gas mark 3 for a further 1¼ hours until the pork is tender. Leave to cool then chill in the refrigerator. Slice very thinly. Mix the mustard powder with just enough water to make a creamy paste to serve with the pork.

Chinese Roast Pork

Serves 6

1.25 kg/3 lb joint of pork, thickly sliced
2 cloves garlic, finely chopped
30 ml/2 tbsp rice wine or dry sherry
15 ml/1 tbsp brown sugar
15 ml/1 tbsp honey
90 ml/6 tbsp soy sauce
2.5 ml/½ tsp five-spice powder

Arrange the pork in a shallow dish. Mix together the remaining ingredients, pour over the pork, cover and marinate in the refrigerator overnight, turning and basting occasionally.

Arrange the pork slices on a rack in a roasting tin filled with a little water and baste well with the marinade. Roast in a preheated oven at 180°C/350°F/gas mark 5 for about 1 hour, basting occasionally, until the pork is cooked.

Pork with Spinach

Serves 6–8

30 ml/2 tbsp groundnut (peanut) oil
1.25 kg/3 lb loin of pork
250 ml/8 fl oz/1 cup chicken stock
15 ml/1 tbsp brown sugar
60 ml/4 tbsp soy sauce
900 g/2 lb spinach

Heat the oil and brown the pork on all sides. Pour off most of the fat. Add the stock, sugar and soy sauce, bring to the boil, cover and simmer for about 2 hours until the pork is cooked. Remove the meat from the pan and leave it to cool slightly, then slice it. Add the spinach to the pan and simmer, stirring gently, until softened. Drain the spinach and arrange on a warmed serving plate. Top with the pork slices and serve.

Deep-Fried Pork Balls

Serves 4

450 g/1 lb minced (ground) pork
1 slice ginger root, minced
15 ml/1 tbsp cornflour (cornstarch)
15 ml/1 tbsp water
2.5 ml/½ tsp salt
10 ml/2 tsp soy sauce
oil for deep-frying

Mix the pork and ginger. Mix the cornflour, water, salt and soy sauce then stir the mixture into the pork and mix well. Shape into walnut-sized balls. Heat the oil and fry the pork balls until they rise to the top of the oil. Remove from the oil and reheat. Return the pork to the pan and fry for 1 minute. Drain well.

Pork and Prawn Egg Rolls

Serves 4

30 ml/2 tbsp groundnut (peanut) oil
225 g/8 oz minced (ground) pork
225 g/8 oz prawns
100 g/4 oz Chinese leaves, shredded
100 g/4 oz bamboo shoots, cut into strips
100 g/4 oz water chestnuts, cut into strips
10 ml/2 tsp soy sauce
5 ml/1 tsp salt
5 ml/1 tsp sugar
3 spring onions (scallions), finely chopped
8 egg roll skins
oil for deep-frying

Heat the oil and fry the pork until sealed. Add the prawns and stir-fry for 1 minute. Add the Chinese leaves, bamboo shoots, water chestnuts, soy sauce, salt and sugar and stir-fry for 1 minute then cover and simmer for 5 minutes. Stir in the spring onions, turn into a colander and leave to drain.

Place a few spoonfuls of the filling mixture in the centre of each egg roll skin, fold up the bottom, fold in the sides, then roll upwards, enclosing the filling. Seal the edge with a little flour and water mixture then leave to dry for 30 minutes. Heat the oil and fry the egg rolls for about 10 minutes until crisp and golden brown. Drain well before serving.

Steamed Minced Pork

Serves 4

450 g/1 lb minced (ground) pork
5 ml/1 tsp cornflour (cornstarch)
2.5 ml/½ tsp salt
10 ml/2 tsp soy sauce

Mix the pork with the remaining ingredients and spread the mixture flat in a shallow ovenproof dish. Place in a steamer over boiling water and steam for about 30 minutes until cooked. Serve hot.

Deep-Fried Pork with Crab Meat

Serves 4

225 g/8 oz crab meat, flaked

100 g/4 oz mushrooms, chopped

100 g/4 oz bamboo shoots, chopped

5 ml/1 tsp cornflour (cornstarch)

2.5 ml/½ tsp salt

225 g/8 oz cooked pork, sliced

1 egg white, lightly beaten

oil for deep-frying

15 ml/1 tbsp chopped fresh flat-leaved
    parsley

Mix together the crab meat, mushrooms, bamboo shoots, most of the cornflour and the salt. Cut the meat into 5 cm/2 in squares. Make into sandwiches with the crab meat mixture. Coat in the egg white. Heat the oil and deep-fry the sandwiches a few at a time until golden brown. Drain well. Serve sprinkled with parsley.

Pork with Bean Sprouts

Serves 4

30 ml/2 tbsp groundnut (peanut) oil

2.5 ml/½ tsp salt

2 cloves garlic, crushed

450 g/1 lb bean sprouts

225 g/8 oz cooked pork, cubed

120 ml/4 fl oz/½ cup chicken stock

15 ml/1 tbsp soy sauce

15 ml/1 tbsp rice wine or dry sherry

5 ml/1 tsp sugar

15 ml/1 tbsp cornflour (cornstarch)

2.5 ml/½ tsp sesame oil

3 spring onions (scallions), chopped

Heat the oil and fry the salt and garlic until lightly browned. Add the bean sprouts and pork and stir-fry for 2 minutes. Add half the stock, bring to the boil, cover and simmer for 3 minutes. Mix the remaining stock with the rest of the ingredients, stir into the pan, return to the boil and simmer for 4 minutes, stirring. Serve sprinkled with spring onion.

Drunken Pork

Serves 6

1.25 kg/3 lb boneless rolled pork joint

30 ml/2 tbsp salt

freshly ground pepper

1 spring onion (scallion), chopped

2 cloves garlic, chopped

1 bottle dry white wine

Place the pork in a pan and add the salt, pepper, spring onion and garlic. Cover with boiling water, return to the boil, cover and simmer for 30 minutes. Remove the pork from the pan, leave to cool and dry for 6 hours or overnight in the refrigerator. Cut the pork into large pieces and place in a large screw top jar. Cover with the wine, seal and store in the refrigerator for at least 1 week.

Steamed Leg of Pork

Serves 6–8

1 small leg of pork
90 ml/6 tbsp soy sauce
450 ml/¾ pt/2 cups water
45 ml/3 tbsp brown sugar
15 ml/1 tbsp rice wine or dry sherry
30 ml/2 tbsp groundnut (peanut) oil
3 cloves garlic, crushed
450 g/1 lb spinach
2.5 ml/½ tsp salt
30 ml/2 tbsp cornflour (cornstarch)

Pierce the pork skin all over with a pointed knife then rub in 30 ml/2 tbsp of soy sauce. Place in a heavy saucepan with the water, bring to the boil, cover and simmer for 40 minutes. Drain, reserving the liquid, and leave the pork to cool then place it in a heatproof bowl.

Mix together 15 ml/1 tbsp of sugar, the wine or sherry and 30ml/2 tbsp of soy sauce then rub over the pork. Heat the oil and fry the garlic until lightly browned. Add the remaining sugar and soy sauce, pour the mixture over the pork and cover the bowl. Stand the bowl in a wok and fill with water to come half way up the sides. Cover and steam for about 1½ hours, topping up with boiling water as necessary. Cut the spinach into 5 cm/2 in pieces then sprinkle with salt. Bring a pan of water to the boil then pour over the spinach. Leave to stand for 2 minutes until thespinach begins to soften then drain and arrange on a warmed serving plate. Place the pork on top. Bring the pork stock to the boil. Blend the cornflour with a little water, stir it into the stock and simmer, stirring, until sauce clears and thickens. Pour over pork and serve.

Stir-Fried Roast Pork with Vegetables

Serves 4

50 g/2 oz/½ cup blanched almonds
30 ml/2 tbsp groundnut (peanut) oil
salt
100 g/4 oz mushrooms, diced
100 g/4 oz bamboo shoots, diced
1 onion, diced
2 stalks celery, diced
100 g/4 oz mangetout (snow peas), diced
4 water chestnuts, diced
1 spring onion (scallion), chopped
120 ml/4 fl oz/½ cup chicken stock
225 g/8 oz Barbecue Roast Pork (page 174), cubed
15 ml/1 tbsp cornflour (cornstarch)
45 ml/3 tbsp water
2.5 ml/½ tsp sugar
freshly ground pepper

Toast the almonds until lightly browned. Heat the oil and salt then add the vegetables and stir-fry for 2 minutes until coated with oil. Add the stock, bring to the boil, cover and simmer for 2 minutes until the vegetables are almost cooked but still crisp. Add the pork and heat through. Mix together the cornflour, water, sugar and pepper and stir into the sauce. Simmer, stirring, until the sauce clears and thickens.

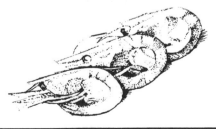

Twice-Cooked Pork

Serves 4

45 ml/3 tbsp groundnut (peanut) oil
6 spring onions (scallions), chopped
1 clove garlic, crushed
1 slice ginger root, chopped
2.5 ml/½ tsp salt
225 g/8 oz cooked pork, cubed
15 ml/1 tbsp soy sauce
15 ml/1 tbsp rice wine or dry sherry
30 ml/2 tbsp chilli bean paste

Heat the oil and fry the spring onions, garlic, ginger and salt until lightly browned. Add the pork and stir-fry for 2 minutes. Add the soy sauce, wine or sherry and chilli bean paste and stir-fry for 3 minutes.

Pork Kidneys with Mangetout

Serves 4

4 pork kidneys, halved and cored
30 ml/2 tbsp groundnut (peanut) oil
2.5 ml/½ tsp salt
1 slice ginger root, minced
3 stalks celery, chopped
1 onion, chopped
30 ml/2 tbsp soy sauce
15 ml/1 tbsp rice wine or dry sherry
5 ml/1 tsp sugar
60 ml/4 tbsp chicken stock
225 g/8 oz mangetout (snow peas)
15 ml/1 tbsp cornflour (cornstarch)
45 ml/3 tbsp water

Parboil the kidneys for 10 minute then drain and rinse in cold water. Heat the oil and fry the salt and ginger for a few seconds. Add the kidneys and stir-fry for 30 seconds until coated with oil. Add the celery and onion and stir-fry for 2 minutes. Add the soy sauce, wine or sherry and sugar and stir-fry for 1 minute. Add the stock, bring to the boil, cover and simmer for 1 minute. Stir in the mangetout, cover and simmer for 1 minute. Mix the cornflour and water then stir it into the sauce and simmer until the sauce clears and thickens. Serve at once.

Red-Cooked Ham with Chestnuts

Serves 4 –6

1.25 kg/3 lb ham
2 spring onions (scallions), halved
2 cloves garlic, crushed
45 ml/3 tbsp brown sugar
30 ml/2 tbsp rice wine or dry sherry
60 ml/4 tbsp soy sauce
450 ml/¾ pt/2 cups water
350 g/12 oz chestnuts

Place the ham in a pan with the spring onions, garlic, sugar, wine or sherry, soy sauce and water. Bring to the boil, cover and simmer for about 1½ hours, turning the ham occasionally. Blanch the chestnuts in boiling water for 5 minutes then drain. Add to the ham, cover and simmer for a further 1 hour, turning the ham once or twice.

Deep-Fried Ham and Egg Balls

Serves 4

225 g/8 oz smoked ham, minced
2 spring onions (scallions), minced
3 eggs, beaten
4 slices stale bread
10 ml/2 tbsp plain (all-purpose) flour
2.5 ml/½ tsp salt
oil for deep-frying

Mix together the ham, spring onions and eggs. Make the bread into crumbs and mix it into the ham with the flour and salt. Shape into walnut-sized balls. Heat the oil and deep-fry the meat balls until golden brown. Drain well on kitchen paper.

Ham and Pineapple

Serves 4

4 Chinese dried mushrooms
15 ml/1 tbsp groundnut (peanut) oil
1 clove garlic, crushed
50 g/2 oz water chestnuts, sliced
50 g/2 oz bamboo shoots
225 g/8 oz ham, chopped
225 g/8 oz canned pineapple chunks in fruit juice
120 ml/4 fl oz/½ cup chicken stock
15 ml/1 tbsp soy sauce
15 ml/1 tbsp cornflour (cornstarch)

Soak the mushrooms in warm water for 30 minutes then drain. Discard the stems and slice the caps. Heat the oil and fry the garlic until lightly browned. Add the mushrooms, water chestnuts and bamboo shoots and stir-fry for 2 minutes. Add the ham and drained pineapple chunks and stir-fry for 1 minute. Add 30 ml/2tbsp of the juice from the pineapple, most of the chicken stock and the soy sauce. Bring to the boil, cover and simmer for 5 minutes. Mix the cornflour with the remaining stock and stir it into the sauce. Simmer, stirring, until the sauce clears and thickens.

Ham and Spinach Stir-Fry

Serves 4

30 ml/2 tbsp groundnut (peanut) oil
2.5 ml/½ tsp salt
1 clove garlic, minced
2 spring onions (scallions), chopped
225 g/8 oz ham, diced
450 g/1 lb spinach, shredded
60 ml/4 tbsp chicken stock
15 ml/1 tbsp cornflour (cornstarch)
15 ml/1 tsp soy sauce
45 ml/3 tbsp water
5 ml/1 tsp sugar

Heat the oil and fry the salt, garlic and spring onions until lightly browned. Add the ham and stir-fry for 1 minute. Add the spinach and stir until coated in oil. Add the stock, bring to the boil, cover and simmer for 2 minutes until the spinach begins to wilt. Mix together the cornflour, soy sauce, water and sugar then stir it into the pan. Simmer, stirring, until the sauce thickens.

Steamed Ham

Serves 6–8

900 g/2 lb fresh ham
30 ml/2 tbsp brown sugar
60 ml/4 tbsp rice wine or dry sherry

Place the ham in a heatproof dish on a rack, cover and steam over boiling water for about 1 hour. Add the sugar and wine or sherry to the dish, cover and steam for a further 1 hour or until the ham is cooked. Leave to cool in the bowl before slicing.

Bacon with Cabbage

Serves 4

4 rashers streaky bacon, rinded and
   chopped
2.5 ml/½ tsp salt
1 slice ginger root, minced
½ cabbage, shredded
75 ml/5 tbsp chicken stock
15 ml/1 tbsp oyster sauce

Fry the bacon until crisp then remove it from. Add the salt and ginger and stir-fry for 2 minutes. Add the cabbage and stir well then stir in the bacon and add the stock, cover and simmer for about 5 minutes until the cabbage is tender but still slightly crisp. Stir in the oyster sauce, cover and simmer for 1 minute before serving.

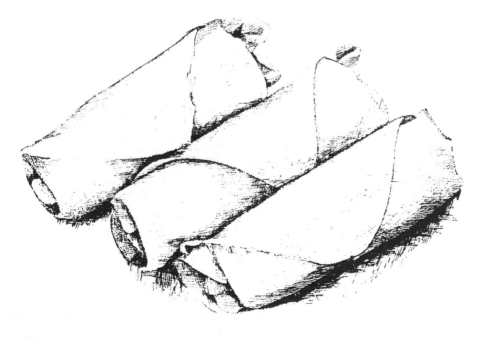

Poultry and Game

Chicken is perfect for Chinese dishes. It tastes good, it is easy to prepare, very inexpensive, and marries well with the traditional Chinese flavouring ingredients. Use free range chicken for the best flavour. For a change, you can also prepare the recipes using turkey now this is available in smaller portions. Duck is also very popular in Chinese cooking and Peking Duck must be many people's favourite Chinese dish.

Almond Chicken

Serves 4–6

375 ml/13 fl oz/1½ cups chicken stock
60 ml/4 tbsp rice wine or dry sherry
45 ml/3 tbsp cornflour (cornstarch)
15 ml/1 tbsp soy sauce
4 chicken breasts
1 egg white
2.5 ml/½ tsp salt
oil for deep-frying
75 g/3 oz/½ cup blanched almonds
1 large carrot, diced
5 ml/1 tsp grated ginger root
6 spring onions (scallions), sliced
3 stalks celery, sliced
100 g/4 oz mushrooms, sliced
100 g/4 oz bamboo shoots, sliced

Mix the stock, half the wine or sherry, 30 ml/2 tbsp of cornflour, and the soy sauce in a saucepan. Bring to the boil, stirring, then simmer for 5 minutes until the mixture thickens. Remove from the heat and keep warm.

Remove the skin and bones from the chicken and cut it into 2.5cm/1 in pieces. Mix the remaining wine or sherry and cornflour, the egg white and salt, add the chicken pieces and stir well. Heat the oil and fry the chicken pieces a few at a time for about 5 minutes until golden brown.

Drain well. Remove all but 30ml/2tbsp of oil from the pan and stir-fry the almonds for 2 minutes until golden. Drain well. Add the carrot and ginger to the pan and stir-fry for 1 minute. Add the remaining vegetables and stir-fry for about 3 minutes until the vegetables are tender but still crisp. Return the chicken and almonds to the pan with the sauce and stir over a moderate heat for a few minutes until heated through.

Chicken with Almonds and Water Chestnuts

Serves 4

6 dried Chinese mushrooms
4 chicken pieces, boned
100 g/4 oz ground almonds
salt and freshly ground pepper
60 ml/4 tbsp groundnut (peanut) oil
100 g/4 oz water chestnuts, sliced
75 ml/5 tbsp chicken stock
30 ml/2 tbsp soy sauce

Soak the mushrooms in warm water for 30 minutes then drain. Discard the stalks and slice the caps. Thinly slice the chicken. Season the almonds generously with salt and pepper and coat the chicken slices in the almonds. Heat the oil and fry the chicken until lightly browned. Add the mushrooms, water chestnuts, stock and soy sauce, bring to the boil, cover and simmer for a few minutes until the chicken is cooked.

Chicken with Almonds and Vegetables

Serves 4

75 ml/5 tbsp groundnut (peanut) oil
4 slices ginger root, minced
5 ml/1 tsp salt
100 g/4 oz Chinese cabbage, shredded
50 g/2 oz bamboo shoots, diced
50 g/2 oz mushrooms, diced
2 stalks celery, diced
3 water chestnuts, diced
120 ml/4 fl oz/½ cup chicken stock
225 g/8 oz chicken breast, diced
15 ml/1 tbsp rice wine or dry sherry
50 g/2 oz mangetout (snow peas)
100 g/4 oz flaked almonds, toasted
10 ml/2 tsp cornflour (cornstarch)
15 ml/1 tbsp water

Heat half the oil and stir-fry the ginger and salt for 30 seconds. Add the cabbage, bamboo shoots, mushrooms, celery and water chestnuts and stir-fry for 2 minutes. Add the stock, bring to the boil, cover and simmer for 2 minutes. Remove the vegetables and sauce from the pan. Heat the remaining oil and fry the chicken for 1 minute. Add the wine or sherry and fry for 1 minute. Return the vegetables to the pan with the mangetout and almonds and simmer for 30 seconds. Blend the cornflour and water to a paste, stir it into the sauce and simmer, stirring,until the sauce thickens.

Anise Chicken

Serves 4

75 ml/5 tbsp groundnut (peanut) oil
2 onions, chopped
1 clove garlic, chopped
2 slices ginger root, chopped
15 ml/1 tbsp plain (all-purpose) flour
30 ml/2 tbsp curry powder
450 g/1 lb chicken, cubed
15 ml/1 tbsp sugar
30 ml/2 tbsp soy sauce
450 ml/¾ pt/2 cups chicken stock
2 cloves star anise
225 g/8 oz potatoes, diced

Heat half the oil and fry the onions until lightly browned then remove them from the pan. Heat the remaining oil and fry the garlic and ginger for 30 seconds. Stir in the flour and curry powder and cook for 2 minutes. Return the onions to the pan, add the chicken and stir-fry for 3 minutes. Add the sugar, soy sauce, stock and anise, bring to the boil, cover and simmer for 15 minutes. Add the potatoes, return to the boil, cover and simmer for a further 20 minutes until tender.

Chicken with Apricots

Serves 4

4 chicken pieces
salt and freshly ground pepper
pinch of ground ginger
60 ml/4 tbsp groundnut (peanut) oil
225 g/8 oz canned apricots, halved
300 ml/½ pt/1¼ cups Sweet and Sour
    Sauce (page 327)
30 ml/2 tbsp flaked almonds, toasted

Season the chicken with salt, pepper
and ginger. Heat the oil and fry the
chicken until lightly browned. Cover
and cook for about 20 minutes until
tender, turning occasionally. Drain
off the oil. Add the apricots and sauce
to the pan, bring to the boil, cover and
simmer gently for about 5 minutes or
until heated through. Garnish with
flaked almonds.

Chicken with Asparagus

Serves 4

45 ml/3 tbsp groundnut (peanut) oil
5 ml/1 tsp salt
1 clove garlic, crushed
1 spring onion (scallion), chopped
1 chicken breast, sliced
30 ml/2 tbsp black bean sauce
350 g/12 oz asparagus, cut into 2.5
    cm/1 in pieces
120 ml/4 fl oz/½ cup chicken stock
5 ml/1 tsp sugar
15 ml/1 tbsp cornflour (cornstarch)
45 ml/3 tbsp water

Heat half the oil and fry the salt, garlic and spring onion until lightly
browned. Add the chicken and fry
until lightly coloured. Add the black
bean sauce and stir to coat the chick-
en. Add the asparagus, stock and
sugar, bring to the boil, cover and
simmer for 5 minutes until the chick-
en is tender. Mix the cornflour and
water to a paste, stir it into the pan
and simmer, stirring, until the sauce
clears and thickens.

Chicken with Aubergine

Serves 4

225 g/8 oz chicken, sliced
15 ml/1 tbsp soy sauce
15 ml/1 tbsp rice wine or dry sherry
15 ml/1 tbsp cornflour (cornstarch)
1 aubergine (eggplant), peeled and cut
    into strips
30 ml/2 tbsp groundnut (peanut) oil
2 dried red chilli peppers
2 cloves garlic, crushed
75 ml/5 tbsp chicken stock

Place the chicken in a bowl. Mix the
soy sauce, wine or sherry and
cornflour, stir into the chicken and
leave to stand for 30 minutes. Blanch
the aubergine in boiling water for 3
minutes then drain well. Heat the oil
and fry the peppers until they darken
then remove and discard them. Add
the garlic and chicken and stir-fry
until lightly coloured. Add the stock
and aubergine, bring to the boil, cover
and simmer for 3 minutes, stirring
occasionally.

Bacon-Wrapped Chicken

Serves 4 –6

225 g/8 oz chicken, cubed
30 ml/2 tbsp soy sauce
15 ml/1 tbsp rice wine or dry sherry
5 ml/1 tsp sugar
5 ml/1 tsp sesame oil
salt and freshly ground pepper
225 g/8 oz bacon rashers
1 eggs, lightly beaten
100 g/4 oz plain (all-purpose) flour
oil for deep-frying
4 tomatoes, sliced

Mix the chicken with the soy sauce, wine or sherry, sugar, sesame oil, salt and pepper. Cover and leave to marinate for 1 hour, stirring occasionally, then remove the chicken and discard the marinade. Cut the bacon into pieces and wrap it around the chicken cubes. Beat the eggs with the flour to make a thick batter, adding a little milk if necessary. Dip the cubes in the batter. Heat the oil and deep-fry the cubes until golden brown and cooked through. Serve garnished with tomatoes.

Chicken with Bamboo Shoots

Serves 4

45 ml/3 tbsp groundnut (peanut) oil
1 clove garlic, crushed
1 spring onion (scallion), chopped
1 slice ginger root, chopped
225 g/8 oz chicken breast, cut into
    slivers
225 g/8 oz bamboo shoots, cut into
    slivers
45 ml/3 tbsp soy sauce
15 ml/1 tbsp rice wine or dry sherry
5 ml/1 tsp cornflour (cornstarch)

Heat the oil and fry the garlic, spring onion and ginger until lightly browned. Add the chicken and stir-fry for 5 minutes. Add the bamboo shoots and stir-fry for 2 minutes. Stir in the soy sauce, wine or sherry and cornflour and stir-fry for about 3 minutes until the chicken is cooked through.

Chicken with Bean Sprouts

Serves 4

45 ml/3 tbsp groundnut (peanut) oil

1 clove garlic, crushed

1 spring onion (scallion), chopped

1 slice ginger root, chopped

225 g/8 oz chicken breast, cut into slivers

225 g/8 oz bean sprouts

45 ml/3 tbsp soy sauce

15 ml/1 tbsp rice wine or dry sherry

5 ml/1 tsp cornflour (cornstarch)

Heat the oil and fry the garlic, spring onion and ginger until lightly browned. Add the chicken and stir-fry for 5 minutes. Add the bean sprouts and stir-fry for 2 minutes. Stir in the soy sauce, wine or sherry and cornflour and stir-fry for about 3 minutes until the chicken is cooked through.

Chicken with Black Bean Sauce

Serves 4

30 ml/2 tbsp groundnut (peanut) oil

5 ml/1 tsp salt

30 ml/2 tbsp black bean sauce

2 cloves garlic, crushed

450 g/1 lb chicken, diced

250 ml/8 fl oz/1 cup stock

1 green pepper, diced

1 onion, chopped

15 ml/1 tbsp soy sauce

freshly ground pepper

15 ml/1 tbsp cornflour (cornstarch)

45 ml/3 tbsp water

Heat the oil and fry the salt, black beans and garlic for 30 seconds. Add the chicken and fry until lightly browned. Stir in the stock, bring to the boil, cover and simmer for 10 minutes. Add the pepper, onion, soy sauce and pepper, cover and simmer for a further 10 minutes. Blend the cornflour and water to a paste, stir into the sauce and simmer, stirring, until the sauce thickens and the chicken is tender.

Chicken with Broccoli

Serves 4

450 g/1 lb chicken meat, diced

225 g/8 oz chicken livers

45 ml/3 tbsp plain (all-purpose) flour

45 ml/3 tbsp groundnut (peanut) oil

1 onion, diced

1 red pepper, diced

1 green pepper, diced

225 g/8 oz broccoli florets

4 slices pineapple, diced

30 ml/2 tbsp tomato purée (paste)

30 ml/2 tbsp hoisin sauce

30 ml/2 tbsp honey

30 ml/2 tbsp soy sauce

300 ml/½ pt/1¼ cups chicken stock

10 ml/2 tsp sesame oil

Toss the chicken and chicken livers in the flour. Heat the oil and stir-fry the liver for 5 minutes then remove from the pan. Add the chicken, cover and fry over a moderate heat for 15 minutes, stirring occasionally. Add the vegetables and pineapple and stir-fry for 8 minutes. Return the livers to the wok, add the remaining ingredients and bring to the boil. Simmer, stirring, until the sauce thickens.

Chicken with Cabbage and Peanuts

Serves 4

45 ml/3 tbsp groundnut (peanut) oil

30 ml/2 tbsp peanuts

450 g/1 lb chicken, diced

¼ cabbage, cut into squares

15 ml/1 tbsp black bean sauce

2 red chilli peppers, minced

5 ml/1 tsp salt

Heat a little oil and fry the peanuts for a few minutes, stirring continuously. Remove, drain then crush. Heat the remaining oil and fry the chicken and cabbage until lightly browned. Remove from the pan. Add the black bean sauce and chilli peppers and stir-fry for 2 minutes. Return the chicken and cabbage to the pan with the crushed peanuts and season with salt. Stir-fry until heated through then serve at once.

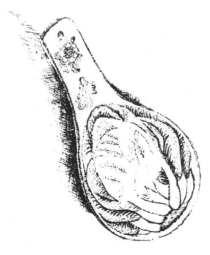

Chicken with Cashews

Serves 4

30 ml/2 tbsp soy sauce

30 ml/2 tbsp cornflour (cornstarch)

15 ml/1 tbsp rice wine or dry sherry

350 g/12 oz chicken, cubed

45 ml/3 tbsp groundnut (peanut) oil

2.5 ml/½ tsp salt

2 cloves garlic, crushed

225 g/8 oz mushrooms, sliced

100 g/4 oz water chestnuts, sliced

100 g/4 oz bamboo shoots

50 g/2 oz mangetout (snow peas)

225 g/8 oz/2 cups cashew nuts

300 ml/½ pt/1¼ cups chicken stock

Mix together the soy sauce, cornflour and wine or sherry, pour over the chicken, cover and leave to marinate for at least 1 hour. Heat 30 ml/2 tbsp of oil with the salt and garlic and fry until the garlic is lightly browned. Add the chicken with the marinade and stir-fry for 2 minutes until the chicken is lightly browned. Add the mushrooms, water chestnuts, bamboo shoots and mangetout and stir-fry for 2 minutes. Meanwhile, heat the remaining oil in a separate pan and fry the cashew nuts over a gentle heat for a few minutes until golden brown. Add them to the pan with the stock, bring to the boil, cover and simmer for 5 minutes. If the sauce has not thickened sufficiently, stir in a little cornflour blended with a spoonful of water and stir until the sauce thickens and clears.

Chicken with Chestnuts

Serves 4

225 g/8 oz chicken, sliced
5 ml/1 tsp salt
15 ml/1 tbsp soy sauce
oil for deep-frying
250 ml/8 fl oz/1 cup chicken stock
200 g/7 oz water chestnuts, chopped
225 g/8 oz chestnuts, chopped
225 g/8 oz mushrooms, quartered
15 ml/1 tbsp chopped fresh parsley

Sprinkle the chicken with salt and soy sauce and rub it well into the chicken. Heat the oil and deep-fry the chicken until golden brown then remove and drain. Place the chicken in a pan with the stock, bring to the boil and simmer for 5 minutes. Add the water chestnuts, chestnuts and mushrooms, cover and simmer for about 20 minutes until everything is tender. Serve garnished with parsley.

Hot Chilli-Chicken

Serves 4

350 g/1 lb chicken meat, cubed
1 egg, lightly beaten
10 ml/2 tsp soy sauce
2.5 ml/½ tsp cornflour (cornstarch)
oil for deep-frying
1 green pepper, diced
4 cloves garlic, crushed
2 red chilli peppers, shredded
5 ml/1 tsp freshly ground pepper
5 ml/1 tsp wine vinegar
5 ml/1 tsp water
2.5 ml/½ tsp sugar
2.5 ml/½ tsp chilli oil
2.5 ml/½ tsp sesame oil

Mix the chicken with the egg, half the soy sauce and the cornflour and leave to stand for 30 minutes. Heat the oil and deep-fry the chicken until golden brown then drain well. Pour off all but 15 ml/1 tbsp of oil from the pan, add the pepper, garlic and chilli peppers and fry for 30 seconds. Add the pepper, wine vinegar, water and sugar and fry for 30 seconds. Return the chicken to the pan and stir-fry for a few minutes until cooked through. Serve sprinkled with chilli and sesame oils.

Stir-Fried Chicken with Chilli

Serves 4

225 g/8 oz chicken, sliced
2.5 ml/½ tsp soy sauce
2.5 ml/½ tsp sesame oil
2.5 ml/½ tsp rice wine or dry sherry
5 ml/1 tsp cornflour (cornstarch)
salt
45 ml/3 tbsp groundnut (peanut) oil
100 g/4 oz spinach
4 spring onions (scallions), chopped
2.5 ml/½ tsp chilli powder
15 ml/1 tbsp water
1 tomato, sliced

Mix the chicken with the soy sauce, sesame oil, wine or sherry, half the cornflour and a pinch of salt. Leave to stand for 30 minutes. Heat 15 ml/1 tbsp of oil and fry the chicken until lightly browned. Remove from the wok. Heat 15 ml/1 tbsp of oil and stir-fry the spinach until wilted then remove it from the wok. Heat the remaining oil and fry the spring onions, chilli powder, water and remaining cornflour for 2 minutes.

Stir in the chicken and stir-fry quickly. Arrange the spinach around a warmed serving plate, top with the chicken and serve garnished with tomatoes.

Chicken Chop Suey

Serves 4

100 g/4 oz Chinese leaves, shredded

100 g/4 oz bamboo shoots, cut into strips

60 ml/4 tbsp groundnut (peanut) oil

3 spring onions (scallions), sliced

2 cloves garlic, crushed

1 slice ginger root, chopped

225 g/8 oz chicken breast, cut into strips

45 ml/3 tbsp soy sauce

15 ml/1 tbsp rice wine or dry sherry

5 ml/1 tsp salt

2.5 ml/½ tsp sugar

freshly ground pepper

15 ml/1 tbsp cornflour (cornstarch)

Blanch the Chinese leaves and bamboo shoots in boiling water for 2 minutes. Drain and pat dry. Heat 45ml/3 tbsp of oil and fry the onions, garlic and ginger until lightly browned. Add the chicken and stir-fry for 4 minutes. Remove from the pan. Heat the remaining oil and stir-fry the vegetables for 3 minutes. Add the chicken, soy sauce, wine or sherry, salt, sugar and a pinch of pepper and stir-fry for 1 minute. Mix the cornflour with a little water, stir it into the sauce and simmer, stirring, until the sauce clears and thickens.

Chicken Chow Mein

Serves 4

30 ml/2 tbsp groundnut (peanut) oil

2 cloves garlic, crushed

450 g/1 lb chicken, sliced

225 g/8 oz bamboo shoots, sliced

100 g/4 oz celery, sliced

225 g/8 oz mushrooms, sliced

450 ml/¾ pt/2 cups chicken stock

225 g/8 oz bean sprouts

4 onions, cut into wedges

30 ml/2 tbsp soy sauce

30 ml/2 tbsp cornflour (cornstarch)

225 g/8 oz dried Chinese noodles

Heat the oil with the garlic until lightly golden then add the chicken and stir-fry for 2 minutes until lightly browned. Add the bamboo shoots, celery and mushrooms and stir fry for 3 minutes. Add most of the stock, bring to the boil, cover and simmer for 8 minutes. Add the bean sprouts and onions and simmer for 2 minutes, stirring, until there is just a little stock remaining. Mix together the remaining stock with the soy sauce and cornflour. Stir it into the pan and simmer, stirring, until the sauce clears and thickens.

Meanwhile, cook the noodles in boiling salted water for a few minutes, according to the instructions on the packet. Drain well then toss with the chicken mixture and serve at once.

Crispy-Fried Spiced Chicken

Serves 4

450 g/1 lb chicken meat, cut into chunks
30 ml/2 tbsp soy sauce
30 ml/2 tbsp plum sauce
45 ml/3 tbsp mango chutney
1 clove garlic, crushed
2.5 ml/½ tsp ground ginger
few drops of brandy
30 ml/2 tbsp cornflour (cornstarch)
2 eggs, beaten
100 g/4 oz/1 cup dried breadcrumbs
30 ml/2 tbsp groundnut (peanut) oil
6 spring onions (scallions), chopped
1 red pepper, diced
1 green pepper, diced
30 ml/2 tbsp soy sauce
30 ml/2 tbsp honey
30 ml/2 tbsp wine vinegar

Place the chicken in a bowl. Mix the sauces, chutney, garlic, ginger and brandy, pour over the chicken, cover and leave to marinate for 2 hours. Drain the chicken then dust it with cornflour. Coat in eggs then breadcrumbs. Heat the oil then fry the chicken until golden brown. Remove from the pan. Add the vegetables and stir-fry for 4 minutes then remove. Drain the oil from the pan then return the chicken and vegetables to the pan with the remaining ingredients. Bring to the boil and heat through before serving.

Fried Chicken with Cucumber

Serves 4

225 g/8 oz chicken meat
1 egg white
2.5 ml/½ tsp cornflour (cornstarch)
salt
½ cucumber
30 ml/2 tbsp groundnut (peanut) oil
100 g/4 oz button mushrooms
50 g/2 oz bamboo shoots, cut into strips
50 g/2 oz ham, diced
15 ml/1 tbsp water
2.5 ml/½ tsp salt
2.5 ml/½ tsp rice wine or dry sherry
2.5 ml/½ tsp sesame oil

Slice the chicken and cut it into chunks. Mix with the egg white, cornflour and salt and leave to stand. Halve the cucumber lengthways and cut diagonally into thick slices. Heat the oil and stir-fry the chicken until lightly browned then remove from the pan. Add the cucumber and bamboo shoots and stir-fry for 1 minute. Return the chicken to the pan with the ham, water, salt and wine or sherry. Bring to the boil and simmer until the chicken is tender. Serve sprinkled with sesame oil.

Chilli-Chicken Curry

Serves 4

120 ml/4 fl oz/½ cup groundnut
    (peanut) oil

4 chicken pieces

1 onion, chopped

5 ml/1 tsp curry powder

5 ml/1 tsp chilli sauce

15 ml/1 tbsp rice wine or dry sherry

2.5 ml/½ tsp salt

600 ml/1 pt/2½ cups chicken stock

15 ml/1 tbsp cornflour (cornstarch)

45 ml/3 tbsp water

5 ml/1 tsp sesame oil

Heat the oil and fry the chicken pieces until golden brown on both sides then remove them from the pan. Add the onion, curry powder and chilli sauce and stir-fry for 1 minute. Add the wine or sherry and salt, stir well, then return the chicken to the pan and stir again. Add the stock, bring to the boil and simmer gently for about 30 minutes until the chicken is tender. If the sauce has not reduced sufficiently, blend the cornflour and water to a paste, stir a little into the sauce and simmer, stirring, until the sauce thickens. Serve sprinkled with sesame oil.

Chinese Chicken Curry

Serves 4

45 ml/3 tbsp curry powder

1 onion, sliced

350 g/12 oz chicken, diced

150 ml/¼ pt/⅔ cup chicken stock

5 ml/1 tsp salt

10 ml/2 tsp cornflour (cornstarch)

15 ml/1 tbsp water

Heat the curry powder and onion in a dry pan for 2 minutes, shaking the pan to coat the onion. Add the chicken and stir until well coated in curry powder. Add the stock and salt, bring to the boil, cover and simmer for about 5 minutes until the chicken is tender. Mix the cornflour and water to a paste, stir into the pan and simmer, stirring, until the sauce thickens.

Quick Curried Chicken

Serves 4

450 g/1 lb chicken breasts, cubed

45 ml/3 tbsp rice wine or dry sherry

50 g/2 oz cornflour (cornstarch)

1 egg white

salt

150 ml/¼ pt/⅔ cup groundnut (peanut)
    oil

15 ml/1 tbsp curry powder

10 ml/2 tsp brown sugar

150 ml/¼ pt/⅔ cup chicken stock

Mix together the chicken cubes and sherry. Reserve 10 ml/2 tsp of the cornflour. Beat the egg white with the remaining cornflour and a pinch of salt then stir it into the chicken until it is well coated. Heat the oil and fry the chicken until cooked and golden. Remove from the pan and drain off all but 15 ml/1 tbsp of the oil. Stir in the reserved cornflour, curry powder and sugar and fry for 1 minute. Stir in the stock, bring to the boil and simmer, stirring continuously, until the sauce thickens. Return the chicken to the pan, stir together and reheat before serving.

Curried Chicken with Potatoes

Serves 4

45 ml/3 tbsp groundnut (peanut) oil

2.5 ml/½ tsp salt

1 clove garlic, crushed

750 g/1½ lb chicken, cubed

225 g/8 oz potatoes, cubed

4 onions, cut into wedges

15 ml/1 tbsp curry powder

450 ml/¾ pt/2 cups chicken stock

225 g/8 oz mushrooms, sliced

Heat the oil with the salt and garlic, add the chicken and fry until lightly browned. Add the potatoes, onions and curry powder and stir-fry for 2 minutes. Add the stock, bring to the boil, cover and simmer for about 20 minutes until the chicken is cooked, stirring occasionally. Add the mushrooms, remove the lid and simmer for a further 10 minutes until the liquid has reduced.

Deep-Fried Chicken Legs

Serves 4

2 large chicken legs, boned

2 spring onions (scallion)

1 slice ginger, beaten flat

120 ml/4 fl oz/½ cup soy sauce

5 ml/1 tsp rice wine or dry sherry

oil for deep-frying

5 ml/1 tsp sesame oil

freshly ground pepper

Spread out the chicken flesh and score it all over. Beat 1 spring onion flat and chop the other. Mix the flattened spring onion with the ginger, soy sauce and wine or sherry. Pour over the chicken and leave to marinate for 30 minutes. Remove and drain. Place on a plate on a steamer rack and steam for 20 minutes.

Heat the oil and deep-fry the chicken for about 5 minutes until golden brown. Remove from the pan, drain well and slice thickly, then arrange the slices on a warmed serving plate. Heat the sesame oil, add the chopped spring onion and pepper, pour over the chicken and serve.

Deep-Fried Chicken with Curry Sauce

Serves 4

1 egg, lightly beaten

30 ml/2 tbsp cornflour (cornstarch)

25 g/1 oz/¼ cup plain (all-purpose) flour

2.5 ml/½ tsp salt

225 g/8 oz chicken, cubed

oil for deep-frying

30 ml/2 tbsp groundnut (peanut) oil

30 ml/2 tbsp curry powder

60 ml/4 tbsp rice wine or dry sherry

Beat the egg with the cornflour, flour and salt to a thick batter. Pour over the chicken and stir well to coat. Heat the oil and deep-fry the chicken until golden brown and cooked through. Meanwhile, heat the oil and fry the curry powder for 1 minute. Stir in the wine or sherry and bring to the boil. Place the chicken on a warmed plate and pour over the curry sauce.

Photograph opposite: Crispy-fried Spiced Chicken (page 190)

Drunken Chicken

Serves 4

450 g/1 lb chicken fillet, cut into chunks
60 ml/4 tbsp soy sauce
30 ml/2 tbsp hoisin sauce
30 ml/2 tbsp plum sauce
30 ml/2 tbsp wine vinegar
2 cloves garlic, crushed
pinch of salt
few drops of chilli oil
2 egg whites
60 ml/4 tsp cornflour (cornstarch)
oil for deep-frying
200 ml/⅓ pt/1¼ cups rice wine or dry sherry

Place the chicken in a bowl. Mix the sauces and wine vinegar, garlic, salt and chilli oil, pour over the chicken and marinate in the refrigerator for 4 hours. Beat the egg whites until stiff and fold in the cornflour. Remove the chicken from the marinade and coat with the egg white mixture. Heat the oil and deep-fry the chicken until cooked through and golden brown. Drain well on kitchen paper and place in a bowl. Pour over the wine or sherry, cover and leave to marinate in the refrigerator for 12 hours. Remove the chicken from the wine and serve cold.

Savoury Chicken with Eggs

Serves 4

30 ml/2 tbsp groundnut (peanut) oil
4 chicken pieces
2 spring onions (scallions), chopped
1 clove garlic, crushed
1 slice ginger root, chopped
175 ml/6 fl oz/⅔ cup soy sauce
30 ml/2 tbsp rice wine or dry sherry
30 ml/2 tbsp brown sugar
5 ml/1 tsp salt
375 ml/13 fl oz/1¼ cups water
4 hard-boiled (hard-cooked) eggs
15 ml/1 tbsp cornflour (cornstarch)

Heat the oil and fry the chicken pieces until golden brown. Add the spring onions, garlic and ginger and fry for 2 minutes. Add the soy sauce, wine or sherry, sugar and salt and stir together well. Add the water and bring to the boil, cover and simmer for 20 minutes. Add the hard-boiled eggs, cover and cook for a further 15 minutes. Mix the cornflour with a little water, stir it into the sauce and simmer, stirring, until the sauce clears and thickens.

Photograph opposite: Honey-roast Duck (page 236)

Chicken Egg Rolls

Serves 4

4 Chinese dried mushrooms
100 g/4 oz chicken, cut into strips
5 ml/1 tsp cornflour (cornstarch)
15 ml/1 tbsp soy sauce
2.5 ml/½ tsp salt
2.5 ml/½ tsp sugar
60 ml/4 tbsp groundnut (peanut) oil
225 g/8 oz bean sprouts
3 spring onions (scallions), chopped
100 g/4 oz spinach
12 egg roll skins (page 282)
1 egg, beaten
oil for deep-frying

Soak the mushrooms in warm water for 30 minutes then drain. Discard the stalks and chop the caps. Place the chicken in a bowl. Mix the cornflour with 5 ml/1 tsp of soy sauce, the salt and sugar and stir into the chicken. Leave to stand for 15 minutes. Heat half the oil and stir-fry the chicken until lightly browned. Blanch the bean sprouts in boiling water for 3 minutes then drain. Heat the remaining oil and fry the spring onions until lightly browned. Stir in the mushrooms, beansprouts, spinach and remaining soy sauce. Add in the chicken and stir-fry for 2 minutes. Leave to cool. Place a little filling on the centre of each skin and brush the edges with beaten egg. Fold in the sides then roll up the egg rolls, sealing the edges with egg. Heat the oil and deep-fry the egg rolls until crisp and golden.

Braised Chicken with Eggs

Serves 4

30 ml/2 tbsp groundnut (peanut) oil
4 chicken breast fillets, cut into strips
1 red pepper, cut into strips
1 green pepper, cut into strips
45 ml/3 tbsp soy sauce
45 ml/3 tbsp rice wine or dry sherry
250 ml/8 fl oz/1 cup chicken stock
100 g/4 oz iceberg lettuce, shredded
5 ml/1 tsp brown sugar
30 ml/2 tbsp hoisin sauce
salt and pepper
15 ml/1 tbsp cornflour (cornstarch)
30 ml/2 tbsp water
4 eggs
30 ml/2 tbsp sherry

Heat the oil and fry the chicken and peppers until golden brown. Add the soy sauce, wine or sherry and stock, bring to the boil, cover and simmer for 30 minutes. Add the lettuce, sugar and hoisin sauce and season with salt and pepper. Mix the cornflour and water, stir it into the sauce and bring to the boil, stirring. Beat the eggs with the sherry and fry as thin omelettes. Sprinkle with salt and pepper and tear into strips. Arrange in a warmed serving dish and spoon over the chicken.

Far Eastern Chicken

Serves 4

60 ml/4 tbsp groundnut (peanut) oil

450 g/1 lb chicken meat, cut into chunks

2 cloves garlic, crushed

2.5 ml/½ tsp salt

2 onions, chopped

2 pieces stem ginger, chopped

45 ml/3 tbsp soy sauce

30 ml/2 tbsp hoisin sauce

45 ml/3 tbsp rice wine or dry sherry

300 ml/½ pt/1¼ cups chicken stock

5 ml/1 tsp freshly ground pepper

6 hard-boiled (hard-cooked) eggs, chopped

15 ml/1 tbsp cornflour (cornstarch)

15 ml/1 tbsp water

Heat the oil and fry the chicken until golden brown. Add the garlic, salt, onions and ginger and fry for 2 minutes. Add the soy sauce, hoisin sauce, wine or sherry, stock and pepper. Bring to the boil, cover and simmer for 30 minutes. Add the eggs. Mix the cornflour and water and stir it into the sauce. Bring to the boil and simmer, stirring, until the sauce thickens.

Chicken Foo Yung

Serves 4

6 eggs, beaten

45 ml/3 tbsp cornflour (cornstarch)

100 g/4 oz mushrooms, roughly chopped

225 g/8 oz chicken breast, diced

1 onion, finely chopped

5 ml/1 tsp salt

45 ml/3 tbsp groundnut (peanut) oil

Beat the eggs then beat in the cornflour. Stir in all the remaining ingredients except the oil. Heat the oil. Pour the mixture into the pan a little at a time to make small pancakes about 7.5 cm/3 in across. Cook until the bottom is golden brown then turn and cook the other side.

Ham and Chicken Foo Yung

Serves 4

6 eggs, beaten

45 ml/3 tbsp cornflour (cornstarch)

100 g/4 oz ham, diced

225 g/8 oz chicken breast, diced

3 spring onions (scallions), finely chopped

5 ml/1 tsp salt

45 ml/3 tbsp groundnut (peanut) oil

Beat the eggs then beat in the cornflour. Stir in all the remaining ingredients except the oil. Heat the oil. Pour the mixture into the pan a little at a time to make small pancakes about 7.5 cm/3 in across. Cook until the bottom is golden brown then turn and cook the other side.

Deep-Fried Chicken with Ginger

Serves 4

1 chicken, halved

4 slices ginger root, crushed

30 ml/2 tbsp rice wine or dry sherry

30 ml/2 tbsp soy sauce

5 ml/1 tsp sugar

oil for deep-frying

Place the chicken in a shallow bowl. Mix the ginger, wine or sherry, soy sauce and sugar, pour over the chicken and rub into the skin. Leave to marinate for 1 hour. Heat the oil and deep-fry the chicken, one half at a time, until lightly coloured. Remove from the oil and leave to cool slightly while you reheat the oil. Return the chicken to the pan and deep-fry until golden brown and cooked through. Drain well before serving.

Ginger Chicken

Serves 4

225 g/8 oz chicken, thinly sliced

1 egg white

pinch of salt

2.5 ml/½ tsp cornflour (cornstarch)

15 ml/1 tbsp groundnut (peanut) oil

10 slices ginger root

6 mushrooms, halved

1 carrot, sliced

2 spring onions (scallions), sliced

5 ml/1 tsp rice wine or dry sherry

5 ml/1 tsp water

2.5 ml/½ tsp sesame oil

Mix the chicken with the egg white, salt and cornflour. Heat half the oil and fry the chicken until lightly browned then remove it from the pan. Heat the remaining oil and fry the ginger, mushrooms, carrot and spring onions for 3 minutes. Return the chicken to the pan with the wine or sherry and water and simmer until the chicken is tender. Serve sprinkled with sesame oil.

Ginger-Chicken with Mushrooms and Chestnuts

Serves 4

60 ml/4 tbsp groundnut (peanut) oil

225 g/8 oz onions, sliced

450 g/1 lb chicken meat, diced

100 g/4 oz mushrooms, sliced

30 ml/2 tbsp plain (all-purpose) flour

60 ml/4 tbsp soy sauce

10 ml/2 tsp sugar

salt and freshly ground pepper

900 ml/1½ pt/3¾ cups hot water

2 slices ginger root, chopped

450 g/1 lb water chestnuts

Heat the half oil and fry the onions for 3 minutes then remove them from the pan. Heat the remaining oil and fry the chicken until lightly browned. Add the mushrooms and cook for 2 minutes. Sprinkle the mixture with flour then stir in the soy sauce, sugar, salt and pepper. Pour in the water and ginger, onions and chestnuts. Bring to the boil, cover and simmer gently for 20 minutes. Remove the lid and continue to simmer gently until the sauce has reduced.

Golden Chicken

Serves 4

8 small chicken pieces

300 ml/½ pt/1¼ cups chicken stock

45 ml/3 tbsp soy sauce

15 ml/1 tbsp rice wine or dry sherry

5 ml/1 tsp sugar

1 sliced ginger root, minced

Place all the ingredients in a large pan, bring to the boil, cover and simmer for about 30 minutes until the chicken is thoroughly cooked. Remove the lid and continue to simmer until the sauce has reduced.

Marinated Golden Chicken Stew

Serves 4

4 chicken pieces

300 ml/½ pt/1¼ cups soy sauce

oil for deep-frying

4 spring onions (scallions), thickly sliced

1 slice ginger root, minced

2 red chilli peppers, sliced

3 cloves star anise

50 g/2 oz bamboo shoots, sliced

150 ml/¼ pt/⅔ cup chicken stock

30 ml/2 tbsp cornflour (cornstarch)

60 ml/4 tbsp water

5 ml/1 tsp sesame oil

Cut the chicken into large chunks and marinate in the soy sauce for 10 minutes. Remove and drain, reserving the soy sauce. Heat the oil and deep-fry the chicken for about 2 minutes until lightly browned. Remove and drain. Pour off all but 30 ml/2tbsp of the oil then add the spring onions, ginger, chilli peppers and star anise and fry for 1 minute. Return the chicken to the pan with the bamboo shoots and reserved soy sauce and add just enough stock to cover the chicken. Bring to the boil and simmer for about 10 minutes until the chicken is tender. Remove the chicken from the sauce with a slotted spoon and arrange on a warmed serving dish. Strain the sauce then return it to the pan. Blend the cornflour and water to a paste, stir into the sauce and simmer, stirring, until the sauce thickens. Pour over the chicken and serve sprinkled with a little sesame oil.

Golden Coins

Serves 4

4 chicken breast fillets
30 ml/2 tbsp honey
30 ml/2 tbsp wine vinegar
30 ml/2 tbsp tomato ketchup (catsup)
30 ml/2 tbsp soy sauce
pinch of salt
2 cloves garlic, crushed
5 ml/1 tsp five-spice powder
45 ml/3 tbsp plain (all-purpose) flour
2 eggs, beaten
5 ml/1 tsp grated root ginger
5 ml/1 tsp grated lemon rind
100 g/4 oz/1 cup dried breadcrumbs
oil for deep-frying

Put the chicken into a bowl. Mix together the honey, wine vinegar, tomato ketchup, soy sauce, salt, garlic and five-spice powder. Pour over the chicken, stir well, cover and marinate in the refrigerator for 12 hours.

Remove the chicken from the marinade and cut into finger thick strips. Dust with flour. Beat the eggs, ginger and lemon rind. Coat the chicken in the mixture then in the breadcrumbs until evenly coated. Heat the oil and deep-fry the chicken until golden brown.

Steamed Chicken with Ham

Serves 4

4 chicken portions
100 g/4 oz smoked ham, chopped
3 spring onions (scallions), chopped
15 ml/1 tbsp groundnut (peanut) oil
salt and freshly ground pepper
15 ml/1 tbsp flat-leaved parsley

Chop the chicken portions into 5 cm/ 1 in chunks and place in an ovenproof bowl with the ham and spring onions. Sprinkle with oil and season with salt and pepper then toss the ingredients together gently. Place the bowl on a rack in a steamer, cover and steam over boiling water for about 40 minutes until the chicken is tender. Serve garnished with parsley.

Chicken with Hoisin Sauce

Serves 4

4 chicken portions, halved
50 g/2 oz/½ cup cornflour (cornstarch)
oil for deep-frying
10 ml/2 tsp grated ginger root
2 onions, chopped
225 g/8 oz broccoli florets
1 red pepper, chopped
225 g/8 oz button mushrooms
250 ml/8 fl oz/1 cup chicken stock
45 ml/3 tbsp rice wine or dry sherry
45 ml/3 tbsp cider vinegar
45 ml/3 tbsp hoisin sauce
20 ml/4 tsp soy sauce

Coat the chicken pieces in half the cornflour. Heat the oil and fry the chicken pieces a few at a time for about 8 minutes until golden brown and cooked through. Remove from the pan and drain on kitchen paper. Remove all but 30 ml/2 tbsp of oil from the pan and stir-fry the ginger for 1 minute. Add the onions and stir-fry for 1 minute. Add the broccoli, pepper and mushrooms and stir-fry for 2 minutes. Combine the stock with the reserved cornflour and remaining ingredients and add to the pan. Bring to the boil, stirring, and cook until the sauce clears. Return the chicken to the wok and cook, stirring, for about 3 minutes until heated through.

Honey Chicken

Serves 4

30 ml/2 tbsp groundnut (peanut) oil
4 chicken pieces
30 ml/2 tbsp soy sauce
120 ml/4 fl oz/½ cup rice wine or dry sherry
30 ml/2 tbsp honey
5 ml/1 tsp salt
1 spring onion (scallion), chopped
1 slice ginger root, finely chopped

Heat the oil and fry the chicken until browned on all sides. Drain off excess oil. Mix together the remaining ingredients and pour them into the pan. Bring to the boil, cover and simmer for about 40 minutes until the chicken is cooked through.

Kung Pao Chicken

Serves 4

450 g/1 lb chicken, cubed
1 egg white
5 ml/1 tsp salt
30 ml/2 tbsp cornflour (cornstarch)
60 ml/4 tbsp groundnut (peanut) oil
25 g/1 oz dried red chilli peppers, trimmed
5 ml/1 tsp minced garlic
15 ml/1 tbsp soy sauce
15 ml/1 tbsp rice wine or dry sherry
5 ml/1 tsp sugar
5 ml/1 tsp wine vinegar
5 ml/1 tsp sesame oil
30 ml/2 tbsp water

Place the chicken in a bowl with the egg white, salt and half the cornflour and leave to marinate for 30 minutes. Heat the oil and fry the chicken until lightly browned then remove it from the pan. Reheat the oil and fry the chilli peppers and garlic for 2 minutes. Return the chicken to the pan with the soy sauce, wine or sherry, sugar, wine vinegar and sesame oil and stir-fry for 2 minutes. Mix the remaining cornflour with the water, stir it into the pan and simmer, stirring, until the sauce clears and thickens.

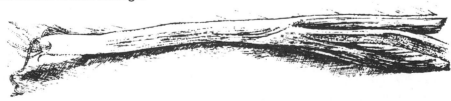

Chicken with Leeks

Serves 4

30 ml/2 tbsp groundnut (peanut) oil

5 ml/1 tsp salt

225 g/8 oz leeks, sliced

1 slice ginger root, chopped

225 g/8 oz chicken, thinly sliced

15 ml/1 tbsp rice wine or dry sherry

15 ml/1 tbsp soy sauce

Heat half the oil and fry the salt and leeks until lightly browned then remove them from the pan. Heat the remaining oil and fry the ginger and chicken until lightly browned. Add the wine or sherry and soy sauce and fry for a further 2 minutes until the chicken is cooked. Return the leeks to the pan and stir together until heated through. Serve at once.

Lemon Chicken

Serves 4

4 boned chicken breasts

2 eggs

50 g/2 oz/½ cup cornflour (cornstarch)

50 g/2 oz/½ cup plain (all-purpose) flour

150 ml/¼ pt/⅔ cup water

groundnut (peanut) oil for deep-frying

250 ml/8 fl oz/1 cup chicken stock (page 21)

60 ml/5 tbsp lemon juice

30 ml/2 tbsp rice wine or dry sherry

30 ml/2 tbsp cornflour (cornstarch)

30 ml/2 tbsp tomato purée (paste)

1 head lettuce

Cut each chicken breast into 4 pieces. Beat the eggs, cornflour and plain flour, adding just enough water to make a thick batter. Place the chicken pieces in the batter and stir until thoroughly coated. Heat the oil and deep-fry the chicken until golden brown and cooked through.

Meanwhile, mix the stock, lemon juice, wine or sherry, cornflour and tomato purée and heat gently, stirring, until the mixture comes to the boil. Simmer gently, stirring continuously, until the sauce thickens and clears. Arrange the chicken on a warmed serving plate on a bed of lettuce leaves and either pour over the sauce or serve it separately.

Lemon Chicken Stir-Fry

Serves 4

450 g/1 lb boned chicken, sliced

30 ml/2 tbsp lemon juice

15 ml/1 tbsp soy sauce

15 ml/1 tbsp rice wine or dry sherry

30 ml/2 tbsp cornflour (cornstarch)

30 ml/2 tbsp groundnut (peanut) oil

2.5 ml/½ tsp salt

2 cloves garlic, crushed

50 g/2 oz water chestnuts, cut into strips

50 g/2 oz bamboo shoots, cut into strips

a few Chinese leaves, cut into strips

60 ml/4 tbsp chicken stock (page 21)

15 ml/1 tbsp tomato purée (paste)

15 ml/1 tbsp sugar

15 ml/1 tbsp lemon juice

Place the chicken in a bowl. Mix together the lemon juice, soy sauce, wine or sherry and 15 ml/1 tbsp cornflour, pour over the chicken and leave to marinate for 1 hour, turning occasionally.

Heat the oil, salt and garlic until the garlic is lightly browned then add the chicken and marinade and stir-fry for about 5 minutes until the chicken is lightly browned. Add the water chestnuts, bamboo shoots and Chinese leaves and stir-fry for a further 3 minutes or until the chicken is just cooked. Add the remaining ingredients and stir-fry for about 3 minutes until the sauce clears and thickens.

Chicken Livers with Bamboo Shoots

Serves 4

225 g/8 oz chicken livers, thickly sliced
45 ml/3 tbsp rice wine or dry sherry
45 ml/3 tbsp groundnut (peanut) oil
15 ml/1 tbsp soy sauce
100 g/4 oz bamboo shoots, sliced
100 g/4 oz water chestnuts, sliced
60 ml/4 tbsp chicken stock
salt and freshly ground pepper

Mix the chicken livers with the wine or sherry and leave to stand for 30 minutes. Heat the oil and fry the chicken livers until lightly browned. Add the marinade, soy sauce, bamboo shoots, water chestnuts and stock. Bring to the boil and season with salt and pepper. Cover and simmer for about 10 minutes until tender.

Deep-Fried Chicken Livers

Serves 4

450 g/1 lb chicken livers, halved
50 g/2 oz/½ cup cornflour (cornstarch)
oil for deep-frying

Pat the chicken livers dry then dust with cornflour, shaking off any excess.

Heat the oil and deep-fry the chicken livers for a few minutes until golden brown and cooked through. Drain on kitchen paper before serving.

Chicken Livers with Mangetout

Serves 4

225 g/8 oz chicken livers, thickly sliced
10 ml/2 tsp cornflour (cornstarch)
10 ml/2 tsp rice wine or dry sherry
15 ml/1 tbsp soy sauce
45 ml/3 tbsp groundnut (peanut) oil
2.5 ml/½ tsp salt
2 slices ginger root, minced
100 g/4 oz mangetout (snow peas)
10 ml/2 tsp cornflour (cornstarch)
60 ml/4 tbsp water

Place the chicken livers in a bowl. Add the cornflour, wine or sherry and soy sauce and toss well to coat. Heat half the oil and fry the salt and ginger until lightly browned. Add the mangetout and stir-fry until well coated with oil then remove from the pan. Heat the remaining oil and fry the chicken livers for 5 minutes until cooked through. Mix the cornflour and water to a paste, stir it into the pan and simmer, stirring, until the sauce clears and thickens. Return the mangetout to the pan and simmer until heated through.

Chicken Livers with Noodle Pancake

Serves 4

30 ml/2 tbsp groundnut (peanut) oil

1 onion, sliced

450 g/1 lb chicken livers, halved

2 stalks celery, sliced

120 ml/4 fl oz/½ cup chicken stock

15 ml/1 tbsp cornflour (cornstarch)

15 ml/1 tbsp soy sauce

30 ml/2 tbsp water

noodle pancake (page 277)

Heat the oil and fry the onion until softened. Add the chicken livers and stir-fry until coloured. Add the celery and stir-fry for 1 minute. Add the stock, bring to the boil, cover and simmer for 5 minutes. Mix the cornflour, soy sauce and water to a paste, stir it into the pan and simmer, stirring, until the sauce clears and thickens. Pour the mixture over the noodle pancake and serve.

Chicken Livers with Oyster Sauce

Serves 4

45 ml/3 tbsp groundnut (peanut) oil

1 onion, chopped

225 g/8 oz chicken livers, halved

100 g/4 oz mushrooms, sliced

30 ml/2 tbsp oyster sauce

15 ml/1 tbsp soy sauce

15 ml/1 tbsp rice wine or dry sherry

120 ml/4 fl oz/½ cup chicken stock

5 ml/1 tsp sugar

15 ml/1 tbsp cornflour (cornstarch)

45 ml/3 tbsp water

Heat half the oil and fry the onion until softened. Add the chicken livers and fry until just coloured. Add the mushrooms and fry for 2 minutes. Mix the oyster sauce, soy sauce, wine or sherry, stock and sugar, pour it into the pan and bring to the boil, stirring. Mix the cornflour and water to a paste, add it to the pan and simmer, stirring until the sauce clears and thickens and the livers are tender.

Chicken Livers with Pineapple

Serves 4

225 g/8 oz chicken livers, halved

45 ml/3 tbsp groundnut (peanut) oil

30 ml/2 tbsp soy sauce

15 ml/1 tbsp cornflour (cornstarch)

15 ml/1 tbsp sugar

15 ml/1 tbsp wine vinegar

salt and freshly ground pepper

100 g/4 oz pineapple chunks

60 ml/4 tbsp chicken stock

Blanch the chicken livers in boiling water for 30 seconds then drain. Heat the oil and stir-fry the chicken livers for 30 seconds. Mix together the soy sauce, cornflour, sugar, wine vinegar, salt and pepper, pour into the pan and stir well to coat the chicken livers. Add the pineapple chunks and stock and stir-fry for about 3 minutes until the livers are cooked.

Sweet and Sour Chicken Livers

Serves 4

30 ml/2 tbsp groundnut (peanut) oil
450 g/1 lb chicken livers, quartered
2 green peppers, cut into chunks
4 slices canned pineapple, cut into chunks
60 ml/4 tbsp chicken stock
30 ml/2 tbsp cornflour (cornstarch)
10 ml/2 tsp soy sauce
100 g/4 oz/½ cup sugar
120 ml/4 fl oz/½ cup wine vinegar
120 ml/4 fl oz/½ cup water

Heat the oil and fry the livers until lightly browned then transfer them to a warmed serving dish. Add the peppers to the pan and fry for 3 minutes. Add the pineapple and stock, bring to the boil, cover and simmer for 15 minutes. Blend the remaining ingredients to a paste, stir into the pan and simmer, stirring, until the sauce thickens. Pour over the chicken livers and serve.

Chicken with Lychees

Serves 4

3 chicken breasts
60 ml/4 tbsp cornflour (cornstarch)
45 ml/3 tbsp groundnut (peanut) oil
5 spring onions (scallions), sliced
1 red pepper, cut into chunks
120 ml/4 fl oz/½ cup tomato sauce
120 ml/4 fl oz/½ cup chicken stock
5 ml/1 tsp sugar
275 g/10 oz peeled lychees

Cut the chicken breasts in half and remove and discard the bones and skin. Cut each breast into 6. Reserve 5 ml/1 tsp of cornflour and toss the chicken in the remainder until it is well coated. Heat the oil and stir-fry the chicken for about 8 minutes until golden brown. Add the spring onions and pepper and stir-fry for 1 minute. Mix together the tomato sauce, half the stock and the sugar and stir it into the wok with the lychees. Bring to the boil, cover and simmer for about 10 minutes until the chicken is cooked through. Mix the reserved cornflour and stock then stir it into the pan. Simmer, stirring, until the sauce clears and thickens.

Chicken with Lychee Sauce

Serves 4

225 g/8 oz chicken
1 spring onion (scallion)
4 water chestnuts
30 ml/2 tbsp cornflour (cornstarch)
45 ml/3 tbsp soy sauce
30 ml/2 tbsp rice wine or dry sherry
2 egg whites
oil for deep-frying
400 g/14 oz canned lychees in syrup
5 tbsp chicken stock

Mince (grind) the chicken with the spring onion and waterchestnut. Mix in half the cornflour, 30 ml/2 tbsp of soy sauce, the wine or sherry and the egg whites. Shape the mixture into walnut-sized balls. Heat the oil and deep-fry the chicken until golden brown. Drain on kitchen paper.

Meanwhile, heat the lychee syrup gently with the stock and reserved soy sauce. Mix the remaining cornflour with a little water, stir it into the pan and simmer, stirring, until the sauce clears and thickens. Stir in the lychees and simmer gently to heat through. Arrange the chicken on a warmed serving plate, pour over the lychees and sauce and serve at once.

Chicken with Mangetout

Serves 4

225 g/8 oz chicken, thinly sliced
5 ml/1 tsp cornflour (cornstarch)
5 ml/1 tsp rice wine or dry sherry
5 ml/1 tsp sesame oil
1 egg white, lightly beaten
45 ml/3 tbsp groundnut (peanut) oil
1 clove garlic, crushed
1 slice ginger root, minced
100 g/4 oz mangetout (snow peas)
120 ml/4 fl oz/½ cup chicken stock
salt and freshly ground pepper

Mix the chicken with the cornflour, wine or sherry, sesame oil and egg white. Heat half the oil and fry the garlic and ginger until lightly browned. Add the chicken and fry until golden then remove from the pan. Heat the remaining oil and fry the mangetout for 2 minutes. Add the stock, bring to the boil, cover and simmer for 2 minutes. Return the chicken to the pan and season with salt and pepper. Simmer gently until heated through.

Chicken with Mangoes

Serves 4

100 g/4 oz/1 cup plain (all-purpose) flour
250 ml/8 fl oz/1 cup water
2.5 ml/½ tsp salt
pinch of baking powder
3 chicken breasts
oil for deep-frying
1 slice ginger root, minced
150 ml/¼ pt/⅔ cup chicken stock
45 ml/3 tbsp wine vinegar
45 ml/3 tbsp rice wine or dry sherry
20 ml/4 tsp soy sauce
10 ml/2 tsp sugar
10 ml/2 tsp cornflour (cornstarch)
5 ml/1 tsp sesame oil
5 spring onions (scallions), sliced
400 g/11 oz canned mangoes, drained and cut into strips

Whisk together the flour, water, salt and baking powder. Leave to stand for 15 minutes. Remove and discard the skin and bones from the chicken. Cut the chicken into thin strips. Mix these into the flour mixture. Heat the oil and fry the chicken for about 5 minutes until golden brown. Remove from the pan and drain on kitchen paper. Remove all but 15 ml/1 tbsp of oil from the wok and stir-fry the ginger until lightly browned. Mix the stock with the wine vinegar, wine or sherry, soy sauce, sugar, cornflour and sesame oil. Add to the pan and bring to the boil, stirring. Add the spring onions and simmer for 3 minutes. Add the chicken and mangoes and simmer, stirring, for 2 minutes.

Chicken-Stuffed Melon

Serves 4

350 g/12 oz chicken meat
6 water chestnuts
2 shelled scallops
4 slices ginger root
5 ml/1 tsp salt
15 ml/1 tbsp soy sauce
600 ml/1 pt/2½ cups chicken stock
8 small or 4 medium cantaloup melons

Finely chop the chicken, chestnuts, scallops and ginger and mix with the salt, soy sauce and stock. Cut the tops off the melons and scoop out the seeds. Serrate the top edges. Fill the melons with the chicken mixture and stand on a rack in a steamer. Steam over boiling water for 40 minutes until the chicken is cooked.

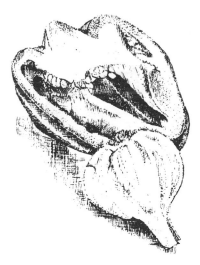

Chicken and Mushroom Stir-Fry

Serves 4

45 ml/3 tbsp groundnut (peanut) oil
1 clove garlic, crushed
1 spring onion (scallion), chopped
1 slice ginger root, minced
225 g/8 oz chicken breast, cut into slivers
225 g/8 oz button mushrooms
45 ml/3 tbsp soy sauce
15 ml/1 tbsp rice wine or dry sherry
5 ml/1 tsp cornflour (cornstarch)

Heat the oil and fry the garlic, spring onion and ginger until lightly browned. Add the chicken and stir-fry for 5 minutes. Add the mushrooms and stir-fry for 3 minutes. Add the soy sauce, wine or sherry and cornflour and stir-fry for about 5 minutes until the chicken is cooked through.

Chicken with Mushrooms and Peanuts

Serves 4

30 ml/2 tbsp groundnut (peanut) oil
2 cloves garlic, crushed
1 slice ginger root, minced
450 g/1 lb boned chicken, cubed
225 g/8 oz button mushrooms
100 g/4 oz bamboo shoots, cut into strips
1 green pepper, cubed
1 red pepper, cubed
250 ml/8 fl oz/1 cup chicken stock (page 21)
30 ml/2 tbsp rice wine or dry sherry
15 ml/1 tbsp soy sauce
15 ml/1 tbsp tabasco sauce
30 ml/2 tbsp cornflour (cornstarch)
30 ml/2 tbsp water

Heat the oil, garlic and ginger until the garlic is lightly golden. Add the chicken and stir-fry until it is lightly browned. Add the mushrooms, bamboo shoots and peppers and stir-fry for 3 minutes. Add the stock, wine or sherry, soy sauce and tabasco sauce and bring to the boil, stirring. Cover and simmer for about 10 minutes until the chicken is thoroughly cooked. Mix together the cornflour and water and stir them into the sauce. Simmer, stirring, until the sauce clears and thickens, adding a little more stock or water if the sauce is too thick.

Stir-Fried Chicken with Mushrooms

Serves 4

6 dried Chinese mushrooms
1 chicken breast, thinly sliced
1 slice ginger root, minced
2 spring onions (scallions), minced
15 ml/1 tbsp cornflour (cornstarch)
15 ml/1 tbsp rice wine or dry sherry
30 ml/2 tbsp water
2.5 ml/½ tsp salt
45 ml/3 tbsp groundnut (peanut) oil
225 g/8 oz mushrooms, sliced
100 g/4 oz bean sprouts
15 ml/1 tbsp soy sauce
5 ml/1 tsp sugar
120 ml/4 fl oz/½ cup chicken stock

Soak the mushrooms in warm water for 30 minutes then drain. Discard the stalks and slice the caps. Place the chicken in a bowl. Mix the ginger, spring onions, cornflour, wine or sherry, water and salt, stir into the chicken and leave to stand for 1 hour. Heat half the oil and stir-fry the chicken until lightly browned then remove it from the pan. Heat the remaining oil and stir-fry the dried and fresh mushrooms and the bean sprouts for 3 minutes. Add the soy sauce, sugar and stock, bring to the boil, cover and simmer for 4 minutes until the vegetables are just tender. Return the chicken to the pan, stir well and reheat gently before serving.

Steamed Chicken with Mushrooms

Serves 4

4 chicken pieces
30 ml/2 tbsp cornflour (cornstarch)
30 ml/2 tbsp soy sauce
3 spring onions (scallions), chopped
2 slices root ginger, chopped
2.5 ml/½ tsp salt
100 g/4 oz mushrooms, sliced

Chop the chicken pieces into 5 cm/2 in chunks and place them in an ovenproof bowl. Mix the cornflour and soy sauce to a paste, stir in the spring onions, ginger and salt and mix well with the chicken. Gently stir in the mushrooms. Place the bowl on a rack in a steamer, cover and steam over boiling water for about 35 minutes until the chicken is tender.

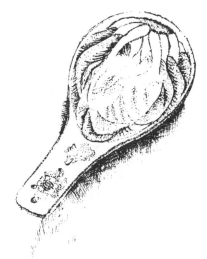

Chicken with Onions

Serves 4

60 ml/4 tbsp groundnut (peanut) oil
2 onions, chopped
450 g/1 lb chicken, sliced
30 ml/2 tbsp rice wine or dry sherry
250 ml/8 fl oz/1 cup chicken stock
45 ml/3 tbsp soy sauce
30 ml/2 tbsp cornflour (cornstarch)
45 ml/3 tbsp water

Heat the oil and fry the onions until lightly browned. Add the chicken and fry until lightly browned. Add the wine or sherry, stock and soy sauce, bring to the boil, cover and simmer for 25 minutes until the chicken is tender. Blend the cornflour and water to a paste, stir it into the pan and simmer, stirring, until the sauce clears and thickens.

Orange and Lemon Chicken

Serves 4

350 g/1 lb chicken meat, cut into strips
30 ml/2 tbsp groundnut (peanut) oil
2 cloves garlic, crushed
2 slices ginger root, minced
grated rind of ½ orange
grated rind of ½ lemon
45 ml/3 tbsp orange juice
45 ml/3 tbsp lemon juice
15 ml/1 tbsp soy sauce
3 spring onions (scallions), chopped
15 ml/1 tbsp cornflour (cornstarch)
45 ml/1 tbsp water

Blanch the chicken in boiling water for 30 seconds then drain. Heat the oil and stir-fry the garlic and ginger for 30 seconds. Add the orange and lemon rind and juice, soy sauce and spring onions and stir-fry for 2 minutes. Add the chicken and simmer for a few minutes until the chicken is tender. Blend the cornflour and water to a paste, stir into the pan and simmer, stirring, until the sauce thickens.

Chicken with Oyster Sauce

Serves 4

30 ml/2 tbsp groundnut (peanut) oil
1 clove garlic, crushed
1 slice ginger, finely chopped
450 g/1 lb chicken, sliced
250 ml/8 fl oz/1 cup chicken stock
30 ml/2 tbsp oyster sauce
15 ml/1 tbsp rice wine or sherry
5 ml/1 tsp sugar

Heat the oil with the garlic and ginger and fry until lightly browned. Add the chicken and stir-fry for about 3 minutes until lightly browned. Add the stock, oyster sauce, wine or sherry and sugar, bring to the boil, stirring, then cover and simmer for about 15 minutes, stirring occasionally, until the chicken is cooked through. Remove the lid and continue to cook, stirring, for about 4 minutes until the sauce has reduced and thickened.

Chicken Parcels

Serves 4

225 g/8 oz chicken
30 ml/2 tbsp rice wine or dry sherry
30 ml/2 tbsp soy sauce
waxed paper or baking parchment
30 ml/2 tbsp groundnut (peanut) oil
oil for deep-frying

Cut the chicken into 5 cm/2 in cubes. Mix the wine or sherry and soy sauce, pour over the chicken and stir well. Cover and leave to stand for 1 hour, stirring occasionally. Cut the paper into 10 cm/4 in squares and brush with oil. Drain the chicken well. Place a piece of paper on the work surface with one corner pointing towards you. Place a piece of chicken on the square just below the centre, fold up the bottom corner and fold up again to encase the chicken. Fold in the sides then fold down the top corner to secure the parcel. Heat the oil and deep-fry the chicken parcels for about 5 minutes until cooked. Serve hot in the parcels for the guests to open themselves.

Chicken with Peanuts

Serves 4

225 g/8 oz chicken, thinly sliced
1 egg white, lightly beaten
10 ml/2 tsp cornflour (cornstarch)
45 ml/3 tbsp groundnut (peanut) oil
1 clove garlic, crushed
1 slice ginger root, minced
2 leeks, chopped
30 ml/2 tbsp soy sauce
15 ml/1 tbsp rice wine or dry sherry
100 g/4 oz/ roasted peanuts

Mix the chicken with the egg white and cornflour until well coated. Heat half the oil and stir-fry the chicken until golden brown then remove from the pan. Heat the remaining oil and fry and garlic and ginger until softened. Add the leeks and fry until lightly browned. Stir in the soy sauce and wine or sherry and simmer for 3 minutes. Return the chicken to the pan with the peanuts and simmer gently until heated through.

Chicken with Peanut Butter

Serves 4

4 chicken breasts, diced
salt and freshly ground pepper
5 ml/1 tsp five spice powder
45 ml/3 tbsp groundnut (peanut) oil
1 onion, diced
2 carrots, diced
1 stick celery, diced
300 ml/½ pt/1¼ cups chicken stock
10 ml/2 tsp tomato purée (paste)
100 g/4 oz peanut butter
15 ml/1 tbsp soy sauce
10 ml/2 tsp cornflour (cornstarch)
pinch of brown sugar
15 ml/1 tbsp chopped chives

Season the chicken with salt, pepper and five-spice powder. Heat the oil and stir-fry the chicken until tender. Remove from the pan. Add the vegetables and fry until tender but still crisp. Mix the stock with the remaining ingredients except the chives, stir into the pan and bring to the boil. Return the chicken to the pan and reheat, stirring. Serve sprinkled with sugar.

Chicken with Peas

Serves 4

60 ml/4 tbsp groundnut (peanut) oil
1 onion, chopped
450 g/1 lb chicken, diced
salt and freshly ground pepper
100 g/4 oz peas
2 stalks celery, chopped
100 g/4 oz mushrooms, chopped
250 ml/8 fl oz/1 cup chicken stock
15 ml/1 tbsp cornflour (cornstarch)
15 ml/1 tbsp soy sauce
60 ml/4 tbsp water

Heat the oil and fry the onion until lightly browned. Add the chicken and fry until coloured. Season with salt and pepper and add the peas, celery and mushrooms and stir well. Add the stock, bring to the boil, cover and simmer for 15 minutes. Blend the cornflour, soy sauce and water to a paste, stir it into the pan and simmer, stirring, until the sauce clears and thickens.

Peking Chicken

Serves 4

4 chicken portions
salt and freshly ground pepper
5 ml/1 tsp sugar
1 spring onion (scallion), chopped
1 slice ginger root, minced
15 ml/1 tbsp soy sauce
15 ml/1 tbsp rice wine or dry sherry
15 ml/1 tbsp cornflour (cornstarch)
oil for deep-frying

Place the chicken portions in a shallow bowl and sprinkle with salt and pepper. Mix the sugar, spring onion, ginger, soy sauce and wine or sherry, rub into the chicken, cover and leave to marinate for 3 hours. Drain the chicken and dust it with cornflour. Heat the oil and deep-fry the chicken until golden brown and cooked through. Drain well before serving.

Chicken with Peppers

Serves 4

60 ml/4 tbsp soy sauce
45 ml/3 tbsp rice wine or dry sherry
45 ml/3 tbsp cornflour (cornstarch)
450 g/1 lb chicken, minced (ground)
60 ml/4 tbsp groundnut (peanut) oil
2.5 ml/½ tsp salt
2 cloves garlic, crushed
2 red peppers, cubed
1 green pepper, cubed
5 ml/1 tsp sugar
300 ml/½ pt/1¼ cups chicken stock

Mix together half the soy sauce, half the wine or sherry and half the cornflour. Pour over the chicken, stir well, and leave to marinate for at least 1 hour. Heat half the oil with the salt and garlic until the garlic is lightly browned. Add the chicken and marinade and stir-fry for about 4 minutes until the chicken turns white then remove from the pan. Add the remaining oil to the pan and stir-fry the peppers for 2 minutes. Add the sugar to the pan with the remaining soy sauce, wine or sherry and cornflour and mix well. Add the stock, bring to the boil then simmer, stirring, until the sauce thickens. Return the chicken to the pan, cover and simmer for 4 minutes until the chicken is cooked through.

Stir-Fried Chicken with Peppers

Serves 4

1 chicken breast, thinly sliced
2 slices ginger root, minced
2 spring onions (scallions), minced
15 ml/1 tbsp cornflour (cornstarch)
30 ml/2 tbsp rice wine or dry sherry
30 ml/2 tbsp water
2.5 ml/½ tsp salt
45 ml/3 tbsp groundnut (peanut) oil
100 g/4 oz water chestnuts, sliced
1 red pepper, cut into strips
1 green pepper, cut into strips
1 yellow pepper, cut into strips
30 ml/2 tbsp soy sauce
120 ml/4 fl oz/½ cup chicken stock

Place the chicken in a bowl. Mix the ginger, spring onions, cornflour, wine or sherry, water and salt, stir into the chicken and leave to stand for 1 hour. Heat half the oil and stir-fry the chicken until lightly browned then remove it from the pan. Heat the remaining oil and stir-fry the water chestnuts and peppers for 2 minutes. Add the soy sauce and stock, bring to the boil, cover and simmer for 5 minutes until the vegetables are just tender. Return the chicken to the pan, stir well and reheat gently before serving.

Chicken and Pineapple

Serves 4

30 ml/2 tbsp groundnut (peanut) oil
5 ml/1 tsp salt
2 cloves garlic, crushed
450 g/1 lb boned chicken, thinly sliced
2 onions, sliced
100 g/4 oz water chestnuts, sliced
100 g/4 oz pineapple chunks
30 ml/2 tbsp rice wine or dry sherry
450 ml/¾ pt/2 cups chicken stock
5 ml/1 tsp sugar
freshly ground pepper
30 ml/2 tbsp pineapple juice
30 ml/2 tbsp soy sauce
30 ml/2 tbsp cornflour (cornstarch)

Heat the oil, salt and garlic until the garlic turns light golden. Add the chicken and stir-fry for 2 minutes. Add the onions, water chestnuts and pineapple and stir-fry for 2 minutes. Add the wine or sherry, stock and sugar and season with pepper. Bring to the boil, cover and simmer for 5 minutes. Mix together the pineapple juice, soy sauce and cornflour. Stir into the pan and simmer, stirring until the sauce thickens and clears.

Chicken with Pineapple and Lychees

Serves 4

30 ml/2 tbsp groundnut (peanut) oil
225 g/8 oz chicken, thinly sliced
1 slice ginger root, minced
15 ml/1 tsp soy sauce
15 ml/1 tbsp rice wine or dry sherry
200 g/7 oz canned pineapple chunks in syrup
200 g/7 oz canned lychees in syrup
15 ml/1 tbsp cornflour (cornstarch)

Heat the oil and fry the chicken until lightly coloured. Add the soy sauce and wine or sherry and stir well. Measure 250 ml/8 floz/1 cup of the mixed pineapple and lychee syrup and reserve 30ml/2 tbsp. Add the rest to the pan, bring to the boil and simmer for a few minutes until the chicken is tender. Add the pineapple chunks and lychees. Mix the cornflour with the reserved syrup, stir into the pan and simmer, stirring, until the sauce clears and thickens.

Chicken with Pork

Serves 4

1 chicken breast, thinly sliced
100 g/4 oz lean pork, thinly sliced
60 ml/4 tbsp soy sauce
15 ml/1 tbsp cornflour (cornstarch)
1 egg white
45 ml/3 tsp groundnut (peanut) oil
3 slices ginger root, chopped
50 g/2 oz bamboo shoots, sliced
225 g/8 oz mushrooms, sliced
225 g/8 oz Chinese leaves, shredded
120 ml/4 fl oz/½ cup chicken stock
30 ml/2 tbsp water

Mix together the chicken and pork. Mix the soy sauce, 5 ml/1 tsp of cornflour and the egg white and stir into the chicken and pork. Leave to stand for 30 minutes. Heat half the oil and fry the chicken and pork until lightly browned then remove them from the pan. Heat the remaining oil and fry the ginger, bamboo shoots, mushrooms and Chinese leaves until well coated in oil. Add the stock and bring to the boil. Return the chicken mixture to the pan, cover and simmer for about 3 minutes until the meats are tender. Blend the remaining cornflour to a paste with the water, stir into the sauce and simmer, stirring, until the sauce thickens. Serve at once.

Braised Chicken with Potatoes

Serves 4

4 chicken pieces
45 ml/3 tbsp groundnut (peanut) oil
1 onion, sliced
1 clove garlic, crushed
2 slices ginger root, minced
450 ml/¾ pt/2 cups water
45 ml/3 tbsp soy sauce
15 ml/1 tbsp brown sugar
2 potatoes, cubed

Chop the chicken into 5 cm/2 in pieces. Heat the oil and fry the onion, garlic and ginger until lightly browned. Add the chicken and fry until lightly browned. Add the water and soy sauce and bring to the boil. Stir in the sugar, cover and simmer for about 30 minutes. Add the potatoes to the pan, cover and simmer for a further 10 minutes until the chicken is tender and the potatoes are cooked.

Five-Spice Chicken with Potatoes

Serves 4

45 ml/3 tbsp groundnut (peanut) oil
450 g/1 lb chicken, cut into chunks
salt
45 ml/3 tbsp yellow bean paste
45 ml/3 tbsp soy sauce
5 ml/1 tsp sugar
5 ml/1 tsp five-spice powder
1 potato, diced
450 ml/¾ pt/2 cups chicken stock

Heat the oil and stir-fry the chicken until lightly browned. Sprinkle with salt then stir in the bean paste, soy sauce, sugar and five-spice powder and stir-fry for 1 minute. Add the potato and stir in well then add the stock, bring to the boil, cover and simmer for about 30 minutes until tender.

Red-Cooked Chicken

Serves 4

450 g/1 lb chicken, sliced
120 ml/4 fl oz/½ cup soy sauce
15 ml/1 tbsp sugar
2 slices ginger root, finely chopped
90 ml/6 tbsp chicken stock
30 ml/2 tbsp rice wine or dry sherry
4 spring onions (scallions), sliced

Place all the ingredients in a pan and bring to the boil. Cover and simmer for about 15 minutes until the chicken is cooked through. Remove the lid and continue to simmer for about 5 minutes, stirring occasionally, until the sauce has thickened. Serve sprinkled with spring onions.

Chicken Rissoles

Serves 4

225 g/8 oz chicken meat, minced (ground)

3 water chestnuts, minced

1 spring onion (scallion), chopped

1 slice ginger root, minced

2 egg whites

5 ml/2 tsp salt

5 ml/1 tsp freshly ground pepper

120 ml/4 fl oz/½ cup groundnut (peanut) oil

5 ml/1 tsp chopped ham

Mix together the chicken, chestnuts, half the spring onion, the ginger, egg whites, salt and pepper. Shape into small balls and press flat. Heat the oil and fry the rissoles until golden brown, turning once. Serve sprinkled with the remaining spring onion and the ham.

Savoury Chicken

Serves 4

30 ml/2 tbsp groundnut (peanut) oil

4 chicken pieces

3 spring onions (scallions), chopped

2 cloves garlic, crushed

1 slice ginger root, chopped

120 ml/4 fl oz/½ cup soy sauce

30 ml/2 tbsp rice wine or dry sherry

30 ml/2 tbsp brown sugar

5 ml/1 tsp salt

375 ml/13 fl oz/1½ cups water

15 ml/1 tbsp cornflour (cornstarch)

Heat the oil and fry the chicken pieces until golden brown. Add the spring onions, garlic and ginger and fry for 2 minutes. Add the soy sauce, wine or sherry, sugar and salt and stir together well. Add the water and bring to the boil, cover and simmer for 40 minutes. Mix the cornflour with a little water, stir it into the sauce and simmer, stirring, until the sauce clears and thickens.

Chicken in Sesame Oil

Serves 4

90 ml/6 tbsp groundnut (peanut) oil

60 ml/4 tbsp sesame oil

5 slices ginger root

4 chicken pieces

600 ml/1 pt/2½ cups rice wine or dry sherry

5 ml/1 tsp sugar

salt and freshly ground pepper

Heat the oils and fry the ginger and chicken until lightly browned. Add the wine or sherry and season with sugar, salt and pepper. Bring to the boil and simmer gently, uncovered, until the chicken is tender and the sauce has reduced. Serve in bowls.

Sherry Chicken

Serves 4

30 ml/2 tbsp groundnut (peanut) oil

4 chicken pieces

120 ml/4 fl oz/½ cup soy sauce

500 ml/17 fl oz/2¼ cups rice wine or dry sherry

30 ml/2 tbsp sugar

5 ml/1 tsp salt

2 cloves garlic, crushed

1 slice ginger root, chopped

Heat the oil and fry the chicken until

browned on all sides. Drain off excess oil and add all the remaining ingredients. Bring to the boil, cover and simmer over a fairly high heat for 25 minutes. Reduce the heat and simmer for a further 15 minutes until the chicken is cooked through and the sauce has reduced.

Chicken with Soy Sauce

Serves 4

350 g/12 oz chicken, diced

2 spring onions (scallions), chopped

3 slices ginger root, minced

15 ml/1 tbsp cornflour (cornstarch)

30 ml/2 tbsp rice wine or dry sherry

30 ml/2 tbsp water

45 ml/3 tbsp groundnut (peanut) oil

60 ml/4 tsp thick soy sauce

5 ml/1 tsp sugar

Mix together the chicken, spring onions, ginger, cornflour, wine or sherry and water and leave to stand for 30 minutes, stirring occasionally. Heat the oil and stir-fry the chicken for about 3 minutes until lightly browned. Add the soy sauce and sugar and stir-fry for about 1 minute until the chicken is cooked through and tender.

Spicy Baked Chicken

Serves 4

150 ml/¼ pt/⅔ cup soy sauce

2 cloves garlic, crushed

50 g/2 oz/¼ cup brown sugar

1 onion, finely chopped

30 ml/2 tbsp tomato purée (paste)

1 slice lemon, chopped

1 slice ginger root, minced

45 ml/3 tbsp rice wine or dry sherry

4 large chicken pieces

Mix together all the ingredients except the chicken. Place the chicken in an ovenproof dish, pour over the mixture, cover and marinate overnight, basting occasionally. Bake the chicken in a preheated oven at 180°C/350°F/gas mark 4 for 40 minutes, turning and basting occasionally. Remove the lid, raise the oven temperature to 200°C/400°F/gas mark 6 and continue to cook for a further 15 minutes until the chicken is cooked through.

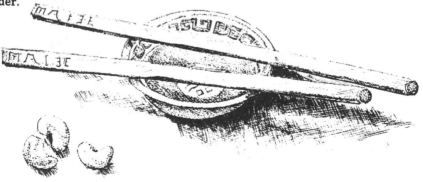

Chicken with Spinach

Serves 4

100 g/4 oz chicken, minced
15 ml/1 tbsp ham fat, minced
175 ml/6 fl oz/¾ cup chicken stock
3 egg whites, lightly beaten
salt
5 ml/1 tsp water
450 g/1 lb spinach, finely chopped
5 ml/1 tsp cornflour (cornstarch)
45 ml/3 tbsp groundnut (peanut) oil

Mix together the chicken, ham fat, 150 ml/¼ pt/⅔ cup of chicken stock, the egg whites, 5 ml/1 tsp of salt and the water. Mix the spinach with the remaining stock, a pinch of salt and the cornflour mixed with a little water. Heat half the oil, add the spinach mixture to the pan and stir constantly over a low heat until heated through. Transfer to a warmed serving plate and keep warm. Heat the remaining oil and fry spoonfuls of the chicken mixture until set and white. Arrange on top of the spinach and serve at once.

Chicken Spring Rolls

Serves 4

15 ml/1 tbsp groundnut (peanut) oil
pinch of salt
1 clove garlic, crushed
225 g/8 oz chicken, cut into strips
100 g/4 oz mushrooms, sliced
175 g/6 oz cabbage, shredded
100 g/4 oz bamboo shoots, shredded
50 g/2 oz water chestnuts, shredded
100 g/4 oz bean sprouts
5 ml/1 tsp sugar
5 ml/1 tsp rice wine or dry sherry
5 ml/1 tsp soy sauce
8 spring roll skins
oil for deep-frying

Heat the oil, salt and garlic and fry gently until the garlic begins to turn golden. Add the chicken and mushrooms and stir-fry for a few minutes until the chicken turns white. Add the cabbage, bamboo shoots, water chestnuts and bean sprouts and stir-fry for 3 minutes. Add the sugar, wine or sherry and soy sauce, stir well, cover and stir-fry for a final 2 minutes. Turn into a colander and leave to drain.

Place a few spoonfuls of the filling mixture in the centre of each spring roll skin, fold up the bottom, fold in the sides, then roll upwards, enclosing the filling. Seal the edge with a little flour and water mixture then leave to dry for 30 minutes. Heat the oil and deep-fry the spring rolls for about 10 minutes until crisp and golden brown. Drain well before serving.

Simple Chicken Stir-Fry

Serves 4

1 chicken breast, thinly sliced
2 slices ginger root, minced
2 spring onions (scallions), minced
15 ml/1 tbsp cornflour (cornstarch)
15 ml/1 tbsp rice wine or dry sherry
30 ml/2 tbsp water
2.5 ml/½ tsp salt
45 ml/3 tbsp groundnut (peanut) oil
100 g/4 oz bamboo shoots, sliced
100 g/4 oz mushrooms, sliced
100 g/4 oz bean sprouts
15 ml/1 tbsp soy sauce
5 ml/1 tsp sugar
120 ml/4 fl oz/½ cup chicken stock

Place the chicken in a bowl. Mix the ginger, spring onions, cornflour, wine or sherry, water and salt, stir into the chicken and leave to stand for 1 hour. Heat half the oil and stir-fry the chicken until lightly browned then remove it from the pan. Heat the remaining oil and stir-fry the bamboo shoots, mushrooms and bean sprouts for 4 minutes. Add the soy sauce, sugar and stock, bring to the boil, cover and simmer for 5 minutes until the vegetables are just tender. Return the chicken to the pan, stir well and reheat gently before serving.

Chicken in Tomato Sauce

Serves 4

30 ml/2 tbsp groundnut (peanut) oil
5 ml/1 tsp salt
2 cloves garlic, crushed
450 g/1 lb chicken, cubed
300 ml/½ pt/1¼ cups chicken stock
120 ml/4 fl oz/½ cup tomato ketchup (catsup)
15 ml/1 tbsp cornflour (cornstarch)
4 spring onions (scallions), sliced

Heat the oil with the salt and garlic until the garlic is lightly golden. Add the chicken and stir-fry until lightly browned. Add most of the stock, bring to the boil, cover and simmer for about 15 minutes until the chicken is tender. Stir the remaining stock with the ketchup and cornflour and stir it into the pan. Simmer, stirring, until the sauce thickens and clears. If the sauce is too thin, leave it simmering for a while until it has reduced. Add the spring onions and simmer for 2 minutes before serving.

Chicken with Tomatoes

Serves 4

225 g/8 oz chicken, diced
15 ml/1 tbsp cornflour (cornstarch)
15 ml/1 tbsp soy sauce
15 ml/1 tbsp rice wine or dry sherry
45 ml/3 tbsp groundnut (peanut) oil
1 onion, diced
60 ml/4 tbsp chicken stock
5 ml/1 tsp salt
5 ml/1 tsp sugar
2 tomatoes, skinned and diced

Mix the chicken with the cornflour, soy sauce and wine or sherry and leave to stand for 30 minutes. Heat the oil and fry the chicken until lightly coloured. Add the onion and stir-fry until softened. Add the stock, salt and sugar, bring to the boil and stir gently over a low heat until the chicken is cooked. Add the tomatoes and stir until heated through.

Poached Chicken with Tomatoes

Serves 4

4 chicken portions
4 tomatoes, skinned and quartered
15 ml/1 tbsp rice wine or dry sherry
15 ml/1 tbsp groundnut (peanut) oil
salt

Place the chicken in a pan and just cover with cold water. Bring to the boil, cover and simmer for 20 minutes. Add the tomatoes, wine or sherry, oil and salt, cover and simmer for a further 10 minutes until the chicken is cooked. Arrange the chicken on a warmed serving plate and chop into serving pieces. Reheat the sauce and pour over the chicken to serve.

Chicken and Tomatoes with Black Bean Sauce

Serves 4

45 ml/3 tbsp groundnut (peanut) oil
1 clove garlic, crushed
45 ml/3 tbsp black bean sauce
225 g/8 oz chicken, diced
15 ml/1 tbsp rice wine or dry sherry
5 ml/1 tsp sugar
15 ml/1 tbsp soy sauce
90 ml/6 tbsp chicken stock
3 tomatoes, skinned and quartered
10 ml/2 tsp cornflour (cornstarch)
45 ml/3 tbsp water

Heat the oil and fry the garlic for 30 seconds. Add the black bean sauce and fry for 30 seconds then add the chicken and stir until well coated in oil. Add the wine or sherry, sugar, soy sauce and stock, bring to the boil, cover and simmer for about 5 minutes until the chicken is cooked. Mix the cornflour and water to a paste, stir it into the pan and simmer, stirring, until the sauce clears and thickens.

Quick-Cooked Chicken with Vegetables

Serves 4

1 egg white
50 g/2 oz cornflour (cornstarch)
225 g/8 oz chicken breasts, cut into strips
75 ml/5 tbsp groundnut (peanut) oil
200 g/7 oz bamboo shoots, cut into strips
50 g/2 oz bean sprouts
1 green pepper, cut into strips
3 spring onions (scallions), sliced
1 slice ginger root, minced
1 clove garlic, minced
15 ml/1 tbsp rice wine or dry sherry

Beat the egg white and cornflour then dip the chicken strips in the mixture. Heat the oil to moderately hot and fry the chicken for a few minutes until just cooked. Remove from the pan and drain well. Add the bamboo shoots, bean sprouts, pepper, onions, ginger and garlic to the pan and stir-fry for 3 minutes. Add the wine or sherry and return the chicken to the pan. Stir together well and heat through before serving.

Walnut Chicken

Serves 4

45 ml/3 tbsp groundnut (peanut) oil
2 spring onions (scallions), chopped
1 slice ginger root, minced
450 g/1 lb chicken breast, very thinly sliced
50 g/2 oz ham, shredded
30 ml/2 tbsp soy sauce
30 ml/2 tbsp rice wine or dry sherry
5 ml/1 tsp sugar
5 ml/1 tsp salt
100 g/4 oz/1 cup walnuts, chopped

Heat the oil and stir-fry the onions and ginger for 1 minute. Add the chicken and ham and stir-fry for 5 minutes until almost cooked. Add the soy sauce, wine or sherry, sugar and salt and stir-fry for 3 minutes. Add the walnuts and stir-fry for 1 minute until the ingredients are thoroughly blended.

Chicken with Walnuts

Serves 4

100 g/4 oz/1 cup shelled walnuts, halved

oil for deep-frying

45 ml/3 tbsp groundnut (peanut) oil

2 slices ginger root, minced

225 g/8 oz chicken, diced

100 g/4 oz bamboo shoots, sliced

75 ml/5 tbsp chicken stock

Prepare the walnuts, heat the oil and deep-fry the walnuts until golden brown then drain well. Heat the groundnut oil and fry the ginger for 30 seconds. Add the chicken and stir-fry until lightly browned. Add the remaining ingredients, bring to the boil and simmer, stirring, until the chicken is cooked.

Chicken with Water Chestnuts

Serves 4

45 ml/3 tbsp groundnut (peanut) oil

2 cloves garlic, crushed

2 spring onions (scallions), chopped

1 slice ginger root, chopped

225 g/8 oz chicken breast, cut into slivers

100 g/4 oz water chestnuts, cut into slivers

45 ml/3 tbsp soy sauce

15 ml/1 tbsp rice wine or dry sherry

5 ml/1 tsp cornflour (cornstarch)

Heat the oil and fry the garlic, spring onions and ginger until lightly browned. Add the chicken and stir-fry for 5 minutes. Add the water chestnuts and stir-fry for 3 minutes. Add the soy sauce, wine or sherry and cornflour and stir-fry for about 5 minutes until the chicken is cooked through.

Savoury Chicken with Water Chestnuts

Serves 4

30 ml/2 tbsp groundnut (peanut) oil

4 chicken pieces

3 spring onions (scallions), chopped

2 cloves garlic, crushed

1 slice ginger root, chopped

250 ml/8 fl oz/1 cup soy sauce

30 ml/2 tbsp rice wine or dry sherry

30 ml/2 tbsp brown sugar

5 ml/1 tsp salt

375 ml/13 fl oz/1¾ cups water

225 g/8 oz water chestnuts, sliced

15 ml/1 tbsp cornflour (cornstarch)

Heat the oil and fry the chicken pieces until golden brown. Add the spring onions, garlic and ginger and fry for 2 minutes. Add the soy sauce, wine or sherry, sugar and salt and stir together well. Add the water and bring to the boil, cover and simmer for 20 minutes. Add the water chestnuts, cover and cook for a further 20 minutes. Mix the cornflour with a little water, stir it into the sauce and simmer, stirring, until the sauce clears and thickens.

Chicken Wontons

Serves 4

4 Chinese dried mushrooms
450 g/1 lb chicken breast, shredded
225 g/8 oz mixed vegetables, chopped
1 spring onion (scallion), chopped
15 ml/1 tbsp soy sauce
2.5 ml/½ tsp salt
40 wonton skins (see page 282)
1 egg, beaten

Soak the mushrooms in warm water for 30 minutes then drain. Discard the stalks and chop the caps. Mix with the chicken, vegetables, soy sauce and salt.

To fold the wontons, hold the skin in the palm of your left hand and spoon a little filling into the centre. Moisten the edges with egg and fold the skin into a triangle, sealing the edges. Moisten the corners with egg and twist them together.

Bring a saucepan of water to the boil. Drop in the wontons and simmer for about 10 minutes until they float to the top.

Crispy Chicken Wings

Serves 4

900 g/2 lb chicken wings
60 ml/4 tbsp rice wine or dry sherry
60 ml/4 tbsp soy sauce
50 g/2 oz/½ cup cornflour (cornstarch)
groundnut (peanut) oil for deep-frying

Place the chicken wings in a bowl. Mix together the remaining ingredients and pour over the chicken wings, stirring well so that they are coated in the sauce. Cover and leave to stand for 30 minutes. Heat the oil and deep-fry the chicken a few at a time until cooked through and dark brown. Drain well on kitchen paper and keep warm while you fry the remaining chicken.

Five-Spice Chicken Wings

Serves 4

30 ml/2 tbsp groundnut (peanut) oil
2 cloves garlic, crushed
450 g/1 lb chicken wings
250 ml/8 fl oz/1 cup chicken stock
30 ml/2 tbsp soy sauce
5 ml/1 tsp sugar
5 ml/1 tsp five-spice powder

Heat the oil and garlic until the garlic is lightly browned. Add the chicken and fry until lightly browned. Add the remaining ingredients, stirring well, and bring to the boil. Cover and simmer for about 15 minutes until the chicken is cooked through. Remove the lid and continue to simmer, stirring occasionally, until almost all the liquid has evaporated. Serve hot or cold.

Marinated Chicken Wings

Serves 4

45 ml/3 tbsp soy sauce

45 ml/3 tbsp rice wine or dry sherry

30 ml/2 tbsp brown sugar

5 ml/1 tsp grated ginger root

2 cloves garlic, crushed

6 spring onions (scallions), sliced

450 g/1 lb chicken wings

30 ml/2 tbsp groundnut (peanut) oil

225 g/8 oz bamboo shoots, sliced

20 ml/4 tsp cornflour (cornstarch)

175 ml/6 fl oz/¾ cup chicken stock

Mix together the soy sauce, wine or sherry, sugar, ginger, garlic and spring onions. Add the chicken wings and stir to coat completely. Cover and leave to stand for 1 hour, stirring occasionally. Heat the oil and stir-fry the bamboo shoots for 2 minutes. Remove them from the pan. Drain the chicken and onions, reserving the marinade. Reheat the oil and stir-fry the chicken until browned on all sides. Cover and cook for a further 20 minutes until the chicken is tender. Blend the cornflour with the stock and the reserved marinade. Pour over the chicken and bring to the boil, stirring, until the sauce thickens. Stir in the bamboo shoots and simmer, stirring, for a further 2 minutes.

Royal Chicken Wings

Serves 4

12 chicken wings

250 ml/8 fl oz/1 cup groundnut (peanut) oil

15 ml/1 tbsp granulated sugar

2 spring onions (scallions), cut into chunks

5 slices root ginger

5 ml/1 tsp salt

45 ml/3 tbsp soy sauce

250 ml/8 fl oz/1 cup rice wine or dry sherry

250 ml/8 fl oz/1 cup chicken stock

10 slices bamboo shoots

15 ml/1 tbsp cornflour (cornstarch)

45 ml/1 tbsp water

2.5 ml/½ tsp sesame oil

Blanch the chicken wings in boiling water for 5 minutes then drain well. Heat the oil, add the sugar and stir until melted and golden brown. Add the chicken, spring onions, ginger, salt, soy sauce, wine and stock, bring to the boil and simmer gently for 20 minutes. Add the bamboo shoots and simmer for 2 minutes or until the liquid has almost all evaporated. Blend the cornflour with the water, stir it into the pan and stir until thick. Transfer the chicken wings to a warmed serving plate and serve sprinkled with sesame oil.

Spiced Chicken Wings

Serves 4

30 ml/2 tbsp groundnut (peanut) oil

5 ml/1 tsp salt

2 cloves garlic, crushed

900 g/2 lb chicken wings

30 ml/2 tbsp rice wine or dry sherry

30 ml/2 tbsp soy sauce

30 ml/2 tbsp tomato purée (paste)

15 ml/1 tbsp Worcestershire sauce

Heat the oil, salt and garlic and fry until the garlic turns light golden. Add the chicken wings and fry, stirring frequently, for about 10 minutes until golden brown and almost cooked through. Add the remaining ingredients and stir-fry for about 5 minutes until the chicken is crispy and thoroughly cooked.

Barbecued Chicken Drumsticks

Serves 4

16 chicken drumsticks

30 ml/2 tbsp rice wine or dry sherry

30 ml/2 tbsp wine vinegar

30 ml/2 tbsp olive oil

salt and freshly ground pepper

120 ml/4 fl oz/½ cup orange juice

30 ml/2 tbsp soy sauce

30 ml/2 tbsp honey

15 ml/1 tbsp lemon juice

2 slices ginger root, minced

120 ml/4 fl oz/½ cup chilli sauce

Mix together all the ingredients except the chilli sauce, cover and leave to marinate in the refrigerator overnight. Remove the chicken from the marinade and barbecue or grill (broil) for about 25 minutes, turning and basting with the chilli sauce as you cook.

Hoisin Chicken Drumsticks

Serves 4

8 chicken drumsticks

600 ml/1 pt/2½ cups chicken stock

salt and freshly ground pepper

250 ml/8 fl oz/1 cup hoisin sauce

30 ml/2 tbsp plain (all-purpose) flour

2 eggs, beaten

100 g/4 oz/1 cup breadcrumbs

oil for deep-frying

Place the drumsticks and stock in a pan, bring to the boil, cover and simmer for 20 minutes until cooked. Remove the chicken from the pan and pat dry on kitchen paper. Place the chicken in a bowl and season with salt and pepper. Pour over the hoisin sauce and leave to marinate for 1 hour. Drain. Toss the chicken in the flour then coat in the eggs and breadcrumbs, then in egg and breadcrumbs again. Heat the oil and fry the chicken for about 5 minutes until golden brown. Drain on kitchen paper and serve hot or cold.

Braised Chicken

Serves 4–6

75 ml/5 tbsp groundnut (peanut) oil
1 chicken
3 spring onions (scallions), sliced
3 slices ginger root
120 ml/4 fl oz/½ cup soy sauce
30 ml/2 tbsp rice wine or dry sherry
5 ml/1 tsp sugar

Heat the oil and fry the chicken until browned. Add the spring onions, ginger, soy sauce and wine or sherry, and bring to the boil. Cover and simmer for 30 minutes, turning occasionally. Add the sugar, cover and simmer for a further 30 minutes until the chicken is cooked.

Crispy Fried Chicken

Serves 4

1 chicken
salt
30 ml/2 tbsp rice wine or dry sherry
3 spring onions (scallions), diced
1 slice ginger root
30 ml/2 tbsp soy sauce
30 ml/2 tbsp sugar
5 ml/1 tsp whole cloves
5 ml/1 tsp salt
5 ml/1 tsp peppercorns
150 ml/¼ pt/⅔ cup chicken stock
oil for deep-frying
1 lettuce, shredded
4 tomatoes, sliced
½ cucumber, sliced

Rub the chicken with salt and leave to stand for 3 hours. Rinse and place in a bowl. Add the wine or sherry, ginger, soy sauce, sugar, cloves, salt, pepper-corns and stock and baste well. Stand the bowl in a steamer, cover and steam for about 2¼ hours until the chicken is thoroughly cooked. Drain. Heat the oil until smoking, then add the chicken and deep-fry until browned. Fry for a further 5 minutes then remove from the oil and drain. Cut into pieces and arrange on a warmed serving plate. Garnish with the lettuce, tomatoes and cucumber and serve with a pepper and salt dip.

Deep-Fried Whole Chicken

Serves 5

1 chicken
10 ml/2 tsp salt
15 ml/1 tbsp rice wine or dry sherry
2 spring onions (scallions), halved
3 slices ginger root, cut into strips
oil for deep-frying

Pat the chicken dry and rub the skin with salt and wine or sherry. Place the spring onions and ginger inside the cavity. Hang the chicken to dry in a cool place for about 3 hours. Heat the oil and place the chicken in a frying basket. Lower gently into the oil and baste continuously inside and out until the chicken is lightly coloured. Remove from the oil and leave to cool slightly while you reheat the oil. Fry again until golden brown. Drain well then chop into pieces.

Photograph opposite (from the top):
Beef Fried Rice (page 269), Special Fried Rice (page 273), Fried Rice and Peas (page 272), Duck Fried Rice (page 270)

Five-Spice Chicken

Serves 4 –6

1 chicken
120 ml/4 fl oz/½ cup soy sauce
2.5 cm/1 in piece ginger root, minced
1 clove garlic, crushed
15 ml/1 tbsp fivespice powder
30 ml/2 tbsp rice wine or dry sherry
30 ml/2 tbsp honey
2.5 ml/½ tsp sesame oil
oil for deep-frying
30 ml/2 tbsp salt
5 ml/1 tsp freshly ground pepper

Place the chicken in a large saucepan and fill with water to come half way up the thigh. Reserve 15 ml/1 tbsp of the soy sauce and add the remainder to the pan with the ginger, garlic and half the five-spice powder. Bring to the boil, cover and simmer for 5 minutes. Turn off the heat and leave the chicken to stand in the water until the water is lukewarm. Drain.

Cut the chicken in half lengthways and place cut side down in a roasting tin. Mix together the remaining soy sauce and five-spice powder with the wine or sherry, honey and sesame oil. Rub the mixture over the chicken and leave to stand for 2 hours, brushing occasionally with the mixture. Heat the oil and deep-fry the chicken halves for about 15 minutes until golden brown and cooked through. Drain on kitchen paper and cut into serving sized pieces.

Meanwhile, mix the salt and pepper and heat in a dry pan for about 2 minutes. Serve as a dip with the chicken.

Ginger and Spring Onion Chicken

Serves 4

1 chicken
2 slices ginger root, cut into strips
salt and freshly ground pepper
90 ml/4 tbsp groundnut (peanut) oil
8 spring onions (scallions), finely chopped
10 ml/2 tsp white wine vinegar
5 ml/1 tsp soy sauce

Place the chicken in a large saucepan, add half the ginger and pour in enough water almost to cover the chicken. Season with salt and pepper. Bring to the boil, cover and simmer for about 1¼ hours until tender. Leave the chicken to stand in the stock until cool. Drain the chicken and refrigerate until cold. Cut into portions.

Grate the remaining ginger and mix with the oil, spring onions, wine vinegar and soy sauce and salt and pepper. Refrigerate for 1 hour. Place the chicken pieces in a serving bowl and pour over the ginger dressing. Serve with steamed rice.

Photograph opposite: Noodle Baskets (page 276)

Poached Chicken

Serves 4

---

1 chicken
1.2 1/2 pts/5 cups chicken stock or water
30 ml/2 tbsp rice wine or dry sherry
4 spring onions (scallions), chopped
1 slice ginger root
5 ml/1 tsp salt

Place the chicken in a large saucepan with all the remaining ingredients. The stock or water should come half way up the thigh. Bring to the boil, cover and simmer gently for about 1 hour until the chicken is thoroughly cooked. Drain, reserving the stock for soups.

Red-Cooked Chicken

Serves 4

---

1 chicken
250 ml/8 fl oz/1 cup soy sauce

Place the chicken in a pan, pour over the soy sauce and top up with water almost to cover the chicken. Bring to the boil, cover and simmer for about 1 hour until the chicken is cooked, turning occasionally.

Red-Cooked Spiced Chicken

Serves 4

---

2 slices ginger root
2 spring onions (scallions)
1 chicken
3 cloves star anise
½ cinnamon stick
15 ml/1 tbsp Szechuan peppercorns
75 ml/5 tbsp soy sauce
75 ml/5 tbsp rice wine or dry sherry
75 ml/5 tbsp sesame oil
15 ml/1 tbsp sugar

Place the ginger and spring onions inside the chicken cavity and place the chicken in a pan. Tie the star anise, cinnamon and peppercorns in a piece of muslin and add it to the pan. Pour over the soy sauce, wine or sherry and sesame oil. Bring to the boil, cover and simmer for about 45 minutes. Add the sugar, cover and simmer for a further 10 minutes until the chicken is cooked through.

Sesame Roast Chicken

Serves 4

---

50 g/2 oz sesame seeds
1 onion, finely chopped
2 cloves garlic, minced
10 ml/2 tsp salt
1 dried red chilli pepper, crushed
pinch of ground cloves
2.5 ml/½ tsp ground cardamom
2.5 ml/½ tsp ground ginger
75 ml/5 tbsp groundnut (peanut) oil
1 chicken

Mix together all the seasonings and oil

and brush over the chicken. Stand it in a roasting tin and add 30 ml/2 tbsp of water to the tin. Roast in a preheated oven at 180°C/350°F/gas mark 4 for about 2 hours, basting and turning the chicken occasionally, until the chicken is golden and cooked through. Add a little more water, if necessary, to prevent burning.

Chicken in Soy Sauce

Serves 4–6

300 ml/½ pt/1¼ cups soy sauce

300 ml/½ pt/1¼ cups rice wine or dry sherry

1 onion, chopped

3 slices root ginger, minced

50 g/2 oz/¼ cup sugar

1 chicken

15 ml/1 tbsp cornflour (cornstarch)

60 ml/4 tbsp water

1 cucumber, peeled and sliced

30 ml/2 tbsp chopped fresh parsley

Mix together the soy sauce, wine or sherry, onion, ginger and sugar in a pan and bring to the boil. Add the chicken, return to the boil, cover and simmer gently for 1 hour, turning the chicken occasionally, until the chicken is cooked. Transfer the chicken to a warmed serving plate and carve. Pour out all but 250 ml/8 fl oz/1 cup of the cooking liquid and bring it back to the boil. Blend the cornflour and water to a paste, stir it into the pan and simmer, stirring, until the sauce clears and thickens. Brush a little of the sauce over the chicken and garnish the chicken with cucumber and parsley. Serve the remaining sauce separately.

Steamed Chicken

Serves 4

1 chicken

45 ml/3 tbsp rice wine or dry sherry

salt

2 slices ginger root

2 spring onions (scallions)

250 ml/8 fl oz/1 cup chicken stock

Place the chicken in an ovenproof bowl and rub with wine or sherry and salt and place the ginger and spring onions inside the cavity. Place the bowl on a rack in a steamer, cover and steam over boiling water for about 1 hour until cooked through. Serve hot or cold.

Steamed Chicken with Anise

Serves 4

250 ml/8 fl oz/1 cup soy sauce

250 ml/8 fl oz/1 cup water

15 ml/1 tbsp brown sugar

4 cloves star anise

1 chicken

Mix the soy sauce, water, sugar and anise in a saucepan and bring to the boil over a gentle heat. Place the chicken in a bowl and baste thoroughly with the mixture inside and out. Reheat the mixture and repeat. Place the chicken in an ovenproof bowl. Place the bowl on a rack in a steamer, cover and steam over boiling water for about 1 hour until cooked through.

Strange-Flavoured Chicken

Serves 4

1 chicken
5 ml/1 tsp minced ginger root
5 ml/1 tsp minced garlic
45 ml/3 tbsp thick soy sauce
5 ml/1 tsp sugar
2.5 ml/½ tsp wine vinegar
10 ml/2 tsp sesame sauce
5 ml/1 tsp freshly ground pepper
10 ml/2 tsp chilli oil
½ lettuce, shredded
15 ml/1 tbsp chopped fresh coriander

Place the chicken in a pan and fill with water to come half way up the chicken legs. Bring to the boil, cover and simmer gently for about 1 hour until the chicken is tender. Remove from the pan and drain well and soak in iced water until the meat cools completely. Drain well and chop into 5 cm/2 in pieces. Mix together all the remaining ingredients and pour over the chicken. Serve garnished with lettuce and coriander.

Crispy Chicken Chunks

Serves 4

100 g/4 oz plain (all-purpose) flour
pinch of salt
15 ml/1 tbsp water
1 egg
350 g/12 oz cooked chicken, cubed
oil for deep-frying

Mix together the flour, salt, water and egg to a fairly stiff batter, adding a little more water if necessary. Dip the chicken pieces into the batter until they are well covered. Heat the oil until very hot and deep-fry the chicken for a few minutes until crispy and golden brown.

Chicken with Green Beans

Serves 4

45 ml/3 tbsp groundnut (peanut) oil
450 g/1 lb cooked chicken, shredded
5 ml/1 tsp salt
2.5 ml/½ tsp freshly ground pepper
225 g/8 oz green beans, cut into pieces
1 stalk celery, diagonally sliced
225 g/8 oz mushrooms, sliced
250 ml/8 fl oz/1 cup chicken stock
30 ml/2 tbsp cornflour (cornstarch)
60 ml/4 tbsp water
10 ml/2 tsp soy sauce

Heat the oil and fry the chicken, salt and pepper until lightly browned. Add the beans, celery and mushrooms and mix well. Add the stock, bring to the boil, cover and simmer for 15 minutes. Mix the cornflour, water and soy sauce to a paste, stir it into the pan and simmer, stirring, until the sauce clears and thickens.

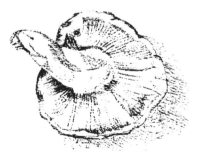

Cooked Chicken with Pineapple

Serves 4

| 45 ml/3 tbsp groundnut (peanut) oil |
| 225 g/8 oz cooked chicken, diced |
| salt and freshly ground pepper |
| 2 stalks celery, diagonally sliced |
| 3 slices pineapple, cut into chunks |
| 120 ml/4 fl oz/½ cup chicken stock |
| 15 ml/1 tbsp soy sauce |
| 10 ml/2 tbsp cornflour (cornstarch) |
| 30 ml/2 tbsp water |

Heat the oil and fry the chicken until lightly browned. Season with salt and pepper, add the celery and stir-fry for 2 minutes. Add the pineapple, stock and soy sauce and stir for a few minutes until heated through. Mix the cornflour and water to a paste, stir into the pan and simmer, stirring, until the sauce clears and thickens.

Chicken with Peppers and Tomatoes

Serves 4

| 45 ml/3 tbsp groundnut (peanut) oil |
| 450 g/1 lb cooked chicken, sliced |
| 10 ml/2 tsp salt |
| 5 ml/1 tsp freshly ground pepper |
| 1 green pepper, cut into chunks |
| 4 large tomatoes, skinned and cut into wedges |
| 250 ml/8 fl oz/1 cup chicken stock |
| 30 ml/2 tbsp cornflour (cornstarch) |
| 15 ml/1 tbsp soy sauce |
| 120 ml/4 fl oz/½ cup water |

Heat the oil and fry the chicken, salt and pepper until browned. Add the peppers and tomatoes. Pour in the stock, bring to the boil, cover and simmer for 15 minutes. Blend the cornflour, soy sauce and water to a paste, stir it into the pan and simmer, stirring, until the sauce clears and thickens.

Sesame Chicken

Serves 4

| 450 g/1 lb cooked chicken, cut into strips |
| 2 slices ginger, finely chopped |
| 1 spring onion (scallion), finely chopped |
| salt and freshly ground pepper |
| 60 ml/4 tbsp rice wine or dry sherry |
| 60 ml/4 tbsp sesame oil |
| 10 ml/2 tsp sugar |
| 5 ml/1 tsp wine vinegar |
| 150 ml/¼ pt/⅔ cup soy sauce |

Arrange the chicken on a serving plate and sprinkle with ginger, spring onion, salt and pepper. Mix together the wine or sherry, sesame oil, sugar, wine vinegar and soy sauce. Pour over the chicken.

Fried Poussins

Serves 4

2 poussins, halved

45 ml/3 tbsp soy sauce

45 ml/3 tbsp rice wine or dry sherry

120 ml/4 fl oz/½ cup groundnut
(peanut) oil

1 spring onion (scallion), finely
chopped

30 ml/2 tbsp chicken stock

10 ml/2 tsp sugar

5 ml/1 tsp chilli oil

5 ml/1 tsp garlic paste

salt and pepper

Place the poussins in a bowl. Mix the soy sauce and wine or sherry, pour over the poussins, cover and marinate for 2 hours, basting frequently. Heat the oil and fry the poussins for about 20 minutes until cooked through. Remove them from the pan and reheat the oil. Return them to the pan and fry until golden brown. Drain off most of the oil. Mix together the remaining ingredients, add to the pan and heat through quickly. Pour over the poussins before serving.

Turkey with Mangetout

Serves 4

60 ml/4 tbsp groundnut (peanut) oil

2 spring onions (scallions), chopped

2 cloves garlic, crushed

1 slice ginger root, minced

225 g/8 oz turkey breast, cut into strips

225 g/8 oz mangetout (snow peas)

100 g/4 oz bamboo shoots, cut into
strips

50 g/2 oz water chestnuts, cut into strips

45 ml/3 tbsp soy sauce

15 ml/1 tbsp rice wine or dry sherry

5 ml/1 tsp sugar

5 ml/1 tsp salt

15 ml/1 tbsp cornflour (cornstarch)

Heat 45 ml/3 tbsp of oil and fry the spring onions, garlic and ginger until lightly browned. Add the turkey and stir-fry for 5 minutes. Remove from the pan and set aside. Heat the remaining oil and stir-fry the mangetout, bamboo shoots and water chestnuts for 3 minutes. Add the soy sauce, wine or sherry, sugar and salt and return the turkey to the pan. Stir-fry for 1 minute. Mix the cornflour with a little water, stir it into the pan and simmer, stirring, until the sauce clears and thickens.

Turkey with Peppers

Serves 4

4 dried Chinese mushrooms
30 ml/2 tbsp groundnut (peanut) oil
1 Chinese cabbage, cut into strips
350 g/12 oz smoked turkey, cut into
    strips
1 onion, sliced
1 red pepper, cut into strips
1 green pepper, cut into strips
120 ml/4 fl oz/½ cup chicken stock
30 ml/2 tbsp tomato purée (paste)
45 ml/3 tbsp wine vinegar
30 ml/2 tbsp soy sauce
15 ml/1 tbsp hoisin sauce
10 ml/2 tsp cornflour (cornstarch)
few drops of chilli oil

Soak the mushrooms in warm water
for 30 minutes then drain. Discard
the stalks and cut the caps into strips.
Heat half the oil and stir-fry the cabbage for about 5 minutes or until
cooked down. Remove from the pan.
Add the turkey and stir-fry for 1
minute. Add the vegetables and stir-
fry for 3 minutes. Mix the stock with
the tomato purée, wine vinegar and
sauces and add to the pan with the
cabbage. Mix the cornflour with a little water, stir it into the pan and
bring to the boil, stirring. Sprinkle
with chilli oil and simmer for 2
minutes, stirring continuously.

Chinese Roast Turkey

Serves 8 – 10

1 small turkey
600 ml/1 pt/2½ cups hot water
10 ml/2 tsp allspice
500 ml/16 fl oz/2 cups soy sauce
5 ml/1 tsp sesame oil
10 ml/2 tsp salt
45 ml/3 tbsp butter

Place the turkey in a pan and pour
over the hot water. Add the
remaining ingredients except the
butter and leave to stand for 1 hour,
turning several times. Remove the
turkey from the liquid and brush with
butter. Place in a roasting tin, cover
loosely with kitchen foil and roast in a
preheated oven at 160°C/325°F/gas
mark 3 for about 4 hours, basting
occasionally with the soy sauce liquid.
Remove the foil and allow the skin to
crisp for the last 30 minutes of
cooking.

Turkey with Walnuts and Mushrooms

Serves 4

450 g/1 lb turkey breast fillet
salt and pepper
juice of 1 orange
15 ml/1 tbsp plain (all-purpose) flour
12 pickled black walnuts with juice
5 ml/1 tsp cornflour (cornstarch)
15 ml/1 tbsp groundnut (peanut) oil
2 spring onions (scallions), diced
225 g/8 oz button mushrooms
45 ml/3 tbsp rice wine or dry sherry
10 ml/2 tsp soy sauce
50 g/2 oz/¼ cup butter
25 g/1 oz pine kernels

Cut the turkey into 1 cm/½ in thick slices. Sprinkle with salt, pepper and orange juice and dust with flour. Drain and halve the walnuts, reserving the liquid, and mix the liquid with the cornflour. Heat the oil and stir-fry the turkey until golden brown. Add the spring onions and mushrooms and stir-fry for 2 minutes. Stir in the wine or sherry and soy sauce and simmer for 30 seconds. Add the walnuts to the cornflour mixture then stir them into the pan and bring to the boil. Add the butter in small flakes but do not allow the mixture to boil. Toast the pine kernels in a dry pan until golden. Transfer the turkey mixture to a warmed serving plate and serve garnished with pine kernels.

Duck with Bamboo Shoots

Serves 4

6 dried Chinese mushrooms
1 duck
50 g/2 oz smoked ham, cut into strips
100 g/4 oz bamboo shoots, cut into strips
2 spring onions (scallions), cut into strips
2 slices ginger root, cut into strips
5 ml/1 tsp salt

Soak the mushrooms in warm water for 30 minutes then drain. Discard the stalks and cut the caps into strips. Place all the ingredients in a heatproof bowl and stand in a pan filled with water to come two-thirds of the way up the bowl. Bring to the boil, cover and simmer for about 2 hours until the duck is cooked, topping up with boiling water as necessary.

Duck with Bean Sprouts

Serves 4

225 g/8 oz bean sprouts
45 ml/3 tbsp groundnut (peanut) oil
450 g/1 lb cooked duck meat
15 ml/1 tbsp oyster sauce
15 ml/1 tbsp rice wine or dry sherry
30 ml/2 tbsp water
2.5 ml/½ tsp salt

Blanch the bean sprouts in boiling water for 2 minutes then drain. Heat the oil, stir-fry the bean sprouts for 30 seconds. Add the duck, stir-fry until heated through. Add the remaining ingredients and stir-fry for 2 minutes to blend the flavours. Serve at once.

Braised Duck

Serves 4

| 4 spring onions (scallions), chopped |
| 1 slice ginger root, minced |
| 120 ml/4 fl oz/½ cup soy sauce |
| 30 ml/2 tbsp rice wine or dry sherry |
| 1 duck |
| 120 ml/4 fl oz/½ cup groundnut (peanut) oil |
| 600 ml/1 pt/2½ cups water |
| 15 ml/1 tbsp brown sugar |

Mix together the spring onions, ginger, soy sauce and wine or sherry and rub it over the duck inside and out. Heat the oil and fry the duck until lightly browned on all sides. Drain off the oil. Add the water and the remaining soy sauce mixture, bring to the boil then cover and simmer for 1 hour. Add the sugar then cover and simmer for a further 40 minutes until the duck is tender.

Steamed Duck with Celery

Serves 4

| 350 g/12 oz cooked duck, sliced |
| 1 head celery |
| 250 ml/8 fl oz/1 cup chicken stock |
| 2.5 ml/½ tsp salt |
| 5 ml/1 tsp sesame oil |
| 1 tomato, cut into wedges |

Arrange the duck on a steamer rack. Trim the celery into 7.5cm/3 in lengths and place in a pan. Pour in the stock, season with salt and place the steamer over the pan. Bring the stock to the boil then simmer gently for about 15 minutes until the celery is tender and the duck heated through. Arrange the duck and celery on a warmed serving plate, sprinkle the celery with sesame oil and serve garnished with tomato wedges.

Duck with Ginger

Serves 4

| 350 g/12 oz duck breast, thinly sliced |
| 1 egg, lightly beaten |
| 5 ml/1 tsp soy sauce |
| 5 ml/1 tsp cornflour (cornstarch) |
| 5 ml/1 tsp groundnut (peanut) oil |
| oil for deep-frying |
| 50 g/2 oz bamboo shoots |
| 50 g/2 oz mangetout (snow peas) |
| 2 slices ginger root, chopped |
| 15 ml/1 tbsp water |
| 2.5 ml/½ tsp sugar |
| 2.5 ml/½ tsp rice wine or dry sherry |
| 2.5 ml/½ tsp sesame oil |

Mix the duck with the egg, soy sauce, cornflour and oil and leave to stand for 10 minutes. Heat the oil and deep-fry the duck and bamboo shoots until cooked and golden brown. Remove from the pan and drain well. Pour out all but 15 ml/1 tbsp of oil from the pan and stir-fry the duck, bamboo shoots, mangetout, ginger, water, sugar and wine or sherry for 2 minutes. Serve sprinkled with sesame oil.

Duck with Green Beans

Serves 4

1 duck
60 ml/4 tbsp groundnut (peanut) oil
2 cloves garlic, crushed
2.5 ml/½ tsp salt
1 onion, chopped
15 ml/1 tbsp grated root ginger
45 ml/3 tbsp soy sauce
120 ml/4 fl oz/½ cup rice wine or dry sherry
60 ml/4 tbsp tomato ketchup (catsup)
45 ml/3 tbsp wine vinegar
300 ml/½ pt/1¼ cups chicken stock
450 g/1 lb green beans, sliced
pinch of freshly ground pepper
5 drops chilli oil
15 ml/1 tbsp cornflour (cornstarch)
30 ml/2 tbsp water

Chop the duck into 8 or 10 pieces. Heat the oil and fry the duck until golden brown. Transfer to a bowl. Add the garlic, salt, onion, ginger, soy sauce, wine or sherry, tomato ketchup and wine vinegar. Mix, cover and marinate in the refrigerator for 3 hours.

Reheat the oil, add the duck, stock and marinade, bring to the boil, cover and simmer for 1 hour. Add the beans, cover and simmer for 15 minutes. Add the pepper and chilli oil. Mix the cornflour with the water, stir it into the pan and simmer, stirring, until the sauce thickens.

Deep-Fried Steamed Duck

Serves 4

1 duck
salt and freshly ground pepper
oil for deep-frying
hoisin sauce

Season the duck with salt and pepper and place in a heatproof bowl. Stand in a pan filled with water to come two-thirds of the way up the bowl, bring to the boil, cover and simmer for about 1½ hours until the duck is tender. Drain and leave to cool.

Heat the oil and deep-fry the duck until crispy and golden brown. Remove and drain well. Chop into bite-sized pieces and serve with hoisin sauce.

Duck with Exotic Fruits

Serves 4

4 duck breast fillets, cut into strips
2.5 ml/½ tsp five-spice powder
30 ml/2 tbsp soy sauce
15 ml/1 tbsp sesame oil
15 ml/1 tbsp groundnut (peanut) oil
3 stalks celery, diced
2 slices pineapple, diced
100 g/4 oz melon, diced
100 g/4 oz lychees, halved
130 ml/4 fl oz/½ cup chicken stock
30 ml/2 tbsp tomato purée (paste)
30 ml/2 tbsp hoisin sauce
10 ml/2 tsp wine vinegar
pinch of brown sugar

Place the duck in a bowl. Mix the five-spice powder, soy sauce and sesame oil, pour over the duck and marinate for 2 hours, stirring occasionally. Heat the oil and stir-fry the duck for 8 minutes. Remove from the pan. Add the celery and fruits and stir-fry for 5 minutes. Return the duck to the pan with the remaining ingredients, bring to the boil and simmer, stirring, for 2 minutes before serving.

Braised Duck with Chinese Leaves

Serves 4

1 duck
30 ml/2 tbsp rice wine or dry sherry
30 ml/2 tbsp hoisin sauce
5 ml/1 tbsp cornflour (cornstarch)
5 ml/1 tsp salt
5 ml/1 tsp sugar
60 ml/4 tbsp groundnut (peanut) oil
4 spring onions (scallions), chopped
2 cloves garlic, crushed
1 slice ginger root, minced
75 ml/5 tbsp soy sauce
600 ml/1 pt/2½ cups water
225 g/8 oz Chinese leaves, shredded

Cut the duck into about 6 pieces. Mix together the wine or sherry, hoisin sauce, cornflour, salt and sugar and rub over the duck. Leave to stand for 1 hour. Heat the oil and fry the spring onions, garlic and ginger for a few seconds. Add the duck and fry until lightly browned on all sides. Drain off any excess fat. Pour in the soy sauce and water, bring to the boil, cover and simmer for about 30 minutes. Add the Chinese leaves, cover again and simmer for a further 30 minutes until the duck is tender.

Drunken Duck

Serves 4

2 spring onions (scallions), chopped
2 cloves garlic, chopped
1.5 l/2½ pts/6 cups water
1 duck
450 ml/¾ pt/2 cups rice wine or dry sherry

Place the spring onions, garlic and water in a large pan and bring to the boil. Add the duck, return to the boil, cover and simmer for 45 minutes. Drain well, reserving the liquid for stock. Leave the duck to cool then refrigerate overnight. Cut the duck into pieces and place them in a large screw-top jar. Pour over the wine or sherry and chill for about 1 week before draining and serving cold.

Five-Spice Duck

Serves 4

150 ml/¼ pt/⅔ cup rice wine or dry sherry
150 ml/¼ pt/⅔ cup soy sauce
1 duck
10 ml/2 tsp five-spice powder

Bring the wine or sherry and soy sauce to the boil. Add the duck and simmer, turning for about 5 minutes. Remove the duck from the pan and rub the five-spice powder into the skin. Return the bird to the pan and add enough water to half cover the duck. Bring to the boil, cover and simmer for about 1½ hours until the duck is tender, turning and basting frequently. Chop the duck into 5 cm/2 in pieces and serve hot or cold.

Stir-Fried Duck with Ginger

Serves 4

1 duck
2 slices ginger root, shredded
2 spring onions (scallions), chopped
15 ml/1 tbsp cornflour (cornstarch)
30 ml/2 tbsp soy sauce
30 ml/2 tbsp rice wine or dry sherry
2.5 ml/½ tsp salt
45 ml/3 tbsp groundnut (peanut) oil

Remove the meat from the bones and cut into pieces. Mix the meat with all the remaining ingredients except the oil. Leave to stand for 1 hour. Heat the oil and stir-fry the duck with the marinade for about 15 minutes until the duck is tender.

Duck with Ham and Leeks

Serves 4

1 duck
450 g/1 lb smoked ham
2 leeks
2 slices ginger root, minced
45 ml/3 tbsp rice wine or dry sherry
45 ml/3 tbsp soy sauce
2.5 ml/½ tsp salt

Place the duck in a pan and just cover with cold water. Bring to the boil, cover and simmer for about 20 minutes. Drain and reserve 450 ml/ ¾ pts/2 cups of stock. Let the duck cool slightly then cut the meat from the bones and cut it into 5 cm/2 in squares. Cut the ham into similar pieces. Cut off long pieces of leek and roll a slice of duck and ham inside the leaf and tie with string. Place in a heatproof bowl. Add the ginger, wine or sherry, soy sauce and salt to the reserved stock and pour it over the duck rolls. Place the bowl in a pan filled with water to come two-thirds of the way up the sides of the bowl. Bring to the boil, cover and simmer for about 1 hour until the duck is tender.

Honey-Roast Duck

Serves 4

1 duck
salt
3 cloves garlic, crushed
3 spring onions (scallions), minced
45 ml/3 tbsp soy sauce
45 ml/3 tbsp rice wine or dry sherry
45 ml/3 tbsp honey
200 ml/7 fl oz/scant 1 cup boiling water

Pat the duck dry and rub with salt inside and out. Mix the garlic, spring onions, soy sauce and wine or sherry then divide the mixture in half. Mix the honey into one half and rub over the duck then leave it to dry. Add the water to the remaining honey mixture. Pour the soy sauce mixture into the cavity of the duck and stand it on a rack in a roasting tin with a little water in the bottom. Roast in a preheated oven at 180°C/350°F/gas mark 4 for about 2 hours until the duck is tender, basting throughout cooking with the remaining honey mixture.

Moist Roast Duck

Serves 4

6 spring onions (scallions), chopped
2 slices ginger root, minced
1 duck
2.5 ml/½ tsp ground anise
15 ml/1 tbsp sugar
45 ml/3 tbsp rice wine or dry sherry
60 ml/4 tbsp soy sauce
250 ml/8 fl oz/1 cup water

Place half the spring onions and ginger in a large heavy-based pan. Place the remainder in the cavity of the duck and add it to the pan. Add all the remaining ingredients except the hoisin sauce, bring to the boil, cover and simmer for about 1½ hours, turning occasionally. Remove the duck from the pan and leave it to dry for about 4 hours.

Place the duck on a rack in a roasting tin filled with a little cold water. Roast in a preheated oven at 230°C/450°F/gas mark 8 for 15 minutes then turn it over and roast for a further 10 minutes until crispy. Meanwhile, reheat the reserved liquid and pour over the duck to serve.

Stir-Fried Duck with Mushrooms

Serves 4

1 duck
75 ml/5 tbsp groundnut (peanut) oil
45 ml/3 tbsp rice wine or dry sherry
15 ml/1 tbsp soy sauce
15 ml/1 tbsp sugar
5 ml/1 tsp salt
pinch of pepper
2 cloves garlic, crushed
225 g/8 oz mushrooms, halved
600 ml/1 pt/2½ cups chicken stock
15 ml/1 tbsp cornflour (cornstarch)
30 ml/2 tbsp water
5 ml/1 tsp sesame oil

Chop the duck into 5 cm/2 in pieces. Heat 45 ml/3 tbsp of oil and fry the duck until lightly browned on all sides. Add the wine or sherry, soy sauce, sugar, salt and pepper and stir-fry for 4 minutes. Remove from the pan. Heat the remaining oil and fry the garlic until lightly browned. Add the mushrooms and stir until coated in oil then return the duck mixture to the pan and add the stock. Bring to the boil, cover and simmer for about 1 hour until the duck is tender. Mix the cornflour and water to a paste then stir it into the mixture and simmer, stirring, until the sauce thickens. Sprinkle with sesame oil and serve.

Duck with Two Mushrooms

Serves 4

6 dried Chinese mushrooms

1 duck

750 ml/1¼ pts/3 cups chicken stock

45 ml/3 tbsp rice wine or dry sherry

5 ml/1 tsp salt

100 g/4 oz bamboo shoots, cut into
    strips

100 g/4 oz button mushrooms

Soak the mushrooms in warm water for 30 minutes then drain. Discard the stalks and halve the caps. Place the duck in a large heatproof bowl with the stock, wine or sherry and salt and stand in a pan filled with water to come two-thirds up the sides of the bowl. Bring to the boil, cover and simmer for about 2 hours until the duck is tender. Remove from the pan and cut the meat from the bone. Transfer the cooking liquid to a separate pan. Arrange the bamboo shoots and both types of mushrooms in the bottom of the steamer bowl, replace the duck meat, cover and steam for a further 30 minutes. Bring the cooking liquid to the boil and pour over the duck to serve.

Braised Duck with Onions

Serves 4

4 dried Chinese mushrooms

1 duck

90 ml/6 tbsp soy sauce

60 ml/4 tbsp groundnut (peanut) oil

1 spring onion (scallion), chopped

1 slice ginger root, minced

45 ml/3 tbsp rice wine or dry sherry

450 g/1 lb onions, sliced

100 g/4 oz bamboo shoots, sliced

15 ml/1 tbsp brown sugar

15 ml/1 tbsp cornflour (cornstarch)

45 ml/3 tbsp water

Soak the mushrooms in warm water for 30 minutes then drain. Discard the stalks and slice the caps. Rub 15 ml/1 tbsp of soy sauce into the duck. Reserve 15 ml/1 tbsp of oil, heat the remaining oil and fry the spring onion and ginger until lightly browned. Add the duck and fry until lightly browned on all sides. Pour off any excess fat. Add the wine or sherry, remaining soy sauce to the pan and just enough water almost to cover the duck. Bring to the boil, cover and simmer for 1 hour, turning occasionally.

Heat the reserved oil and fry the onions until softened. Remove from the heat and stir in the bamboo shoots and mushrooms then add them to the duck, cover and simmer for a further 30 minutes until the duck is tender. Remove the duck from the pan, cut into serving pieces and arrange on a warmed serving plate. Bring the liquids in the pan to the boil, add the sugar and cornflour and simmer, stirring, until the mixture boils and thickens. Pour over the duck to serve.

Duck with Orange

Serves 4

1 duck

3 spring onions (scallions), cut into chunks

2 slices ginger root, cut into strips

1 slice orange rind

salt and freshly ground pepper

Place the duck in a large pan, just cover with water and bring to the boil. Add the spring onions, ginger and orange rind, cover and simmer for about 1½ hours until the duck is tender. Season with salt and pepper, drain and serve.

Orange-Roast Duck

Serves 4

1 duck

2 cloves garlic, halved

45 ml/3 tbsp groundnut (peanut) oil

1 onion

1 orange

120 ml/4 fl oz/½ cup rice wine or dry sherry

2 slices ginger root, minced

5 ml/1 tsp salt

Rub the garlic over the duck inside and out then brush it with oil. Pierce the peeled onion with a fork, place it and the unpeeled orange inside the duck cavity and seal with a skewer. Stand the duck on a rack over a roasting tin filled with a little hot water and roast in a preheated oven at 160°C/325°F/gas mark 3 for about 2 hours. Discard the liquids and return the duck to the roasting tin. Pour over the wine or sherry and sprinkle with the ginger and salt. Return to the oven for a further 30 minutes. Discard the onion and orange and cut the duck into serving pieces. Pour the pan juices over the duck to serve.

Duck with Pears and Chestnuts

Serves 4

225 g/8 oz chestnuts, shelled

1 duck

45 ml/3 tbsp groundnut (peanut) oil

250 ml/8 fl oz/1 cup chicken stock

45 ml/3 tbsp soy sauce

15 ml/1 tbsp rice wine or dry sherry

5 ml/1 tsp salt

1 slice ginger root, minced

1 large pear, peeled and thickly sliced

15 ml/1 tbsp sugar

Boil the chestnuts for 15 minutes then drain. Chop the duck into 5 cm/2 in pieces. Heat the oil and fry the duck until lightly browned on all sides. Drain off any excess oil then add the stock, soy sauce, wine or sherry, salt and ginger. Bring to the boil, cover and simmer for 25 minutes, stirring occasionally. Add the chestnuts, cover and simmer for a further 15 minutes. Sprinkle the pear with sugar, add to the pan and simmer for about 5 minutes until heated through.

Peking Duck

Serves 6

1 duck
250 ml/8 fl oz/1 cup water
120 ml/4 fl oz/½ cup honey
120 ml/4 fl oz/½ cup sesame oil
For the pancakes:
250 ml/8 fl oz/1 cup water
225 g/8 oz/2 cups plain (all-purpose) flour
groundnut (peanut) oil for frying
For the dips:
120 ml/4 fl oz/½ cup hoisin sauce
30 ml/2 tbsp brown sugar
30 ml/2 tbsp soy sauce
5 ml/1 tsp sesame oil
6 spring onions (scallions), sliced lengthways
1 cucumber, cut into strips

The duck should be whole with the skin intact. Tie the neck tightly with string and sew up or skewer the bottom opening. Cut a small slit in the side of the neck, insert a straw and blow air under the skin until it is inflated. Suspend the duck over a basin and leave to hang for 1 hour.

Bring a pan of water to the boil, insert the duck and boil for 1 minute then remove and dry well. Bring the water to the boil and stir in the honey. Rub the mixture over the duck skin until it is saturated. Hang the duck over a basin in a cool, airy place for about 8 hours until the skin is hard.

Suspend the duck or place on a rack over a roasting tin and roast in a preheated oven at 180°C/350°F/gas mark 4 for about 1½ hours, basting regularly with sesame oil.

To make the pancakes, boil the water then gradually add the flour.

Knead lightly until the dough is soft, cover with a damp cloth and leave to stand for 15 minutes. Roll out on a floured surface and shape into a long cylinder. Cut into 2.5 cm/1 in slices then flatten until about 5 mm/¼ in thick and brush the tops with oil. Stack in pairs with the oiled surfaces touching and dust the outsides lightly with flour. Roll out the pairs to about 10 cm/4 in across and cook in pairs for about 1 minute on each side until lightly browned. Separate and stack until ready to serve.

Prepare the dips by mixing half the hoisin sauce with the sugar and mixing the remaining hoisin sauce with the soy sauce and sesame oil.

Remove the duck from the oven, cut off the skin and cut it into squares, and cube the meat. Arrange on separate plates and serve with the pancakes, dips and accompaniments.

Braised Duck with Pineapple

Serves 4

1 duck
400 g/14 oz canned pineapple chunks in syrup
45 ml/3 tbsp soy sauce
5 ml/1 tsp salt
pinch of freshly ground pepper

Place the duck in a heavy-based pan, just cover with water, bring to the boil then cover and simmer for 1 hour. Drain the pineapple syrup into the pan with the soy sauce, salt and pepper, cover and simmer for a further 30 minutes. Add the pineapple pieces and simmer for a further 15 minutes until the duck is tender.

Stir-Fried Duck with Pineapple

Serves 4

1 duck
45 ml/3 tbsp cornflour (cornstarch)
45 ml/3 tbsp soy sauce
225 g/8 oz canned pineapple in syrup
45 ml/3 tbsp groundnut (peanut) oil
2 slices ginger root, cut into strips
15 ml/1 tbsp rice wine or dry sherry
5 ml/1 tsp salt

Cut the meat from the bone and cut it into pieces. Mix the soy sauce with 30 ml/2 tbsp of cornflour and mix into the duck until well coated. Leave to stand for 1 hour, stirring occasionally. Crush the pineapple and syrup and heat gently in a pan. Mix the remaining cornflour with a little water, stir into the pan and simmer, stirring, until the sauce thickens. Keep warm. Heat the oil and fry the ginger until lightly browned then discard the ginger. Add the duck and stir-fry until lightly browned on all sides. Add the wine or sherry and salt and stir-fry for a further few minutes until the duck is cooked. Arrange the duck on a warmed serving plate, pour over the sauce and serve at once.

Pineapple and Ginger Duck

Serves 4

1 duck
100 g/4 oz preserved ginger in syrup
200 g/7 oz canned pineapple chunks in syrup
5 ml/1 tsp salt
15 ml/1 tbsp cornflour (cornstarch)
30 ml/2 tbsp water

Place the duck in a heatproof bowl and stand it in a pan filled with water to come two-thirds of the way up the sides of the bowl. Bring to the boil, cover and simmer for about 2 hours until the duck is tender. Remove the duck and leave to cool slightly. Remove the skin and bone and cut the duck into pieces. Arrange on a serving plate and keep them warm.

Drain the syrup from the ginger and pineapple into a pan, add the salt, cornflour and water. Bring to the boil, stirring and simmer for a few minutes, stirring, until the sauce clears and thickens. Add the ginger and pineapple, stir through then pour over the duck to serve.

Duck with Pineapple and Lychees

Serves 4

4 duck breasts
15 ml/1 tbsp soy sauce
1 clove star anise
1 slice ginger root
groundnut (peanut) oil for deep-frying
90 ml/6 tbsp wine vinegar
100 g/4 oz/½ cup brown sugar
250 ml/8 fl oz/½ cup chicken stock
15 ml/1 tbsp tomato ketchup (catsup)
200 g/7 oz canned pineapple chunks in
　syrup
15 ml/1 tbsp cornflour (cornstarch)
6 canned lychees
6 maraschino cherries

Place the ducks, soy sauce, anise and ginger in a saucepan and just cover with cold water. Bring to the boil, skim, then cover and simmer for about 45 minutes until the duck is cooked. Drain and pat dry. Deep-fry in hot oil until crispy.

Meanwhile, mix the wine vinegar, sugar, stock, tomato ketchup and 30 ml/2tbsp of the pineapple syrup in a pan, bring to the boil and simmer for about 5 minutes until thick. Stir in the fruit and heat through before pouring over the duck to serve.

Duck with Pork and Chestnuts

Serves 4

6 dried Chinese mushrooms
1 duck
225 g/8 oz chestnuts, shelled
225 g/8 oz lean pork, cubed
3 spring onions (scallions), chopped
1 slice ginger root, minced
250 ml/8 fl oz/1 cup soy sauce
900 ml/1½ pts/3¾ cups water

Soak the mushrooms in warm water for 30 minutes then drain. Discard the stalks and slice the caps. Place in a large pan with all the remaining ingredients, bring to the boil, cover and simmer for about 1½ hours until the duck is cooked.

Duck with Potatoes

Serves 4

75 ml/5 tbsp groundnut (peanut) oil
1 duck
3 cloves garlic, crushed
30 ml/2 tbsp black bean sauce
10 ml/2 tsp salt
1.2 l/2 pts/5 cups water
2 leeks, thickly sliced
15 ml/1 tbsp sugar
45 ml/3 tbsp soy sauce
60 ml/4 tbsp rice wine or dry sherry
1 clove star anise
900 g/2 lb potatoes, thickly sliced
½ head Chinese leaves
15 l/1 tbsp cornflour (cornstarch)
30 l/2 tbsp water
sprigs flat-leaf parsley

Heat 60 ml/4 tbsp of oil and fry the duck until browned on all sides. Tie or sew up the neck end and stand the duck, neck down, in a deep bowl. Heat the remaining oil and fry the garlic until lightly browned. Add the black bean sauce and salt and fry for 1 minute. Add the water, leeks, sugar, soy sauce, wine or sherry and star anise and bring to the boil. Pour 120 ml/8 fl oz/1 cup of the mixture into the duck cavity and tie or sew up to secure. Bring the remaining mixture in the pan to the boil. Add the duck and potatoes, cover and simmer for 40 minutes, turning the duck once. Arrange the Chinese leaves on a serving plate. Remove the duck from the pan, chop into 5 cm/2 in pieces and arrange on the serving plate with the potatoes. Mix the cornflour to a paste with the water, stir it into the pan and simmer, stirring, until the sauce thickens. Pour over the duck and serve garnished with parsley.

Red-Cooked Duck

Serves 4

1 duck
4 spring onions (scallions), cut into chunks
2 slices ginger root, cut into strips
90 ml/6 tbsp soy sauce
45 ml/3 tbsp rice wine or dry sherry
10 ml/2 tsp salt
10 ml/2 tsp sugar

Place the duck in a heavy pan, just cover with water and bring to the boil. Add the spring onions, ginger, wine or sherry and salt, cover and simmer for about 1 hour. Add the sugar and simmer for a further 45 minutes until the duck is tender. Slice the duck on to a serving plate and serve hot or cold, with or without the sauce.

Rice Wine Roast Duck

Serves 4

1 duck
500 ml/14 fl oz/1¼ cups rice wine or dry sherry
5 ml/1 tsp salt
45 ml/3 tbsp soy sauce

Place the duck in a heavy-based pan with the sherry and salt, bring to the boil, cover and simmer for 20 minutes. Drain the duck, reserving the liquid, and rub it with soy sauce. Place on a rack in a roasting tin filled with a little hot water and roast in a preheated oven at 180°C/350°F/gas mark 4 for about 1 hour, basting regularly with the reserved wine liquid.

Steamed Duck with Rice Wine

Serves 4

1 duck

4 spring onions (scallions), halved

1 slice ginger root, chopped

250 ml/8 fl oz/1 cup rice wine or dry sherry

30 ml/2 tbsp soy sauce

pinch of salt

Blanch the duck in boiling water for 5 minutes then drain. Place in a heatproof bowl with the remaining ingredients. Stand the bowl in a pan filled with water to come two-thirds of the way up the sides of the bowl. Bring to the boil, cover and simmer for about 2 hours until the duck is tender. Discard the spring onions and ginger before serving.

Savoury Duck

Serves 4

45 ml/3 tbsp groundnut (peanut) oil

4 duck breasts

3 spring onions (scallions), sliced

2 cloves garlic, crushed

1 slice ginger root, chopped

250 ml/8 fl oz/1 cup soy sauce

30 ml/2 tbsp rice wine or dry sherry

30 ml/2 tbsp brown sugar

5 ml/1 tsp salt

450 ml/¾ pt/2 cups water

15 ml/1 tbsp cornflour (cornstarch)

Heat the oil and fry the duck breasts until golden brown. Add the spring onions, garlic and ginger and fry for 2 minutes. Add the soy sauce, wine or sherry, sugar and salt and mix well. Add the water, bring to the boil, cover and simmer for about 1¾ hours until the meat is very tender. Mix the cornflour with a little water then stir it into the pan and simmer, stirring, until the sauce thickens.

Savoury Duck with Green Beans

Serves 4

45 ml/3 tbsp groundnut (peanut) oil

4 duck breasts

3 spring onions (scallions), sliced

2 cloves garlic, crushed

1 slice ginger root, chopped

250 ml/8 fl oz/1 cup soy sauce

30 ml/2 tbsp rice wine or dry sherry

30 ml/2 tbsp brown sugar

5 ml/1 tsp salt

450 ml/¾ pt/2 cups water

225 g/8 oz green beans

15 ml/1 tbsp cornflour (cornstarch)

Heat the oil and fry the duck breasts until golden brown. Add the spring onions, garlic and ginger and fry for 2 minutes. Add the soy sauce, wine or sherry, sugar and salt and mix well. Add the water, bring to the boil, cover and simmer for about 45 minutes. Add the beans, cover and simmer for a further 20 minutes. Mix the cornflour with a little water then stir it into the pan and simmer, stirring, until the sauce thickens.

Slow-Cooked Duck

Serves 4

1 duck
50 g/2 oz/½ cup cornflour (cornstarch)
oil for deep-frying
2 cloves garlic, crushed
30 ml/2 tbsp rice wine or dry sherry
30 ml/2 tbsp soy sauce
5 ml/1 tsp grated ginger root
750 ml/1¼ pts/3 cups chicken stock
4 dried Chinese mushrooms
225 g/8 oz bamboo shoots, sliced
225 g/8 oz water chestnuts, sliced
10 ml/2 tsp sugar
pinch of pepper
5 spring onions (scallions), sliced

Cut the duck into serving-size pieces. Reserve 30 ml/2 tbsp of cornflour and coat the duck in the remaining cornflour. Dust off the excess. Heat the oil and fry the garlic and duck until lightly browned. Remove from the pan and drain on kitchen paper. Place the duck in a large pan. Mix together the wine or sherry, 15 ml/1 tbsp of soy sauce and the ginger. Add to the pan and cook over a high heat for 2 minutes. Add half the stock, bring to the boil, cover and simmer for about 1 hour until the duck is tender.

Meanwhile, soak the mushrooms in warm water for 30 minutes then drain. Discard the stalks and slice the caps. Add the mushrooms, bamboo shoots and water chestnuts to the duck and cook, stirring frequently, for 5 minutes. Skim off any fat from the liquid. Blend the remaining stock, cornflour and soy sauce with the sugar and pepper and stir into the pan. Bring to the boil, stirring, then simmer for about 5 minutes until the sauce thickens. Transfer to a warmed serving bowl and serve garnished with spring onions.

Stir-Fried Duck

Serves 4

1 egg white, lightly beaten
20 ml/1½ tbsp cornflour (cornstarch)
salt
450 g/1 lb duck breasts, thinly sliced
45 ml/3 tbsp groundnut (peanut) oil
2 spring onions (scallions), cut into
    strips
1 green pepper, cut into strips
5 ml/1 tsp rice wine or dry sherry
75 ml/5 tbsp chicken stock
2.5 ml/½ tsp sugar

Beat the egg white with 15 ml/1 tbsp of cornflour and a pinch of salt. Add the sliced duck and mix until the duck is coated. Heat the oil and fry the duck until cooked through and golden. Remove the duck from the pan and drain off all but 30 ml/2 tbsp of the oil. Add the spring onions and pepper and stir-fry for 3 minutes. Add the wine or sherry, stock and sugar and bring to the boil. Mix the remaining cornflour with a little water, stir it into the sauce and simmer, stirring, until the sauce thickens. Stir in the duck, heat through and serve.

Duck with Sweet Potatoes

Serves 4

| 1 duck |
| 250 ml/8 fl oz/1 cup groundnut (peanut) oil |
| 225 g/8 oz sweet potatoes, peeled and cubed |
| 2 cloves garlic, crushed |
| 1 slice ginger root, minced |
| 2.5 ml/½ tsp cinnamon |
| 2.5 ml/½ tsp ground cloves |
| pinch of ground anise |
| 5 ml/1 tsp sugar |
| 15 ml/1 tbsp soy sauce |
| 250 ml/8 fl oz/1 cup chicken stock |
| 15 ml/1 tbsp cornflour (cornstarch) |
| 30 ml/2 tbsp water |

Chop the duck into 5 cm/2 in pieces. Heat the oil and deep-fry the potatoes until golden brown. Remove them from the pan and drain off all but 30 ml/2 tbsp of oil. Add the garlic and ginger and stir-fry for 30 seconds. Add the duck and fry until lightly browned on all sides. Add the spices, sugar, soy sauce and stock and bring to the boil. Add the potatoes, cover and simmer for about 20 minutes until the duck is tender. Blend the cornflour to a paste with the water then stir it into the pan and simmer, stirring, until the sauce thickens.

Sweet and Sour Duck

Serves 4

| 1 duck |
| 1.2 1/2 pts/5 cups chicken stock |
| 2 onions |
| 2 carrots |
| 2 cloves garlic, sliced |
| 15 ml/1 tbsp pickling spice |
| 10 ml/2 tsp salt |
| 10 ml/2 tsp groundnut (peanut) oil |
| 6 spring onions (scallions), chopped |
| 1 mango, peeled and cubed |
| 12 lychees, halved |
| 15 ml/1 tbsp cornflour (cornstarch) |
| 15 ml/1 tbsp wine vinegar |
| 10 ml/2 tsp tomato purée (paste) |
| 15 ml/1 tbsp soy sauce |
| 5 ml/1 tsp five-spice powder |
| 300 ml/½ pt/1¼ cups chicken stock |

Arrange the duck in a steam basket over a pan containing the stock, onions, carrots, garlic, pickling spice and salt. Cover and steam for 2½ hours. Cool the duck, cover and chill for 6 hours. Remove the meat from the bones and cut it into cubes. Heat the oil and fry the duck and spring onions until crisp. Stir in the remaining ingredients, bring to the boil and simmer for 2 minutes, stirring, until the sauce thickens.

Tangerine Duck

Serves 4

| 1 duck |
| 60 ml/4 tbsp groundnut (peanut) oil |
| 1 piece dried tangerine peel |
| 900 ml/1½ pts/3¾ cups chicken stock |
| 5 ml/1 tsp salt |

Hang the duck to dry for 2 hours. Heat half the oil and fry the duck until lightly browned. Transfer to a large heatproof bowl. Heat the remaining oil and fry the tangerine peel for 2 minutes then place it inside the duck. Pour the stock over the duck and season with salt. Place the bowl on a rack in a steamer, cover and steam for about 2 hours until the duck is tender.

Duck with Vegetables

Serves 4

1 large duck, chopped into 16 pieces
salt
300 ml/½ pt/1¼ cups water
300 ml/½ pt/1¼ cups dry white wine
120 ml/4 fl oz/½ cup wine vinegar
45 ml/3 tbsp soy sauce
30 ml/2 tbsp plum sauce
30 ml/2 tbsp hoisin sauce
5 ml/1 tsp five-spice powder
6 spring onions (scallions), chopped
2 carrots, chopped
5 cm/2 in white radish, chopped
50 g/2 oz Chinese cabbage, diced
freshly ground pepper
5 ml/1 tsp sugar

Put the duck pieces in a bowl, sprinkle with salt and add the water and wine. Add the wine vinegar, soy sauce, plum sauce, hoisin sauce and five-spice powder, bring to the boil, cover and simmer for about 1 hour. Add the vegetables to the pan, remove the lid and simmer for a further 10 minutes. Season with salt, pepper and sugar then leave to cool. Cover and refrigerate overnight. Skim off any fat then reheat the duck in the sauce for 20 minutes.

Stir-Fried Duck with Vegetables

Serves 4

4 dried Chinese mushrooms
1 duck
10 ml/2 tsp cornflour (cornstarch)
15 ml/1 tbsp soy sauce
45 ml/3 tbsp groundnut (peanut) oil
100 g/4 oz bamboo shoots, cut into strips
50 g/2 oz water chestnuts, cut into strips
120 ml/4 fl oz/½ cup chicken stock
15 ml/1 tbsp rice wine or dry sherry
5 ml/1 tsp salt

Soak the mushrooms in warm water for 30 minutes then drain. Discard the stalks and dice the caps. Remove the meat from the bones and cut into pieces. Mix the cornflour and soy sauce, add to the duck meat and leave to stand for 1 hour. Heat the oil and fry the duck until lightly browned on all sides. Remove from the pan. Add the mushrooms, bamboo shoots and water chestnuts to the pan and stir-fry for 3 minutes. Add the stock, wine or sherry and salt, bring to the boil and simmer for 3 minutes. Return the duck to the pan, cover and simmer for a further 10 minutes until the duck is tender.

White-Cooked Duck

Serves 4

1 slice ginger root, chopped

250 1/8 fl oz/1 cup rice wine or dry
    sherry

salt and freshly ground pepper

1 duck

3 spring onions (scallions), chopped

5 ml/1 tsp salt

100 g/4 oz bamboo shoots, sliced

100 g/4 oz smoked ham, sliced

Mix the ginger, 15 ml/1 tbsp wine or
sherry, a little salt and pepper. Rub
over the duck and leave to stand for 1
hour. Place the bird in a heavy-based
pan with the marinade and add the
spring onions and salt. Add enough
cold water just to cover the duck,
bring to the boil, cover and simmer for
about 2 hours until the duck is tender.
Add the bamboo shoots and ham and
simmer for a further 10 minutes.

Duck with Wine

Serves 4

1 duck

15 ml/1 tbsp yellow bean sauce

1 onion, sliced

1 bottle dry white wine

Rub the duck inside and out with the
yellow bean paste. Place the onion
inside the cavity. Bring the wine to
the boil in a large pan, add the duck,
return to the boil, cover and simmer
as gently as possible for about 3 hours
until the duck is tender. Drain and
slice to serve.

Wine-Vapour Duck

Serves 4

1 duck

celery salt

200 ml/7 fl oz/scant 1 cup rice wine or
    dry sherry

30 ml/2 tbsp chopped fresh parsley

Rub the duck with celery salt inside
and out then place it in a deep
ovenproof dish. Place an ovenproof
cup containing the wine into the
cavity of the duck. Place the dish on a
rack in a steamer, cover and steam
over boiling water for about 2 hours
until the duck is tender.

Fried Pheasant

Serves 4

900 g/2 lb pheasant

30 ml/2 tbsp soy sauce

4 eggs, beaten

120 ml/4 fl oz/½ cup groundnut
    (peanut) oil

Bone the pheasant and slice the meat.
Mix with the soy sauce and leave to
stand for 30 minutes. Drain the
pheasant then dip it in the eggs. Heat
the oil and fry the pheasant quickly
until golden brown. Drain well before
serving.

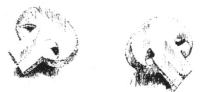

Pheasant with Almonds

Serves 4

45 ml/3 tbsp groundnut (peanut) oil
2 spring onions (scallions), chopped
1 slice ginger root, minced
225 g/8 oz pheasant, very thinly sliced
50 g/2 oz ham, shredded
30 ml/2 tbsp soy sauce
30 ml/2 tbsp rice wine or dry sherry
5 ml/1 tsp sugar
5 ml/1 tsp freshly ground pepper
2.5 ml/½ tsp salt
100 g/4 oz/1 cup flaked almonds

Heat the oil and fry the spring onions and ginger until lightly browned. Add the pheasant and ham and stir-fry for 5 minutes until almost cooked. Add the soy sauce, wine or sherry, sugar, pepper and salt and stir-fry for 2 minutes. Add the almonds and stir-fry for 1 minute until the ingredients are thoroughly blended.

Venison with Dried Mushrooms

Serves 4

8 dried Chinese mushrooms
450 g/1 lb venison fillet, cut into strips
15 ml/1 tbsp juniper berries, ground
15 ml/1 tsp sesame oil
30 ml/2 tbsp soy sauce
30 ml/2 tbsp hoisin sauce
5 ml/1 tsp five-spice powder
30 ml/2 tbsp groundnut (peanut) oil
6 spring onions (scallions), chopped
30 ml/2 tbsp honey
30 ml/2 tbsp wine vinegar

Soak the mushrooms in warm water for 30 minutes then drain. Discard the stalks and slice the caps. Place the venison in a bowl. Mix the juniper berries, sesame oil, soy sauce, hoisin sauce and five-spice powder, pour over the venison and marinate for at least 3 hours, stirring occasionally. Heat the oil and stir-fry the meat for 8 minutes until cooked. Remove from the pan. Add the spring onions and mushrooms to the pan and stir-fry for 3 minutes. Return the meat to the pan with the honey and wine vinegar and heat through, stirring.

Eggs

Chinese omelette and soufflé dishes are excellent for light lunches or as part of a large meal. They are simple and easy to digest, as well as having just that little bit extra flavour. Other Chinese dishes include strips of omelette in the dish or as a garnish.

Salted Eggs

Makes 6

1.2 1/2 pts/5 cups water
100 g/4 oz rock salt
6 duck eggs

Bring the water to the boil with the salt and stir until the salt has dissolved. Leave to cool. Pour the salt water into a large jar, add the eggs, cover and leave to stand for 1 month. Hard-boil the eggs before steaming with rice.

Soy Eggs

Serves 4

4 eggs
120 ml/4 fl oz/½ cup soy sauce
120 ml/4 fl oz/½ cup water
50 g/2 oz/¼ cup brown sugar
½ head lettuce, shredded
2 tomatoes, sliced

Place the eggs in a saucepan, cover with cold water, bring to the boil and boil for 10 minutes. Drain and cool under running water. Return the eggs to the pan and add the soy sauce, water and sugar. Bring to the boil, cover and simmer for 1 hour. Arrange the lettuce on a serving plate. Quarter the eggs and place on top of the lettuce. Serve garnished with tomatoes.

Tea Eggs

Serves 4 –6

6 eggs
10 ml/2 tsp salt
3 China tea bags
45 ml/3 tbsp soy sauce
1 clove star anise, broken apart

Place the eggs in a pan, cover with cold water then bring to a slow boil and simmer for 15 minutes. Remove from the heat and place the eggs in cold water until cool. Leave to stand for 5 minutes. Remove the eggs from the pan and gently crack the shells but do not remove them. Return the eggs to the pan and cover with cold water. Add the remaining ingredients, bring to the boil then simmer for 1½ hours. Cool and remove the shell.

Egg Custard

Serves 4

4 eggs, beaten
375 ml/13 fl oz/1½ cups chicken stock
2.5 ml/½ tsp salt
1 spring onion (scallion), minced
100 g/4 oz peeled prawns, roughly
    chopped
15 ml/1 tbsp soy sauce
15 ml/1 tbsp groundnut (peanut) oil

Mix all the ingredients except the oil

in a deep bowl and stand the bowl in a roasting tin filled with 2.5 cm/1 in of water. Cover and steam for 15 minutes. Heat the oil and pour it over the custard. Cover and steam for a further 15 minutes.

Steamed Eggs

Serves 4

250 ml/8 fl oz/1 cup chicken stock

4 eggs, lightly beaten

15 ml/1 tbsp rice wine or dry sherry

5 ml/1 tsp groundnut (peanut) oil

2.5 ml/½ tsp salt

2.5 ml/½ tsp sugar

2 spring onions (scallions), chopped

15 ml/1 tbsp soy sauce

Beat the eggs lightly with the wine or sherry, oil, salt, sugar and spring onions. Warm the stock then slowly stir it into the egg mixture and pour into a shallow ovenproof dish. Place the dish on a rack in a steamer, cover and steam for about 30 minutes over gently simmering water until the mixture is the consistency of thick custard. Sprinkle with soy sauce before serving.

Steamed Eggs with Fish

Serves 4

225 g/8 oz sole fillets, cut into strips

30 ml/2 tbsp cornflour (cornstarch)

½ small green pepper, finely chopped

1 spring onion (scallion), finely
  chopped

30 ml/2 tbsp groundnut (peanut) oil

120 ml/4 fl oz/½ cup chicken stock

3 eggs, lightly beaten

pinch of salt

Dust the strips of fish lightly in cornflour then shake off any excess. Arrange them in a shallow ovenproof dish. Sprinkle with the pepper, spring onion and oil. Warm the chicken stock, stir it into the eggs and season with salt then pour the mixture over the fish. Place the dish on a rack in a steamer, cover and steam for about 40 minutes over gently simmering water until the fish is cooked and the eggs are just set.

Steamed Eggs with Ham and Fish

Serves 4 –6

6 eggs, separated

225 g/8 oz minced (ground) cod

375 ml/13 fl oz/1½ cups warm water

pinch of salt

50 g/2 oz smoked ham, chopped

15 ml/1 tbsp groundnut (peanut) oil

sprigs flat-leaf parsley

Mix the egg white with the fish, half the water and a little salt and pour the mixture into a shallow ovenproof dish. Mix the egg yolks with the remaining water, the ham and a little salt and pour it on top of the egg white mixture. Place the dish on a rack in a steamer, cover and steam over gently simmering water for about 20 minutes until the eggs are set. Heat the oil to smoking point, pour it over the eggs and serve garnished with parsley.

Steamed Eggs with Pork

Serves 4

45 ml/3 tbsp groundnut (peanut) oil
225 g/8 oz lean pork, minced (ground)
100 g/4 oz water chestnuts, minced
    (ground)
1 spring onion (scallion), chopped
30 ml/2 tbsp soy sauce
5 ml/1 tsp salt
120 ml/4 fl oz/½ cup chicken stock
4 eggs, lightly beaten

Heat the oil and fry the pork, water chestnuts and spring onions until lightly coloured. Stir in the soy sauce and salt then drain off any excess oil and spoon into a shallow ovenproof dish. Warm the stock then stir it into the eggs and pour over the meat mixture. Place the dish on a rack in a steamer, cover and steam over gently simmering water for about 30 minutes until the eggs are just set.

Deep-Fried Pork Eggs

Serves 4

100 g/4 oz minced (ground) pork
2 spring onions (scallions) minced
15 ml/1 tbsp cornflour (cornstarch)
15 ml/1 tbsp rice wine or dry sherry
15 ml/1 tbsp soy sauce
2.5 ml/½ tsp salt
4 hardboiled (hardcooked) eggs
oil for deepfrying
½ head lettuce, shredded

Mix together the pork, spring onions, cornflour, wine or sherry, soy sauce and salt. Shape around the eggs to coat them completely. Heat the oil and deep-fry the eggs until the coat-ing is golden brown and cooked through. Remove and drain well then serve on a bed of lettuce.

Soy-Sauce Fried Eggs

Serves 4

45 ml/3 tbsp groundnut (peanut) oil
4 eggs
15 ml/1 tbsp soy sauce
½ head lettuce, shredded

Heat the oil until very hot and break the eggs into the pan. Cook until the underside is lightly browned them sprinkle generously with soy sauce and turn over without breaking the yolk. Fry for a further 1 minute. Arrange the lettuce on a serving plate and place the eggs on top to serve.

Half-Moon Eggs

Serves 4

45 ml/3 tbsp groundnut (peanut) oil
4 eggs
salt and freshly ground pepper
15 ml/1 tbsp soy sauce
15 ml/1 tbsp chopped fresh flat-leaved
    parsley

Heat the oil until very hot and break the eggs into the pan. Cook until the underside is lightly browned then sprinkle with salt, pepper and soy sauce. Fold the egg in half and press down gently so that it holds together. Cook for a further 2 minutes until golden brown on both sides then serve sprinkled with parsley.

Fried Eggs with Vegetables

Serves 4

4 dried Chinese mushrooms
30 ml/2 tbsp groundnut (peanut) oil
2.5 ml/½ tsp salt
3 spring onions (scallions), chopped
50 g/2 oz bamboo shoots, sliced
50 g/2 oz water chestnuts, sliced
90 ml/6 tbsp chicken stock
10 ml/2 tsp cornflour (cornstarch)
15 ml/1 tbsp water
5 ml/1 tsp sugar
oil for deep-frying
4 eggs
¼ head lettuce, shredded

Soak the mushrooms in warm water for 30 minutes then drain. Discard the stalks and slice the caps. Heat the oil and salt and stir-fry the spring onions for 30 seconds. Add the bamboo shoots and water chestnuts and stir-fry for 2 minutes. Add the stock, bring to the boil, cover and simmer for 2 minutes. Blend the cornflour and water to a paste and stir it into the pan with the sugar. Simmer, stirring, until the sauce thickens. Meanwhile, heat the oil and deep-fry the eggs for a few minutes until the edges begin to brown. Arrange the lettuce on a serving plate, top with the eggs and pour over the hot sauce.

Chinese Omelette

Serves 4

4 eggs
salt and freshly ground pepper
30 ml/2 tbsp groundnut (peanut) oil

Beat the eggs lightly and season with salt and pepper. Heat the oil then pour the eggs into the pan and tilt the pan so that the egg covers the surface. Lift the edges of the omelette as the eggs set so that the uncooked egg can run underneath. Cook until just set then fold in half and serve at once.

Chinese Omelette with Bean Sprouts

Serves 4

100 g/4 oz bean sprouts
4 eggs
salt and freshly ground pepper
30 ml/2 tbsp groundnut (peanut) oil
½ small green pepper, chopped
2 spring onions (scallions), chopped

Blanch the bean sprouts in boiling water for 2 minutes then drain well. Beat the eggs lightly and season with salt and pepper. Heat the oil and stir-fry the pepper and spring onions for 1 minute. Add the bean sprouts and stir until coated with oil. Pour the eggs into the pan and tilt the pan so that the egg covers the surface. Lift the edges of the omelette as the eggs set so that the uncooked egg can run underneath. Cook until just set then fold in half and serve at once.

Cauliflower Omelette

Serves 4

1 cauliflower, broken into florets
225 g/8 oz chicken meat, minced (ground)
5 ml/1 tsp salt
3 egg whites, lightly beaten
2.5 ml/½ tsp celery salt
45 ml/3 tbsp chicken stock
45 ml/3 tbsp groundnut (peanut) oil

Blanch the cauliflower florets in boiling water for 10 minutes then drain well. Mix the chicken, salt, egg whites, celery salt and stock. Beat with an electric whisk until the mixture forms soft peaks. Heat the oil, add the chicken mixture and stir-fry for about 2 minutes. Add the cauliflower and stir-fry for a further 2 minutes before serving.

Crab Omelette with Brown Sauce

Serves 4

15 ml/1 tbsp groundnut (peanut) oil
4 eggs, beaten
2.5 ml/½ tsp salt
200 g/7 oz crab meat, flaked
175 ml/6 fl oz/¾ cup chicken stock
15 ml/1 tbsp soy sauce
10 ml/2 tsp cornflour (cornstarch)
45 ml/3 tbsp cooked green peas

Heat the oil. Beat the eggs and salt and stir in the crab meat. Pour into the pan and cook, lifting the edges of the omelette as the eggs set so that the uncooked egg can run underneath. Cook until just set then fold in half and transfer to a warmed serving plate. Meanwhile, heat the stock with the soy sauce and cornflour, stirring until the mixture boils and thickens. Simmer for 2 minutes then stir in the peas. Pour over the omelette just before serving.

Omelette with Ham and Water Chestnuts

Serves 2

30 ml/2 tbsp groundnut (peanut) oil
1 onion, chopped
1 clove garlic, crushed
50 g/2 oz ham, chopped
50 g/2 oz water chestnuts, chopped
15 ml/1 tbsp soy sauce
50 g/2 oz Cheddar cheese
3 eggs, beaten

Heat half the oil and fry the onion, garlic, ham, water chestnuts and soy sauce until lightly browned. Remove them from the pan. Heat the remaining oil, add the eggs and draw the egg into the centre as it begins to set so that the uncooked egg can run underneath. When the egg is just set, spoon the ham mixture onto half the omelette, top with the cheese and fold over the other half of the omelette. Cover and cook for 2 minutes then turn and cook for a further 2 minutes until golden brown.

Omelette with Lobster

Serves 4

4 eggs

salt and freshly ground pepper

30 ml/2 tbsp groundnut (peanut) oil

3 spring onions (scallions), chopped

100 g/4 oz lobster meat, chopped

Beat the eggs lightly and season with salt and pepper. Heat the oil and stir-fry the spring onions for 1 minute. Add the lobster and stir until coated with oil. Pour the eggs into the pan and tilt the pan so that the egg covers the surface. Lift the edges of the omelette as the eggs set so that the uncooked egg can run underneath. Cook until just set then fold in half and serve at once.

Oyster Omelette

Serves 4

4 eggs

120 ml/4 fl oz/½ cup milk

12 shelled oysters

3 spring onions (scallions), chopped

salt and freshly ground pepper

30 ml/2 tbsp groundnut (peanut) oil

50 g/2 oz lean pork, shredded

50 g/2 oz mushrooms, sliced

50 g/2 oz bamboo shoots, sliced

Lightly beat the eggs with the milk, oysters, spring onions, salt and pepper. Heat the oil and stir-fry the pork until lightly browned. Add the mushrooms and bamboo shoots and stir-fry for 2 minutes. Pour the egg mixture into the pan and cook, lifting the edges of the omelette as the eggs set so that the uncooked egg can run un-derneath. Cook until just set then fold in half, turn the omelette over and cook until lightly browned on the other side. Serve at once.

Omelette with Prawns

Serves 4

4 eggs

15 ml/1 tbsp rice wine or dry sherry

salt and freshly ground pepper

30 ml/2 tbsp groundnut (peanut) oil

1 slice ginger root, minced

225 g/8 oz peeled prawns

Beat the eggs lightly with the wine or sherry and season with salt and pepper. Heat the oil and stir-fry the ginger until lightly browned. Add the prawns and stir until coated with oil. Pour the eggs into the pan and tilt the pan so that the egg covers the surface. Lift the edges of the omelette as the eggs set so that the uncooked egg can run underneath. Cook until just set then fold in half and serve at once.

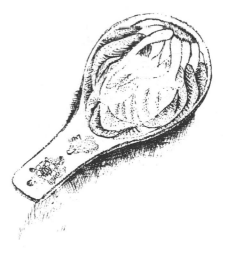

Omelette with Scallops

Serves 4

4 eggs
5 ml/1 tsp soy sauce
salt and freshly ground pepper
30 ml/2 tbsp groundnut (peanut) oil
3 spring onions (scallions), chopped
225 g/8 oz scallops, halved

Beat the eggs lightly with the soy sauce and season with salt and pepper. Heat the oil and stir-fry the spring onions until lightly browned. Add the scallops and stir-fry for 3 minutes. Pour the eggs into the pan and tilt the pan so that the egg covers the surface. Lift the edges of the omelette as the eggs set so that the uncooked egg can run underneath. Cook until just set then fold in half and serve at once.

Omelette with Tofu

Serves 4

4 eggs
salt and freshly ground pepper
30 ml/2 tbsp groundnut (peanut) oil
225 g/8 oz tofu, mashed

Beat the eggs lightly and season with salt and pepper. Heat the oil then add the tofu and stir-fry until heated through. Pour the eggs into the pan and tilt the pan so that the egg covers the surface. Lift the edges of the omelette as the eggs set so that the uncooked egg can run underneath. Cook until just set then fold in half and serve at once.

Pork Stuffed Omelette

Serves 4

50 g/2 oz bean sprouts
60 ml/4 tbsp groundnut (peanut) oil
225 g/8 oz lean pork, diced
3 spring onions (scallions), chopped
1 stalk celery, chopped
15 ml/1 tbsp soy sauce
5 ml/1 tsp sugar
4 eggs, lightly beaten
salt

Blanch the bean sprouts in boiling water for 3 minutes then drain well. Heat half the oil and stir-fry the pork until lightly browned. Add the spring onions and celery and stir-fry for 1 minute. Add the soy sauce and sugar and stir-fry for 2 minutes. Remove from the pan. Season the beaten eggs with salt. Heat the remaining oil and pour the eggs into the pan, tilting the pan so that the egg covers the surface. Lift the edges of the omelette as the eggs set so that the uncooked egg can run underneath. Spoon the filling on to half the omelette and fold in half. Cook until just set then serve at once.

Photograph opposite: Straw Mushrooms in Oyster Sauce (page 303)

Prawn Stuffed Omelette

Serves 4

30 ml/2 tbsp groundnut (peanut) oil
2 stalks celery, chopped
2 spring onions (scallions), chopped
225 g/8 oz peeled prawns, halved
4 eggs, lightly beaten
salt

Heat half the oil and stir-fry the celery and onions until lightly browned. Add the prawns and stir-fry until heated through. Remove from the pan. Season the beaten eggs with salt. Heat the remaining oil and pour the eggs into the pan, tilting the pan so that the egg covers the surface. Lift the edges of the omelette as the eggs set so that the uncooked egg can run underneath. Spoon the filling on to half the omelette and fold in half. Cook until just set then serve at once.

Steamed Omelette Rolls with Chicken Filling

Serves 4

4 eggs, lightly beaten
salt
15 ml/1 tbsp groundnut (peanut) oil
100 g/4 oz cooked chicken, minced
2 slices ginger root, minced
1 onion, chopped
120 ml/4 fl oz/½ cup chicken stock
15 ml/1 tbsp rice wine or dry sherry

Photograph opposite: Four-jewelled Tofu (page 317)

Beat the eggs and season with salt. Heat a little oil and pour in one quarter of the eggs, tilting to spread the mixture over the pan. Fry until lightly browned on one side and just set then turn upside down on to a plate. Cook the remaining 4 omelettes. Mix the chicken, ginger and onion. Spoon the mixture equally between the omelettes, roll them up, secure with cocktail sticks and arrange the rolls in a shallow ovenproof dish. Place on a rack in a steamer, cover and steam for 15 minutes. Transfer to a warmed serving plate and cut into thick slices. Meanwhile, heat the stock and sherry and season with salt. Pour over the omelettes and serve.

Oyster Pancakes

Serves 4-6

12 oysters
4 eggs, lightly beaten
3 spring onions (scallions), sliced
salt and freshly ground pepper
6 ml/4 tbsp plain (all-purpose) flour
2.5 ml/½ tsp baking powder
45 ml/3 tbsp groundnut (peanut) oil

Shell the oysters, reserving 60 ml/4 tbsp of the liquor, and chop them coarsely. Mix the eggs with the oysters, spring onions, salt and pepper. Mix together the flour and baking powder, blend it to a paste with the oyster liquor then stir the mixture into the eggs. Heat a little oil and fry spoonfuls of the batter to make small pancakes. Cook until lightly browned on each side then add a little more oil to the pan and continue until all the mixture has been used.

Prawn Pancakes

Serves 4

50 g/4 oz peeled prawns, minced
4 eggs, lightly beaten
75 g/3 oz/⅓cup plain (all-purpose) flour
salt and freshly ground pepper
120 ml/4 fl oz/½ cup chicken stock
2 spring onions (scallions), chopped
30 ml/2 tbsp groundnut (peanut) oil

Mix together all the ingredients except the oil. Heat a little of the oil, pour in one quarter of the batter, tilting the pan to spread it over the base. Cook until lightly browned on the underside then turn and brown the other side. Remove from the pan and continue to cook the remaining pancakes.

Chinese Scrambled Eggs

Serves 4

4 eggs, beaten
2 spring onions (scallions), chopped
pinch of salt
5 ml/1 tsp soy sauce (optional)
30 ml/2 tbsp groundnut (peanut) oil

Beat the eggs with the spring onions, salt and soy sauce, if using. Heat the oil then pour in the egg mixture. Stir gently with a fork until the eggs are just set. Serve at once.

Scrambled Eggs with Fish

Serves 4

225 g/8 oz fish fillet
30 ml/2 tbsp groundnut (peanut) oil
1 slice ginger root, minced
2 spring onions (scallions), chopped
4 eggs, lightly beaten
salt and freshly ground pepper

Place the fish in an ovenproof bowl and place on a rack in a steamer. Cover and steam for about 20 minutes then remove the skin and flake the flesh. Heat the oil and stir-fry the ginger and spring onions until lightly browned. Add the fish and stir until coated with oil. Season the eggs with salt and pepper then pour them into the pan and stir gently with a fork until the eggs are just set. Serve at once.

Scrambled Eggs with Mushrooms

Serves 4

30 ml/2 tbsp groundnut (peanut) oil
4 eggs, beaten
3 spring onions (scallions), chopped
pinch of salt
5 ml/1 tsp soy sauce
100 g/4 oz mushrooms, roughly
    chopped

Heat half the oil and gently fry the mushrooms for a few minutes until heated through then remove them from the pan. Beat the eggs with the spring onions, salt and soy sauce. Heat the remaining oil then pour in the egg mixture. Stir gently with a fork until the eggs begin to set, then return the mushrooms to the pan and cook until the eggs are just set. Serve at once.

Scrambled Eggs with Oyster Sauce

Serves 4

4 eggs, beaten
3 spring onions (scallions), chopped
salt and freshly ground pepper
5 ml/1 tsp soy sauce
30 ml/2 tbsp groundnut (peanut) oil
15 ml/1 tbsp oyster sauce
100 g/4 oz cooked ham, shredded
2 sprigs flat-leaved parsley

Beat the eggs with the spring onions, salt, pepper and soy sauce. Stir in half the oil. Heat the remaining oil then pour in the egg mixture. Stir gently with a fork until the eggs begin to set, then stir in the oyster sauce and cook until the eggs are just set. Serve garnished with the ham and parsley.

Scrambled Eggs with Pork

Serves 4

225 g/8 oz lean pork, cut into slivers
30 ml/2 tbsp soy sauce
30 ml/2 tbsp groundnut (peanut) oil
2 spring onions (scallions), chopped
4 eggs, beaten
pinch of salt
5 ml/1 tsp soy sauce

Mix together the pork and soy sauce so that the pork is well coated. Heat the oil and stir-fry the pork until lightly browned. Add the spring onions and stir-fry for 1 minute. Beat the eggs with the spring onions, salt

and soy sauce then pour the egg mixture into the pan. Stir gently with a fork until the eggs are just set. Serve at once.

Scrambled Eggs with Pork and Prawns

Serves 4

100 g/4 oz minced (ground) pork
225 g/8 oz peeled prawns
2 spring onions (scallions), chopped
1 slice ginger root, minced
5 ml/1 tsp cornflour (cornstarch)
15 ml/1 tbsp rice wine or dry sherry
15 ml/1 tbsp soy sauce
salt and freshly ground pepper
45 ml/3 tbsp groundnut (peanut) oil
4 eggs, lightly beaten

Mix together the pork, prawns, spring onions, ginger, cornflour, wine or sherry, soy sauce, salt and pepper. Heat the oil and stir fry the pork mixture until lightly browned. Pour in the eggs and stir gently with a fork until the eggs are just set. Serve at once.

Scrambled Eggs with Spinach

Serves 4

45 ml/3 tbsp groundnut (peanut) oil
225 g/8 oz spinach
4 eggs, beaten
2 spring onions (scallions), chopped
pinch of salt

Heat half the oil and stir-fry the spinach for a few minutes until it turns bright green but does not wilt. Remove it from the pan and chop it finely. Beat the eggs with the spring onions, salt and soy sauce, if using. Stir in the spinach. Heat the oil then pour in the egg mixture. Stir gently with a fork until the eggs are just set. Serve at once.

Scrambled Eggs with Spring Onions

Serves 4

4 eggs, beaten
8 spring onions (scallions), chopped
salt and freshly ground pepper
5 ml/1 tsp soy sauce
30 ml/2 tbsp groundnut (peanut) oil

Beat the eggs with the spring onions, salt, pepper and soy sauce. Heat the oil then pour in the egg mixture. Stir gently with a fork until the eggs are just set. Serve at once.

Scrambled Eggs with Tomatoes

Serves 4

4 eggs, beaten
2 spring onions (scallions), chopped
pinch of salt
30 ml/2 tbsp groundnut (peanut) oil
3 tomatoes, skinned and chopped

Beat the eggs with the spring onions and salt. Heat the oil then pour in the egg mixture. Stir gently until the eggs begin to set, then mix in the tomatoes and continue to cook, stirring, until just set. Serve at once.

Scrambled Eggs with Vegetables

Serves 4

30 ml/2 tbsp groundnut (peanut) oil
5 ml/1 tsp sesame oil
1 green pepper, diced
1 clove garlic, chopped
100 g/4 oz mangetout (snow peas), halved
4 eggs, beaten
2 spring onions (scallions), chopped
pinch of salt
5 ml/1 tsp soy sauce

Heat half the groundnut (peanut) oil with the sesame oil and stir-fry the pepper and garlic until lightly browned. Add the mangetout and stir-fry for 1 minute. Beat the eggs with the spring onions, salt and soy sauce then pour the mixture into the pan. Stir gently with a fork until the eggs are just set. Serve at once.

Chicken Soufflé

Serves 4

100 g/4 oz chicken breast, minced (ground)
45 ml/3 tbsp chicken stock
2.5 ml/½ tsp salt
4 egg whites
75 ml/5 tbsp groundnut (peanut) oil

Mix the chicken, stock and salt together well. Whisk the egg whites until stiff and fold them into the mixture. Heat the oil to smoking point, add the mixture and stir well then lower the heat and continue to cook, stirring gently, until the mixture is just firm.

Crab Soufflé

Serves 4

100 g/4 oz crab meat, flaked
salt
15 ml/1 tbsp cornflour (cornstarch)
120 ml/4 fl oz/½ cup milk
4 egg whites
75 ml/5 tbsp groundnut (peanut) oil

Mix the crab meat, salt, cornflour and mix together well. Whisk the egg whites until stiff then fold them into the mixture. Heat the oil to smoking point, add the mixture and stir well then lower the heat and continue to cook, stirring gently, until the mixture is just firm.

Crab and Ginger Soufflé

Serves 4

75 ml/5 tbsp groundnut (peanut) oil
2 slices ginger root, minced
1 spring onion (scallion), minced
100 g/4 oz crab meat, flaked
salt
15 ml/1 tbsp rice wine or dry sherry
120 ml/4 fl oz/½ cup milk
60 ml/4 tbsp chicken stock
15 ml/2 tbsp cornflour (cornstarch)
4 egg whites
5 ml/1 tsp sesame oil

Heat half the oil and stir-fry the ginger and onion until softened. Stir in the crab meat and salt, remove from the heat and leave to cool slightly. Mix the wine or sherry, milk, stock and cornflour then stir this into the crab meat mixture. Whisk the egg whites until stiff then fold them into the mixture. Heat the remaining oil to smoking point, add the mixture and stir well then lower the heat and continue to cook, stirring gently, until the mixture is just firm.

Fish Soufflé

Serves 4

3 eggs, separated
5 ml/1 tsp soy sauce
5 ml/1 tsp sugar
salt and freshly ground pepper
450 g/1 lb fish fillets
45 ml/3 tbsp groundnut (peanut) oil

Mix the egg yolks with the soy sauce, sugar, salt and pepper. Cut the fish into large pieces. Dip the fish into the mixture until well coated. Heat the oil and fry the fish until lightly browned on the underside. Meanwhile, whisk the egg whites until stiff. Turn the fish over and spoon the egg white on to the top of the fish. Cook for 2 minutes until the underside is lightly browned then turn again and cook for a further 1 minute until the egg white is set and golden brown. Serve with tomato sauce.

Prawn Soufflé

Serves 4

225 g/8 oz peeled prawns, chopped
1 slice ginger root, minced
15 ml/1 tbsp rice wine or dry sherry
15 ml/1 tbsp soy sauce
salt and freshly ground pepper
4 eggs whites
45 ml/3 tbsp groundnut (peanut) oil

Mix together the prawns, ginger, wine or sherry, soy sauce, salt and pepper. Whisk the egg whites until stiff then fold them into the mixture. Heat the oil to smoking point, add the mixture and stir well then lower the heat and continue to cook, stirring gently, until the mixture is just firm.

Prawn Soufflé with Bean Sprouts

Serves 4

100 g/4 oz bean sprouts
100 g/4 oz peeled prawns, coarsely chopped
2 spring onions (scallions), chopped
5 ml/1 tsp cornflour (cornstarch)
15 ml/1 tbsp rice wine or dry sherry
120 ml/4 fl oz/½ cup chicken stock
salt
4 egg whites
45 ml/3 tbsp groundnut (peanut) oil

Blanch the bean sprouts in boiling water for 2 minutes then drain and keep warm. Meanwhile, mix the prawns, onions, cornflour, wine or sherry and stock and season with salt. Whisk the egg whites until stiff then fold them into the mixture. Heat the oil to smoking point, add the mixture and stir well then lower the heat and continue to cook, stirring gently, until the mixture is just firm. Place on a warmed serving dish and top with the bean sprouts.

Vegetable Soufflé

Serves 4

5 eggs, separated
3 potatoes, grated
1 small onion, finely chopped
15 ml/1 tbsp chopped fresh parsley
5 ml/1 tsp soy sauce
salt and freshly ground pepper

Beat the egg whites until stiff. Beat the egg yolks until pale and thick then add the potatoes, onion, parsley and soy sauce and stir together well.

Fold in the egg whites. Pour into a greased soufflé dish and bake in a preheated oven at 180°C/350°F/gas mark 4 for about 40 minutes.

Egg Foo Yung

Serves 4

4 eggs, lightly beaten
salt
100 g/4 oz cooked chicken, chopped
1 onion, chopped
2 stalks celery, chopped
50 g/2 oz mushrooms, chopped
30 ml/2 tbsp groundnut (peanut) oil
egg foo yung sauce (page 322)

Mix together the eggs, salt, chicken, onion, celery and mushrooms. Heat a little of the oil and spoon one quarter of the mixture into the pan. Fry until the underside is lightly browned then turn and brown the other side. Serve with egg foo yung sauce.

Deep-Fried Egg Foo Yung

Serves 4

4 eggs, lightly beaten
5 ml/1 tsp salt
100 g/4 oz smoked ham, chopped
100 g/4 oz mushrooms, chopped
15 ml/1 tbsp soy sauce
oil for deep-frying

Mix the eggs with the salt, ham, mushrooms and soy sauce. Heat the oil and carefully drop spoonfuls of the mixture into the oil. Cook until they rise to the surface turn them over until they are brown on both sides. Remove from the oil and drain while you cook the remaining pancakes.

Crab Foo Yung with Mushrooms

Serves 4

6 eggs, beaten
45 ml/3 tbsp cornflour (cornstarch)
100 g/4 oz crab meat
100 g/4 oz mushrooms, diced
100 g/4 oz frozen peas
2 spring onions (scallions), chopped
5 ml/1 tsp salt
45 ml/3 tbsp groundnut (peanut) oil

Beat the eggs then beat in the cornflour. Add all the remaining ingredients except the oil. Heat a little of the oil and pour the mixture into the pan a little at a time to make small pancakes about 7.5 cm/3 in across. Fry until the bottom is lightly browned then turn and brown the other side. Continue until you have used all the mixture.

Ham Egg Foo Yung

Serves 4

60 ml/4 tbsp groundnut (peanut) oil
50 g/2 oz bamboo shoots, diced
50 g/2 oz water chestnuts, diced
2 spring onions (scallions), chopped
2 stalks celery, diced
50 g/2 oz smoked ham, diced
15 ml/1 tbsp soy sauce
2.5 ml/½ tsp sugar
2.5 ml/½ tsp salt
4 eggs, lightly beaten

Heat half the oil and stir-fry the bamboo shoots, water chestnuts, spring onions and celery for about 2 minutes. Stir in the ham, soy sauce, sugar and salt, remove from the pan and leave to cool slightly. Stir the mixture into the beaten eggs. Heat a little of the remaining oil and pour the mixture into the pan a little at a time to make small pancakes about 7.5 cm/3in across. Fry until the bottom is lightly browned then turn and brown the other side. Continue until you have used all the mixture.

Roast Pork Egg Foo Yung

Serves 4

4 dried Chinese mushrooms
60 ml/3 tbsp groundnut (peanut) oil
100 g/4 oz roast pork, shredded
100 g/4 oz Chinese cabbage, shredded
50 g/2 oz bamboo shoots, sliced
50 g/2 oz water chestnuts, sliced
4 eggs, lightly beaten
salt and freshly ground pepper

Soak the mushrooms in warm water for 30 minutes then drain. Discard the stalks and slice the caps. Heat 30 ml/2 tbsp of oil and stir-fry the mushrooms, pork, cabbage, bamboo shoots and water chestnuts for 3 minutes. Remove from the pan and leave to cool slightly then mix them into the eggs and season with salt and pepper. Heat a little of the remaining oil and pour the mixture into the pan a little at a time to make small pancakes about 7.5 cm/3 in across. Fry until the bottom is lightly browned then turn and brown the other side. Continue until you have used all the mixture.

Pork and Prawn Egg Foo Yung

Serves 4

45 ml/3 tbsp groundnut (peanut) oil
100 g/4 oz lean pork, cut into slivers
1 onion, chopped
225 g/8 oz peeled prawns, cut into
    slivers
50 g/2 oz Chinese cabbage, shredded
4 eggs, lightly beaten
salt and freshly ground pepper

Heat 30 ml/2 tbsp of oil and stir-fry the pork and onion until lightly browned. Add the prawns and stir-fry until coated with oil then add the cabbage, stir well, cover and simmer for 3 minutes. Remove from the pan and leave to cool slightly. Add the meat mixture to the eggs and season with salt and pepper. Heat a little of the remaining oil and pour the mixture into the pan a little at a time to make small pancakes about 7.5 cm/3in across. Fry until the bottom is lightly browned then turn and brown the other side. Continue until you have used all the mixture.

Rice

Almost every Chinese meal includes at least one rice dish; it marries perfectly with the rich and varied tastes of the other dishes. It is also a very economical way of eating as the Chinese eat a great deal of rice with their meals. There are many ways to cook rice; it is not difficult, but you may find you need a little practice to get it absolutely right. The most important thing is knowing when the rice is ready. It should not be hard or mushy but firm to the bite, *al dente*.

White Rice

Serves 4

225 g/8 oz/1 cup long-grain rice
15 ml/1 tbsp oil
750 ml/1¼ pts/3 cups water

Wash the rice then place it in a saucepan. Add the water to the oil then add it to the pan so that it comes about 2.5 cm/1 in above the rice. Bring to the boil, cover with a tight-fitting lid, reduce the heat and simmer gently for 20 minutes.

Boiled Brown Rice

Serves 4

225 g/8 oz/1 cup long-grain brown rice
5 ml/1 tsp salt
900 ml/1½ pts/3¾ cups water

Wash the rice then place it in a saucepan. Add the salt and water so that it comes about 3 cm/1¼ in above the rice. Bring to the boil, cover with a tight-fitting lid, reduce the heat and simmer gently for 30 minutes, making sure that it does not boil dry.

Rice with Beef

Serves 4

225 g/8 oz/1 cup long-grain rice
100 g/4 oz minced (ground) beef
1 slice ginger root, minced
15 ml/1 tbsp soy sauce
15 ml/1 tbsp rice wine or dry sherry
5 ml/1 tsp groundnut (peanut) oil
2.5 ml/½ tsp sugar
2.5 ml/½ tsp salt

Place the rice in a large pan and bring to the boil. Cover and simmer for about 10 minutes until most of the liquid has been absorbed. Mix together the remaining ingredients, arrange on top of the rice, cover and cook for a further 20 minutes over a low heat until cooked. Stir the ingredients together before serving.

Chicken Liver Rice

Serves 4

225 g/8 oz/1 cup long-grain rice
375 ml/13 fl oz/1⅔ cups chicken stock
salt
2 cooked chicken livers, thinly sliced

Place the rice and stock in a large pan and bring to the boil. Cover and simmer for about 10 minutes until the rice is almost tender. Remove the lid and continue to simmer until most of the stock has been absorbed. Season to taste with salt, stir in the chicken livers and heat through gently before serving.

Chicken and Mushroom Rice

Serves 4

225 g/8 oz/1 cup long-grain rice
100 g/4 oz chicken meat, shredded
100 g/4 oz mushrooms, diced
5 ml/1 tsp cornflour (cornstarch)
5 ml/1 tsp soy sauce
5 ml/1 tsp rice wine or dry sherry
pinch of salt
15 ml/1 tbsp chopped spring onions
    (scallions)
15 ml/1 tbsp oyster sauce

Place the rice in a large pan and bring to the boil. Cover and simmer for about 10 minutes until most of the liquid has been absorbed. Mix together all the remaining ingredients except the spring onions and oyster sauce, arrange on top of the rice, cover and cook for a further 20 minutes over a low heat until cooked. Stir the ingredients together and sprinkle with spring onions and oyster sauce before serving.

Coconut Rice

Serves 4

225 g/8 oz/1 cup Thai scented rice
1 l/1¾ pts/4¼ cups coconut milk
150 ml/¼ pt/⅔ cup coconut cream
1 sprig coriander, chopped
pinch of salt

Bring all the ingredients to the boil in a pan, cover and leave the rice to swell over a low heat for about 25 minutes, stirring occasionally.

Crab Meat Rice

Serves 4

225 g/8 oz/1 cup long-grain rice
100 g/4 oz crab meat, flaked
2 slices ginger root, minced
15 ml/1 tbsp soy sauce
15 ml/1 tbsp rice wine or dry sherry
5 ml/1 tsp groundnut (peanut) oil
5 ml/1 tsp cornflour (cornstarch)
salt and freshly ground pepper

Place the rice in a large pan and bring to the boil. Cover and simmer for about 10 minutes until most of the liquid has been absorbed. Mix together the remaining ingredients, arrange on top of the rice, cover and cook for a further 20 minutes over a low heat until cooked. Stir the ingredients together before serving.

Rice with Peas

Serves 4

225 g/8 oz/1 cup long-grain rice
350 g/12 oz peas
30 ml/2 tbsp soy sauce

Place the rice and stock in a large pan and bring to the boil. Add the peas, cover and simmer for about 20 minutes until the rice is almost tender. Remove the lid and continue to simmer until most of the liquid has been absorbed. Cover and leave to stand off the heat for 5 minutes then serve sprinkled with soy sauce.

Pepper Rice

Serves 4

225 g/8 oz/1 cup long-grain rice
2 spring onions (scallions), minced
1 red pepper, diced
45 ml/3 tbsp soy sauce
30 ml/2 tbsp groundnut (peanut) oil
5 ml/1 tsp sugar

Place the rice in a pan, cover with cold water, bring to the boil, cover and simmer for about 20 minutes until tender. Drain well then stir in the spring onions, pepper, soy sauce, oil and sugar. Transfer to a warmed serving bowl and serve at once.

Poached Egg Rice

Serves 4

225 g/8 oz/1 cup long-grain rice
4 eggs
15 ml/1 tbsp oyster sauce

Place the rice in a pan, cover with cold water, bring to the boil, cover and simmer for about 10 minutes until tender. Drain and arrange on a warmed serving plate. Meanwhile, bring a pan of water to the boil, carefully break in the eggs and poach for a few minutes until the whites are set but the eggs are still moist. Lift out of the pan with a slotted spoon and arrange on top of the rice. Serve sprinkled with oyster sauce.

Singapore-Style Rice

Serves 4

225 g/8 oz/1 cup long-grain rice
5 ml/1 tsp salt
1.2 litres/2 pts/5 cups water

Wash the rice then place it in a saucepan with the salt and water. Bring to the boil then reduce the heat and simmer for about 15 minutes until the rice is tender. Drain in a colander and rinse with hot water before serving.

Slow Boat Rice

Serves 4

225 g/8 oz/1 cup long-grain rice
5 ml/1 tsp salt
15 ml/1 tbsp oil
750 ml/1¼ pts/3 cups water

Wash the rice then place it in an ovenproof dish with the salt, oil and water. Cover and bake in a preheated oven at 120°C/250°F/gas mark ¼ for about 1 hour until all the water has been absorbed.

Steamed Oven Rice

Serves 4

225 g/8 oz/1 cup long-grain rice
5 ml/1 tsp salt
450 ml/¾ pt/2 cups water

Place the rice, salt and water in a casserole dish, cover and bake in a preheated oven at 180°C/350°F/gas mark 4 for about 30 minutes.

Reheating Rice

There are several ways of reheating rice successfully, so you can always prepare a large quantity then reheat it for subsequent meals.

Place the rice in a pan with 5 ml/1 tsp water, cover and simmer gently for about 10 minutes until the rice has reheated.

Place the rice in a colander over a pan of hot water and cover. Bring the water to the boil and steam for about 5 minutes.

Place the rice in the top of a double boiler and bring the water in the bottom to the boil. Cover and simmer for about 15 minutes until the rice is heated through.

Place the rice in a saucepan with 1.2 litres/2 pts/5 cups water, bring to the boil then simmer for 2 minutes. Strain thoroughly.

Fried Rice

Serves 4

225 g/8 oz/1 cup long-grain rice
750 ml/1¼ pts/3 cups water
30 ml/2 tbsp groundnut (peanut) oil
1 egg, beaten
2 cloves garlic, crushed
pinch of salt
1 onion, finely chopped
3 spring onions (scallions), chopped
2.5 ml/½ tsp black treacle

Place the rice and water in a saucepan, bring to the boil, cover and simmer for about 20 minutes until the rice is cooked. Drain well. Heat 5 ml/1 tsp oil and pour in the egg. Cook until it sets on the base then turn and continue to cook until set. Remove from the pan and cut into strips. Add the remaining oil to the pan with the garlic and salt and fry until the garlic turns light golden. Add the onion and rice and stir-fry for 2 minutes. Add the spring onions and stir-fry for 2 minutes. Stir in the black treacle until the rice is covered then stir in the egg strips and serve.

Almond Fried Rice

Serves 4

250 ml/8 fl oz/1 cup groundnut (peanut) oil
50 g/2 oz/½ cup flaked almonds
4 eggs, beaten
450 g/1 lb/3 cups cooked longgrain rice
5 ml/1 tsp salt
3 slices cooked ham, cut into strips
2 shallots, finely chopped
15 ml/1 tbsp soy sauce

Heat the oil and fry the almonds until golden brown. Remove from the pan and drain on kitchen paper. Pour most of the oil out of the pan then reheat and pour in the eggs, stirring continuously. Add the rice and salt and cook for 5 minutes, lifting and stirring quickly so that the rice grains are coated with the egg. Stir in the ham, shallots and soy sauce and cook for a further 2 minutes. Fold in most of the almonds and serve garnished with the remaining almonds.

Fried Rice with Bacon and Egg

Serves 4

45 ml/3 tbsp groundnut (peanut) oil
225 g/8 oz bacon, chopped
1 onion, finely chopped
3 eggs, beaten
225 g/8 oz cooked long-grain rice

Heat the oil and fry the bacon and onion until lightly browned. Add the eggs and stir-fry until the eggs are almost cooked. Add the rice and stir-fry until the rice is heated through.

Beef Fried Rice

Serves 4

225 g/8 oz lean beef, cut into strips
15 ml/1 tbsp cornflour (cornstarch)
15 ml/1 tbsp soy sauce
15 ml/1 tbsp rice wine or dry sherry
5 ml/1 tsp sugar
75 ml/5 tbsp groundnut (peanut) oil
1 onion, chopped
450 g/1 lb/3 cups cooked long-grain rice
45 ml/3 tbsp chicken stock

Mix the beef with the cornflour, soy sauce, wine or sherry and sugar. Heat half the oil and fry the onion until translucent. Add the beef and stir-fry for 2 minutes. Remove from the pan. Heat the remaining oil, add the rice and stir-fry for 2 minutes. Add the stock and heat through. Add half the beef and onion mixture and stir until hot then transfer to a warmed serving plate and top with the remaining beef and onions.

Fried Rice with Minced Beef

Serves 4

30 ml/2 tbsp groundnut (peanut) oil
1 clove garlic, crushed
pinch of salt
30 ml/2 tbsp soy sauce
30 ml/2 tbsp hoisin sauce
450 g/1 lb minced (ground) beef
1 onion, diced
1 carrot, diced
1 leek, diced
450 g/1 lb cooked long-grain rice

Heat the oil and fry the garlic and salt until lightly browned. Add the soy and hoisin sauces and stir until heated through. Add the beef and fry until brown and crumbly. Add the vegetables and fry until tender, stirring frequently. Add the rice and fry, stirring continuously, until heated through and coated in the sauces.

Fried Rice with Beef and Onions

Serves 4

450 g/1 lb lean beef, thinly sliced
45 ml/3 tbsp soy sauce
15 ml/1 tbsp rice wine or dry sherry
salt and freshly ground pepper
15 ml/1 tbsp cornflour (cornstarch)
45 ml/3 tbsp groundnut (peanut) oil
1 onion, chopped
225 g/8 oz cooked long-grain rice

Marinate the beef in the soy sauce, wine or sherry, salt, pepper and cornflour for 15 minutes. Heat the oil and fry the onion until lightly browned. Add the beef and marinade and stir-fry for 3 minutes. Add the rice and stir-fry until heated through.

Chicken Fried Rice

Serves 4

225 g/8 oz/1 cup long-grain rice
750 ml/1¼ pts/3 cups water
30 ml/2 tbsp groundnut (peanut) oil
2 cloves garlic, crushed
pinch of salt
1 onion, finely chopped
3 spring onions (scallions), chopped
100 g/4 oz cooked chicken, shredded
15 ml/1 tbsp soy sauce

Place the rice and water in a saucepan, bring to the boil, cover and simmer for about 20 minutes until the rice is cooked. Drain well. Heat the oil and fry the garlic and salt until the garlic turns light golden. Add the onion and stir-fry for 1 minute. Add the rice and stir-fry for 2 minutes. Add the spring onions and chicken and stir-fry for 2 minutes. Stir in the soy sauce until the rice is covered.

Duck Fried Rice

Serves 4

4 Chinese dried mushrooms
45 ml/3 tbsp groundnut (peanut) oil
2 spring onions (scallions), sliced
225 g/8 oz Chinese cabbage, shredded
100 g/4 oz cooked duck, shredded
45 ml/3 tbsp soy sauce
15 ml/1 tbsp rice wine or dry sherry
350 g/12 oz cooked long-grain rice
45 ml/3 tbsp chicken stock

Soak the mushrooms in warm water for 30 minutes then drain. Discard the stalks and chop the caps. Heat half the oil and fry the spring onions until translucent. Add the Chinese cabbage and stir-fry for 1 minute. Add the duck, soy sauce and wine or sherry and stir-fry for 3 minutes. Remove from the pan. Heat the remaining oil and stir-fry the rice until coated with oil. Add the stock, bring to the boil and stir-fry for 2 minutes. Return the duck mixture to the pan and stir until heated through before serving.

Ham Fried Rice

Serves 4

30 ml/2 tbsp groundnut (peanut) oil
1 egg, beaten
1 clove garlic, crushed
350 g/12 oz cooked long-grain rice
1 onion, finely chopped
1 green pepper, chopped
100 g/4 oz ham, chopped
50 g/2 oz water chestnuts, sliced
50 g/2 oz bamboo shoots, chopped
15 ml/1 tbsp soy sauce
15 ml/1 tbsp rice wine or dry sherry
15 ml/1 tbsp oyster sauce

Heat a little of the oil in a pan and add the egg, tilting the pan so that it spreads across the pan. Cook until the underside is lightly browned, then turn it and cook the other side. Remove it from the pan and cut it in and fry the garlic until lightly browned. Add the rice, onion and pepper and stir-fry for 3 minutes. Add the ham, waterchestnuts and bamboo shoots and stir-fry for 5 minutes. Add the remaining ingredients and stir-fry for about 4 minutes. Serve sprinkled with the egg strips.

Smoked Ham Rice with Stock

Serves 4

30 ml/2 tbsp groundnut (peanut) oil
3 eggs, beaten
350 g/12 oz cooked longgrain rice
600 ml/1 pt/2½ cups chicken stock
100 g/4 oz smoked ham, shredded
100 g/4 oz bamboo shoots, sliced

Heat the oil then pour in the eggs. When they begin to set, add the rice and stir fry for 2 minutes. Add the stock and ham and bring to the boil. Simmer for 2 minutes then add the bamboo shoots and serve.

Pork Fried Rice

Serves 4

45 ml/3 tbsp groundnut (peanut) oil
3 spring onions (scallions), chopped
100 g/4 oz roast pork, diced
350 g/12 oz cooked long-grain rice
30 ml/2 tbsp soy sauce
2.5 ml/½ tsp salt
2 eggs, beaten

Heat the oil and stir-fry the spring onions until translucent. Add the pork and stir until coated with oil. Add the rice, soy sauce and salt and stir-fry for 3 minutes. Add the eggs and fold in until they begin to set.

Pork and Prawn Fried Rice

Serves 4

45 ml/3 tbsp groundnut (peanut) oil
2.5 ml/½ tsp salt
2 spring onions (scallions), chopped
350 g/12 oz cooked long-grain rice
100 g/4 oz roast pork
225 g/8 oz peeled prawns
50 g/2 oz Chinese leaves, shredded
45 ml/3 tbsp soy sauce

Heat the oil and fry the salt and spring onions until lightly browned. Add the rice and stir-fry to break up the grains. Add the pork and stir-fry for 2 minutes. Add the prawns, Chinese leaves and soy sauce and stir-fry until heated through.

Prawn Fried Rice

Serves 4

225 g/8 oz/1 cup long-grain rice
750 ml/1¼ pts/3 cups water
30 ml/2 tbsp groundnut (peanut) oil
2 cloves garlic, crushed
pinch of salt
1 onion, finely chopped
225 g/8 oz peeled prawns
5 ml/1 tsp soy sauce

Place the rice and water in a saucepan, bring to the boil, cover and simmer for about 20 minutes until the rice is cooked. Drain well. Heat the oil with the garlic and salt and fry until the garlic turns light golden. Add the rice and onion and stir-fry for 2 minutes. Add the prawns and stir-fry for 2 minutes. Stir in the soy sauce before serving.

Fried Rice and Peas

Serves 4

30 ml/2 tbsp groundnut (peanut) oil
2 cloves garlic, crushed
5 ml/1 tsp salt
350 g/12 oz cooked long-grain rice
225 g/8 oz blanched or frozen peas, thawed
4 spring onions (scallions), finely chopped
30 ml/2 tbsp finely chopped fresh parsley

Heat the oil and fry the garlic and salt until lightly browned. Add the rice and stir-fry for 2 minutes. Add the peas, onions and parsley and stir-fry for a few minutes until heated through. Serve hot or cold.

Salmon Fried Rice

Serves 4

30 ml/2 tbsp groundnut (peanut) oil
2 cloves garlic, chopped
2 spring onions (scallions), sliced
50 g/2 oz salmon, chopped
75 g/3 oz spinach, chopped
150 g/5 oz cooked long-grain rice

Heat the oil and fry the garlic and spring onions for 30 seconds. Add the salmon and fry for 1 minute. Add the spinach and fry for 1 minute. Add the rice and stir-fry until heated through and well mixed.

Special Fried Rice

Serves 4

60 ml/4 tbsp groundnut (peanut) oil
1 onion, finely chopped
100 g/4 oz bacon, chopped
50 g/2 oz ham, chopped
50 g/2 oz cooked chicken, shredded
50 g/2 oz peeled prawns
60 ml/4 tbsp soy sauce
30 ml/2 tbsp rice wine or dry sherry
salt and freshly ground pepper
15 ml/1 tbsp cornflour (cornstarch)
225 g/8 oz cooked long grain rice
2 eggs, beaten
100 g/4 oz mushrooms, sliced
50 g/2 oz frozen peas

Heat the oil and fry the onion and bacon until lightly browned. Add the ham and chicken and stir-fry for 2 minutes. Add the prawns, soy sauce, wine or sherry, salt, pepper and cornflour and stir-fry for 2 minutes. Add the rice and stir-fry for 2 minutes. Add the eggs, mushrooms and peas and stir-fry for 2 minutes until hot.

Ten Precious Rice

Serves 6–8

45 ml/3 tbsp groundnut (peanut) oil
1 spring onion (scallion), chopped
100 g/4 oz lean pork, shredded
1 chicken breast, shredded
100 g/4 oz ham, shredded
30 ml/2 tbsp soy sauce
30 ml/2 tbsp rice wine or dry sherry
5 ml/1 tsp salt
350 g/12 oz cooked long grain rice
250 ml/8 fl oz/1 cup chicken stock
100 g/4 oz bamboo shoots, cut into strips
50 g/2 oz water chestnuts, sliced

Heat the oil and fry the spring onion until translucent. Add the pork and stir-fry for 2 minutes. Add the chicken and ham and stir-fry for 2 minutes. Stir in the soy sauce, sherry and salt. Stir in the rice and stock and bring to the boil. Add the bamboo shoots and water chestnuts, cover and simmer for 30 minutes.

Fried Tuna Rice

Serves 4

30 ml/2 tbsp groundnut (peanut) oil
2 onions, sliced
1 green pepper, chopped
450 g/1 lb/3 cups cooked long grain rice
salt
3 eggs, beaten
300 g/12 oz canned tuna, flaked
30 ml/2 tbsp soy sauce
2 shallots, finely chopped

Heat the oil and fry the onions until soft. Add the pepper and fry for 1 minute. Push to one side of the pan. Add the rice, sprinkle with salt and stir-fry for 2 minutes, gradually mixing in the pepper and onions. Make a well in the centre of the rice, pour in a little more oil and pour in the eggs. Stir until almost scrambled and mix in with the rice. Cook for a further 3 minutes. Add the tuna and soy sauce and heat through thoroughly. Serve sprinkled with the chopped shallots.

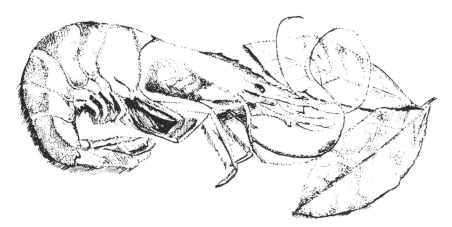

Noodles and Pastry

Noodles are often served with a Chinese meal instead of, or aswell as a rice dish. You can often substitute noodles in rice dishes and they will taste equally delicious. You will also find many other classic dishes, such as Chow Mein, in the relevant chapters of the book.

Wonton skins and other Chinese pastries are available from supermarkets and Oriental stores, but it can be fun to make your own.

Boiled Egg Noodles

Serves 4

10 ml/2 tsp salt
450 g/1 lb egg noodles
30 ml/2 tbsp groundnut (peanut) oil

Bring a pan of water to the boil, add the salt and toss in the noodles. Return to the boil and boil for about 10 minutes until tender but still firm. Drain well, rinse in cold water, drain, then rinse in hot water. Toss with the oil before serving.

Steamed Egg Noodles

Serves 4

10 ml/2 tsp salt
450 g/1 lb thin egg noodles

Bring a saucepan of water to the boil, add the salt and toss inthe noodles. Stir well then drain. Arrange the noodles in a colander, place in a steamer and steam over boiling water for about 20 minutes until just tender.

Tossed Noodles

10 ml/2 tsp salt
450 g/1 lb egg noodles
30 ml/2 tbsp groundnut (peanut) oil
stir-fried dish

Bring a saucepan of water to the boil, add the salt and toss inthe noodles. Return to the boil and boil for about 10 minutes until tender but still firm. Drain well, rinse in cold water, drain, then rinse in hot water. Toss with the oil then toss gently with any stir-fried mixture and heat through gently to blend the flavours together.

Fried Noodles

Serves 4

225 g/8 oz thin egg noodles
salt
oil for deepfrying

Cook the noodles in boiling salted water according to the instructions on the packet. Drain well. Arrange several layers of kitchen paper on a baking sheet, spread out the noodles and leave to dry for several hours. Heat the oil and fry spoonfuls of the noodles at a time for about 30 seconds until golden. Drain on kitchen paper.

Soft-Fried Noodles

Serves 4

350 g/12 oz egg noodles
75 ml/5 tbsp groundnut (peanut) oil
salt

Bring a pan of water to the boil, add the noodles and boil until the noodles are just tender. Drain and rinse in cold water, then hot water then drain again. Toss in 15 ml/1 tbsp of oil then leave to cool and chill in the refrigerator. Heat the remaining oil almost to smoking point. Add the noodles and stir gently until coated with oil. Reduce the heat and continue to stir for a few minutes until the noodles are golden brown on the outside but soft inside.

Stewed Noodles

Serves 4

450 g/1 lb egg noodles
5 ml/1 tsp salt
30 ml/2 tbsp groundnut (peanut) oil
3 spring onions (scallions), cut into strips
1 clove garlic, crushed
2 slices ginger root, minced
100 g/4 oz lean pork, cut into strips
100 g/4 oz ham, cut into strips
100 g/4 oz peeled prawns
450 ml/¾ pt/2 cups chicken stock
30 ml/2 tbsp soy sauce

Bring a pan of water to the boil, add the salt and toss in the noodles. Return to the boil and boil for about 5 minutes then drain and rinse in cold water.

Meanwhile, heat the oil and fry the spring onions, garlic and ginger until lightly browned. Add the pork and stir-fry until lightly coloured. Add the ham and prawns and stir in the stock, soy sauce and noodles. Bring to the boil, cover and simmer for 10 minutes.

Cold Noodles

Serves 4

450 g/1 lb egg noodles
5 ml/1 tsp salt
15 ml/1 tbsp groundnut (peanut) oil
225 g/8 oz bean sprouts
225 g/8 oz roast pork, shredded
1 cucumber, cut into strips
12 radishes, cut into strips

Bring a pan of water to the boil, add the salt and toss in the noodles. Return to the boil and boil for about 10 minutes until tender but still firm. Drain well, rinse in cold water then drain again. Toss with the oil then arrange in a serving dish. Arrange the other ingredients in small dishes surrounding the noodles. Guests serve a selection of ingredients into small bowls.

Noodle Baskets

Serves 4

225 g/8 oz thin egg noodles
salt
oil for deep-frying

Cook the noodles in boiling salted water according to the instructions on the packet. Drain well. Arrange several layers of kitchen paper on a baking sheet, spread out the noodles and leave to dry for several hours. Brush the inside of a medium-sized strainer with a little oil. Spread an even layer of noodles about 1 cm/½ in thick in the strainer. Brush the outside of a smaller strainer with oil and press lightly into the larger one. Heat the oil, lower the two strainers into the oil and fry for about 1 minute until the noodles are golden. Carefully remove the strainers, running a knife around the edges of the noodles if necessary to loosen them.

Noodle Pancake

Serves 4

225 g/8 oz egg noodles
5 ml/1 tsp salt
75 ml/5 tbsp groundnut (peanut) oil

Bring a saucepan of water to the boil, add the salt and toss in the noodles. Return to the boil and boil for about 10 minutes until tender but still firm. Drain well, rinse in cold water, drain, then rinse in hot water. Toss with 15 ml/1 tbsp of oil. Heat the remaining oil. Add the noodles to the pan to make a thick pancake. Fry until lightly browned on the underside then turn and fry until lightly browned but soft in the centre.

Braised Noodles

Serves 4

4 dried Chinese mushrooms
450 g/1 lb egg noodles
30 ml/2 tbsp groundnut (peanut) oil
5 ml/1 tsp salt
3 spring onions (scallions), chopped
100 g/4 oz lean pork, cut into strips
100 g/4 oz cauliflower florets
15 ml/1 tbsp cornflour (cornstarch)
250 ml/8 fl oz/1 cup chicken stock
15 ml/1 tbsp sesame oil

Soak the mushrooms in warm water for 30 minutes then drain. Discard the stalks and slice the caps. Bring a saucepan of water to the boil, add the noodles and boil for 5 minutes then drain. Heat the oil and fry the salt and spring onions for 30 seconds. Add the pork and stir-fry until lightly coloured. Add the cauliflower and mushrooms and stir-fry for 3 minutes. Mix the cornflour and stock, stir it into the pan, bring to the boil, cover and simmer for 10 minutes, stirring occasionally. Heat the sesame oil in a separate pan, add the noodles and stir gently over a medium heat until lightly browned. Transfer to a warmed serving dish, pour over the pork mixture and serve.

Beef Noodles

Serves 4

350 g/12 oz egg noodles

45 ml/3 tbsp groundnut (peanut) oil

450 g/1 lb minced (ground) beef

salt and freshly ground pepper

1 clove garlic, crushed

1 onion, finely chopped

250 ml/8 fl oz/1 cup beef stock

100 g/4 oz mushrooms, sliced

2 stalks celery, chopped

1 green pepper, chopped

30 ml/2 tbsp cornflour (cornstarch)

60 ml/4 tbsp water

15 ml/1 tbsp soy sauce

Cook the noodles in boiling water for about 8 minutes until just tender then drain. Meanwhile, heat the oil and fry the beef, salt, pepper, garlic and onion until lightly browned. Add the stock, mushrooms, celery and pepper, bring to the boil, cover and simmer for 5 minutes. Blend the cornflour, water and soy sauceto a paste, stir into the pan and simmer, stirring, until the sauce thickens. Arrange the noodles on a warmed serving plateand pour over the beef and sauce.

Noodles with Chicken

Serves 4

350 g/12 oz egg noodles

100 g/4 oz bean sprouts

45 ml/3 tbsp groundnut (peanut) oil

2.5 ml/½ tsp salt

2 cloves garlic, minced

2 spring onions (scallions), chopped

100 g/4 oz cooked chicken, diced

5 ml/1 tsp sesame oil

Bring a saucepan of water to the boil, add the noodles and boil until they are just tender. Blanch the bean sprouts in boiling water for 3 minutes then drain. Heat the oil and fry the salt, garlic and spring onions until softened. Add the chicken and stir-fry until heated through. Add the bean sprouts and heat through. Drain the noodles well, rinse in cold water then hot water. Toss in sesame oil and arrange on a warmed serving plate. Top with the chicken mixture and serve.

Noodles with Crab Meat

Serves 4

350 g/12 oz egg noodles

45 ml/3 tbsp groundnut (peanut) oil

3 spring onions (scallions), chopped

2 slices ginger root, cut into strips

350 g/12 oz crab meat, flaked

5 ml/1 tsp salt

15 ml/1 tbsp rice wine or dry sherry

15 ml/1 tbsp cornflour (cornstarch)

30 ml/2 tbsp water

30 ml/2 tbsp wine vinegar

Bring a pan of water to the boil, add the noodles and boil for 10 minutes until just tender. Mean-while, heat 30 ml/2 tbsp of the oil and fry the spring onions and ginger until lightly browned. Add the crab meat and salt, stir-fry for 2 minutes. Add the wine or sherry stir-fry for 1 minute. Mix the cornflour and water to a paste, stir it into the pan and simmer, stirring, until thickened. Drain the noodles and rinse in cold water then hot water. Toss in the remaining oil and arrange on a warmed serving plate. Top with the crab meat mixture and serve sprinkled with wine vinegar.

Noodles in Curry Sauce

Serves 4

450 g/1 lb egg noodles
5 ml/1 tsp salt
30 ml/2 tbsp curry powder
1 onion, sliced
75 ml/5 tbsp chicken stock
100 g/4 oz roast pork, shredded
120 ml/4 fl oz/½ cup tomato ketchup (catsup)
15 ml/1 tbsp hoisin sauce
salt and freshly ground pepper

Bring a pan of water to the boil, add the salt and toss in the noodles. Return to the boil and boil for about 10 minutes until tender but still firm. Drain well, rinse in cold water, drain,then rinse in hot water. Meanwhile, cook the curry powder in adry pan for 2 minutes, shaking the pan. Add the onion and stir until well coated. Stir in the stock then add the pork and bring to the boil. Stir in the tomato ketchup, hoisin sauce, salt and pepper and simmer, stirring, until heated through. Arrange the noodles in a warmed serving dish, pour over the sauce and serve.

Dan-Dan Noodles

Serves 4

100 g/4 oz egg noodles
45 ml/3 tbsp mustard
60 ml/4 tbsp sesame sauce
60 ml/4 tbsp groundnut (peanut) oil
20 ml/4 tsp salt
4 spring onions (scallions), minced
60 ml/4 tbsp soy sauce
60 ml/4 tbsp peanuts, ground
60 ml/4 tbsp chicken stock

Cook the noodles in boiling water for about 10 minutes until tender then drain well. Mix together the remaining ingredients, pour over the noodles and toss together well before serving.

Noodles with Egg Sauce

Serves 4

225 g/8 oz egg noodles
750 ml/1¼ pts/3 cups chicken stock
45 ml/3 tbsp soy sauce
45 ml/3 tbsp rice wine or dry sherry
15 ml/1 tbsp groundnut (peanut) oil
3 spring onions (scallions), cut into strips
3 eggs, beaten

Bring a pan of water to the boil, add the noodles, bring back to the boil and simmer for 10 minutes until just tender. Drain and arrange in a warmed serving bowl. Meanwhile, bring the stock to the boil with the soy sauce and wine or sherry. In a separate pan, heat the oil and fry the spring onions until softened. Add the eggs then stir in the hot stock and continue to stir over a medium heat until the mixture comes to the boil. Pour the sauce over the noodles and serve.

Ginger and Spring Onion Noodles

Serves 4

900 ml/1½ pts/4¼ cups chicken stock
15 ml/1 tbsp groundnut (peanut) oil
225 g/8 oz egg noodles
2.5 ml/½ tsp sesame oil
4 spring onions (scallions), shredded
2 slices ginger root, shredded
15 ml/1 tbsp oyster sauce

Bring the stock to the boil, add the oil and noodles and simmer, uncovered, for about 15 minutes until tender. Transfer the noodles to a warmed serving plate and add the sesame oil, spring onions and ginger to the wok. Simmer, uncovered, for 5 minutes until the vegetables are slightly softened and the stock reduced. Spoon the vegetables over the noodles with a little of the stock. Sprinkle with oyster sauce and serve at once.

Hot and Sour Noodles

Serves 4

225 g/8 oz egg noodles
15 ml/1 tbsp soy sauce
15 ml/1 tbsp chilli oil
15 l/1 tbsp red wine vinegar
1 clove garlic, crushed
2 spring onions (scallions), minced
5 ml/1 tsp freshly ground pepper

Cook the noodles in boiling water for about 10 minutes until tender. Drain well and transfer to a warmed serving dish. Mix together the remaining ingredients, pour over the noodles and toss together well before serving.

Noodles in Meat Sauce

Serves 4

4 dried Chinese mushrooms
30 ml/2 tbsp groundnut (peanut) oil
225 g/8 oz lean pork, sliced
100 g/4 oz mushrooms, sliced
4 spring onions (scallions), sliced
15 ml/1 tbsp soy sauce
15 ml/1 tbsp rice wine or dry sherry
600 ml/1 pt/2½ cups chicken stock
350 g/12 oz egg noodles
30 ml/2 tbsp cornflour (cornstarch)
2 eggs, lightly beaten
salt and freshly ground pepper

Soak the mushrooms in warm water for 30 minutes then drain. Discard the stalks and slice the caps. Heat the oil and fry the pork until lightly coloured. Add the dried and fresh mushrooms and spring onions and stir-fry for 2 minutes. Add the soy sauce, wine or sherry and stock, bring to the boil, cover and simmer for 30 minutes.

Meanwhile, bring a pan of water to the boil, add the noodles and boil for about 10 minutes until the noodles are tender but still firm. Drain, rinse in cold then hot water then drain again and arrange on in a warmed serving dish. Blend the cornflour with a little water, stir it into the pan and simmer, stirring, until the sauce clears and thickens. Gradually stir in the eggs and season with salt and pepper. Pour the sauce over the noodles to serve.

Noodles with Poached Eggs

Serves 4

350 g/12 oz rice noodles
4 eggs
30 ml/2 tbsp groundnut (peanut) oil
1 clove garlic, minced
100 g/4 oz cooked ham, finely chopped
45 ml/3 tbsp tomato purée (paste)
120 ml/4 fl oz/½ cup water
5 ml/1 tsp sugar
5 ml/1 tsp salt
soy sauce

Bring a pan of water to the boil, add the noodles and simmer for about 8 minutes until just cooked. Drain and rinse in cold water. Arrange in nest shapes on a warmed serving plate. Meanwhile, poach the eggs and place one on each nest. Heat the oil and stir fry the garlic for 30 seconds. Add the ham and stir-fry for 1 minute. Add all the remaining ingredients except the soy sauce and stir-fry until heated through. Pour over the eggs, sprinkle with soy sauce and serve at once.

Noodles with Pork and Vegetables

Serves 4

350 g/12 oz rice noodles
75 ml/5 tbsp groundnut (peanut) oil
225 g/8 oz lean pork, shredded
100 g/4 oz bamboo shoots, shredded
100 g/4 oz Chinese cabbage, shredded
450 ml/¾ pt/2 cups chicken stock
10 ml/2 tsp cornflour (cornstarch)
45 ml/3 tbsp water

Parboil the noodles for about 6 minutes until cooked but still firm then drain. Heat 45 ml/3 tbsp of oil and stir-fry the pork for 2 minutes. Add the bamboo shoots and cabbage and stir-fry for 1 minute. Add the stock, bring to the boil, cover and simmer for 4 minutes. Mix the cornflour and water, stir it into the pan and simmer, stirring, until the sauce thickens. Heat the remaining oil and fry the noodles until lightly browned. Transfer to a warmed serving plate, top with the pork mixture and serve.

Transparent Noodles with Minced Pork

Serves 4

200 g/7 oz transparent noodles
oil for deep-frying
75 ml/5 tbsp groundnut (peanut) oil
225 g/8 oz minced (ground) pork
25 g/1 oz chilli bean paste
2 spring onions (scallions), chopped
1 clove garlic, chopped
1 slice ginger root, chopped
5 ml/1 tsp chilli powder
250 ml/8 fl oz/1 cup chicken stock
30 ml/2 tbsp rice wine or dry sherry
30 ml/2 tbsp soy sauce
salt

Heat the oil until boiling and deepfry the noodles until they expand. Remove and drain. Heat the 75 ml/5 tbsp of oil and fry the pork until browned. Stir in the bean paste, spring onions, garlic, ginger and chilli powder and fry for 2 minutes. Mix in the stock, wine or sherry, soy sauce and noodles and simmer until the sauce thickens. Season to taste with salt before serving.

Egg Roll Skins

Makes 12

225 g/8 oz/2 cups plain (allpurpose)
    flour

1 egg, beaten

2.5 ml/½ tsp salt

120 ml/4 fl oz/½ cup iced water

Mix all the ingredients together then
knead until smooth and elastic.
Cover with a damp cloth and chill for
30 minutes. Roll out on a floured surface until paper thin then cut into
squares.

Cooked Egg Roll Skins

Makes 12

175 g/6 oz/1½ cups plain (all-purpose)
    flour

2.5 ml½ tsp salt

2 eggs, beaten

375 ml/13 fl oz/1½ cups water

Mix the flour and salt then blend in
the eggs. Gradually add the water to
make a smooth batter. Lightly grease
a small frying pan then pour in 30
ml/2 tbsp of batter and tilt the pan to
spread it evenly over the surface.
When the dough shrinks from the
sides of the pan, remove it and cover
with a damp cloth while you cook the
remaining skins.

Chinese Pancakes

Serves 4

250 ml/8 fl oz/1 cup water

225 g/8 oz/2 cups plain (allpurpose)
    flour

groundnut (peanut) oil for frying

Boil the water then gradually add the
flour. Knead lightly until the dough
is soft, cover with a damp cloth and
leave to stand for 15 minutes. Roll
out on a floured surface and shape
into a long cylinder. Cut into 2.5 cm/
1 in slices then flatten until about 5
mm/¼ in thick and brush the tops
with oil. Stack in pairs with the oiled
surfaces touching and dust the outsides lightly with flour. Roll out the
pairs to about 10 cm/4 in across and
cookin pairs for about 1 minute on
each side until lightly browned.
Separate and stack until ready to
serve.

Wonton Skins

Makes about 40

450 g/1 lb/2 cups plain (all-purpose)
    flour

5 ml/1 tsp salt

1 egg, beaten

45 ml/3 tbsp water

Sift the flour and salt then make a
well in the centre. Blend in the egg,
sprinkle with water and knead the
mixture to a smooth dough. Place in a
bowl, cover with a damp cloth and
chill for 1 hour.

Roll out the dough on a floured
surface until it is wafer thin and even.
Cut into 7.5 cm/3 in strips, dust lightly with flour and stack then cut into
squares. Cover with a damp cloth
until ready to use.

Vegetables

Many Chinese recipes include a range of vegetables in the main dish, but you can prepare simple vegetables in a Chinese style to make a sidedish to accompany a meat course, or as attractive and delicious meals in their own right.

Asparagus with Clams

Serves 4

120 ml/4 fl oz/½ cup groundnut (peanut) oil

1 red chilli pepper, cut into strips

2 spring onions (scallions), cut into strips

2 slices ginger root, shredded

225 g/8 oz asparagus, cut into pieces

30 ml/2 tbsp thick soy sauce

2.5 ml/½ tsp sesame oil

225 g/8 oz clams, soaked and scrubbed

Heat the oil and stir-fry the chilli pepper, spring onions and ginger for 30 seconds. Add the asparagus and soy sauce, cover and simmer until the asparagus is almost tender. Add the sesame oil and clams, cover and cook until the clams open. Discard any clams that have not opened and serve at once.

Asparagus with Egg Sauce

Serves 4

450 g/1 lb asparagus

45 ml/3 tbsp groundnut (peanut) oil

30 ml/2 tbsp rice wine or dry sherry

salt

250 ml/8 fl oz/1 cup chicken stock

15 ml/1 tbsp cornflour (cornstarch)

1 egg, lightly beaten

Trim the asparagus and cut into 5 cm/2 in pieces. Heat the oil and stir-fry the asparagus for about 4 minutes until tender but still crisp. Sprinkle with wine or sherry and salt. Meanwhile, bring the stock and cornflour to the boil, stirring, and season with salt. Mix a little of the warm stock into the egg, then mix the egg into the pan and simmer, stirring, until the sauce thickens. Arrange the asparagus on a warmed serving plate, pour over the sauce and serve at once.

Asparagus with Mushrooms and Spring Onions

Serves 4

10 dried Chinese mushrooms

225 g/8 oz asparagus

1 bunch spring onions (scallions), trimmed

600 ml/1 pt/2½ cups chicken stock

5 ml/1 tsp cornflour (cornstarch)

15 ml/1 tbsp water

5 ml/1 tsp salt

Soak the mushrooms in warm water for 30 minutes then drain. Discard the stalks. Arrange the mushrooms in the centre of a strainer then arrange the spring onions and asparagus in a circle radiating out from the centre. Bring the stock to the boil then lower the strainer into the stock, cover and simmer gently for about 10 minutes until the vegetables are just tender. Remove the vegetables and invert them on to a warmed serving plate to maintain the pattern. Bring the stock to the boil. Blend the water, cornflour and salt to a paste, stir it into the stock and simmer, stirring, until the sauce thickens slightly. Spoon over the vegetables and serve at once.

Asparagus Stir-Fry

Serves 4

45 ml/3 tbsp groundnut (peanut) oil

1 spring onion (scallion), chopped

450 g/1 lb asparagus

30 ml/2 tbsp soy sauce

5 ml/1 tsp sugar

120 ml/4 fl oz/½ cup chicken stock

5 ml/1 tsp cornflour (cornstarch)

Heat the oil and fry the spring onion until lightly browned. Add the asparagus and stir-fry for 3 minutes. Add the remaining ingredients and stir-fry for 4 minutes.

Sweet and Sour Asparagus

Serves 4

30 ml/2 tbsp groundnut (peanut) oil

450 g/1 lb asparagus, cut in diagonal pieces

60 ml/4 tbsp wine vinegar

50 g/2 oz/¼ cup brown sugar

15 ml/1 tbsp soy sauce

15 ml/1 tbsp rice wine or dry sherry

5 ml/1 tsp salt

15 ml/1 tbsp cornflour (cornstarch)

Heat the oil and stir-fry the asparagus for 4 minutes. Add the wine vinegar, sugar, soy sauce, wine or sherry and salt and stir-fry for 2 minutes. Mix the cornflour with a little water, stir it into the pan and stir-fry for 1 minute.

Aubergine with Basil

Serves 4

60 ml/4 tbsp groundnut (peanut) oil

2 aubergines (eggplants)

60 ml/4 tbsp water

2 cloves garlic, crushed

1 red chilli pepper, diagonally sliced

45 ml/3 tbsp soy sauce

1 large bunch basil

Heat the oil and fry the aubergine until lightly browned. Add the water, garlic, chilli pepper and soy sauce and stir-fry until the aubergine changes colour. Add the basil and stir-fry until the leaves are wilted. Serve at once.

Braised Aubergine

Serves 4

1 aubergine (eggplant)

oil for deep-frying

15 ml/1 tbsp groundnut (peanut) oil

3 spring onions (scallions), chopped

1 slice ginger root, chopped

90 ml/6 tbsp chicken stock

15 ml/1 tbsp rice wine or dry sherry

15 ml/1 tbsp soy sauce

15 ml/1 tbsp black bean sauce

15 ml/1 tbsp brown sugar

Peel the aubergine and cut it into large cubes. Heat the oil and deep-fry the aubergine until soft and lightly browned. Remove and drain well.

Heat the oil and fry the spring onions and ginger until lightly browned. Add the aubergine and stir well. Add the stock, wine or sherry, soy sauce, black bean sauce and sugar. Stir-fry for 2 minutes.

Braised Aubergine with Tomatoes

Serves 4

6 slices bacon

2 cloves garlic, crushed

2 spring onions (scallions), chopped

1 aubergine (eggplant), peeled and diced

4 tomatoes, skinned and quartered

salt and freshly ground pepper

Cut the rind off the bacon and cut into chunks. Fry until lightly browned. Add the garlic and spring onions and stir-fry for 2 minutes. Add the aubergine and stir-fry for about 5 minutes until slightly soft. Carefully mix in the tomatoes and season with salt and pepper. Stir gently over a low heat until heated through.

Steamed Aubergine

Serves 4

1 aubergine (eggplant)

30 ml/2 tbsp soy sauce

5 ml/1 tsp groundnut (peanut) oil

Score the aubergine skin a few times and place it in an ovenproof dish. Place on a rack in a steamer and steam over gently simmering water for about 25 minutes until soft. Leave to cool slightly then peel off the skin and tear the flesh into shreds. Sprinkle with soy sauce and oil and stir well. Serve hot or cold.

Stuffed Aubergine

Serves 4

4 dried Chinese mushrooms
225 g/8 oz minced (ground) pork
2 spring onions (scallions), minced
1 slice ginger root, minced
30 ml/2 tbsp soy sauce
15 ml/1 tbsp rice wine or dry sherry
5 ml/1 tsp sugar
1 aubergine (eggplant), halved lengthways

Soak the mushrooms in warm water for 30 minutes then drain. Discard the stalks and chop the caps. Mix with the pork, spring onions, ginger, soy sauce, wine or sherry and sugar. Scoop out the seeds of the aubergine to make a hollow shape. Stuff with the pork mixture and arrange in an ovenproof dish. Place on a rack in a steamer and steam over gently simmering water for 30 minutes until tender.

Stir-Fried Aubergine

Serves 4–6

4 dried Chinese mushrooms
1 aubergine (eggplant), peeled and diced
30 ml/2 tbsp cornflour (cornstarch)
oil for deep-frying
45 ml/3 tbsp groundnut (peanut) oil
50 g/2 oz cooked chicken, diced
50 g/2 oz smoked ham, diced
50 g/2 oz bamboo shoots, chopped
50 g/2 oz/¼ cup chopped mixed nuts
5 ml/1 tsp salt
5 ml/1 tsp sugar
30 ml/2 tbsp soy sauce
30 ml/2 tbsp rice wine or dry sherry

Soak the mushrooms in warm water for 30 minutes then drain. Discard the stalks and slice the caps. Toss the aubergine lightly in cornflour. Heat the oil and deep-fry the aubergine until golden. Remove from the pan and drain well. Heat the oil and stir-fry the chicken, ham, bamboo shoots and nuts. Add the remaining ingredients and stir-fry for a 3 minutes. Return the aubergine to the pan and stir-fry until heated through.

Bamboo Shoots with Chicken

Serves 4

50 g/2 oz chicken meat, minced (ground)
50 g/2 oz smoked ham, minced (ground)
50 g/2 oz water chestnuts, minced (ground)
2 egg whites
15 ml/1 tbsp cornflour (cornstarch)
225 g/8 oz bamboo shoots, cut into thick strips
15 ml/1 tbsp chopped flat leaved parsley

Mix together the chicken, ham and water chestnuts. Mix together the egg whites and cornflour then stir them into the minced ingredients. Stir the bamboo shoots into the mixture until well coated then arrange in an ovenproof dish. Place on a rack in a steamer, cover and steam over gently simmering water for 15 minutes. Serve garnished with parsley.

Deep-Fried Bamboo Shoots

Serves 4

oil for deep-frying

225 g/8 oz bamboo shoots, cut into strips

15 ml/1 tbsp groundnut (peanut) oil

15 ml/1 tbsp brown sugar

15 ml/1 tbsp soy sauce

10 ml/2 tsp cornflour (cornstarch)

90 ml/6 tbsp water

Heat the oil and deep fry the bamboo shoots until golden. Drain well. Heat the groundnut (peanut) oil and stir-fry the bamboo shoots until coated with oil. Mix together the sugar, soy sauce, cornflour and water, stir into the pan and stir-fry until heated through.

Fried Bamboo Shoots

Serves 4

90 ml/6 tbsp groundnut (peanut) oil

1 spring onion, cut into strips

1 clove garlic, crushed

1 red chilli pepper, cut into strips

225 g/8 oz bamboo shoots

15 ml/1 tbsp thick soy sauce

2.5 ml/½ tsp sesame oil

Heat the oil and stir-fry the spring onion, garlic and chilli pepper for 30 seconds. Add the bamboo shoots and stir-fry until just tender and well coated in the spices. Add the soy sauce and sesame oil and stir-fry for a further 3 minutes. Serve at once.

Bamboo Shoots with Mushrooms

Serves 4

8 dried Chinese mushrooms

45 ml/3 tbsp groundnut (peanut) oil

350 g/12 oz bamboo shoots, cut into strips

30 ml/2 tbsp soy sauce

5 ml/1 tsp brown sugar

15 ml/1 tbsp cornflour (cornstarch)

45 ml/3 tbsp water

Soak the mushrooms in warm water for 30 minutes then drain. Discard the stalks and slice the caps. Heat the oil and stir-fry the mushrooms for 2 minutes. Add the bamboo shoots and stir-fry for 3 minutes. Add the soy sauce and sugar and stir well until heated through. Transfer the vegetables to a warmed serving plate using a slotted spoon. Mix the cornflour and water to a paste and stir it into the pan. Simmer, stirring, until the sauce clears and thickens then pour it over the vegetables and serve at once.

Bamboo Shoots with Dried Mushrooms

Serves 4

6 Chinese dried mushrooms
250 ml/8 fl oz/1 cup chicken stock
15 ml/1 tbsp rice wine or dry sherry
15 ml/1 tbsp soy sauce
15 ml/1 tbsp groundnut (peanut) oil
225 g/8 oz bamboo shoots, sliced
15 ml/1 tbsp cornflour (cornstarch)

Soak the mushrooms in warm water for 30 minutes then drain. Discard the stems and slice the caps. Place the mushroom caps in a pan with half the stock, the wine or sherry and soy sauce. Bring to the boil, cover and simmer for about 10 minutes until thick. Add the oil and stir over a medium heat for 2 minutes. Add the bamboo shoots and stir-fry for 3 minutes. Mix the cornflour into the remaining stock and stir it into the pan. Bring to the boil, stirring, then simmer for about 4 minutes until the sauce thickens and clears.

Bamboo Shoots in Oyster Sauce

Serves 4

15 ml/1 tbsp groundnut (peanut) oil
350 g/12 oz bamboo shoots, cut into
    strips
250 ml/8 fl oz/1 cup chicken stock
15 ml/1 tbsp oyster sauce
5 ml/1 tsp soy sauce
2.5 ml/½ tsp brown sugar
2.5 ml/½ tsp sesame oil

Heat the oil and stir-fry the bamboo shoots for 1 minute. Add the stock, oyster sauce, soy sauce and sugar and bring to the boil. Simmer for about 10 minutes until the bamboo shoots are tender and the liquid has reduced. Serve sprinkled with sesame oil.

Bamboo Shoots with Sesame Oil

Serves 4

100 g/4 oz bean sprouts
45 ml/3 tbsp groundnut (peanut) oil
225 g/8 oz bamboo shoots
5 ml/1 tsp salt
5 ml/1 tsp sesame oil

Cook the bean sprouts in boiling water for about 10 minutes until tender but still crisp. Drain well. Meanwhile, heat the oil and stir-fry the bamboo shoots for about 5 minutes until tender but still crisp. Sprinkle with salt, mix well then arrange with the bean sprouts on a warmed serving plate. Sprinkle with sesame oil and serve.

Bamboo Shoots with Spinach

Serves 4

45 ml/3 tbsp groundnut (peanut) oil
450 g/1 lb bamboo shoots
5 ml/1 tsp rice wine or dry sherry
pinch of salt
120 ml/4 fl oz/½ cup chicken stock
100 g/4 oz spinach
2.5 ml/½ tsp sesame oil

Photograph opposite: Rice Salad (page 342)

Heat the oil and fry the bamboo shoots for about 1 minute. Add the wine or sherry, salt and stock, bring to the boil and simmer for 3 minutes. Add the spinach and simmer until the spinach has wilted and the liquid reduced slightly. Transfer to a warmed serving bowl and serve sprinkled with sesame oil.

Broad Bean Sauté

Serves 4

---

450 g/1 lb shelled broad beans
60 ml/4 tbsp groundnut (peanut) oil
5 ml/1 tsp salt
10 ml/2 tsp brown sugar
75 ml/5 tbsp chicken stock
salt
2 spring onions (scallions), chopped

Place the beans in a pan, just cover with water, bring to the boil and simmer until tender. Drain well.

Heat the oil then add the beans and stir until well coated with oil. Add the sugar and stock and season to taste with salt. Stir-fry for 3 minutes. Stir in the spring onions and serve.

Green Beans with Chilli

Serves 4

---

45 ml/3 tbsp groundnut (peanut) oil
2 dried red chilli peppers
2 onions, chopped
450 g/1 lb green beans

Heat the oil with the chilli peppers and fry until they change colour then remove them from the pan. Add the onions and stir-fry until lightly browned. Meanwhile, blanch the beans in boiling water for 2 minutes then drain well. Add to the onions and stir-fry for 10 minutes until tender but still crisp and well coated in the spiced oil.

Spiced Green Beans

Serves 4

---

450 g/1 lb green beans
15 ml/1 tbsp salt
5 ml/1 tsp ground anise
5 ml/1 tsp freshly ground red pepper

Place all the ingredients in a large pan and just cover with water. Bring to the boil and simmer for about 8 minutes until the beans are just tender. Drain well before serving.

Stir-Fried Green Beans

Serves 4

---

45 ml/3 tbsp groundnut (peanut) oil
5 ml/1 tsp salt
450 g/1 lb string beans, cut into pieces
120 ml/4 fl oz/½ cup chicken stock
15 ml/1 tbsp soy sauce

Heat the oil and salt then add the beans and stir-fry for 2 minutes. Add the stock and soy sauce, bring to the boil, cover and simmer for about 5 minutes until the beans are tender but still slightly crisp.

Photograph opposite: Honeyed Bananas (page 345)

Sautéed Bean Sprouts

Serves 4

15 ml/1 tbsp groundnut (peanut) oil
450 g/1 lb bean sprouts
15 ml/1 tbsp soy sauce
salt and freshly ground pepper

Heat the oil and stir-fry the bean sprouts for about 3 minutes. Add the soy sauce, salt and pepper and stir together well. Cover and simmer for 5 minutes then remove the lid and simmer for a further 1 minute.

Bean Sprout Stir-Fry

Serves 4

15 ml/1 tbsp groundnut (peanut) oil
2.5 ml/½ tsp salt
1 clove garlic, crushed
450 g/1 lb bean sprouts
3 spring onions (scallions), chopped
60 ml/4 tbsp chicken stock
5 ml/1 tsp sugar
5 ml/1 tsp soy sauce

Heat the oil, salt and garlic until the garlic turns light golden. Add the bean sprouts and spring onions and stir-fry for 2 minutes. Add the remaining ingredients and stir-fry for a few minutes until all the liquid has evaporated.

Bean Sprouts and Celery

Serves 4

450 g/1 lb bean sprouts
45 ml/3 tbsp groundnut (peanut) oil
4 stalks celery, cut into strips
5 ml/1 tsp salt
15 ml/1 tbsp soy sauce
90 ml/6 tbsp chicken stock

Blanch the bean sprouts in boiling water for 3 minutes then drain. Heat the oil and stir-fry the celery for 1 minute. Add the bean sprouts and stir-fry for 1 minute. Add the remaining ingredients, bring to the boil, cover and simmer for 3 minutes before serving.

Bean Sprouts and Peppers

Serves 4

225 g/8 oz bean sprouts
45 ml/3 tbsp groundnut (peanut) oil
2 dried chilli peppers
1 slice ginger root, minced
1 red pepper, cut into strips
1 green pepper, cut into strips
90 ml/6 tbsp chicken stock

Blanch the bean sprouts in boiling water for 3 minutes then drain. Heat the oil and fry the whole chilli peppers for about 3 minutes then discard the peppers. Add the ginger and peppers to the pan and stir-fry for 3 minutes. Add the bean sprouts and stir-fry for 2 minutes. Add the stock, bring to the boil, cover and simmer for 3 minutes before serving.

Bean Sprouts with Pork

Serves 4

450 g/1 lb bean sprouts
100 g/4 oz lean pork, cut into strips
15 ml/1 tbsp cornflour (cornstarch)
15 ml/1 tbsp rice wine
15 ml/1 tbsp soy sauce
5 ml/1 tsp sugar
2.5 ml/½ tsp salt
30 ml/2 tbsp groundnut (peanut) oil
75 ml/5 tbsp chicken stock

Blanch the bean sprouts in boiling water for 3 minutes then drain. Toss the pork with the cornflour, wine or sherry, soy sauce, sugar and salt then leave to stand for 30 minutes. Heat half the oil and stir-fry the bean sprouts for 1 minute. Remove from the pan. Heat the remaining oil and stir-fry the pork until lightly browned. Add the stock, cover and simmer for 3 minutes. Return the bean sprouts to the pan and stir until heated through. Serve at once.

Broccoli Stir-Fry

Serves 4

45 ml/3 tbsp groundnut (peanut) oil
1 spring onion (scallion), chopped
450 g/1 lb broccoli florets
30 ml/2 tbsp soy sauce
5 ml/1 tsp sugar
120 ml/4 fl oz/½ cup chicken stock
5 ml/1 tsp cornflour (cornstarch)

Heat the oil and fry the spring onion until lightly browned. Add the broccoli and stir-fry for 3 minutes. Add the remaining ingredients and stir-fry for 2 minutes.

Broccoli in Brown Sauce

Serves 4

225 g/8 oz broccoli florets
30 ml/2 tbsp groundnut (peanut) oil
1 clove garlic, crushed
100 g/4 oz bamboo shoots, sliced
250 ml/8 fl oz/1 cup chicken stock
15 ml/1 tbsp soy sauce
15 ml/1 tbsp oyster sauce
15 ml/1 tbsp cornflour (cornstarch)
30 ml/2 tbsp rice wine or dry sherry

Parboil the broccoli in boiling water for 4 minutes then drain well. Heat the oil and fry the garlic until golden brown. Add the broccoli and bamboo shoots and stir-fry for 1 minute. Add the stock, soy sauce and oyster sauce, bring to the boil, cover and simmer for 4 minutes. Mix the cornflour and wine or sherry, stir it into the pan and simmer, stirring, until the sauce has thickened.

Cabbage with Bacon Shreds

Serves 4

350 g/12 oz cabbage, finely shredded
salt
3 slices streaky bacon, rinded and cut
    into strips
30 ml/2 tbsp groundnut (peanut) oil
2 cloves garlic
5 ml/1 tsp grated ginger root
5 ml/1 tsp sugar
120 ml/4 fl oz/½ cup chicken or
    vegetable stock

Sprinkle the cabbage with salt and leave to stand for 15 minutes. Fry the bacon until crisp. Heat the oil and fry the garlic until lightly browned then discard. Add the cabbage to the pan with the ginger and sugar and stir-fry for 2 minutes. Add the stock and bacon and stir-fry for a further 2 minutes. Serve with fried rice.

Creamed Cabbage

Serves 4

450 g/1 lb Chinese cabbage
45 ml/3 tbsp groundnut (peanut) oil
250 ml/8 fl oz/1 cup chicken stock
salt
15 ml/1 tbsp cornflour (cornstarch)
50 g/2 oz smoked ham, diced

Cut the cabbage into 5 cm/2 in strips. Heat the oil and stir-fry the cabbage for 3 minutes. Add the stock and season with salt. Bring to the boil, cover and simmer for 4 minutes. Mix the cornflour with a little water, stir it into the pan and simmer, stirring, until the sauce thickens. Transfer to a warmed serving plate and serve sprinkled with ham.

Chinese Cabbage with Mushrooms

Serves 4

6 dried Chinese mushrooms
45 ml/3 tbsp groundnut (peanut) oil
1 Chinese cabbage, diced
1 red pepper, diced
1 green pepper, diced
225 g/8 oz garlic sausage, diced
120 ml/4 fl oz/½ cup chicken stock
45 ml/3 tbsp wine vinegar
20 ml/4 tsp soy sauce
20 ml/4 tsp honey
5 ml/1 tsp cornflour (cornstarch)
salt and freshly ground pepper
20 ml/2 tbsp chopped chives

Soak the mushrooms in warm water for 30 minutes then drain. Discard the stalks and chop the caps. Heat the oil and stir-fry the mushrooms, cabbage and peppers for 5 minutes. Add the garlic sausage and fry briefly. Mix the stock with the wine vinegar, soy sauce, honey and cornflour. Stir into the pan and bring to the boil. Season with salt and pepper and simmer, stirring, until the sauce thickens. Serve sprinkled with chives.

Spicy Cabbage Stir-Fry

Serves 4

450 g/1 lb cabbage, shredded
30 ml/2 tbsp groundnut (peanut) oil
2 cloves garlic, crushed
1 slice ginger root, minced
15 ml/1 tbsp oyster sauce
15 ml/1 tbsp soy sauce
15 ml/1 tbsp chilli bean sauce
5 ml/1 tsp sesame oil

Blanch the cabbage in boiling salted water for 2 minutes. Drain well. Heat the oil and stir-fry the garlic and ginger for a few seconds until lightly browned. Add the cabbage and stir-fry for 2 minutes. Add the remaining ingredients and stir-fry for a further 2 minutes.

Sweet and Sour Cabbage

Serves 4

15 ml/1 tbsp groundnut (peanut) oil
1 head cabbage, shredded
5 ml/1 tsp salt
30 ml/2 tbsp wine vinegar
30 ml/2 tbsp sugar
15 ml/1 tbsp soy sauce
15 ml/1 tbsp cornflour (cornstarch)
45 ml/3 tbsp water

Heat the oil and stir-fry the cabbage for 3 minutes. Add the salt and continue to stir-fry until the cabbage is just tender. Blend the wine vinegar, sugar, soy sauce, cornflour and water to a paste, add it to the pan and simmer, stirring, until the sauce coats the cabbage.

Sweet and Sour Red Cabbage

Serves 4

30 ml/2 tbsp groundnut (peanut) oil
450 g/1 lb red cabbage, shredded
50 g/2 oz/¼ cup brown sugar
45 ml/3 tbsp wine vinegar
15 ml/1 tbsp soy sauce
5 ml/1 tsp salt
15 ml/1 tbsp cornflour (cornstarch)

Heat the oil and stir-fry the cabbage for 4 minutes. Add the sugar, wine vinegar, soy sauce and salt and stir-fry for 2 minutes. Mix the cornflour with a little water and stir-fry for 1 minute.

Crispy Seaweed

Serves 4

750 g/1½ lb spring greens, very finely shredded
Oil for deep-frying
5 ml/1 tsp salt
10 ml/2 tsp caster sugar

Rinse the greens then dry thoroughly. Heat the oil and deep-fry the greens in batches over a medium heat until they float to the surface. Remove from the oil and drain well on kitchen paper. Sprinkle with salt and sugar and toss together gently. Serve cold.

Carrots with Honey

Serves 4

1 kg/2 lb small spring carrots
20 ml/4 tsp groundnut (peanut) oil
20 ml/4 tsp unsalted butter
15 ml/1 tbsp water
10 ml/2 tsp honey
15 ml/1 tbsp chopped fresh coriander
100 g/4 oz pine kernels
salt and freshly ground pepper

Wash the carrots and cut the green down to 5 mm/¼ in. Heat the oil and butter, add the water and honey and bring to the boil. Add the carrots and cook for about 4 minutes. Add the coriander and pine kernels and season with salt and pepper.

Carrot and Pepper Stir-Fry

Serves 4

30 ml/2 tbsp groundnut (peanut) oil
2.5 ml/½ tsp salt
4 carrots, sliced
1 green pepper, cut into strips
30 ml/2 tbsp sugar
15 ml/1 tbsp wine vinegar
250 ml/8 fl oz/1 cup chicken tock
15 ml/1 tbsp cornflour (cornstarch)

Heat the oil and salt then add the carrots and pepper and stir-fry for 3 minutes. Add the sugar, wine vinegar and half the stock, bring to the boil, cover and simmer for 5 minutes. Stir the cornflour into the remaining stock, add to the pan and simmer, stirring, until the sauce thickens and clears.

Stir-Fried Cauliflower

Serves 4

450 g/1 lb cauliflower florets
45 ml/3 tbsp groundnut (peanut) oil
1 spring onion (scallion), chopped
120 ml/4 fl oz/½ cup chicken stock
5 ml/1 tsp cornflour (cornstarch)

Blanch the cauliflower in boiling water for 2 minutes then drain well. Heat the oil and fry the spring onion until lightly browned. Add the cauliflower and stir-fry for 4 minutes. Add the remaining ingredients and stir-fry for 2 minutes.

Cauliflower with Mushrooms

Serves 4

6 dried Chinese mushrooms
1 small cauliflower
45 ml/3 tbsp groundnut (peanut) oil
100 g/4 oz water chestnuts, sliced
45 ml/3 tbsp soy sauce
15 ml/1 tbsp rice wine or dry sherry
5 ml/1 tsp cornflour (cornstarch)
30 ml/2 tbsp water

Soak the mushrooms in warm water for 30 minutes then drain, reserving 120 ml/4 fl oz/½ cup of liquid. Discard the stalks and slice the caps. Cut the cauliflower into small florets. Heat the oil and stir-fry the mushrooms until coated with oil. Add the water chestnuts and stir-fry for 1 minute. Mix the soy sauce and wine or sherry with the mushroom liquid and add it to the pan with the cauliflower. Bring to the boil, cover and simmer for 5 minutes. Blend the cornflour and water to a paste, stir into the sauce and simmer, stirring, until the sauce thickens.

Celery Stir-Fry

Serves 4

| 30 ml/2 tbsp groundnut (peanut) oil |
| 6 spring onions (scallions), chopped |
| ½ head celery, cut into chunks |
| 15 ml/1 tbsp soy sauce |
| 5 ml/1 tsp salt |

Heat the oil and fry the spring onions until lightly browned. Add the celery and stir until well coated with oil. Add the soy sauce and salt, stir well, cover and simmer for 3 minutes.

Celery and Mushrooms

Serves 4

| 45 ml/3 tbsp groundnut (peanut) oil |
| 6 stalks celery, diagonally sliced |
| 225 g/8 oz mushrooms, sliced |
| 30 ml/2 tbsp rice wine or dry sherry |
| salt and freshly ground pepper |

Heat the oil and stir-fry the celery for 3 minutes. Add the mushrooms and stirfry for 2 minutes. Add the wine or sherry and season with salt and pepper. Stir-fry for a few minutes until heated through.

Stir-Fried Chinese Leaves

Serves 4

| 15 ml/1 tbsp groundnut (peanut) oil |
| 1 clove garlic, chopped |
| 3 spring onions (scallions), chopped |
| 350 g/12 oz Chinese leaves, shredded |
| 2.5 ml/½ tsp salt |
| 450 ml/¾ pt boiling water |

Heat the oil and fry the garlic and onion until lightly browned. Add the Chinese leaves and salt and stir well. Add the boiling water, return to the boil, cover and simmer for about 5 minutes until the Chinese leaves are tender but still crisp. Drain well.

Chinese Leaves in Milk

Serves 4

| 350 g/12 oz Chinese leaves, shredded |
| 45 ml/3 tbsp groundnut (peanut) oil |
| 3 spring onions (scallions), chopped |
| 15 ml/1 tbsp rice wine or dry sherry |
| 90 ml/6 tbsp chicken stock |
| salt |
| 90 ml/6 tbsp milk |
| 15 ml/1 tbsp cornflour (cornstarch) |
| 5 ml/1 tsp sesame oil |

Steam the Chinese leaves for about 5 minutes until just tender. Heat the oil and fry the spring onions until lightly browned. Add the wine or sherry and chicken stock and season with salt. Stir in the cabbage, cover and simmer gently for 5 minutes. Mix the milk and cornflour, stir into pan and simmer, stirring, for 2 minutes. Serve sprinkled with sesame oil.

Chinese Leaves with Mushrooms

Serves 4

50 g/2 oz Chinese dried mushrooms
450 g/1 lb Chinese leaves
45 ml/3 tbsp groundnut (peanut) oil
120 ml/4 fl oz/½ cup chicken stock
15 ml/1 tbsp soy sauce
5 ml/1 tsp salt
5 ml/1 tsp sugar
15 ml/1 tbsp cornflour (cornstarch)
10 ml/2 tsp sesame oil

Soak the mushrooms in warm water for 30 minutes then drain. Discard the stems and slice the caps. Cut the head of Chinese leaves into thick slices. Heat half the oil, add the Chinese leaves and stir-fry for 2 minutes. Add the chicken stock, soysauce, salt and sugar and stir-fry for about 4 minutes. Add the mushrooms and stir-fry until the vegetables are tender. Mix the cornflour with a little water, stir it into the sauce and simmer, stirring until the sauce clears and thickens. Serve sprinkled with sesame oil.

Chinese Leaves with Scallops

Serves 4

4 hearts Chinese leaves
600 ml/1 pt/2½ cups chicken stock
100 g/4 oz shelled scallops, sliced
5 ml/1 tsp cornflour (cornstarch)

Place the Chinese leaves and stock in a pan, bring to the boil and simmer for about 10 minutes until just tender. Transfer the Chinese leaves to a warmed serving plate and keep them warm. Pour out all but 250 ml/8 fl oz/1 cup of the stock. Add the scallops and simmer for a few minutes until the scallops are tender. Blend the cornflour with a little water, stir it into the pan and simmer, stirring, until the sauce thickens slightly. Pour over the Chinese leaves and serve.

Steamed Chinese Leaves

Serves 4

450 g/1 lb Chinese leaves, separated
15 ml/1 tbsp cornflour (cornstarch)
5 ml/1 tsp salt
300 ml/½ pt/1¼ cups chicken stock

Arrange the leaves in an ovenproof bowl, place it on a rack in a steamer and steam over gently boiling water for 15 minutes. Meanwhile, blend the cornflour, salt and stock over a gentle heat, bring to the boil and simmer, stirring, until the mixture thickens. Arrange the Chinese leaves on a warmed serving plate, pour over the sauce and serve.

Chinese Leaves with Water Chestnuts

Serves 4

450 g/1 lb Chinese leaves, shredded
45 ml/3 tbsp groundnut (peanut) oil
100 g/4 oz water chestnuts, sliced
250 ml/8 fl oz/1 cup chicken stock
15 ml/1 tbsp soy sauce
15 ml/1 tbsp cornflour (cornstarch)
15 ml/1 tbsp water

Blanch the Chinese leaves in boiling water for 2 minutes then drain. Heat the oil and stir-fry the water chestnuts for 2 minutes. Add the Chinese leaves and stir-fry for 3 minutes. Add the chicken stock and soy sauce, bring to the boil, cover and simmer for 5 minutes. Mix the cornflour and water to a paste, stir into the pan and simmer, stirring, until the sauce clears and thickens.

Courgette Stir-Fry

Serves 4

45 ml/3 tbsp groundnut (peanut) oil
1 spring onion (scallion), chopped
450 g/1 lb courgettes (zucchini), thickly sliced
30 ml/2 tbsp soy sauce
5 ml/1 tsp sugar
120 ml/4 fl oz/½ cup chicken stock
5 ml/1 tsp cornflour (cornstarch)

Heat the oil and fry the spring onion until lightly browned. Add the courgettes and stir-fry for 3 minutes. Add the remaining ingredients and stir-fry for 4 minutes.

Courgettes in Black Bean Sauce

Serves 4

30 ml/2 tbsp groundnut (peanut) oil
1 clove garlic, crushed
5 ml/1 tsp salt
15 ml/1 tbsp chilli bean sauce
450 g/1 lb courgettes (zucchini), thickly sliced
30 ml/2 tbsp rice wine or dry sherry
45 ml/3 tbsp water
15 ml/1 tbsp sesame oil

Heat the oil and fry the garlic, salt and chilli bean sauce for a few seconds. Add the courgettes and stir-fry for 3 minutes until lightly browned. Add the remaining ingredients, including sesame oil to taste, and stir-fry for 1 minute.

Stuffed Courgette Bites

Serves 4

4 large courgettes (zucchini)
225 g/8 oz minced (ground) pork
225 g/8 oz crab meat, flaked
2 eggs, beaten
30 ml/2 tbsp soy sauce
30 ml/2 tbsp oyster sauce
pinch of ground ginger
salt and freshly ground pepper
75 ml/5 tbsp cornflour (cornstarch)
50 g/2 oz/½ cup breadcrumbs
oil for deep-frying

Cut the courgettes in half lengthways and remove the seeds and cores with a spoon. Mix the pork, crab meat, eggs, sauces, ginger, salt and pepper. Bind with the cornflour and breadcrumbs. Cover and chill for 30 minutes. Fill the courgettes with the mixture then cut them into chunks. Heat the oil and deep-fry the courgettes until golden. Drain on kitchen - paper before serving.

Cucumber with Prawns

Serves 4

45 ml/3 tbsp groundnut (peanut) oil
100 g/4 oz peeled prawns
1 cucumber, peeled and thickly sliced
30 ml/2 tbsp soy sauce
5 ml/1 tsp rice wine or dry sherry
5 ml/1 tsp brown sugar
salt
45 ml/3 tbsp water

Heat the oil and stir-fry the prawns for 30 seconds. Add the cucumber and stir-fry for 1 minute. Add the soy sauce, wine or sherry and sugar and season with salt. Stir-fry for 3 minutes, adding a little water if necessary. Serve immediately.

Cucumbers with Sesame Oil

Serves 4

1 large cucumber
salt
30 ml/2 tbsp sesame oil
2.5 ml/½ tsp sugar

Peel the cucumber and cut in half lengthways. Scoop out the seeds then cut into thick slices. Arrange the cucumber slices in a colander and sprinkle generously with salt. Leave to stand for 1 hour then press out as much moisture as possible. Heat the oil and stir-fry the cucumbers for 2 minutes until softened. Stir in the sugar and serve at once.

Stuffed Cucumbers

Serves 4

225 g/8 oz minced (ground) pork
1 egg, beaten
30 ml/2 tbsp cornflour (cornstarch)
15 ml/1 tbsp rice wine or dry sherry
30 ml/2 tbsp soy sauce
salt and freshly ground pepper
2 large cucumbers
30 ml/2 tbsp plain (all-purpose) flour
45 ml/2 tbsp groundnut (peanut) oil
150 ml/¼ pt/⅔ cup chicken stock
30 ml/2 tbsp water

Mix together the pork, egg, half the cornflour, the wine or sherry and half the soy sauce and season with salt and pepper. Peel the cucumbers then cut into 5 cm/2 in chunks. Scoop out some of the seeds to make hollows and fill with stuffing, pressing it down. Dust with flour. Heat the oil and fry the cucumber pieces, stuffing side down, until lightly browned. Turn over and cook until the other side is browned. Add the stock and soy sauce, bring to the boil, cover and simmer for 20 minutes until tender, turning occasionally. Transfer the cucumbers to a warmed serving plate. Mix the remaining cornflour with the water, stir it into the pan and simmer, stirring, until the sauce clears and thickens. Pour over the cucumbers and serve.

Stir-Fried Dandelion Leaves

Serves 4

30 ml/2 tbsp groundnut (peanut) oil
450 g/1 lb dandelion leaves
5 ml/1 tsp salt
15 ml/1 tbsp sugar

Heat the oil, add the dandelion leaves, salt and sugar and stir-fry over a moderate heat for 5 minutes. Serve at once.

Braised Lettuce

Serves 4

1 head crisp lettuce
15 ml/1 tbsp groundnut (peanut) oil
2.5 ml/½ tsp salt
1 clove garlic, crushed
60 ml/4 tsp chicken stock
5 ml/1 tsp soy sauce

Separate the lettuce into leaves. Heat the oil and fry the salt and garlic until lightly browned. Add the lettuce and simmer for 1 minute, stirring to coat the lettuce in oil. Add the stock and simmer for 2 minutes. Serve sprinkled with soy sauce.

Stir-Fried Lettuce with Ginger

Serves 4

45 ml/3 tbsp groundnut (peanut) oil
2 cloves garlic, crushed
1 cm/½ in slice ginger root, finely chopped
1 head lettuce, shredded

Heat the oil and fry the garlic and ginger until light golden. Add the lettuce and stir-fry for about 2 minutes until glossy and slightly wilted. Serve at once.

Mangetout with Bamboo Shoots

Serves 4

30 ml/2 tbsp groundnut (peanut) oil
100 g/4 oz minced (ground) pork
100 g/4 oz mushrooms
225 g/8 oz bamboo shoots, sliced
225 g/8 oz mangetout (snow peas)
15 ml/1 tbsp soy sauce
15 ml/1 tbsp cornflour (cornstarch)
5 ml/1 tsp sugar
120 ml/4 fl oz/½ cup chicken stock

Heat the oil and fry the pork until lightly browned. Stir in the mushrooms and bamboo shoots and stir-fry for 2 minutes. Add the mangetout and stir-fry for 2 minutes. Sprinkle with soy sauce. Mix the cornflour, sugar and stock to a paste, stir into the pan and simmer, stirring, until the sauce thickens.

Mangetout with Mushrooms and Ginger

Serves 4

45 ml/3 tbsp groundnut (peanut) oil
3 spring onions (scallions), sliced
1 slice ginger root, minced
225 g/8 oz mushrooms, halved
300 ml/½ pt/⅔ cup chicken stock
10 ml/2 tsp cornflour (cornstarch)
15 ml/1 tbsp water
15 ml/1 tbsp oyster sauce
225 g/8 oz mangetout (snow peas)

Heat the oil and fry the spring onions and ginger until lightly browned. Add the mushrooms and stir-fry for 3 minutes. Add the stock, bring to the boil, cover and simmer for 3 minutes. Blend the cornflour to a paste with the water and oyster sauce, stir it into the pan and simmer, stirring, until the sauce thickens. Stir in the mangetout and heat through before serving.

Chinese Marrow

Serves 4

60 ml/4 tbsp groundnut (peanut) oil
450 g/1 lb marrow, thinly sliced
30 ml/2 tbsp soy sauce
10 ml/2 tsp salt
freshly ground pepper

Heat the oil and stir-fry the marrow slices for 2 minutes. Add the soy sauce, salt and a pinch of pepper and stir-fry for a further 4 minutes.

Stuffed Marrow

Serves 4

450 g/1 lb fish fillets, flaked
5 ml/1 tsp salt
2 spring onions (scallions), chopped
100 g/4 oz smoked ham, chopped
50 g/2 oz/½ cup chopped almonds
1 marrow, halved
oil for deep-frying
250 ml/8 fl oz/1 cup chicken stock
30 ml/2 tbsp cornflour (cornstarch)
15 ml/1 tbsp soy sauce
5 ml/1 tsp sugar
60 ml/4 tbsp water
5 ml/1 tsp sesame oil
15 ml/1 tbsp chopped flat-leaved
   parsley

Mix the fish, salt, spring onions, ham and almonds. Scoop out the seeds of the marrow and some of the flesh to make a hollow. Press the fish mixture into the marrow. Heat the oil and deep-fry the marrow halves, one at a time if necessary, until golden brown. Transfer to a clean pan and add the stock. Bring to the boil, cover and simmer for 40 minutes. Blend the cornflour, soy sauce, sugar, water and sesame oil to a paste, stir into the pan and simmer, stirring, until the sauce clears and thickens. Serve garnished with parsley.

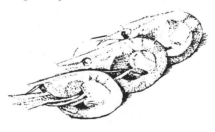

Mushrooms with Anchovy Sauce

Serves 4

15 ml/1 tbsp groundnut (peanut) oil
450 g/1 lb button mushrooms
2 shallots, sliced
1 stick lemon grass, chopped
1 large tomato, diced
60 ml/4 tbsp chopped flat-leaved parsley
20 ml/4 tsp anchovy paste
50 g/2 oz/¼ cup butter
salt and freshly ground pepper
4 slices bread
8 anchovy fillets

Heat the oil and fry the mushrooms, shallots and lemon grass until lightly browned. Add the tomato and half the parsley and stir well. Mix in the anchovy paste and the butter, cut into flakes. Season with salt and pepper. Toast the bread then sprinkle with the remaining parsley. Arrange the anchovy fillets on top and serve with the mushrooms.

Mushrooms and Bamboo Shoots

Serves 4

45 ml/3 tbsp groundnut (peanut) oil
5 ml/1 tsp salt
1 clove garlic, crushed
225 g/8 oz bamboo shoots, sliced
225 g/8 oz mushrooms, sliced
45 ml/3 tbsp soy sauce
15 ml/1 tbsp rice wine or dry sherry
15 ml/1 tbsp sugar
15 ml/1 tbsp cornflour (cornstarch)
90 ml/6 tbsp chicken stock

Heat the oil and fry the salt and garlic until the garlic turns light golden. Add the bamboo shoots and mushrooms and stir-fry for 3 minutes. Add the soy sauce, wine or sherry and sugar and stir-fry for 3 minutes. Mix the cornflour and stock and stir it into the pan. Bring to the boil, stirring, then simmer for a few minutes until the sauce thickens and clears.

Mushrooms with Bamboo Shoots and Mangetout

Serves 4

8 dried Chinese mushrooms
30 ml/2 tbsp groundnut (peanut) oil
100 g/4 oz mangetout (snow peas)
100 g/4 oz bamboo shoots, sliced
60 ml/4 tbsp stock
30 ml/2 tbsp soy sauce
5 ml/1 tsp sugar

Soak the mushrooms in warm water for 30 minutes then drain. Discard the stalks and slice the caps. Heat the oil and fry the mangetout for about 30 seconds then remove from the pan. Add the mushrooms and bamboo shoots and stir-fry until well coated with oil. Add the stock, soy sauce and sugar, bring to the boil, cover and simmer gently for 3 minutes. Return the mangetout to the pan and simmer, uncovered, until heated through. Serve at once.

Mushrooms with Mangetout

Serves 4

30 ml/2 tbsp groundnut (peanut) oil
225 g/8 oz button mushrooms
450 g/1 lb mangetout (snow peas)
15 ml/1 tbsp soy sauce
10 ml/2 tsp sesame oil
5 ml/1 tsp brown sugar

Heat the oil and fry the mushrooms for 5 minutes. Add the mangetout and stir-fry for 1 minute. Add the remaining ingredients and stir-fry for 4 minutes.

Spicy Mushrooms

Serves 4

15 ml/1 tbsp groundnut (peanut) oil
1 clove garlic, finely chopped
1 slice ginger root, minced
2 spring onions (scallions), chopped
225 g/8 oz button mushrooms
15 ml/1 tbsp hoisin sauce
15 ml/1 tbsp rice wine or dry sherry
45 ml/3 tbsp chicken stock
5 ml/1 tsp sesame oil

Heat the oil and stir-fry the garlic, ginger and spring onions for 2 minutes. Add the mushrooms and stir-fry for 2 minutes. Add the remaining ingredients and stir-fry for 5 minutes.

Steamed Mushrooms

Serves 4

18 dried Chinese mushrooms
450 ml/¾ pt/2 cups stock
30 ml/2 tbsp groundnut (peanut) oil
5 ml/1 tsp sugar

Soak the mushrooms in warm water for 30 minutes then drain, reserving 250 ml/8 fl oz/1 cup of soaking liquid. Discard the stalks and arrange the caps in a heatproof bowl. Add the remaining ingredients, stand the bowl on a rack in a steamer, cover and steam over boiling water for about 1 hour.

Steamed Stuffed Mushrooms

Serves 4

450 g/1 lb large mushrooms
225 g/8 oz minced (ground) pork
225 g/8 oz peeled prawns, finely
    chopped
4 water chestnuts, finely chopped
15 ml/1 tbsp cornflour (cornstarch)
5 ml/1 tsp salt
5 ml/1 tsp sugar
30 ml/2 tbsp soy sauce
120 ml/4 fl oz/½ cup

Remove the stalks from the mushrooms. Chop the stalks and mix them with the remaining ingredients. Arrange the mushroom caps on an ovenproof plate and top with the stuffing mixture, pressing it down into a dome shape. Spoon a little stock over each one, reserving a little stock. Place the plate on a rack in a steamer, cover and steam over gently simmering water for about 45 minutes until the mushrooms are cooked, basting with a little more stock during cooking if necessary.

Straw Mushrooms in Oyster Sauce

Serves 4

| 15 ml/1 tbsp groundnut (peanut) oil |
| 225 g/8 oz straw mushrooms |
| 120 ml/4 fl oz/½ cup chicken stock |
| 2.5 ml/½ tsp sugar |
| 5 ml/1 tsp oyster sauce |
| 5 ml/1 tsp cornflour (cornstarch) |
| 15 ml/1 tbsp water |

Heat the oil and fry the mushrooms gently until well coated. Add the stock, sugar and oyster sauce, bring to the boil then simmer gently until the mushrooms are tender. Mix the cornflour and water to a paste, stir into the pan and simmer, stirring, until the sauce clears and thickens.

Baked Onions

Serves 4

| 8 large onions |
| salt and freshly ground pepper |
| 30 ml/2 tbsp groundnut (peanut) oil |
| 120 ml/4 fl oz/½ cup water |
| 15 ml/1 tbsp cornflour (cornstarch) |
| 15 ml/1 tbsp chopped fresh parsley |

Put the onions in a pan and just cover with boiling salted water. Cover and simmer for 5 minutes then drain. Arrange the onions in an ovenproof dish, season with salt and pepper and brush with oil. Pour in the water, cover and bake in a pre-heated oven

at 190°C/375°F/gas mark 5 for 1 hour. Blend the cornflour with a little water and stir it into the onion liquid. Bake for a further 5 minutes, stirring occasionally, until the sauce thickens. Serve garnished with parsley.

Curried Onions with Peas

Serves 4

| 450 g/1 lb pearl onions |
| 10 ml/2 tsp salt |
| 225 g/8 oz peas |
| 45 ml/3 tbsp groundnut (peanut) oil |
| 10 ml/2 tsp curry powder |
| freshly ground pepper |

Place the onions in a pan and just cover with boiling water. Season with 5 ml/1 tsp of salt and boil for 5 minutes. Cover and boil for a further 10 minutes. Add the peas and cook for a further 5 minutes then drain. Heat the oil and fry the curry powder, remaining salt and remaining pepper for 30 seconds. Add the drained vegetables and stir-fry until hot and glazed with the curry oil.

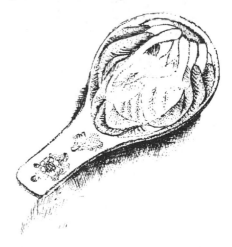

Pearl Onions in Orange-Ginger Sauce

Serves 4

3 oranges

2 red chilli peppers

15 ml/1 tbsp walnut oil

450 g/1 lb pearl onions

1 slice ginger root, chopped

10 ml/2 tsp sugar

10 ml/2 tsp cider vinegar

15 ml/1 tbsp red peppercorns

salt

5 ml/1 tsp grated lemon rind

a few coriander leaves

Using a zester, cut the orange peel into narrow slivers. Halve the oranges and squeeze the juice. Halve the chilli peppers and remove the seeds. Heat the oil and stir-fry the onions, ginger and chilli peppers for 1 minute. Add the sugar then simmer until the onions are translucent. Mix in the orange juice, cider vinegar, peppercorns and orange rind and season with salt. Stir in the lemon rind and most of the coriander leaves. Arrange on a warmed serving plate and garnish with the remaining coriander leaves.

Onion Custard

Serves 4

4 rashers bacon

450 g/1 lb onions, sliced

50 g/2 oz/½ cup cornflour (cornstarch)

2 eggs, lightly beaten

120 ml/4 fl oz/½ cup water

pinch of grated nutmeg

10 ml/2 tsp salt

Fry the bacon until crisp then drain and chop. Add the onions to the pan and fry until softened. Beat the cornflour with the eggs and water and season with nutmeg and salt. Mix the bacon with the onions and place in a greased ovenproof dish. Top with the egg mixture and stand the dish in a roasting tin half filled with water. Bake in a pre-heated oven at 180°C/350°F/gas mark 4 for 45 minutes until the custard is set.

Pak Choi

Serves 4

45 ml/3 tbsp groundnut (peanut) oil

2 spring onions (scallions), chopped

450 g/1 lb pak choi, shredded

15 ml/1 tbsp soy sauce

2.5 ml/½ tsp sugar

120 ml/4 fl oz/½ cup chicken stock

5 ml/1 tsp cornflour (cornstarch)

Heat the oil and fry the spring onions until lightly browned. Add the pak choi and stir-fry for 3 minutes. Add the remaining ingredients and stir-fry for 2 minutes.

Peas with Mushrooms

Serves 4

45 ml/3 tbsp groundnut (peanut) oil

1 spring onion (scallion), chopped

225 g/8 oz mushrooms, halved

225 g/8 oz frozen peas

30 ml/2 tbsp soy sauce

5 ml/1 tsp sugar

120 ml/4 fl oz/½ cup chicken stock

5 ml/1 tsp cornflour (cornstarch)

Heat the oil and fry the spring onion until lightly browned. Add the mushrooms and stir-fry for 3 minutes. Add the peas and stir-fry for 4 minutes. Add the remaining ingredients and stir-fry for 2 minutes.

Stir-Fried Peppers

Serves 4

30 ml/2 tbsp groundnut (peanut) oil
2 green peppers, cubed
2 red peppers, cubed
15 ml/1 tbsp chicken stock or water
5 ml/1 tsp salt
5 ml/1 tsp brown sugar

Heat the oil until very hot, add the peppers and stir-fry until the skins wrinkle slightly. Add the stock or water, salt and sugar and stir-fry for 2 minutes.

Pepper and Bean Stir-Fry

Serves 4

30 ml/2 tbsp groundnut (peanut) oil
2 cloves garlic, crushed
5 ml/1 tsp salt
2 red peppers, cut into strips
225 g/8 oz French beans
5 ml/1 tsp sugar
30 ml/2 tbsp water

Heat the oil and stir-fry the garlic, salt, peppers and beans for 3 minutes. Add the sugar and water and stir-fry for about 5 minutes until the vegetables are tender but still crisp.

Fish-Stuffed Peppers

Serves 4

225 g/8 oz fish fillets, flaked
2 spring onions (scallions), minced
30 ml/2 tbsp cornflour (cornstarch)
15 ml/1 tbsp groundnut (peanut) oil
30 ml/2 tbsp water
salt and freshly ground pepper
4 green peppers
120 ml/4 fl oz/½ cup chicken stock
2.5 ml/½ tsp salt
60 ml/4 tbsp water

Mix together the fish, spring onions, half the cornflour, the oil and water and season with salt and pepper. Cut the tops off the peppers and scoop out the seeds. Fill with the stuffing mixture and replace the tops as lids. Stand the peppers upright in a pan and add the stock. Bring to the boil and season with salt and pepper. Cover and simmer for 1 hour. Transfer the peppers to a warmed serving dish. Blend the remaining cornflour and water to a paste, stir into the pan and bring to the boil. Simmer, stirring, until the sauce clears and thickens. Pour over the peppers and serve at once.

Pork-Stuffed Peppers

Serves 4

30 ml/2 tbsp groundnut (peanut) oil
225 g/8 oz minced (ground) pork
2 spring onions (scallions), chopped
4 water chestnuts, chopped
30 ml/2 tbsp soy sauce
salt and freshly ground pepper
4 green peppers
120 ml/4 fl oz/½ cup chicken stock
2.5 ml/½ tsp salt
15 ml/1 tbsp cornflour (cornstarch)
60 ml/4 tbsp water

Heat the oil and fry the pork, spring onions and water chestnuts until lightly browned. Remove from the heat, stir half the soy sauce and season with salt and pepper. Cut the tops off the peppers and scoop out the seeds. Fill with the stuffing mixture and replace the tops as lids. Stand the peppers upright in a pan and add the stock. Bring to the boil and season with salt and pepper. Cover and simmer for 1 hour. Transfer the peppers to a warmed serving dish. Blend the cornflour, remaining soy sauce and water to a paste, stir into the pan and bring to the boil. Simmer, stirring, until the sauce clears and thickens. Pour over the peppers and serve at once.

Vegetable-Stuffed Peppers

Serves 4

30 ml/2 tbsp groundnut (peanut) oil
2 carrots, grated
1 onion, grated
45 ml/3 tbsp tomato ketchup (catsup)
5 ml/1 tsp sugar
salt and freshly ground pepper
4 green peppers
120 ml/4 fl oz/½ cup chicken stock
2.5 ml/½ tsp salt
15 ml/1 tbsp cornflour (cornstarch)
15 ml/1 tbsp soy sauce
60 ml/4 tbsp water

Heat the oil and fry the carrots and onions until slightly softened. Remove from the heat and stir in the tomato ketchup and sugar. Season with salt and pepper. Cut the tops off the peppers and scoop out the seeds. Fill with the stuffing mixture and replace the tops as lids. Stand the peppers upright in a pan and add the stock. Bring to the boil and season with salt and pepper. Cover and simmer for 1 hour. Transfer the peppers to a warmed serving dish. Blend the cornflour, soy sauce and water to a paste, stir into the pan and bring to the boil. Simmer, stirring, until the sauce clears and thickens. Pour over the peppers and serve at once.

Deep-Fried Potatoes and Carrots

Serves 4

2 carrots, diced
450 g/1 lb potatoes
15 ml/1 tbsp cornflour (cornstarch)
oil for deep-frying
30 ml/2 tbsp groundnut (peanut) oil
5 ml/1 tsp salt
15 ml/1 tbsp rice wine or dry sherry
120 ml/4 fl oz/½ cup chicken stock
5 ml/1 tsp sugar
5 ml/1 tsp soy sauce

Blanch the carrots in boiling water for 3 minutes then drain. Cut the potatoes into chips and dust with a little cornflour. Heat the oil and deep-fry until crisp then drain. Heat the oil and salt and stir-fry the carrots until coated with oil. Add the wine or sherry and stock, bring to the boil, cover and simmer for 2 minutes. Blend the remaining cornflour to a paste with the sugar and soy sauce. Stir into the pan and simmer, stirring, until the sauce thickens. Add the potatoes and reheat. Serve at once.

Potato Sauté

Serves 4

350 g/12 oz potatoes, peeled and cut into matchsticks
30 ml/2 tbsp groundnut (peanut) oil
1 clove garlic, crushed
3 spring onions (scallions), chopped
15 ml/1 tbsp soy sauce
5 ml/1 tsp wine vinegar
salt and freshly ground pepper

Blanch the potatoes in boiling water for 20 seconds then drain. Heat the oil and fry the garlic and spring onions until lightly browned. Add the potatoes and stir-fry for 2 minutes. Add the soy sauce and wine vinegar and season to taste with salt and pepper. Fry for a few minutes until the potatoes are cooked and lightly browned.

Spiced Potatoes

Serves 4

30 ml/2 tbsp groundnut (peanut) oil
350 g/12 oz potatoes, peeled and diced
1 clove garlic, crushed
2.5 ml/½ tsp salt
2 spring onions (scallions), chopped
2 dried chilli peppers, seeded and chopped

Heat the oil and fry the potatoes until lightly golden. Remove them from the pan. Reheat the oil and fry the garlic, salt, spring onions and chilli peppers until lightly browned. Return the potatoes to the pan and stir-fry until the potatoes are cooked.

Pumpkin with Rice Noodles

Serves 4

350 g/12 oz rice noodles
15 ml/1 tbsp groundnut (peanut) oil
2 spring onions (scallions), sliced
225 g/8 oz pumpkin, cubed
250 ml/8 fl oz/1 cup chicken stock
2.5 ml/½ tsp sugar
salt and freshly ground pepper
100 g/4 oz peeled prawns

Blanch the noodles in boiling water for 2 minutes then drain. Heat the oil and stir-fry the spring onions for 30 seconds. Add the pumpkin and stir-fry for 1 minute. Add the stock and noodles, bring to the boil and simmer, uncovered, for about 5 minutes until the pumpkin is almost cooked. Add the sugar and season with salt and pepper. Simmer for about 10 minutes until the noodles are just tender and the liquid has reduced slightly. Add the prawns and heat through before serving.

Shallots in Malt Beer

Serves 4

15 ml/1 tbsp walnut oil
450 g/1 lb shallots
10 ml/2 tsp brown sugar
5 ml/1 tsp red peppercorns
250 ml/8 fl oz/1 cup malt beer
45 ml/3 tbsp balsamic vinegar
salt and freshly ground pepper
2.5 ml/½ tsp paprika
1 lamb's lettuce

Heat the oil and fry the shallots until golden brown. Add the sugar and stir-fry until translucent. Add the peppercorns, beer and balsamic vinegar and simmer for 1 minute. Season with salt, pepper and paprika. Arrange the lettuce leaves around the edge of a warmed serving plate and spoon the shallots into the centre.

Spinach with Garlic

Serves 4

30 ml/2 tbsp groundnut (peanut) oil
450 g/1 lb spinach leaves
2.5 ml/½ tsp salt
3 cloves garlic, crushed
15 ml/1 tbsp soy sauce

Heat the oil, add the spinach and salt and stir-fry for 3 minutes until the spinach begins to wilt. Add the garlic and soy sauce and stir-fry for 3 minutes before serving.

Spinach with Mushrooms

Serves 4 –6

8 dried Chinese mushrooms
75 ml/5 tbsp groundnut (peanut) oil
60 ml/4 tbsp soy sauce
15 ml/1 tbsp rice wine or dry sherry
5 ml/1 tsp sugar
salt
15 ml/1 tbsp cornflour (cornstarch)
15 ml/1 tbsp water
450 g/1 lb spinach

Soak the mushrooms in warm water for 30 minutes then drain, reserving 120 ml/4 fl oz/½ cup of soaking liquid. Discard the stalks and cut the caps in half, if large. Heat half the oil and fry the mushrooms for 2 minutes. Stir in the soy sauce, wine or sherry, sugar and a pinch of salt and mix well. Add the mushroom liquid, bring to the boil, cover and simmer for 10 minutes. Blend the cornflour and water to a paste, stir it into the sauce and simmer, stirring, until the sauce thickens. Leave over a very low heat to keep warm. Meanwhile, heat the remaining oil in a separate pan, add the spinach and stir-fry for about 2 minutes until softened. Transfer to a warmed serving dish, pour over the mushrooms and serve.

Spinach with Ginger

Serves 4

30 ml/2 tbsp groundnut (peanut) oil
1 slice ginger root, minced
1 clove garlic, crushed
5 ml/1 tsp salt
450 g/1 lb spinach
5 ml/1 tsp sugar
10 ml/2 tsp sesame oil

Heat the oil and stir-fry the ginger, garlic and salt until lightly browned. Add the spinach and stir-fry for 3 minutes until wilted. Add the sugar and sesame oil and stir-fry for 3 minutes. Serve hot or cold.

Spinach with Peanuts

Serves 4

30 ml/2 tbsp peanuts
450 g/1 lb spinach, shredded
2.5 ml/½ tsp salt
100 g/4 oz smoked ham, chopped
15 ml/1 tbsp groundnut (peanut) oil

Toast the peanuts in a dry pan then chop coarsely. Blanch the spinach in boiling water for 2 minutes then drain well and chop. Mix in the peanuts, salt, ham and oil and serve at once.

Vegetable Chow Mein

Serves 4

6 dried Chinese mushrooms
450 g/1 lb spinach
45 ml/3 tbsp groundnut (peanut) oil
100 g/4 oz bamboo shoots, sliced
2.5 ml/½ tsp salt
30 ml/2 tbsp soy sauce
soft-fried noodles (page 276)

Soak the mushrooms in warm water for 30 minutes then drain. Discard the stalks and slice the caps. Halve the spinach leaves. Heat the oil and stir-fry the mushrooms and bamboo shoots for 4 minutes. Add the spinach, salt and soy sauce and stir-fry for 1 minute. Add the drained noodles and stir gently until heated through.

Vegetables with Honey

Serves 4

15 ml/1 tbsp groundnut (peanut) oil
1 slice ginger root, chopped
2 cloves garlic, chopped
100 g/4 oz baby sweetcorn
2 spring onions (scallions), sliced
1 red pepper, diced
1 green pepper, diced
100 g/4 oz mushrooms, halved
15 ml/1 tbsp honey
15 ml/1 tbsp fruit vinegar
10 ml/2 tsp soy sauce
salt and freshly ground pepper

Heat the oil and fry the ginger and garlic until lightly browned. Add the vegetables and stir-fry for 1 minute. Add the honey, fruit vinegar and soy sauce and season with salt and pepper. Stir together well and heat through before serving.

Fried Spring Vegetables

Serves 4

45 ml/3 tbsp groundnut (peanut) oil
2 cloves garlic, crushed
salt
30 ml/2 tbsp soy sauce
30 ml/2 tbsp hoisin sauce
6 spring onions (scallions), chopped
1 red pepper, chopped
1 green pepper, chopped
100 g/4 oz bean sprouts
225 g/8 oz mangetout (snow peas), cut into 4
5 ml/1 tsp tomato purée (paste)
5 ml/1 tsp cornflour (cornstarch)
120 ml/4 fl oz/½ cup chicken stock
few drops of lemon juice
60 ml/4 tbsp chopped chives

Heat the oil and fry the garlic and salt until lightly browned. Add the soy and hoisin sauces and stir-fry for 1 minute. Add the peppers, bean sprouts and mangetout and cook, stirring, until they are just tender but still crisp. Stir the tomato purée and cornflour into the stock then add it to the pan. Bring to the boil and simmer, stirring, until the sauce thickens. Sprinkle with lemon juice, stir, then serve sprinkled with chives.

Marinated Steamed Vegetables

Serves 4

30 ml/2 tbsp groundnut (peanut) oil
225 g/8 oz broccoli florets
225 g/8 oz cauliflower florets
100 g/4 oz oyster mushrooms
2 carrots, thinly sliced
1 stick celery, thinly sliced
120 ml/4 fl oz/½ cup dry white wine
30 ml/2 tbsp plum sauce
30 ml/2 tbsp soy sauce
juice of 1 orange
5 ml/1 tsp freshly ground pepper
30 ml/2 tbsp wine vinegar

Heat the oil and stir-fry the vegetables for about 5 minutes then transfer them to a bowl. Add the wine, plum sauce, soy sauce, orange juice and pepper and toss well to mix. Cover and refrigerate overnight.

Place the marinated vegetables in a steamer, cover and cook over gently boiling water to which the wine vinegar has been added for about 15 minutes.

Mixed Vegetables

Serves 4

2 onions
30 ml/2 tbsp groundnut (peanut) oil
15 ml/1 tbsp grated ginger root
225 g/8 oz broccoli florets
225 g/8 oz spinach, chopped
225 g/8 oz mangetout (snow peas)
4 stalks celery, diagonally sliced
6 spring onions (scallions), diagonally sliced
175 ml/6 fl oz/¾ cup vegetable stock

Cut the onions into wedges and separate the layers. Heat the oil and stir-fry the onions, ginger and broccoli for 1 minute. Add the remaining vegetables and toss lightly. Add the stock and toss until the vegetables are completely coated. Bring to the boil, cover and simmer for 3 minutes until the vegetables are tender but still crisp.

Mixed Vegetables with Ginger

Serves 4

100 g/4 oz cauliflower florets
45 ml/3 tbsp groundnut (peanut) oil
2 slices ginger root, minced
1 spring onion (scallion), chopped
100 g/4 oz bamboo shoots, sliced
100 g/4 oz mushrooms, sliced
100 g/4 oz Chinese cabbage, shredded
30 ml/2 tbsp soy sauce
120 ml/4 fl oz/½ cup chicken stock
salt and freshly ground pepper

Blanch the cauliflower in boiling water for 3 minutes then drain. Heat the oil and stir-fry the ginger for 1 minute. Add the vegetables and stir-fry for 3 minutes until coated with oil. Add the soy sauce and stock and season with salt and pepper. Stir-fry for a further 2 minutes until the vegetables are just tender but still crisp.

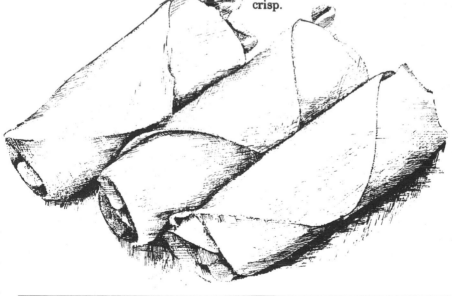

Vegetable Spring Rolls

Serves 4

6 Chinese dried mushrooms
30 ml/2 tbsp groundnut (peanut) oil
2.5 ml/½ tsp salt
2 cloves garlic, finely chopped
2 stalks celery, chopped
1 green pepper, sliced
50 g/2 oz bamboo shoots, sliced
100 g/4 oz Chinese leaves, shredded
100 g/4 oz bean sprouts
4 water chestnuts, cut into strips
3 spring onions (scallions), chopped
15 ml/1 tbsp soy sauce
5 ml/1 tsp sugar
8 spring roll skins
groundnut (peanut) oil for frying

Soak the mushrooms in warm water for 30 minutes then drain. Discard the stems and chop the caps. Heat the oil, salt and garlic until the garlic turns golden then add the mushrooms and stir-fry for 2 minutes. Add the celery, pepper and bamboo shoots and stir-fry for 3 minutes. Add the cabbage, bean sprouts, chestnuts and spring onions and stir-fry for 2 minutes. Stir in the soy sauce and sugar, remove from the heat and leave to stand for 2 minutes. Turn into a colander and leave to drain. Place a few spoonfuls of the filling mixture in the centre of each spring roll skin, fold up the bottom, fold in the sides,then roll upwards, enclosing the filling. Seal the edge with a little flour and water mixture then leave to dry for 30 minutes. Heat the oil and fry the spring rolls for about 10 minutes until crisp and golden brown. Drain well before serving.

Simple Stir-Fried Vegetables

Serves 4

45 ml/3 tbsp groundnut (peanut) oil
5 ml/1 tsp salt
2 slices ginger root, minced
450 g/1 lb mixed vegetables such as sliced bamboo shoots, blanched bean sprouts, broccoli florets, sliced carrots, cauliflower florets, diced peppers
120 ml/4 fl oz/½ cup chicken or vegetable stock
15 ml/1 tbsp soy sauce
5 ml/1 tsp sugar

Heat the oil and stir-fry the salt and ginger until lightly browned. Add the vegetables and stir-fry for 3 minutes until well coated with oil. Add the stock, soy sauce and sugar and stir-fry for about 2 minutes until heated through.

Vegetable Surprises

Serves 4

225 g/8 oz broccoli florets
225 g/8 oz cauliflower florets
225 g/8 oz brussels sprouts
30 ml/2 tbsp honey
30 ml/2 tbsp soy sauce
30 ml/2 tbsp wine vinegar
5 ml/1 tsp five-spice powder
salt and freshly ground pepper
225 g/8 oz/2 cups plain (all-purpose) flour
250 ml/8 fl oz/1 cup dry white wine
2 eggs, separated
15 ml/1 tbsp grated lemon rind
oil for deep-frying

Blanch the vegetables for 1 minute in boiling water then drain. Mix together the honey, soy sauce, wine vinegar, five-spice powder, salt and pepper. Place the vegetables in the marinade, cover and chill for 2 hours, stirring occasionally. Mix the flour, wine and egg yolks until smooth. Whisk the egg whites until stiff then fold them into the batter. Season with salt, pepper and lemon rind. Drain the vegetables and coat them in the batter. Heat the oil and deep-fry until golden brown. Drain on kitchen paper before serving.

Sweet and Sour Mixed Vegetables

Serves 4

45 ml/3 tbsp groundnut (peanut) oil
2.5 ml/½ tsp salt
2 cloves garlic, crushed
2 carrots, sliced
1 green pepper, cubed
100 g/4 oz bamboo shoots, cut into strips
1 onion, cut into wedges
100 g/4 oz water chestnuts, cut into strips
100 g/4 oz/½ cup sugar
60 ml/4 tbsp chicken stock
60 ml/4 tbsp wine vinegar
30 ml/2 tbsp soy sauce
15 ml/1 tbsp cornflour (cornstarch)

Heat the oil, salt and garlic until the garlic turns light golden. Add the carrots, pepper, bamboo shoots and onions and stir-fry for 3 minutes. Add the water chestnuts and stir-fry for 2 minutes. Mix together the sugar, stock, wine vinegar, soy sauce and cornflour then stir it into the pan. Cook, stirring, until the sauce thickens and clears.

Vegetables in Tomato Sauce

Serves 4

30 ml/2 tbsp groundnut (peanut) oil

2 cloves garlic, crushed

5 ml/1 tsp salt

100 g/4 oz smoked bacon, diced

30 ml/2 tbsp tomato purée (paste)

30 ml/2 tbsp soy sauce

30 ml/2 tbsp honey

30 ml/2 tbsp hoisin sauce

300 ml/½ pt/1¼ cups vegetable stock

1 red pepper, cut into strips

1 green pepper, cut into strips

1 stick celery, cut into strips

100 g/4 oz bean sprouts

100 g/4 oz green peas

10 ml/2 tsp wine vinegar

Heat the oil and fry the garlic and salt until lightly browned. Add the bacon and fry until crisp. Blend together the tomato purée, soy sauce, honey, hoisin sauce and stock. Add the vegetables to the pan and stir-fry for 2 minutes until coated in oil. Add the stock mixture, bring to the boil, cover and simmer for about 20 minutes until cooked.

Water Chestnut Cakes

Serves 4

100 g/4 oz sesame seeds

900 g/2 lb water chestnuts

15 ml/1 tbsp plain (all-purpose) flour

5 ml/1 tsp salt

freshly ground pepper

225 g/8 oz red bean paste

oil for deep-frying

120 ml/4 fl oz/½ cup vegetable stock

15 ml/1 tbsp sesame oil

5 ml/1 tsp cinnamon

Toast the sesame seeds in a dry pan until lightly browned. Mince the water chestnuts and drain off a little of the water. Mix with the flour, salt and pepper and shape into small balls. Press a little bean paste into the centre of each one. Coat the cakes in sesame seeds. Heat the oil and deep-fry the cakes for about 3 minutes then remove from the pan and drain. Pour off all but 30 ml/2 tbsp of oil from the pan then return the cakes to the pan and fry over a low heat for 4 minutes. Add the remaining ingredients, bring to a simmer and simmer until most of the liquid has been absorbed. Transfer to a warmed serving plate and serve at once.

Tofu

Tofu is actually the Japanese word for bean curd, but it has been adopted as the most common name for this nutritious food. Although it has a fairly bland taste on its own, it readily absorbs the flavours of other foods or seasoning ingredients so is very versatile in the kitchen.

Battered Tofu

Serves 4

2 dried Chinese mushrooms
450 g/1 lb tofu
1 egg
1 spring onion, chopped
5 ml/1 tsp ground coriander
5 ml/1 tsp grated cheese
30 ml/2 tbsp cornflour (cornstarch)
salt and freshly ground pepper
275 g/10 oz plain (all-purpose) flour
5 ml/1 tsp baking powder
175 ml/6 fl oz/¾ cup water
oil for deep-frying

Soak the mushrooms in warm water for 30 minutes then drain. Discard the stalks and mince the caps with the tofu, egg, spring onion, coriander, cheese, cornflour, salt and pepper. The mixture should be sticky. Press on to a plate and steam over gently simmering water for about 10 minutes. Cut the tofu into squares. Mix the flour, baking powder and water to a sticky batter and use to coat the tofu. Heat the oil and deep-fry the squares until lightly golden. Drain well before serving.

Tofu with Black Bean Sauce

Serves 4

30 ml/2 tbsp groundnut (peanut) oil
2 cloves garlic, crushed
4 spring onions (scallions), sliced
60 ml/4 tbsp black bean sauce
450 g/1 lb tofu, cubed
15 ml/1 tbsp chicken stock
15 ml/1 tbsp soy sauce
15 ml/1 tbsp rice wine or dry sherry

Heat the oil and fry the garlic until light golden. Add the spring onions and stir-fry for 1 minute. Add the tofu and stir-fry carefully for 2 minutes until golden. Add the stock, soy sauce and wine or sherry, bring to the boil and stir-fry for about 1 minute.

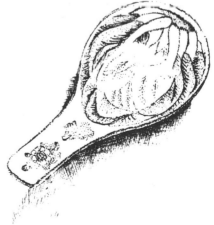

Tofu with Chilli Sauce

Serves 4

450 g/1 lb tofu, cubed
30 ml/2 tbsp groundnut (peanut) oil
100 g/4 oz minced (ground) pork
30 ml/2 tbsp chilli sauce
5 ml/1 tsp minced ginger root
450 ml/¾ pt/2 cups chicken stock
15 ml/1 tbsp soy sauce
15 ml/1 tbsp rice wine or dry sherry
5 ml/1 tsp cornflour (cornstarch)
15 ml/1 tbsp water
2.5 ml/½ tsp sesame oil
1 spring onion, finely chopped
freshly ground pepper

Blanch the tofu in boiling water for 2 minutes then drain. Heat the oil and fry the pork, chilli sauce and ginger until the pork is well cooked. Add the stock, tofu, soy sauce and wine or sherry, bring to the boil and simmer gently until almost all the liquid has evaporated. Blend the cornflour and water to a paste, stir it into the pan and simmer, stirring, until thickened. Transfer to a warmed serving dish and serve sprinkled with sesame oil, spring onions and pepper.

Tofu with Chinese Mushrooms

Serves 4

4 dried Chinese mushrooms
60 ml/4 tbsp groundnut (peanut) oil
450 g/1 lb tofu, cut into squares
2 spring onions (scallions), thickly
    sliced
3 slices ginger root, chopped
3 slices ham, shredded
100 g/4 oz peeled prawns
250 ml/8 fl oz/1 cup chicken stock
45 ml/3 tbsp soy sauce
15 ml/1 tbsp rice wine or dry sherry
2.5 ml/½ tsp salt
2.5 ml/½ tsp sugar

Soak the mushrooms in warm water for 30 minutes then drain. Discard the stalks and quarter the caps. Heat the oil and fry the tofu until golden brown then remove from the pan. Reheat the oil and fry the spring onions and ginger for 30 seconds. Add the tofu, ham, prawns, stock, soy sauce, wine or sherry, salt and sugar, bring to the boil, cover and simmer for about 10 minutes. Remove the lid and simmer until the sauce is reduced. Transfer to a warmed serving dish and serve at once.

Tofu with Crab Meat

Serves 4

45 ml/3 tbsp groundnut (peanut) oil
1 clove garlic, crushed
2 spring onions (scallions), chopped
1 slice ginger root, chopped
225 g/8 oz tofu, cubed
225 g/8 oz crab meat
5 ml/1 tsp sugar
175 ml/6 fl oz/¾ cup chicken stock
15 ml/1 tbsp cornflour (cornstarch)

Heat the oil and fry the garlic, spring onions and ginger until lightly browned. Add the tofu and stir-fry for 4 minutes. Add the crab meat, sugar and stock, bring to the boil then simmer for 4 minutes. Mix the cornflour with a little water, stir it into the sauce and simmer, stirring, until the sauce clears and thickens.

Deep-Fried Tofu

Serves 4

oil for deep-frying
350 g/12 oz tofu, cubed
salt

Heat the oil and deep-fry the tofu until puffed and golden brown. Arrange on a warmed serving plate and sprinkle generously with salt before serving.

Four-Jewelled Tofu

Serves 4

6 dried Chinese mushrooms
45 ml/3 tbsp groundnut (peanut) oil
100 g/4 oz broccoli florets
2.5 ml/½ tsp fish sauce
2.5 ml/½ tsp rice wine or dry sherry
2.5 ml/½ tsp cornflour (cornstarch)
120 ml/4 fl oz/½ cup chicken stock
450 g/1 oz tofu, cubed
100 g/4 oz peeled prawns
100 g/4 oz chicken, shredded
½ small carrot, shredded
15 ml/1 tbsp oyster sauce
15 ml/1 tbsp soy sauce

Soak the mushrooms in warm water for 30 minutes then drain. Discard the stalks and halve the caps. Heat 15 ml/1 tbsp of oil and fry the mushroom caps until tender then remove from the pan. Meanwhile, blanch the broccoli in boiling water until almost tender then drain well. Heat 15 ml/1 tbsp of oil in the wok and cook the broccoli with the fish sauce, wine or sherry, cornflour and chicken stock until just tender. Remove from the wok. Heat the remaining oil and stir-fry the tofu until lightly browned. Add the prawns, chicken and carrot and stir-fry for 3 minutes. Return the broccoli mixture to the pan with the oyster and soy sauce and cook for a few minutes until tender.

Tofu with Oyster Sauce

Serves 4

30 ml/2 tbsp groundnut (peanut) oil
225 g/8 oz tofu, cubed
225 g/8 oz mushrooms, sliced
6 spring onions (scallions), cut into chunks
3 stalks celery, sliced
1 red pepper, cut into chunks
120 ml/4 fl oz/½ cup water
15 ml/1 tbsp cornflour (cornstarch)
30 ml/2 tbsp oyster sauce
15 ml/1 tbsp rice wine or dry sherry
15 ml/1 tbsp soy sauce

Heat half the oil and fry the tofu until lightly browned. Remove from the pan. Heat the remaining oil and fry the mushrooms, spring onions, celery and pepper for 2 minutes. Return the tofu to the pan and toss lightly to combine the ingredients. Blend the water, cornflour, oyster sauce, wine or sherry and soy sauce. Pour the mixture into the wok and bring to the boil, stirring continuously. Simmer, stirring, for 2 minutes before serving.

Peng Tofu

Serves 4

120 ml/4 fl oz/½ cup oil
450 g/1 lb tofu, thickly sliced
15 ml/1 tbsp shredded pork
3 spring onions (scallions), shredded
1 red chilli pepper, shredded
15 ml/1 tbsp black bean sauce
450 ml/¾ pt/2 cups stock
60 ml/4 tbsp soy sauce
2.5 ml/½ tsp sugar
pinch of salt
5 ml/1 tsp cornflour (cornstarch)
5 ml/1 tsp sesame oil

Heat the oil and fry the tofu until golden brown. Remove from the pan and drain. Pour off all but 30 ml/ 2 tbsp of oil and fry the pork, spring onions, chilli and black bean sauce for 30 seconds. Return the tofu to the pan with the stock, soy sauce, sugar and salt. Bring to the boil and simmer for 10 minutes. Blend the cornflour to a paste with a little water, stir it into the pan and simmer, stirring, for 1 minute. Serve sprinkled with sesame oil.

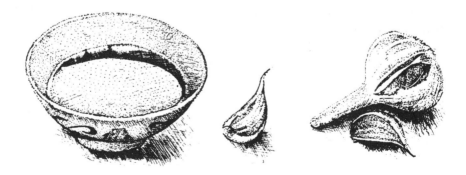

Peppers with Tofu

Serves 4

1 large red pepper
1 large green pepper
150 g/5 oz onions
1 bunch basil
1 bunch parsley
2 beef tomatoes, skinned
salt and freshly ground pepper
pinch of sambal oelek
10 ml/2 tsp soy sauce
15 ml/1 tbsp olive oil
225 g/8 oz tofu, cubed

Cut the peppers into strips and the onion into rings. Reserve a few basil and parsley leaves for garnish and chop the rest finely. Quarter the tomatoes, remove the seeds and purée the flesh with the salt, pepper sambal oelek and soy sauce. Heat the oil and fry the tofu until golden brown. Add the peppers and onions and stir-fry for 3 minutes. Add the tomato purée and simmer for 1 minute. Stir in the chopped herbs and serve garnished with the reserved herbs.

Tofu with Prawns

Serves 4

45 ml/3 tbsp groundnut (peanut) oil
1 clove garlic, crushed
5 ml/1 tsp salt
225 g/8 oz tofu, cubed
225 g/8 oz peeled prawns
30 ml/2 tbsp rice wine or dry sherry
30 ml/2 tbsp soy sauce
250 ml/8 fl oz/1 cup chicken stock
30 ml/2 tbsp cornflour (cornstarch)

Heat the oil and fry the garlic and salt until lightly browned. Add the tofu and stir-fry for 2 minutes. Add the prawns, wine or sherry and soy sauce and stir until the tofu and prawns are well coated in the flavoured oil. Add most of the chicken stock, bring to the boil, cover and simmer for 3 minutes. Mix the cornflour with the remaining stock, stir it into the pan and simmer, stirring, until the sauce clears and thickens.

Pork-Stuffed Tofu

Serves 4

225 g/8 oz minced (ground) pork
2 spring onions (scallions) chopped
15 ml/1 tbsp soy sauce
15 ml/1 tbsp rice wine or dry sherry
5 ml/1 tsp sesame oil
450 g/1 lb tofu

Mix together the pork, spring onions, half the soy sauce, the wine or sherry and the sesame oil. Cut the tofu into 8 large rectangles and scoop out a hollow in the top of each piece. Stuff with the pork mixture and arrange in a shallow ovenproof dish. Sprinkle with the remaining soy sauce. Place on a rack in a steamer and steam over gently simmering water for about 30 minutes.

Tofu with Spring Onion

Serves 4

60 ml/4 tbsp groundnut (peanut) oil

8 spring onions (scallions), cut into
  chunks

450g/1 lb tofu, cubed

45 ml/3 tbsp soy sauce

10 ml / ½ tsp salt

Heat the oil and fry the spring onions
for 2 minutes. Add the tofu stir-fry for
2 minutes. Add the soy sauce and salt
stir-fry for a further 1 minute.

Chinese Tofu

Serves 4

45 ml/3tbsp groundnut (peanut) oil

5 ml/1 tsp salt

450 g/1 lb tofu, cubed

30 ml/2 tbsp soy sauce

120 ml/4 fl oz/ ½ cup chicken stock

5 ml/1 tsp sugar

Heat the oil and salt and fry the tofu
for about 4 minutes until golden
brown on all sides. Add the soy sauce,
stock and sugar, bring to the boil and
stir-fry for about 2 minutes.

Tofu Stir-Fry

Serves 4

45 ml/3 tbsp groundnut (peanut) oil

1 spring onion (scallion), chopped

1 clove garlic, crushed

450 g/1 lb tofu, cubed

45 ml/3 tbsp soy sauce

15 ml/1 tbsp rice wine or dry sherry

2.5 ml/½ tsp salt

15 ml/1 tbsp cornflour (cornstarch)

Heat the oil and fry the spring onion
and garlic until lightly browned. Add
the tofu and fry until golden. Add the
remaining ingredients, bring to the
boil, cover and simmer for 5 minutes.

Tofu Balls with Vegetables

Serves 4

450 g/1 lb tofu

75 g/3 oz minced (ground) chicken

4 water chestnuts, minced

45 ml/3 tbsp cornflour (cornstarch)

oil for deep-frying

100 g/4 oz/1 cup plain (all-purpose)
  flour

45 ml/3tbsp water

2 carrots, cut into strips

100 g/4 oz mangetout (snow peas)

250 ml/8 fl oz/1 cup chicken stock

5 ml/1 tsp salt

Mash the tofu and place it in a
strainer or colander to drain. Mix
with the chicken, water chestnuts and
30 ml/2 tbsp of cornflour and shape
into balls about the size of ping-pong
balls. Mix the flour with enough
water to make a thick batter. Dip the
tofu balls in the batter. Heat the oil
and deep-fry the tofu until golden
brown. Remove and drain.

Spoon 30 ml/2 tbsp of oil into a
wok and fry the carrots and mangetout for 2 minutes. Add the stock and
salt and bring to the boil. Add the
tofu balls and simmer until heated
through. Blend the remaining
cornflour to a paste with a little
water, stir it into the pan and simmer,
until the sauce thickens slightly.
Serve at once.

Sauces

Many Chinese dishes come complete with their own sauces which are part of the recipe itself. You can adapt such sauces by modifying and experimenting with the ingredients in the recipe to suit your own favourite tastes. Here are some additional savoury and sweet sauces which can be combined with a range of ingredients to make new and tasty meals.

Beef Sauce

30 ml/2 tbsp groundnut (peanut) oil
2.5 ml/½ tsp salt
1 clove garlic, crushed
1 onion, chopped
100g/4 oz minced (ground) beef
175 ml/6 fl oz/¾ cup beef stock
5 ml/1 tsp sugar
1 tomato, skinned and cut into wedges
15 ml/1 tbsp cornflour (cornstarch)
45 ml/3 tbsp water
15 ml/1 tbsp chopped fresh parsley

Heat the oil and fry the salt, garlic and onion until lightly browned. Add the beef and stir-fry until lightly browned. Add the stock, sugar and tomato and bring to the boil, stirring. Mix the cornflour and water to a paste then stir it into the pan and simmer, stirring, until the sauce thickens. Pour over noodles and serve garnished with parsley.

Brown Sauce

Serves 4

15 ml/1 tbsp groundnut (peanut) oil
1 spring onion (scallion), minced
10 ml/2 tsp brown sugar
15 ml/1 tbsp soy sauce
30 ml/2 tbsp water

Heat the oil and stir-fry the spring onion until lightly browned. Add the sugar, soy sauce and water and stir-fry for a few seconds until heated through. Sprinkle over fried eggs to serve.

Celery Sauce

Serves 4

2 stalks celery, thinly sliced
4 spring onions (scallions), minced
250 ml/8 fl oz/1 cup chicken stock
30 ml/2 tbsp groundnut (peanut) oil
30 ml/2 tbsp soy sauce
15 ml/1 tbsp rice wine or dry sherry
15 ml/1 tbsp cornflour (cornstarch)
45 ml/3 tbsp water

Mix all the ingredients except the cornflour and water in a pan and bring slowly to the boil. Cover and simmer for 15 minutes. Mix the cornflour and water to a paste, stir into the pan and simmer, stirring, until the sauce thickens.

Chicken Sauce

Serves 4

250 ml/8 fl oz / 1 cup chicken stock
2.5 ml/1/2 salt
5 ml/1 tsp soy sauce
15 ml/1 tbsp cornflour (cornstarch)
45 ml/3 tbsp water

Bring the stock to the boil with the salt and soy sauce. Mix the cornflour and water to paste, stir it into the pan and simmer, stirring, until the sauce thickens. Pour over chicken or vegetables to serve.

Chicken Stock Sauce

Serves 4

15 ml/1 tbsp groundnut (peanut) oil
20 ml/1¼ tbsp cornflour (cornstarch)
450 ml/¾ pt/2 cups chicken stock

Heat the oil. Blend together the cornflour and stock, add to the pan and simmer, stirring, until the sauce thickens. Pour over noodles to serve.

Coconut Cream and Coconut Milk

Serves 4

225 g/8 oz desiccated coconut

Place the coconut in a large bowl and pour on enough warm water to cover. leave to stand for 1 hour. Squeeze the coconut through a piece of muslin in a fine sieve to collect the coconut cream.

Mix the remaining dessicated coconut with a further 500 ml/17 fl oz/ 2 ¼ cups of warm water and leave to stand for a further 1 hour. Squeeze out the liquor again to make coconut milk.

Egg Foo Yung Sauce

Serves 4

175 ml/6 fl oz/¾cup chicken stock
5 ml/ 1 tsp soy sauce
10 ml/2 tsp cornflour (cornstarch)
salt

Heat the stock with the soy sauce. Blend the cornflour to a paste with a little of the stock then stir it into the mixture and season with salt. Heat, stirring, for 1 minute then spoon over the egg foo yung.

Egg Yolk Sauce

Serves 4

2 egg yolks
250 ml/8 fl oz/1 cup water
30 ml/2 tsp groundnut (peanut) oil
10 ml/2 tsp cornflour (cornstarch)
2.5/¼ tsp salt

Beat the egg yolks with 60 ml/4 tbsp of water. Heat the oil, stir in the cornflour and cook over a low heat until smooth. Stir in the remaining water and salt and heat gently, stirring, until the mixture is smooth and bubbling. Gradually pour in the egg mixture in a thin stream, stirring continuously. Simmer over a low heat, stirring, until the sauce is smooth and creamy. Pour over chicken or vegetables to serve.

Fish Sauce

Serves 4

4 Chinese dried mushrooms
6 dried lily buds
15 ml/1 tbsp soy sauce
15 ml/1 tbsp rice wine or dry sherry
2.5 ml / ½ tsp salt
2.5/½ tsp sugar
30 ml/2 tbsp groundnut (peanut) oil
1 slice ginger root, minced
100 g/4 oz lean pork, cut into strips
50 g/2 oz bamboo shoots, cut into strips
50 g/2 oz Chinese leaves, shredded
375 ml/13 fl oz/1½ cups water
15 ml/1 tbsp cornflour (cornstarch)

Soak the mushrooms and lily buds separately in warm water for 30 minutes then drain. Discard the mushroom stalks and slice the caps. Halve the lily buds then mix then with the soy sauce, wine or sherry, salt and sugar. Heat the oil and fry the ginger until lightly browned. Add the pork and stir-fry for 3 minutes. Add the mushrooms, bamboo shoots and Chinese leaves and stir-fry for 2 minutes. Add the water and bring to the boil, cover and simmer for 2 minutes. Stir in the lily bud mixture and heat through. Blend the cornflour to a paste with a little water, stir into the pan and simmer, stirring, until the sauce thickens. Pour over fried fish to serve.

Sauce for Fried Fish

Serves 4

1 slice ginger root, minced
30 ml/2 tbsp brown sugar
15 ml/ 1 tbsp groundnut (peanut) oil
60 ml/4 tbsp chicken stock
15 ml/1 tbsp cornflour (cornstarch)
45 ml/3 tbsp water

Mix together the ginger, sugar, oil and stock then bring to the boil, stirring. Mix the cornflour and water, stir into the pan and simmer, stirring, until the sauce thickens. Pour over fried fish to serve.

Ham Sauce

Serves 4

30 ml/2 tbsp groundnut (peanut) oil
2 stalks celery, chopped
1 onion, chopped
100 g/4 oz ham, chopped
250 ml/8 fl oz/1 cup chicken stock
5 ml/1 tsp cornflour (cornstarch)
60 ml/4 tbsp water
1 egg beaten

Heat the oil and fry the celery, onion and ham and stir-fry for 2 minutes. Add the stock, bring to the boil, cover and simmer for 3 minutes. Mix the cornflour and water to a paste then blend in the egg. Pour into the pan and simmer, stirring, until the sauce thickens. Pour over the noodles to serve.

Sauce for Lobster

Serves 4

30 ml/2 tbsp groundnut (peanut) oil
1 clove garlic, crushed
15 ml/1 tbsp black bean sauce
100 g/4 oz minced (ground) pork
2 spring onions (scallions), chopped
15 ml/1 tbsp soy sauce
15 ml/1 tbsp rice wine or dry sherry
5 ml/1 tsp sugar
120 ml/4 fl oz/½ cup water
15 ml/1 tbsp cornflour (cornstarch)
2 eggs, beaten

Heat the oil and fry the garlic and black bean sauce for 30 seconds. Stir in the pork and stir-fry for 2 minutes. Add the spring onions, soy sauce, wine or sherry, sugar and water, bring to a simmer, cover and simmer for 3 minutes. Mix the cornflour with a little water then stir it into the pan. Simmer, stirring, until the sauce thickens. Stir the eggs into the pan then remove from the heat. Pour over lobster or prawn dishes to serve.

Milk Sauce

Serves 4

375 ml/13 fl oz/1½ cups milk
30 ml/2 tbsp butter
15 ml/1 tbsp rice wine or dry sherry
5 ml/1 tsp sugar
2.5 ml/½ tsp salt
15 ml/1 tbsp cornflour (cornstarch)
45 ml/3 tbsp water

Heat the milk to just below boiling. Stir in the butter, wine or sherry, sugar and salt and heat through gently. Mix the cornflour and water to a paste, stir it into the sauce and simmer, stirring, until the sauce thickens. Pour over chicken or vegetables to serve.

Mushroom Sauce

Serves 4

12 Chinese dried mushrooms
45 ml/3 tbsp groundnut (peanut) oil
60 ml/4 tbsp soy sauce
15 ml/1 tbsp rice wine or dry sherry
2.5 ml/½ tsp salt
15 ml/1 tbsp sugar
15 ml/1 tbsp cornflour (cornstarch)

Soak the mushrooms in warm water for 30 minutes then drain, reserving 120 ml/4 fl oz/½ cup of the liquid. Discard the stalks and halve the caps. Heat 30 ml/2 tbsp of oil and stir-fry the mushrooms for 2 minutes. Add the soy sauce, wine or sherry and salt. Stir in the remaining oil, mushroom liquid and sugar, cover and simmer for 30 minutes, stirring occasionally. Blend the cornflour to a paste with a little water then stir it into the pan and simmer, stirring, until the sauce thickens. Pour over rice to serve.

Mushroom Sauce with Tomato

Serves 4

6 Chinese dried mushrooms

5 ml/1 tsp sugar

30 ml/2 tbsp butter

3 spring onions (scallions), chopped

1 clove garlic, crushed

1 large tomato, skinned and chopped

salt

5 ml/1 tsp cornflour (cornstarch)

Soak the mushrooms in warm water with the sugar for 30 minutes then drain, reserving the liquid. Discard the stems and slice the caps. Melt the butter and fry the spring onions and garlic until softened. Add the mushrooms and liquid, tomato and a pinch of salt. Bring to the boil and simmer for 10 minutes until the vegetables are cooked. Blend the cornflour with a little cold water, stir it into the sauce and simmer, stirring, until the sauce thickens.

Oyster Sauce

Makes about 300 ml/½ pt/1¼ cups

15 oysters

45 ml/3 tbsp soy sauce

Shell the oysters, reserving the liquid. Mince the oysters finely and place them and their liquid in a pan. Bring to the boil, cover and simmer gently for 30 minutes. Strain, discard the oysters, and stir the soy sauce into the liquid. Store in a screwtop jar in the refrigerator.

Peanut Sauce

Serves 4

100 g/4 oz peanut butter

120 ml/4 fl oz/½ cup chicken stock

120 ml/4 fl oz/½ cup groundnut (peanut) oil

15 ml/1 tbsp lemon juice

15 ml/1 tbsp soy sauce

2.5 ml/½ tsp salt

2.5 ml/½ tsp chilli powder

2.5 ml/½ tsp sugar

Mix all the ingredients together thoroughly in a small saucepan over a low heat, stirring continuously. When the ingredients have all mixed together, remove from the heat and leave to cool. Store in the refrigerator in an air-tight jar and stir well before using.

Peking Sauce

Serves 4

30 ml/2 tbsp groundnut (peanut) oil

100 g/4 oz lean minced (ground) pork

4 spring onions (scallions), finely chopped

120 ml/4 fl oz/½ cup yellow bean paste

30 ml/2 tbsp soy sauce

15 ml/1 tbsp hoisin sauce

375 ml/13 fl oz/1½ cups water

Heat the oil and fry the pork until lightly browned. Stir in the spring onions and stir-fry for 1 minute. Stir in the bean paste, soy sauce, hoisin sauce and water and simmer, stirring, for 2 minutes. Pour over noodles to serve.

Pineapple Sauce

Serves 4

45 ml/3 tbsp sugar

45 ml/3 tbsp wine vinegar

15 ml/1 tbsp cornflour (cornstarch)

120 ml/4 fl oz/½ cup pineapple juice

pinch of salt

Mix together all the ingredients and simmer, stirring, until the sauce thickens. Pour over cooked carrots or cabbage to serve.

Plum Sauce

Makes about 750 g/1½ lb

225 g/8 oz plums, peeled, stoned and roughly chopped

225 g/8 oz dried apricots, soaked and roughly chopped

2 canned pimentos, drained and chopped

225 g/8 oz/1 cup brown sugar

120 ml/4 fl oz/½ cup wine vinegar

60 ml/4 tbsp apple purée

Combine all the ingredients in a pan and bring slowly to the boil, stirring. Cover and simmer gently for about 1 hour, stirring occasionally, and adding a little water if the sauce becomes too thick. Pour into warm jars, seal, label and store in a cool place for a few weeks before using.

Pork Sauce

Serves 4

30 ml/2 tbsp oil

2 spring onions (scallions), chopped

2 cloves garlic, crushed

225 g/8 oz minced (ground) pork

225 g/8 oz mixed vegetables, diced

10 ml/2 tsp brown sugar

15 ml/1 tbsp rice wine or dry sherry

15 ml/1 tbsp soy sauce

90 ml/6 tbsp tomato purée (paste)

450 ml/¾ pt/2 cups chicken stock

15 ml/1 tbsp cornflour (cornstarch)

Heat the oil and fry the spring onions and garlic until lightly browned. Add the pork and stir-fry for 3 minutes. Add the vegetables and stir-fry for 2 minutes. Add the sugar, wine or sherry, soy sauce, tomato purée and stock, bring to the boil, cover and simmer for 4 minutes. Mix the cornflour to a paste with a little water then stir it into the pan. Simmer, stirring, until the sauce thickens. Pour over noodles to serve.

Sweet and Sour Sauce

Serves 4

250 ml/8 fl oz/1 cup water
100 g/4 oz/½ cup sugar
120 ml/4 fl oz/½ cup wine vinegar
30 ml/2 tbsp tomato purée (paste)
15 ml/1 tbsp cornflour (cornstarch)
15 ml/1 tbsp soy sauce

Bring three-quarters of the water to the boil. Stir in the sugar and stir until the sugar dissolves. Add the wine vinegar and stir for 1 minute. Mix the remaining water with the tomato purée, cornflour and soy sauce, stir into the pan and simmer, stirring, until the sauce thickens.

Sweet and Sour Egg Sauce

Serves 4

15 ml/1 tbsp sugar
15 ml/1 tbsp wine vinegar
30 ml/2 tbsp soy sauce

Mix all the ingredients together and simmer, stirring, until well blended. Pour over fried eggs to serve.

Sweet and Spicy Sauce

Serves 4

15 ml/1 tbsp cornflour (cornstarch)
45 ml/3 tbsp sugar
45 ml/3 tbsp wine vinegar
120 ml/4 fl oz/½ cup water
pinch of salt

Mix together all the ingredients in a pan and simmer, stirring, until the sauce thickens. Pour over cooked carrots or cabbage to serve.

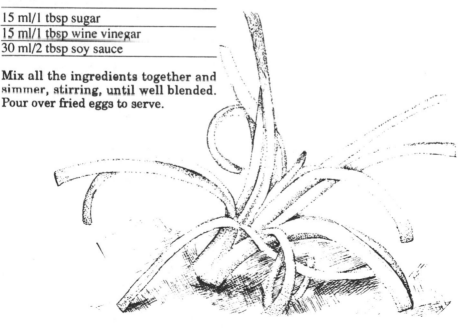

Marinades and Condiments

Many Chinese dishes, especially stir-fried dishes which are cooked quickly over a high heat, gain some of their most interesting flavours from marinating the main ingredients before cooking. This allows the flavours to develop before they are quickly sealed in the hot pan.

Fried or roasted Chinese foods are often served with side dishes of spice or seasoning mixtures into which you dip the food before eating.

Barbecue Marinade

Makes 375 ml/13 fl oz/⅔ cup

2 cloves garlic, crushed
1 slice ginger root, minced
250 ml/8 fl oz/1 cup soy sauce
15 ml/1 tbsp brown sugar
15 ml/1 tbsp rice wine or dry sherry

Mix all the ingredients and pour over spare ribs. Leave to stand for 1 hour, basting occasionally, then drain and cook. Baste with the marinade while cooking or use as the base for a sauce.

Chicken Stock Marinade

Makes 350 ml/13 fl oz/1½ cups

3 cloves garlic, crushed
1 slice ginger root, minced
250 ml/8 fl oz/1 cup chicken stock
60 ml/4 tbsp soy sauce
30 ml/2 tbsp rice wine or dry sherry
15 ml/1 tbsp brown sugar

Mix together all the ingredients and pour over spare ribs. Leave to stand for 1 hour, basting occasionally, then drain and cook. Baste with the marinade while cooking, or use as the base for a sauce.

Five-Spice Marinade

Makes 120 ml/4 fl oz/½ cup

2 cloves garlic, crushed
60 ml/4 tbsp soy sauce
30 ml/2 tbsp groundnut (peanut) oil
5 ml/1 tsp five-spice powder
5 ml/1 tsp salt
5 ml/1 tsp sugar
freshly ground pepper

Mix together the ingredients rub the mixture over chicken, inside and out. Leave to stand for 1 hour, basting occasionally, then drain and cook. Baste with the marinade while cooking.

Five-Spice Marinade for Pork

Makes 60 ml/4 tbsp

5 ml/1 tsp sugar
2.5 ml/½ tsp five-spice powder
2.5 ml/½ tsp salt
pinch of freshly ground pepper
30 ml/2 tbsp soy sauce
15 ml/1 tbsp rice wine or dry sherry

Mix together the sugar, five-spice powder, salt and pepper and rub the mixture over pork strips. Leave to stand for 2 hours. Add the soy sauce and wine or sherry and leave to stand for a further 30 minutes.

Garlic Marinade

Makes 250 ml/8 fl oz/1 cup

3 cloves garlic, crushed

2 spring onions (scallions), chopped

2 slices ginger root, minced

120 ml/4 fl oz/½ cup soy sauce

45 ml/3 tbsp sugar

2.5 ml/½ tsp sesame oil

Mix together all the ingredients and rub over pork strips. Leave to marinate for 2 hours, then drain and cook.

Hoisin Sauce Marinade

Makes 250 ml/8 fl oz/1 cup

120 ml/4 fl oz/½ cup hoisin sauce

120 ml/4 fl oz/½ cup water

Mix together the hoisin sauce and water and brush over chicken. Leave to stand for 2 hours, basting occasionally, then drain and cook. Baste with the marinade while cooking.

Hoisin and Chilli Marinade

Makes 120 ml/4 fl oz/½ cup

2 cloves garlic, crushed

2.5 cm/1 in garlic root, minced

1 spring onion (scallion), finely chopped

60 ml/4 tbsp rice wine or dry sherry

30 ml/2 tbsp soy sauce

15 ml/1 tbsp hoisin sauce

15 ml/1 tsp chilli sauce

15 ml/1 tbsp honey

2.5 ml/½ tsp salt

Mix together all the ingredients and rub over pork. Leave to stand for 2 hours, then drain and cook. Baste with the marinade while cooking.

Hoisin and Sherry Marinade

Makes 120 ml/4 fl oz/½ cup

75 ml/5 tbsp hoisin sauce

45 ml/3 tbsp soy sauce

30 ml/2 tbsp rice wine or dry sherry

30 ml/2 tbsp brown sugar

2.5 ml/½ tsp five-spice powder

Mix all the ingredients together and rub over spare ribs. Leave to stand for 2 hours, basting occasionally, then drain and cook. Baste with the marinade while cooking.

Honey Marinade

Makes 120 ml/4 fl oz/½ cup

5 ml/1 tsp salt
60 ml/4 tbsp soy sauce
30 ml/2 tbsp rice wine or dry sherry
30 ml/2 tbsp honey
15 ml/1 tbsp brown sugar
2 cloves garlic, crushed

Rub strips of pork with salt and leave to stand for 2 hours. Mix the remaining ingredients and pour over the pork. Leave to stand for 1 hour, basting frequently, then drain and cook.

Orange Marinade

Makes 450 ml/¾ pt/2 cups

1 strip orange peel
1 clove garlic, crushed
375 ml/13 fl oz/1½ cups chicken stock
120 ml/4 fl oz/½ cup soy sauce
15 ml/1 tbsp sugar
5 ml/1 tsp salt
freshly ground pepper
2.5 ml/½ tsp sesame oil

Soak the orange peel in warm water until slightly softened then mince and mix with the garlic. Bring the stock almost to the boil, then blend in the remaining ingredients. Pour over chicken and leave to stand for 2 hours, basting occasionally, then drain and cook. Baste with the marinade while cooking.

Pineapple Marinade

Makes 400 ml/14 fl oz/¾ cup

1 clove garlic, crushed
250 ml/8 fl oz/1 cup soy sauce
120 ml/4 fl oz/½ cup pineapple juice
60 ml/4 tbsp rice wine or dry sherry
30 ml/2 tbsp brown sugar

Mix together all the ingredients and pour over spare ribs. Leave to stand for 1 hour, basting occasionally, then drain and cook. Baste with the marinade while cooking, or use as the base for a sauce.

Rice Wine Marinade

Makes 250 ml/8 fl oz/1 cup

2 spring onions (scallions), chopped
1 slice ginger root, minced
120 ml/4 fl oz/½ cup
60 ml/4 tbsp rice wine or dry sherry
30 ml/2 tbsp chicken stock
30 ml/2 tbsp brown sugar
10 ml/2 tsp honey
2.5 ml/½ tsp salt
pinch of freshly ground pepper

Mix together all the ingredients and pour over pork. Leave to marinate for 2 hours, then drain and cook. Baste with the marinade while cooking, or use as the base for a sauce.

Soy Sauce Marinade

Makes 250 ml/8 fl oz/1 cup

120 ml/4 fl oz/½ cup water
60 ml/4 tbsp soy sauce
30 ml/2 tbsp sugar
5 ml/1 tsp salt

Heat the water then blend in the remaining ingredients and pour over pork strips. Leave to stand for 2 hours, basting frequently, then drain and cook.

Soy and Ginger Marinade

Makes 120 ml/4 fl oz/½ cup

2 cloves garlic, crushed
1 slice ginger root, minced
60 ml/4 tbsp soy sauce
15 ml/1 tbsp brown sugar
5 ml/1 tsp salt
pinch of freshly ground pepper

Mix all the ingredients together and rub over spare ribs. Leave to stand for 1 hour, basting occasionally, then drain and cook. Baste with the marinade while cooking.

Soy and Wine Marinade

Makes 250 ml/8 fl oz/1 cup

15 ml/1 tbsp sugar
5 ml/1 tsp salt
2 cloves garlic, crushed
1 spring onion (scallion), chopped
120 ml/4 fl oz/½ cup soy sauce
60 ml/4 tbsp rice wine or dry sherry
15 ml/1 tbsp honey

Mix the salt and sugar and rub over pork strips. Leave to stand for 30 minutes. Mix the remaining ingredients and pour over the pork. Leave to stand for 1 hour, then drain and cook.

Spicy Marinade

Makes 60 ml/4 tbsp

1 clove garlic, crushed
30 ml/2 tbsp soy sauce
15 ml/1 tsp rice wine or dry sherry
5 ml/1 tsp sugar
5 ml/1 tsp salt
2.5 ml/½ tsp cinnamon
pinch of freshly ground pepper
pinch of ground cloves

Mix together all the ingredients and rub over pork strips. Leave to stand for 1½ hours, then grill or fry as directed in the recipe.

Spring Onion Marinade

Makes 375 ml/13 fl oz/1½ cups

4 spring onions (scallions), chopped
2 cloves garlic, minced
1 slice ginger root, minced
5 ml/1 tsp salt
250 ml/8 fl oz/1 cup soy sauce
30 ml/2 tbsp rice wine or dry sherry
15 ml/1 tbsp honey

Mix together all the ingredients, blending well. Rub the marinade over chicken, inside and out, and leave to stand for 1 hour, basting occasionally, then drain and cook. Baste with the marinade while cooking.

Sugar Marinade

Makes 120 ml/4 fl oz/½ cup

1 slice ginger root, minced
60 ml/4 tbsp brown sugar
45 ml/3 tbsp soy sauce
2.5 ml/½ tsp five-spice powder
5 ml/1 tsp rice wine or dry sherry

Mix all the ingredients together and rub over spare ribs. Leave to stand for 1 hour, basting occasionally, then drain and cook. Baste with the marinade while cooking.

Cantonese Salt

Makes about 75 ml/5 tbsp

60 ml/4 tbsp salt
10 ml/2 tsp Szechuan peppercorns

Heat the salt and peppercorns in a dry pan over a low heat, shaking continuously, for about 5 minutes until lightly browned. Crush the peppercorns then store the mixture in a screw-top jar. Serve with fried or roasted foods.

Cinnamon Spice

Makes about 75 ml/5 tbsp

30 ml/2 tbsp ground cinnamon
15 ml/1 tbsp ground ginger
2.5 ml/½ tsp freshly ground pepper

Heat all the ingredients in a dry pan over a low heat, shaking continuously, for a few minutes until the mixture is hot. Store in a screw-top jar and serve with chicken dishes.

Chilli Oil

Makes about 250 ml/8 fl oz/1 cup

250 ml/8 fl oz/1 cup groundnut (peanut) oil
4 fresh red chilli peppers

Heat the oil and chilli peppers over a gentle heat until the oil darkens. Strain and store ready for use. You can vary the strength of the oil according to your taste by adding more or fewer chilli peppers.

Five-Spice Mix

Makes about 75 ml/5 tbsp

60 ml/4 tbsp salt
5 ml/1 tsp sugar
5 ml/1 tsp five-spice powder
5 ml/1 tsp cinnamon

Heat the salt in a dry pan over a low heat, shaking continuously, for about 5 minutes until lightly browned. Add the remaining ingredients then store the mixture in a screw-top jar. Serve with chicken dishes.

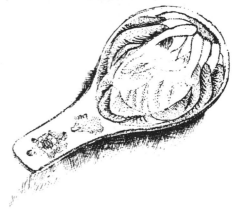

Dips and Dressings

It is interesting to serve some side dishes and dips with Chinese meals to give added interest and authenticity to your meal. Choose your side dishes carefully so that they complement the main courses.

Many salads or vegetable dishes can be tossed with simple dressings to add interest and Chinese appeal to a range of salad ingredients.

Garlic Dip

Makes about 250 ml/8 fl oz/1 cup

4 cloves garlic, crushed
120 ml/4 fl oz/½ cup soy sauce
15 ml/1 tbsp tabasco sauce
pinch of sugar

Blend all the ingredients together well and serve with roast chicken.

Garlic Dip with Soy Sauce

Makes about 120 ml/4 fl oz/½ cup

4 cloves garlic, crushed
60 ml/4 tbsp soy sauce
10 ml/2 tsp brown sugar
10 ml/2 tsp chilli oil (see page 322)

Blend all the ingredients together well and serve with fried or roast chicken dishes.

Ginger Dip

Makes about 120 ml/4 fl oz/½ cup

90 ml/6 tbsp soy sauce
30 ml/2 tbsp wine vinegar
15 ml/1 tbsp brown sugar
1 slice ginger root, minced

Blend all the ingredients together well and serve with prawn or seafood dishes.

Hoisin Dip

Makes about 90 ml/6 tbsp

90 ml/6 tbsp hoisin sauce
5 ml/1 tsp sesame oil

Blend the ingredients together well and serve with pork dishes.

Hot Chilli Dip

Makes about 120 ml/4 fl oz/½ cup

90 ml/6 tbsp chilli sauce
60 ml/4 tbsp soy sauce
2.5 ml/½ tsp mustard powder

Blend all the ingredients together well and serve with pork or chicken dishes.

Mustard Dip

Makes about 120 ml/4 fl oz/½ cup

120 ml/4 fl oz/½ cup made mustard
60 ml/4 tbsp soy sauce
2.5 ml/½ tsp salt

Blend all the ingredients together well and serve with pork dishes.

Peanut Dip

Makes about 75 ml/5 tbsp

30 ml/2 tbsp groundnut (peanut) oil
15 ml/1 tbsp peanut butter
15 ml/1 tbsp soy sauce
5 ml/1 tsp salt
5 ml/1 tsp chilli sauce
5 ml/1 tsp sesame oil

Blend all the ingredients together well and serve with tofu or chicken dishes.

Rice Wine Dip

Makes about 250 ml/8 fl oz/1 cup

120 ml/4 fl oz/½ cup rice wine or dry sherry
60 ml/4 tbsp soy sauce
5 ml/1 tsp brown sugar

Blend all the ingredients together well and serve with fried or roast chicken dishes.

Seafood Dip

Makes about 120 ml/4 fl oz/½ cup

120 ml/4 fl oz/½ cup wine vinegar
1 slice ginger root, minced

Blend the ingredients together well and serve with fish or seafood dishes.

Sesame Dip

Makes about 120 ml/4 fl oz/½ cup

120 ml/4 fl oz/½ cup soy sauce
5 ml/1 tsp sesame oil
1 clove garlic, crushed

Blend all the ingredients together well and serve with pork dishes.

Sesame and Hoisin Dip

Makes about 90 ml/6 tbsp

30 ml/2 tbsp hoisin sauce
15 ml/1 tbsp brown sugar
15 ml/1 tbsp water
15 ml/1 tbsp sesame oil

Blend all the ingredients together well and serve with prawn or seafood dishes.

Soy Sauce Dip

Makes about 250 ml/8 fl oz/1 cup

90 ml/6 tbsp groundnut (peanut) oil
120 ml/4 fl oz/½ cup soy sauce

Heat the oil to smoking point then remove from the heat. Stir in the soy sauce and serve with chicken dishes.

Soy Sauce and Mustard Dip

Makes about 75 ml/5 tbsp

45 ml/3 tbsp soy sauce
10 ml/2 tsp mustard powder
5 ml/1 tsp sesame oil

Blend all the ingredients together well and serve with chicken or tofu.

Tomato and Chilli Dip

Makes about 120 ml/4 fl oz/½ cup

60 ml/4 tbsp tomato ketchup (catsup)
30 ml/2 tbsp chilli sauce
5 ml/1 tsp hoisin sauce

Mix all the ingredients together well and serve with prawn or seafood dishes.

Mustard Dressing

Makes about 90 ml/6 tbsp

30 ml/2 tbsp soy sauce
30 ml/2 tbsp wine vinegar
15 ml/1 tbsp mustard powder
5 ml/1 tsp brown sugar
2.5 ml/½ tsp sesame oil

Mix together all the ingredients until well blended. Chill for several hours before using to dress cold chicken dishes.

Oil and Vinegar Dressing

Makes about 90 ml/6 tbsp

60 ml/4 tbsp groundnut (peanut) oil
30 ml/2 tbsp wine vinegar
5 ml/1 tsp brown sugar
salt and freshly ground pepper
few drops of sesame oil

Blend all the ingredients together well.

Peanut Mayonnaise

Makes about 250 ml/8 fl oz/1 cup

30 ml/2 tbsp wine vinegar
75 ml/5 tbsp water
5 ml/1 tsp groundnut (peanut) oil
60 ml/4 tbsp peanut butter
2.5 ml/½ tsp salt
2.5 ml/½ tsp sesame oil
freshly ground Szechuan pepper

Gradually blend all the ingredients together, seasoning with pepper and extra salt to taste.

Salad Dressing

Serves 4

45 ml/3 tbsp groundnut (peanut) oil
45 ml/3 tbsp soy sauce
45 ml/3 tbsp rice wine or dry sherry
45 ml/3 tbsp wine vinegar
45 ml/3 tbsp orange juice
45 ml/3 tbsp lemon juice
15 ml/1 tbsp sugar
salt and freshly ground pepper
15 ml/1 tbsp sesame seeds
15 ml/1 tbsp chopped ginger root
15 ml/1 tbsp chopped garlic

Blend all the ingredients together well and serve in a sauceboat with cold vegetables or green salads.

Soy and Groundnut Dressing

Makes about 90ml/6tbsp

60ml/4tbsp soy sauce
30ml/2tbsp groundnut (peanut) oil
5ml/1tsp salt
5ml/1tsp sugar

Mix all the ingredients together well. Pour over meat or fish.

Soy and Sesame Dressing

Makes about 90ml/6tbsp

90ml/6tbsp soy sauce
5ml/1tsp sesame oil

Blend the ingredients together well and pour over cold meat or fish.

Soy and Vinegar Dressing

Makes about 120ml/4 fl oz/½ cup

45ml/3tbsp soy sauce
45ml/3tbsp wine vinegar
45ml/3tbsp groundnut (peanut) oil
15ml/1tbsp brown sugar

Blend the ingredients together well and pour over cold vegetable dishes.

Salads

You can combine almost any Chinese-style ingredients to make a tasty and attractive salad to serve with your Chinese meals. Dress the salad with one of the soy sauce and vinegar dressings from the recipes in this chapter.

Asparagus Salad

Serves 4

450g/1lb asparagus
30ml/2tbsp soy sauce
10ml/2tsp wine vinegar
5ml/1tsp sesame oil
5ml/1tsp sugar

Par-boil the asparagus in boiling water for 3 minutes then rinse with cold water. Drain well and leave to cool. Mix together the remaining ingredients, pour over the asparagus and chill for 20 minutes before serving.

Aubergine Salad

Serves 4–6

1 aubergine (eggplant), halved
1 clove garlic, halved
30ml/2tbsp wine vinegar
15ml/1tbsp groundnut (peanut) oil
2.5ml/½ tsp salt
pinch of freshly ground pepper
½ lettuce, separated into leaves

Place the aubergine in a dish on a steaming rack and steam for about 30 minutes until tender. Leave to cool slightly then peel. Rub the cut side of the garlic across the inside of a bowl. Mix together the remaining ingredients, pour over the aubergine and toss together. Cover and refrigerate overnight. Arrange the lettuce on a serving plate and spoon the aubergine on top.

Bean and Pepper Salad

Serves 4

225g/8oz green beans
2 red peppers, cut into strips
10ml/2tsp sesame oil
5ml/1tsp minced ginger root
5ml/1tsp sugar
salt

Blanch the beans and peppers in boiling water for 30 seconds then drain well. Mix together the sesame oil, ginger, sugar and a pinch of salt and pour over the vegetables. Toss together well before serving.

Bean Sprout Salad

Serves 4

450g/1lb bean sprouts
30ml/2tbsp soy sauce
5ml/1tsp sesame oil
5ml/1tsp sugar

Blanch the bean sprouts in boiling water for 20 seconds. Drain and leave to cool. Mix all the remaining ingredients, pour them over the bean sprouts, toss well and chill for 20 minutes before serving.

Carrot and Celery Salad

Serves 4

4 stalks celery, shredded
2 carrots, shredded
2 slices ginger root, shredded
10ml/2tsp salt
600ml/1pt/2 ½ cups iced water
30ml/2tbsp soy sauce
2.5ml/½ tsp sesame oil

Mix the celery, carrots and ginger in a bowl. Dissolve the salt in the water, pour over the vegetables and leave to stand for 1 hour. Drain well and arrange in a serving bowl. Sprinkle with soy sauce and toss together well then sprinkle with sesame oil and serve at once.

Celery Salad

Serves 4

½ head celery, cut into chunks
50g/2oz peeled prawns
1 slice ginger root, minced
30m/2 tbsp soy sauce
10m/2 tsp wine vinegar
10m/2 tsp sesame oil
5ml/1tsp salt

Blanch the celery in boiling water for 30 seconds. Drain and pat dry then mix with the prawns. Mix together the remaining ingredients, pour over the celery and toss together well.

Chicken Salad

Serves 4

350g/12oz cooked chicken, cut into strips
3 stalks celery, diagonally sliced
2 cloves garlic, crushed
15ml/1tbsp soy sauce
5ml/1tsp salt
2.5ml/½ tsp freshly ground pepper
15ml/1tbsp sesame oil
5ml/1tsp wine vinegar

Mix all the ingredients together well and chill before serving.

Sesame Chicken Salad

Serves 4

15ml/1tbsp sesame seeds
3 chicken breasts
1.5lt/2 ½ pts/6 cups water
30ml/2tbsp soy sauce
2.5ml/½ tsp salt
2.5ml/½ tsp five-spice powder
3 stalks celery, sliced
15ml/1tbsp sesame oil
15ml/1tbsp groundnut (peanut) oil
pinch of ground ginger
pinch of freshly ground pepper

Toast the sesame seeds in a dry pan until golden brown. Place the chicken, water, 15ml/1tbsp soy sauce, salt and five-spice powder in a large saucepan. Bring to the boil, cover and simmer for 20 minutes. Remove from the heat and leave the chicken to stand in the water for 1 hour.

Remover the chicken, reserving the stock and drain. Remove and discard the bones and cut the meat into thick slices. Bring the stock back to the boil, add the celery and cook for about 3 minutes until it is tender but still crisp. Drain well. Mix together the remaining soy sauce with the oils, ginger and pepper and add the chicken and celery. Toss well, transfer to a serving dish and serve sprinkled with sesame seeds.

Chinese Leaf Salad

Serves 4

1 head Chinese leaves, shredded
30ml/2tbsp soy sauce
15ml/1tbsp sesame oil
5ml/1tsp sugar
salt

Blanch the Chinese leaves in boiling water for 30 seconds then drain well. Mix the soy sauce, sesame oil, sugar and a pinch of salt. Pour over the Chinese leaves and toss well before serving.

Crab Meat Salad

1 cos lettuce
225g/8oz crab meat
100g/4oz water chestnuts, cut into strips
100g/4oz bean sprouts
100g/4oz Chinese leaves, shredded
For the dressing:
90ml/6tbsp olive oil
30ml/2tbsp cider vinegar
15ml/1tbsp tarragon vinegar
5ml/1tsp soy sauce
15ml/1tbsp chopped green pepper
15ml/1tbsp chopped cucumber
5ml/1tsp chopped fresh parsley
5ml/1tsp chopped fresh chives
4 sprigs watercress

Arrange the salad ingredients in a bowl. Mix together all the dressing ingredients, pour over the salad and toss together gently. Garnish with the watercress.

Crab Meat and Cucumber Rings

Serves 4

200g/7oz canned crab meat, flaked
50g/2oz cottage cheese
15ml/1tbsp chopped fresh chives
5 olives, chopped
5ml/1tsp horseradish sauce
5ml/1tsp soy sauce
1 clove garlic, crushed
15ml/1tbsp chilli sauce
1 large cucumber, thickly sliced
salt

Mix together all the ingredients except the cucumber. Arrange the cucumber slices on a flat platter and sprinkle lightly with salt. Spoon the crab meat mixture on top of the cucumber and serve as a salad or cocktail snack.

Cucumber Salad

Serves 4

2 cucumbers, peeled and seeded
10ml/2tsp salt
½ small onion, finely chopped
1 clove garlic, crushed
1 red chilli pepper, seeded and finely
    chopped
30ml/2tbsp wine vinegar
15ml/1tsp sesame oil
10ml/2tsp soy sauce
10ml/2tsp sugar

Chop the cucumbers roughly then place them in a colander and sprinkle with salt. Leave for 30 minutes. Rinse the cucumber and pat dry. Mix together the remaining ingredients and pour over the cucumbers in a bowl. Cover and leave to stand for 30 minutes before serving.

Shredded Cucumber Salad

Serves 4

1 cucumber, peeled and grated
salt
1 clove garlic, crushed
15ml/1tbsp soy sauce
15ml/1tsp groundnut (peanut) oil
2.5ml/½ tsp sugar

Sprinkle the cucumber with salt and leave to stand for 1 hour. Rinse and drain well. Mix together the remaining ingredients, pour over the cucumber and toss together well. Serve at once.

Smashed Cucumber

Serves 4

1 cucumber
1 slice ginger root, minced
30ml/2tbsp brown sugar
60ml/4tbsp wine vinegar

Peel and slice the cucumber, then smash the slices with a mallet or the bottom of a mug, leaving the slices just intact. Arrange in a serving bowl and refrigerate. Mix the remaining ingredients in a pan over a low heat and stir until the sugar dissolves. Spoon over the cucumber and serve at once.

Smashed Cucumber with Spring Onions

Serves 4

1 cucumber
2 spring onions (scallions), minced
120ml/4fl oz/½ cup wine vinegar
salt and freshly ground pepper

Peel and slice the cucumber then smash the slices with a mallet or the bottom of a mug, leaving the slices just intact. Arrange in a serving bowl and refrigerate. Mix the spring onions with the wine vinegar and leave to stand for 30 minutes. Pour over the cucumber and season with salt and pepper.

Cucumber Salad with Spring Onion Dressing

Serves 4

1 cucumber, sliced
salt
5ml/1tsp sugar
60ml/4tbsp groundnut (peanut) oil
4 spring onions (scallions), chopped

Place the cucumber in a colander and sprinkle generously with salt. Mix well then leave to stand for 30 minutes. Rinse lightly in cold water and drain off the excess. Place in a bowl and stir in the sugar. Heat the oil until moderately hot then remove from the heat and stir in the spring onions. Pour over the cucumber and toss well before serving.

Marinated Cucumber

Serves 4

1 cucumber, thinly sliced
5ml/1tsp salt
120ml/4fl oz/½ cup wine vinegar
45ml/3tbsp sugar
75ml/5tbsp water

Sprinkle the cucumber with salt and leave to stand for 30 minutes. Heat the vinegar then stir in the sugar and water, stirring until the sugar dissolves. Bring to the boil and boil for 2 minutes. Remove from the heat and leave to cool. Add the cucumbers and leave to stand for several hours before serving.

Green Pepper Salad

Serves 4

2 green peppers, cut into strips
15ml/1tbsp sesame oil
10ml/2tsp brown sugar
2.5ml/½ tsp salt

Blanch the peppers in boiling water for 30 seconds then drain well. Mix together the sesame oil, sugar and salt, pour over the peppers and toss together well before serving.

Pork Salad

Serves 4

450g/1lb green beans
10ml/2tsp salt
250ml/8fl oz/1 cup wine vinegar
450g/1lb cooked pork, thinly sliced
120ml/4fl oz/½ cup mild mustard
30ml/2tbsp chopped flat-leaved parsley

Blanch the beans in boiling water for about 10 minutes until just tender but still crisp. Drain well. Mix with half the salt and half the wine vinegar and leave to marinate for 2 hours. Meanwhile, mix the remaining salt and wine vinegar with the pork and mustard and leave to marinate. Mix the pork with the beans and serve garnished with parsley.

Rice Salad

Serves 4

225 g/8 oz cooked long-grain rice

4 spring onion (scallions), chopped

30 ml/2 tbsp groundnut (peanut) oil

5 ml/1 tsp sesame oil

250 ml/8 fl oz/1 cup wine vinegar

5 ml/1 tsp sugar

2.5 ml/½ tsp mustard powder

2.5 ml/½ tsp paprika

100 g/4 oz canned sardines, drained

100 g/4 oz peeled prawns

1 head lettuce

2 hard-boiled (hard-cooked) eggs, chopped

4 small Chinese pickles, chopped

30 ml/2 tbsp chilli sauce

15 ml/1 tbsp capers

5 ml/1 tsp chopped fresh parsley

Mix the rice and spring onions. Mix together the oil, sesame oil, 45 ml/ 3 tbsp of wine vinegar, sugar, mustard and paprika. Pour half the dressing over the rice and mix well. Place the sardines and prawns in a bowl, pour over the remaining wine vinegar and leave to stand for 10 minutes then drain. Arrange the lettuce leaves on a serving plate and mound the rice on top.

Arrange the sardine mixture on top and sprinkle with eggs and pickles. Mix the chilli sauce, eggs and capers into the remaining dressing and serve with the salad.

Shanghai Salad

Serves 4

450 g/1 lb cooked veal, diced

60 ml/4 tbsp French dressing

5 ml/1 tsp soy sauce

100 g/4 oz bean sprouts

50 g/2 oz Chinese mixed pickles, cut into strips

1 onion, thinly sliced

175 ml/6 fl oz/¾ cup mayonaise

salt and freshly ground pepper

Place the veal in a bowl. Mix the French dressing and soy sauce, toss with the veal, cover and leave in the refrigerator overnight. Mix together the remaining ingredients and stir them carefully into the veal.

Spinach Salad

Serves 4

450 g/1 lb spinach, cut into strips

30 ml/2 tbsp soy sauce

15 ml/1 tbsp wine vinegar

5 ml/1 tsp sugar

10 ml/2 tsp sesame oil

5 ml/1tsp peanut butter

Blanch the spinach in boiling water for 2 minutes then drain and rinse in cold water. Mix together the dressing ingredients, pour over the spinach and toss together well. Chill for 20 minutes before serving.

Chilled Tomato Salad

Serves 4

8 ripe tomatoes, skinned and quartered
45 ml/3 tbsp sugar
10 ml/2 tsp Worcestershire sauce

Place the tomatoes in a bowl and sprinkle with sugar and Worcestershire sauce. Chill thoroughly before serving.

Tomato and Onion Salad

Serves 4

450 g/1 lb tomatoes, thinly sliced
2 onions, thinly sliced
30 ml/2 tbsp soy sauce
10 ml/2 tsp wine vinegar
5 ml/1 tsp sesame oil
5 ml/1 tsp sugar

Layer the tomatoes and onions in a bowl. Mix the remaining ingredients and pour then over the tomatoes and onions. Chill for 20 minutes before serving.

Tuna Salad

Serves 4

200 g/7 oz canned tuna, drained and
   flaked
2 spring onions (scallions), chopped
1 green pepper, chopped
1 stalk celery, diagonally sliced
100 g/4 oz bean sprouts
5 ml/1 tsp salt
300 ml/½ pt/1¼ cups mayonaise

Mix together all the ingredients carefully and chill well before serving.

Desserts, Cakes and Confectionery

Chinese cuisine tends to concentrate on the variety of main courses rather than on desserts, so there are few classic Chinese dessert recipes, although the deliciously sweet toffee apples and bananas will be familiar to those who have dined in a Chinese restaurant. The best desserts to choose to complete your Chinese meal are simple and light dishes, often using fruit, which come as a refreshing conclusion to the variety, spice and intensity of the main courses.

Baking is not generally common in China, either – in fact, many people do not have an oven. Almond biscuits are the most famous Chinese biscuits, although you could easily adapt the recipe to use other nuts. The sponge cake is a steamed recipe which you can prepare in a wok with a steamer rack, or in an ordinary saucepan.

Almond Milk Jelly with Lychees

Serves 4 –6

75 ml/5 tbsp water
15 g/½ oz gelatine
250 ml/8 fl oz/1 cup milk
50 g/2 oz/¼ cup brown sugar
5 ml/1 tsp almond essence (extract)
400 g/14 oz canned lychees in syrup

Mix together the water and gelatine and heat gently over a bowl of warm water until the gelatine dissolves. Bring the milk to the boil then stir in the sugar until it dissolves. Stir in the gelatine mixture then the almond essence. Remove from the heat and continue to stir until all the ingredients are well mixed. Pour into a dish and cool then chill until set.

Cut into cubes and arrange in dessert bowls then top with the lychees and syrup.

Toffee Apples

Serves 4

3 firm dessert apples, peeled and cut into wedges
50 g/2 oz plain (all-purpose) flour
1 egg
5 ml/1 tsp sesame oil
300 ml/½ pt/⅓ cup groundnut (peanut) oil
175 g/6 oz sugar
30 ml/2 tbsp sesame seeds

Mix together the flour, egg and sesame oil to a smooth batter. Add the apples. Heat the groundnut (peanut) oil and deep-fry a few pieces of fruit at a time for about 2 minutes until golden brown. Drain on kitchen paper and keep them warm while you fry the remaining fruit pieces.

Reheat the oil and deep-fry the fruit for a further 2 minutes then drain on kitchen paper. Meanwhile, mix the sugar, sesame seeds and 30 ml/2 tbsp oil from the deep-frying pan and heat until the mixture begins to caramelise. Stir the fruit into the caramel a few at a time then place then in iced water to harden. Remove from the water and serve at once.

Honeyed Bananas

Serves 4

30 ml/2 tbsp groundnut (peanut) oil
4 firm bananas, halved lengthways
350 g/12 oz/1 cup brown sugar
120 ml/4 oz/½ cup honey
120 ml/4 fl oz/½ cup water
5 ml/1 tsp wine vinegar

Heat the oil and fry the bananas until lighly browned. Remove from the pan and cut into 2.5 cm/1 in pieces. Place the honey, sugar, water and wine vinegar in a pan and heat gently until the mixture starts to thicken. When the mixture forms threads when a little is dropped into cold water, add the bananas and stir gently until they are completely coated. Dip the bananas into iced water to set them.

Candied Peel

Serves 4

rind of 1 lemon
rind of 1 orange
rind of 1 grapefruit
450 g/1 lb sugar
250 ml/8 fl oz/1 cup water
pinch of salt

Cut the rinds into thin strips and place in a pan. Cover with water, add the salt, bring to the boil and simmer for 30 minutes then drain. Mix the sugar with the water, bring to the boil and simmer until a syrup is formed. Add the rinds and simmer until the rinds are tender and clear. Remove from the pot and spread out on non-stick paper to dry. Store the excess syrup for future use.

Glazed Chestnuts

Serves 4

450 g/1 lb chestnuts
450 g/1 lb/2 cups sugar
250 g/9 oz/¾ cup honey

Soak the chestnuts in water to cover. Drain, shell and pat dry. Mix the sugar and honey and cook over a low heat, stirring continuously, until the mixture forms a syrup. Add the chestnuts, stir well, cover and simmer very gently for about 2 hours until tender, stirring frequently. Arrange the chestnuts separately on a greased serving plate and leave to cool before serving.

Sweet Chestnut Balls

Serves 4–6

450 g/1 lb chestnuts
75 g/3 oz/¼ cup honey
75 g/3 oz/½ cup icing sugar
2.5 ml/1/2 tsp cinnamon

Score the chestnuts, plunge into boiling water and cook for about 20 minutes until the shells burst. Drain, cool and shell. Mince the chestnuts, blend with the honey and shaped into balls. Mix the sugar and cinnamon and roll the chestnut balls in to mixture until coated.

Egg Custards

Serves 4

375 g/12 oz/ 3 cups plain (all-purpose) flour
5 ml/1 tsp salt
225 g/8 oz/1 cup lard
60-90 ml/4-6 tbsp hot water
3 eggs
75 g/3 oz/⅓ cup sugar
375 ml/13 fl oz/1½ cups milk

Mix together the flour and half the salt then rub in the lard until the mixture resembles breadcrumbs. Mix in enough water to form a soft dough. Cut the dough in half and roll out each half on a floured surface to 5 mm/⅛ in thick. Cut out 12 x 8 cm/3 in circles and press the circles into greased muffin tins. Beat the eggs then stir in the sugar and remaining salt. Gradually blend in the milk. Spoon the mixture into the pastry cases and bake in a preheated oven at 180°C/350°F/gas mark 4 for about 30 minutes until set. Remove the tarts from the tin and cool on a wire rack.

Fruits with Almond Cream

Serves 4

1 sachet gelatine
175 ml/6 fl oz/¾ cup water
100 g/4 oz/½ cup sugar
175 ml/6 fl oz/¾ cup boiling water
300 ml/½ pt/1¼ cups evaporated milk
2.5 ml/½ tsp vanilla essence (extract)
2.5 ml/½ tsp almond essence (extract)
2 kiwi fruits, peeled and sliced
4 strawberries

Sprinkle the gelatine on to the cold water in a bowl and leave to stand for 1 minute. Add the sugar and stir until the gelatine dissolves. Stir the gelatine mixture into the boiling water. Mix together the evaporated milk, vanilla and almond essences and pour into the gelatine mixture. Divide the mixture between 4 serving dishes and refrigerate for about 3 hours until set. Serve garnished with kiwi fruits and strawberries.

Canton Fruit Cup

Serves 4

200 g/7 oz pineapple chunks
2 oranges, peeled and cut into segments
2 bananas, sliced
1 piece preserved ginger in syrup, minced

Mix all the ingredients together and chill. Serve in glass sundae dishes.

Sweet Ginger Balls

Serves 4

450 g/1 lb/4 cups strong plain (all-purpose) flour

30 ml/2 tbsp butter

15 ml/1 tbsp caster sugar

2.5 ml/½ tsp salt

1 sachet easy-mix yeast

300 ml/½ pt/1¼ cups warm milk or water

25 g/1 oz/¼ cup walnuts, chopped

50 g/2 oz/⅓ cup chopped mixed peel

50 g/2 oz/¼ cup glacè cherries

50 g/2 oz/⅓ cup dates, chopped

15 ml/1 tbsp rice wine or dry sherry

pinch of ground ginger

Sift the flour into a bowl. Rub in the butter then add the sugar, salt and yeast. Work in the warm milk or water and knead to a smooth dough. Cover and leave in a warm place for 45 minutes. Mix together all the remaining ingredients. Knead the dough and shape it into 18 small balls. Press them flat, spoon some of the mixture into each and close the dough around the filling. Place the balls in a steamer basket, cover and leave to rise in a warm place for 30 minutes. Simmer over slightly sweetened water for about 30 minutes.

Ice Cream Puffs

Serves 4 –6

1.2/1/2 pts/5 cups vanilla ice cream

4 eggs, beaten

25 g/1 oz/¼ cup plain (all-purpose) flour

2.5 ml/½ tsp baking powder

oil for deep-frying

Divide the ice cream into scoops and freeze until very hard. Beat the eggs, flour and baking powder, coat the ice cream with the mixture and freeze again until hard. Heat the oil and dip the ice cream again in the batter mixture. Deep-fry for a few seconds until the pastry covering puff up. Serve immediately.

Lychees with Papaya Sauce

Serves 4

450 g/1 lb lychees

450 g/1 lb papaya, peeled and seeded

45 ml/3 tbsp sugar

If you have fresh lychees, peel and stone them. Canned lychees should be drained thoroughly. Arrange them in a glass bowl. Purée the papaya flesh then stir in the sugar. Spoon the papaya over the lychees and chill before serving.

Chocolate Lychees

Serves 4

500 g/1 lb 2 oz canned lychees, drained
175 g/6 oz plain chocolate
15 ml/1 tbsp vegetable fat

Spread the lychees between several layers of kitchen paper and leave to stand for about 1 hour until dry. Melt the chocolate and fat in the top of a double boiler over boiling water. Remove from the heat and leave to cool slightly. Dip each lychee in chocolate to coat it completely. Carefully lift the lychees out of the chocolate and place round side up on greased baking parchment or greaseproof paper. Drizzle the remaining chocolate over the lychees and refrigerate until cold.

Mandarin Liqueur Sorbet with Lychees

Serves 4

450 ml/3/4 pt/2 cups water
100 g/4 oz/½ cup sugar
550 g/1¼ lb canned mandarin oranges
    in syrup
60 ml/4 tbsp lemon juice
30 ml/2 tbsp orange liqueur
500 g/1 lb 2 oz canned lychees in syrup

Place the water and sugar in a pan and cook over a low heat, stirring continuously, until the mixture boils. Boil, without stirring, for 3 minutes then remove from the heat and leave to cool. Purée 1 can of mandarins with their syrup until smooth. Strain. Stir the purée, lemon juice and liqueur into the cooled syrup. Pour into a large freezer dish and freeze for at least 3 hours until firm. Refrigerate the remaining mandarins and lychees until cold. To serve, drain the mandarins and lychees, reserving the lychee syrup. Spoon the fruit and lychee syrup into serving dishes. Remove the sorbet from the freezer and flake it lightly with a fork. Spoon over the fruit and serve.

Mango Fool

Serves 4

450 g/ 1 lb mangoes, peeled and sliced
30 ml/2 tbsp sugar
250 ml/8 fl oz/1 cup double cream

Purée the mango flesh then stir in the sugar. Whip the cream until stiff, then stir it into the mango purée.

Champagne Melon

Serves 4 –6

1 small melon
120 ml/4 fl oz/½ cup water
100 g/4 oz/½ cup sugar
60 ml/4 tbsp ginger wine
1 bottle Champagne or sparkling wine
450 g/1 lb seedless grapes
1 egg white
225 g/8 fl oz/1 cup caster sugar

Cut the melon in half and remove the seeds. Shape into balls using a melon baller or cut into cubes. Place in a bowl, cover with clingfilm and refrigerate until cold. Mix together the water, sugar and ginger wine in a small saucepan and cook over a low heat, stirring until the sugar dissolves. Bring to the boil and boil for 3 minutes then remove from the heat. Leave to cool and refrigerate until cold. Chill the Champagne or wine. Cut the grapes into small bunches, leaving a large enough stem section on each to hook over the rim of the glass. Beat the egg white until frothy. Brush over the grapes then dip them in caster sugar, turning to coat them completely. Place on a large plate and leave to dry for 2 hours.

Divide the melon balls between 6 large dessert glasses. Spoon about 30 ml/2 tbsp of the ginger syrup into each glass and fill with Champagne or wine. Hang a bunch of grapes over the outside edge of each glass and serve at once.

Peanut Crisps

Serves 4

50 g/2 oz sesame seeds
450 g/1 lb/2 cups sugar
75 ml/5 tbsp wine vinegar
20 ml/4 tsp water
225 g/8 oz/2 cups roast unsalted skinned peanuts

Toast the sesame seeds in a dry pan until golden. Mix the sugar, wine vinegar and water in a saucepan and cook over a low heat, stirring as the sugar dissolves. Bring to the boil without stirring. Boil, without stirring, for about 10 minutes until the mixture is golden and reaches 149°C/300°F or hard-crack stage. While the sugar is boiling, grease a large baking tin. Sprinkle half the sesame seeds and all the peanuts evenly into the tin. Pour the sugar over the nuts and smooth the surface with the back of a greased wooden spoon. Sprinkle with the remaining sesame seeds and leave to cool slightly. While still warm, cut into squares then leave to cool completely.

Sweet Peanut Soup

Serves 4 –6

1.5/1/2 ½ pts/6 cups water
10 ml/2 tsp bicarbonate of soda (baking
    soda)
225 g/8 oz peanuts
225 g/8 oz/1 cup brown sugar

Heat the water to lukewarm then stir in the bicarbonate of soda. Add the peanuts and bring to the boil. Cover and simmer for about 1 ½ hours until soft. Add the sugar and simmer gently, stirring, until the sugar has dissolved. Serve hot in small bowls.

Steamed Pears

Serves 4

4 pears, peeled
60 ml/4 tbsp honey

Slice off the tops of the pears about 2.5 cm/1 in from the top and reserve the tops. Core the pears from the top, shaping a deep hole without cutting through the base. Fill with honey and replace the tops. Stand the pears in a container on a rack in a wok or a pan with water in the bottom to come just below the steaming rack. Bring the water to the boil, cover and steam for about 20 minutes, topping up with boiling water as necessary, until the pears are cooked. The length of time will depend on the size and ripeness of the pears.

Pear Compote

Serves 4

6 large pears, peeled
75 g/3 oz/½ cup chopped dates
50 g/2 oz/½ cup chopped walnuts
90 ml/6 tbsp honey

Core the pears from the top to form a cavity without cutting through to the base. Stand the pears in a container on a rack in a wok or pan with water in the bottom to come just below the steaming rack. Fill the pears with the dates and walnuts and coat with honey. Bring the water to the boil, cover and steam for about 20 minutes, topping up with boiling water as necessary, until the pears are cooked. The length of time will depend on the size and ripeness of the pears.

Pearl Barley Pudding

Serves 4

100 g/4 oz/1 cup pearl barley
450 ml/¾ pt/2 cups water
salt
225 g/8 oz/2 cups brown sugar
450 ml/¾ pt/2 cups milk
100 g/4 oz/1 cup walnuts
50 g/2 oz/⅓ cup raisins
2.5 ml/½ tsp cinnamon

Place the pearl barley, water and salt in a pan, bring to the boil, cover and simmer for 1 hour. Transfer the barley to the top of a double boiler and stir in the sugar and milk. Bring the water in the bottom to the boil and cook for 3 hours over a low heat. Blanch the walnuts in boiling water for 5 minutes then drain and chop. Add to the barley mixture with the raisins and simmer for a further 15 minutes.

Peking Dust

Serves 6

450 g/1 lb chestnuts
milk
5 ml/1 tsp vanilla essence (extract)
25 g/1 oz/2 tbsp butter
50 g/2 oz/¼ cup sugar
15 ml/1 tbsp brandy
½ egg white
pinch of cream of tartar
pinch of salt
120 ml/4 fl oz/½ cup double (heavy) cream, whipped
50 g/2 oz/¼ cup icing sugar
50 g/2 oz maraschino cherries

Shell the chestnuts, place in a pan of cold water and bring to the boil. Simmer for 3 minutes then drain. Cover the chestnuts with milk and add half the vanilla essence. Heat gently but do not boil. Cover and simmer for about 20 minutes until the chestnuts are tender. Drain, discarding the milk. Mash the chestnuts with the butter, half the sugar and the brandy. Beat the egg white with the cream of tartar then fold in the salt and the remaining sugar and vanilla essence. Spoon the mixture into a piping bag and squeeze into a nest shape on a foil-lined baking tray. Bake in a preheated oven at 140°C/275°F/gas mark 1 for about 40 minutes until golden. Leave to cool slightly then transfer to a serving plate. Spoon the chestnut mixture into a clean piping bag and squeeze it out in thin threads over the egg nest to form a mound on top. Whip the cream with the icing sugar and garnish the nest with cream and cherries.

Precious Fruit

Serves 4

600 ml/1 pt/2 ½ cups fruit juice
450 g/1 lb mixed fresh fruit (apples,
  satsumas, bananas), sliced
100 g/4 oz/½ cup brown sugar
400 ml/14 fl oz/ 1¾ cups water
30 ml/2 tbsp cornflour (cornstarch)

Bring the fruit juice to the boil. Add the fruit and sugar and stir until the sugar dissolves. Mix the remaining water and cornflour and stir it into the pan. Bring almost to boiling, stirring continuously, but do not allow the mixture to boil. Serve hot in soup bowls.

Raspberry Fool

Serves 4

350 g/12 oz raspberries
30 ml/2 tbsp sugar
250 ml/8 fl oz/1 cup double cream

Purée the raspberries then rub them through a sieve if you prefer not to have pips in the fool. Stir in the sugar. Whip the cream until stiff then gently fold it into the raspberries.

Raspberry Sorbet

Serves 4

375 g/12 oz raspberries
250 ml/8 fl oz/1 cup water
175 g/6 oz/¾ cup sugar
30 ml/2 tbsp lemon juice
30 ml/2 tbsp orange liqueur
2 egg whites
pinch of cream of tartar

Purée the raspberries with the water, half the sugar, the lemon juice and liqueur. Rub through a sieve into a freezer dish and freeze for about 4 hours until firm. Beat the egg whites and cream of tartar until frothy. Gradually add the remaining sugar and whisk until the whites are stiff but not dry. Remove the raspberry mixture from the freezer and flake it with a fork. Spoon the egg whites over the top and fold them into the raspberry sorbet gently but thoroughly. Freeze for at least 2 hours until firm.

Rice Pudding with Candied Fruits

Serves 4

150 g/5 oz/ short-grain rice
150 ml/¼ pt/ ⅔ cup water
150 ml/¼ pt/⅔ cup rice wine or dry
    sherry
150 ml/¼ pt/⅔ cup milk
50 g/2 oz/¼ cup sugar
25 g/1 oz candied ginger, chopped
25 g/1 oz candied pineapple, chopped
25 g/1 oz glacé cherries, chopped
25 g/1 oz chopped mixed peel
120 ml/4 fl oz/½ cup double cream
300 ml/1/2 pt/1¼ cups whiping cream,
    whipped
50 g/2 oz candied kumquats or other
    fruits, sliced

Soak the rice in the water for 2 hours.
Bring to the boil with the wine or
sherry and milk and simmer for about
20 minutes until tender. Add the
sugar, fruits and cream and leave to
cool. When cold, blend in the whipped
cream and decorate with kumquats.

Split Pea Pudding

Serves 4

675 g/1½ lb split peas
500 ml/17 fl oz/2¼ cups water
100 g/4 oz/½ cup brown sugar
30 ml/2 tbsp cornflour (cornstarch)
60 ml/4 tbsp water
100 g/4 oz maraschino cherries

Soak the split peas overnight in the
water. Bring to the boil in the same
water, cover and simmer for about 2
hours until tender. Rub through a
fine sieve then stir in the sugar and
return to a very low heat. Mix the
cornflour with the water then stir into
the pan. Pour into a shallow rectangular cake tin and leave to cool then
chill until set. Cut into cubes, pile
into a bowl and serve garnished with
cherries.

Water Chestnut Pudding

Serves 4

100 g/4 oz/1 cup water chestnut flour
120 ml/4 fl oz/½ cup water
100 g/4 oz/½ cup brown sugar
600 ml/1 pt/ 2 ½ cups water

Mix the chestnut flour with the first
quantity of water and place in a
heatproof bowl. Blend in the sugar
and remaining water then cover the
bowl. Place on a steaming rack over
boiling water and steam for 1 hour.
Serve hot or cold.

Sweet Puréed Water Chestnuts

Serves 4

450 g/1 lb water chestnuts

225 g/8 oz sugar

600 ml/1 pt/2 ½ cups water

2 glacé cherries, sliced

Purée the water chestnuts in a food processor. Dissolve the sugar in the water over a low heat then stir in the water chestnuts and simmer gently until heated through and thickened. Serve at once.

Water Melon in Ginger Wine

Serves 4

½ water melon

250 ml/8 fl oz/1 cup water

120 ml/4 fl oz/½ cup ginger wine

30 ml/2 tbsp sugar

25 g/1 oz candied ginger, cut into
    slivers

Shape the melon into balls, using a melon baller, removing the seeds as necessary. Mix together the water, ginger wine and sugar in a small pan. Cook over a medium heat, stirring until the sugar dissolves and the mixture is hot. Remove from the heat. Stir in the ginger, pour over the melon then cool and refrigerate for several hours, preferably overnight, before serving.

Almond Biscuits

Makes 12

100 g/4 oz self-raising flour

5 ml/1 tsp baking powder

50 g/2 oz lard

100 g/4 oz sugar

2 eggs, beaten

12 almonds

Mix the flour and baking powder then rub in the large until the mixture resembles breadcrumbs. Mix in the sugar and 1 egg to form a thick paste. Divide into 12 balls and press into circles on a greased baking tray. Press an almond on to the top of each one. Glaze with the remaining egg and bake in a preheated oven at 200°C/400°F/gas mark 6 for 20 minutes until golden brown. Cool on a wire rack.

Sesame Seed Biscuits

Serves 4

45 ml/3 tbsp sesame seeds
120 ml/4 fl oz/½ cup groundnut
    (peanut) oil
225 g/8 oz/1 cup sugar
1 egg
450 g/1 lb plain (all-purpose) flour
5 ml/1 tsp baking powder
pinch of salt
5 ml/1 tsp grated nutmeg

Heat a pan and gently toast the sesame seeds until lightly browned. Beat together the oil and sugar then blend in the egg and most of the sesame seeds. Mix the flour, baking powder, salt and nutmeg and gradually blend it into the mixture. Knead well, adding a little water if necessary to make a firm dough, then chill for 2 hours.

Roll out the dough and use a pastry cutter to cut into about 35 biscuits. Sprinkle with the remaining sesame seeds and press them in lightly. Bake on a greased baking tray in a preheated oven at 180°C/350°F/gas mark 4 for about 15 minutes until golden brown.

Steamed Lemon Cake

Serves 4

6 eggs, separated
225 g/8 oz/1 cup sugar
45 ml/3 tbsp water
175 g/6 oz/1½ cup plain (all-purpose)
    flour
2.5 ml/½ tsp baking powder
2.5 ml/½ tsp vanilla essence (extract)
5 ml/1 tsp lemon essence (extract)

Beat the egg yolks, sugar and water until pale and fluffy. Gradually beat in the flour and baking powder then the vanilla and lemon essence. Beat the egg whites until stiff and fold them into the mixture using a metal spoon. Pour the batter into a greased and lined 20 cm/8 in square cake tin and stand the tin on a steamer rack in a wok or pan over simmering water. Cover and simmer for about 25 minutes until a skewer inserted in the centre comes out clean. Leave to cool slightly in the tin then turn out and serve hot, cut into squares.

Sugared Nuts

Serves 4

225 g/8 oz shelled walnuts
300 ml/½ pt/1¼ cups boiling water
100 g/4 oz/½ cup sugar
120 ml/4 fl oz/½ cup groundnut
    (peanut) oil

Place the walnuts in a bowl and pour over the boiling water. Leave to stand for 30 minutes then drain and dry well. Mix the sugar and oil over a low heat, stirring until the sugar dissolves. Add the nuts and stir until well coated.

Chinese Nut Meringue

Serves 4

100 g/4 oz/½ cup butter
100 g/4 oz/½ cup brown sugar
3 eggs, separated
few drops of vanilla essence (extract)
225 g/8 oz plain (all-purpose) flour
10 ml/2 tsp baking powder
pinch of salt
45 ml/3 tbsp milk
175 g/6 oz/1¼ cups mixed nuts
25 g/1 oz/2 tbsp caster sugar

Cream the butter and sugar then add the egg yolks and 1 egg white and beat well. Add the vanilla essence, flour, baking powder, salt and milk. Spread the mixture into a greased rectangular baking tin and sprinkle with the nuts. Beat the remaining egg whites until stiff, add the caster sugar and beat again until stiff. Spread over the mixture and bake in a preheated oven at 180°C/350°F/gas mark 4 for 35 minutes. cool and cut into squares.

Preserves

Preserves are not a feature of Chinese cuisine, but there are a few which you might be interested to try.

Pickled Cabbage

Makes 450g/1lb

30ml/2tbsp groundnut (peanut) oil
450g/1lb white cabbage, cubed
15ml/1tbsp brown sugar
15ml/1tbsp soy sauce
30ml/2tbsp wine vinegar
2.5ml/½ tsp salt

Heat half the oil and stir-fry the cabbage for about 3 minutes until translucent but still crisp. Transfer to a bowl. Heat the remaining oil and heat the sugar, sauce, wine vinegar and salt, stirring until the sugar dissolves. Pour over the cabbage and toss. Transfer to a screw-top jar and refrigerate overnight.

Pickled Celery

Makes 225g/8oz

6 stalks celery, cut into chunks
15 ml/1 tbsp soy sauce
15ml/1tbsp wine vinegar
2.5ml/1/2tsp salt
2.5ml/1/2tsp sugar
few drops of sesame oil

Blanch the celery in boiling water for 2 minutes then drain well. Mix together the remaining ingredients, pour over the celery and toss. Cover and chill for about 20 minutes.

Preserved Kumquats

Makes 900g/2lb

675g/1½ lb kumquats
600ml/1pt/2 ½ cups water
225g/8oz/1 cup sugar
50g/2oz stem ginger, minced
juice of 1 lime

Puncture each kumquat in 4 places with a large needle. Place all the ingredients in a large pan, bring to the boil then simmer until the liquid becomes thick and translucent. Seal in warmed jars.

Mango Pickle

Makes 450g/1lb

450g/1lb unripe mango, peeled and sliced
10ml/2tsp salt
pinch of freshly ground pepper
60ml/4 tbsp wine vinegar
10ml/2 tsp sugar

Season the mango with salt and pepper and add the vinegar and sugar. Stir well and leave to marinate for at least 2 hours before serving with fish or cold meats.

Turnip Pickle

Makes 450g/1lb

450g/1lb turnips, sliced
90ml/6tbsp wine vinegar
25g/1oz/2tbsp sugar
10ml/2tsp salt
10ml/2tsp minced ginger root
45ml/3tbsp soy sauce
45ml/3tbsp rice wine or dry sherry

Mix all the ingredients together well and place in a screw-top jar. Cover and store in the refrigerator for 3 days before serving with duck or pork.

Chinese Pickled Vegetables

Makes 450g/1lb

100 g/4 oz salt
50 g/2 oz dried red chilli peppers
10 ml/2 tsp peppercorns
30 ml/2 tbsp wine vinegar
50 g/2 oz ginger root, sliced
50 g/2 oz/¼ cup brown sugar
2 1/3 ½ pts/8 ½ cups boiled water
1 cucumber, cubed
1 head celery, roughly chopped
1 head Chinese leaves, cut into chunks
100 g/4 oz shallots
1 leek, sliced
1 red pepper, cut into chunks
1 green pepper, cut into chunks
100 g/4 oz green beans, cut into chunks

Mix all the spice ingredients with the water in a large jar. Add the prepared vegetables, stir well, seal and store in a cool place for at least 5 days before serving.

Nibbles and Drinks

Chinese have enjoyed tea as a refreshing drink since the end of the sixth century and tea is now the most common drink in Chinese homes. There are two types - green and black - which differ because of the way the leaves are dried and each has its own special flavour. Many Chinese teas are available in supermarkets and delicatessens, some of the most popular being Lapsang Souchong, Jasmine and Oolong.

The Chinese also make some sweet teas which are served as a refreshing sweet dessert drink at the end of a meal.

Fried Cashews

Serves 4

groundnut (peanut) oil for deep-frying
225 g/8 oz cashew nuts
2.5 ml/½ tsp five-spice powder
pinch of chilli powder
salt and freshly ground pepper

Heat the oil then fry the nuts until lightly browned. Transfer the nuts to a hot frying pan, add the spices and toss over a medium heat for a few minutes until well coated. Cool before serving.

Crispy Pine Nuts

Serves 4

50 g/2 oz brown sugar
450 ml/¾ pt/2 cups water
100 g/4 oz pine nuts
oil for deep-frying

Dissolve the sugar in the water over a low heat, add the pine nuts and bring to the boil. Simmer for 3 minutes then remove from the heat and leave to stand for 6 hours. Drain well and leave to dry.

Heat the oil until moderately hot and deep-fry the pine nuts until golden brown. Drain well then spread out and leave to cool, stirring occasionally so that they do not stick together.

Roasted Spiced Nuts

Serves 4

10 ml/2 tsp salt
60 ml/4 tbsp water
2.5 ml/½ tsp five-spice powder
450 g/1lb/4 cups shelled peanuts

Dissolve the salt in the water over a gentle heat, then stir in the five-spice powder. Mix in the peanuts and stir together well. Spread the peanuts out in a roasting tin and roast in a pre-heated oven at 140°C/275°F/gas mark 1 for about 1 hour until golden, stirring occasionally.

Orange Tea

Serves 4

3 oranges
30 ml/2 tbsp cornflour (cornstarch)
100 g/4 oz/½ cup sugar
750 ml/1¼ pts/3 cups water

Peel and seed the oranges, removing the pith and membranes. Catch the juice and chop the flesh roughly. Mix the cornflour, sugar and water and bring to the boil, stirring continuously. Add the orange juice and flesh and heat through gently, stirring. Serve hot in small bowls.

Almond Custard Tea

Serves 4

100 g/4 oz/½ cup long-grain rice
100 g/4 oz ground almonds
1.5 1/2¾ pts/6 cups water
100 g/4 oz/½ cup sugar
2.5 ml/½ tsp salt
5 ml/1tsp vanilla essence (extract)

Soak the rice overnight in cold water to cover then drain well. Add the almonds and the water and soak for 1 hour then stir well. Strain and squeeze the liquid into the top of a double boiler over gently simmering water. Simmer gently, stirring, until the mixture thickens then stir in the sugar, salt and vanilla essence, bring to the boil and serve warm in small bowls.

Grapefruit Tea

Serves 4

1l/1¾ pts/4 cups water
450 g/1lb canned grapefruit segments in
    syrup
100 g/4 oz/½ cup brown sugar
30 ml/2 tbsp cornflour (cornstarch)

Bring half the water to the boil, add the grapefruit and syrup and the sugar and stir until the sugar dissolves then add the remaining water. Blend the cornflour with a little cold water then stir it into the mixture and bring to the boil. Simmer, stirring, until the mixture thickens. Serve hot in small bowls.

Hot Lotus Tea

Serves 4–6

900 ml/1½ pts/3¾ cups water
2.5 ml/½ tsp bicarbonate of soda
    (baking soda)
450 g/1 lb lotus seeds
1.2 1/2 pts/5 cups water
225 g/8 oz brown sugar
2 eggs, lightly beaten

Bring the water to the boil, stir in the bicarbonate of soda, pour over the lotus seeds and leave to stand for 10 minutes. Rub the seeds with your fingers to remove the husks. Rinse and drain. Bring the second quantity of water to the boil, stir in the sugar until dissolved then add the lotus seeds, cover and simmer for 1 hour. Gradually stir in the eggs, remove from the heat and serve at once.

Pineapple Tea

Serves 4

100 g/4 oz/½ cup brown sugar
75 g/3 oz/¼ cup honey
75 ml/1¼ pts/3 cups water
450g/1lb canned pineapple in syrup,
    crushed

Mix all the ingredients together in a pan, bring to the boil then simmer gently for 15 minutes, stirring frequently. Serve hot in small bowls.

Walnut Tea

Serves 4

45 g/1lb shelled walnuts
60 ml/4 tbsp vegetable oil
600 ml/1pt/2 ½ cups water
100 g/4 oz/½ cup sugar
pinch of salt
30 ml/2 tbsp cornflour (cornstarch)

Place the walnuts in a pan, cover with water, bring to the boil and simmer for 10 minutes. Remove from the heat and leave to cool. Rub off the walnut skins then drain the walnuts on kitchen paper. Heat the oil in a wok and fry the walnuts for a few minutes until golden brown. Drain and leave to cool. Grind them finely in a blender or crush with a rolling pin.

Bring the water, sugar to taste, and salt to the boil and stir in the walnuts. Mix the cornflour with a little water then stir into the tea. Simmer, stirring, until heated through and translucent. Serve after a banquet.

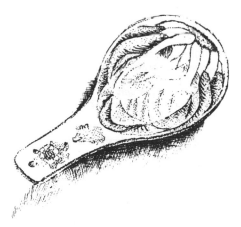

Index

Abalone
  abalone with asparagus 79
  abalone with chicken 78
  abalone with mushroom soup 22
  abalone with mushrooms 79
  abalone with oyster sauce 80
  marinated abalone 9
Almonds
  almond biscuits 354
  almond chicken 182
  almond custard tea 360
  almond fish rolls 39
  almond fried rice 268-9
  almond milk jelly with lychees 344
  chicken with almonds and vegetables 183
  chicken with almonds and vater chestnuts 182-3
  fruits with almond cream 346
  pheasant with almonds 249
  pork with almonds 144
  prawns with almonds 58
Anise
  anise chicken 183
  anise prawns 58
  braised anise beef 96
  steamed chicken with anise 227
Appetisers *see* under individual ingredients
Apples
  toffee apples 344
Apricots
  chicken with apricots 184
Asparagus
  abalone with asparagus 79
  asparagus with clams 283
  asparagus with egg sauce 283
  asparagus with mushrooms and spring onions 284
  asparagus salad 337
  asparagus stir-fry 284
  beef with asparagus 96
  chicken with asparagus 184
  chicken and asparagus soup 22
  lamb with asparagus 132
  prawns with asparagus 58
  sweet and sour asparagus 284
Aubergines
  aubergine with basil 285
  aubergine salad 337
  braised aubergine 285
  chicken with aubergine 184
  steamed aubergine 285
  stir-fry aubergine 286
  stuffed aubergine 286

Bacon
  bacon with cabbage 181
  bacon-wrapped chicken 185
  cabbage with bacon shreds 292
  chicken with bacon 12
  fried rice with bacon and egg 269
  oysters with bacon 89
  prawns with bacon 58
Bamboo shoots
  bamboo shoots with chicken 286
  bamboo shoots with dried mushrooms 288
  bamboo shoots with mushrooms 287
  bamboo shoots in oyster sauce 288
  bamboo shoots with sesame oil 288
  bamboo shoots with spinach 288-9
  beef with bamboo shoots 97
  beef with bamboo shoots and mushrooms 97
  braised bamboo shoots 9
  chicken and bamboo shoot soup 24
  chicken with bamboo shoots 185
  chicken livers with bamboo shoots 201
  cod with bamboo shoots 39
  deep-fried bamboo shoots 287
  duck with bamboo shoots 232
  fried bamboo shoots 287
  mangetout with bamboo shoots 299
  mushrooms and bamboo shoots 301
  mushrooms with bamboo shoots and mangetout 301
  pork with bamboo shoots 143
  prawns with bamboo shoots 59
  scallops with bamboo shoots 90
Bananas
  chicken and banana fries 12
  honey bananas 345
Barley
  pearl barley pudding 351
Basil
  aubergine with basil 285
Bass
  baked whole fish 35
  braised soy fish 35
  soy fish with oyster sauce 35
  steamed bass 36
  sweet and sour fish 36-7
Bean sprouts
  bean sprout and pork soup 21
  bean sprout salad 337
  bean sprout stir-fry 290
  bean sprouts and celery 290
  bean sprouts and peppers 290
  bean sprouts with pork 291

beef with bean sprouts 98
chicken with bean sprouts 186
Chinese omelette with bean sprouts 253
clams with bean sprouts 80
crab foo yung with bean sprouts 82-3
duck with bean sprouts 232
fish with bean sprouts 40
pork with bean sprouts 144
pork with bean sprouts 177
prawn soufflé with bean sprouts 262
prawns with bean sprouts 60
sautéed bean sprouts 290
squid with bean sprouts 93
Beef
baked beef curry 106
barbecued beef 99
beef with asparagus 96
beef balls with glutinous rice 128
beef with bamboo shoots 97
beef with bamboo shoots and mushrooms 97
beef with bean sprouts 98
beef with broccoli 98
beef with carrots 100
beef with cashews 100
beef with cauliflower 101
beef with celery 101
beef with Chinese cabbage 103
beef and Chinese leaves soup 23
beef with Chinese pickles 115
beef chop suey 104
beef chow mein 105
beef with cucumber 104
beef with dried orange rind 113
beef dumplings 126
beef fried rice 269
beef with garlic 107
beef with ginger 107
beef with green beans 108
beef with mangetout 109
beef noodles 278
beef with onions 112
beef with oyster sauce 113
beef and peas 112
beef with pepper 114
beef with peppers 114-5
beef in red sauce 127
beef with rice noodles 112
beef rolls 130
beef soup 22-3
beef and spinach balls 131
beef and spring onions with fish sauce 119
beef stew 120

beef stir-fry 121
beef tenderloin 122
beef toasts 123
beef with tomatoes 123
beef with vegetables 124
black bean beef with spring onions 118
braised anise beef 96
braised beef with mushrooms 111
braised curried beef 106-7
Cantonese beef 99
chilli beef 103
Chinese braised beef 97
crispy beef with curry sauce 106
crispy meatballs 126
deep-fried beef slivers with celery 102
family-style shredded beef 117
fried rice with beef and onions 270
fried rice with minced beef 269
hot beef 108
hot beef shreds 109
marinated beef with spinach 118
marinated braised beef 110
marinated stir-fried beef 110
meatballs with sweet and sour sauce 128
minced beef with cashew nuts 127
pepper steak 114
piquant beef soup 23
red-cooked beef with ginger 108
red-cooked beef with turnips 124
rice with beef 265
savoury beef 116
sesame beef with broccoli 99
shredded beef 116-17
shredded beef with chicken and celery 102
shredded spiced beef 117
shredded tofu-chilli beef 123
slow beef casserole 101
steak with potatoes 116
steak strips 121
steamed beef 119
steamed beef with sweet potatoes 122
steamed meat pudding 129
steamed minced beef 129
stewed beef 125
stewed beef brisket 120
stir-fried beef and mushrooms 110
stir-fried beef with noodles 111
stir-fried beef shred with green peppers 115
stir-fried beef with spring onions 119
stir-fried beef with tofu 131
stir-fried curried beef 107
stir-fried mince with oyster sauce 130

stir-fried onion crackle beef 113
stuffed steak 125
Beer, malt
shallots in malt beer 308
Biscuits
almond biscuits 354
sesame seed biscuits 355
Black bean sauce
prawns with black bean sauce 60
Brisket
stewed beef brisket 120
Broad beans
broad bean sauté 289
Broccoli
beef with broccoli 98
broccoli in brown sauce 291
broccoli stir-fry 291
chicken with broccoli 186
lamb with broccoli 133
monkfish with broccoli 52
scallops with broccoli 91
sesame beef with broccoli 99

Cabbage
bacon with cabbage 181
beef with Chinese cabbage 103
cabbage with bacon shreds 292
cabbage soup 23
chicken with cabbage and peanuts 187
creamed cabbage 292
lamb with cabbage 134
marinated pork with cabbage 147
mushroom and cabbage soup 28-9
pickled cabbage 357
pork with cabbage 146
pork with cabbage and tomatoes 146
spicy cabbage stir-fry 293
sweet and sour cabbage 293
sweet and sour red cabbage 293
Cakes
crab cakes 82
steamed lemon cake 355
steamed meat cake 156
water chestnut cakes 314
candied peel 345
Carp
braised fish with mushrooms 36
braised spiced carp 37
carp with tofu 38
pork-stuffed fish 37
sweet and sour carp 38
Carrots
beef with carrots 100

carrot and celery salad 338
carrot and pepper stir-fry 294
carrots with honey 294
deep-fried potatoes and carrots 307
pork with spinach and carrots 163
trout with carrots 56
Cashew nuts
beef with cashews 100
chicken with cashews 187
fried cashews 359
minced beef with cashew nuts 127
Casserole
slow beef casserole 101
Cauliflower
beef with cauliflower 101
cauliflower with mushrooms 294-5
cauliflower omelette 254
prawns and cauliflower 11
stir-fried cauliflower 294
Celery
bean sprouts and celery 290
beef with celery 101
carrot and celery salad 338
celery and mushrooms 295
celery salad 338
celery stir-fry 295
deep-fried beef slivers with celery 102
eel with celery 47
pickled celery 357
pork with celery 147
prawns with celery 60-1
shredded beef with chicken and celery 102
steamed duck with celery 233
Champagne
champagne melon 349
Chestnuts
duck with pears and chestnuts 239
duck with pork and chestnuts 242
glazed chestnuts 345
Peking dust 351
pork with chestnuts and mushrooms 148
red-cooked ham with chestnuts 179
sweet chestnut balls 345
Chicken
abalone with chicken 78
almond chicken 182
anise chicken 183
bacon-wrapped chicken 185
bamboo shoots with chicken 286
barbecued chicken drumsticks 223
braised chicken 224

braised chicken with eggs 194
braised chicken with potatoes 213
chicken with almonds and vegetables 183
chicken with almonds and water chestnuts 182-3
chicken with apricots 184
chicken with asparagus 184
chicken with asparagus soup 22
chicken with aubergine 184
chicken with bacon 12
chicken with bamboo shoot soup 24
chicken with bamboo shoots 185
chicken and banana fries 12
chicken with bean sprouts 186
chicken with black bean sauce 186
chicken with broccoli 186
chicken with cabbage and peanuts 187
chicken with cashews 187
chicken with chestnuts 188
chicken chop suey 189
chicken chow mein 189
chicken and coconut soup 25
chicken and corn soup 24
chicken with cucumber 9
chicken egg rolls 194
chicken foo yung 195
chicken fried rice 270
chicken with ginger 12-13
chicken and ginger soup 24
chicken with green beans 228
chicken and ham 13
chicken with hoisin sauce 198-9
chicken with leeks 200
chicken liver with oyster sauce 202
chicken liver rice 266
chicken livers with bamboo shoots 201
chicken livers with mangetout 201
chicken liver with noodle pancake 202
chicken livers with pineapple 202
chicken with lychee sauce 204
chicken with lychees 203
chicken with mangetout 204
chicken with mangoes 205
chicken with mushroom rice 266
chicken and mushroom stir-fry 206
chicken with mushrooms and peanuts 206
chicken with onions 207
chicken with oyster sauce 208
chicken parcels 209
chicken with peanut butter 209
chicken with peanuts 209
chicken with peas 210

chicken with peppers 210
chicken with peppers and tomatoes 229
chicken and pineapple 211
chicken with pineapple and lychees 212
chicken with pork 212
chicken and rice soup 25
chicken rissoles 214
chicken salad 338
chicken sesame 10
chicken in sesame oil 214
chicken soufflé 261
chicken soup with Chinese mushrooms 25
chicken with soy sauce 215
chicken in soy sauce 227
chicken with spinach 216
chicken spring rolls 216
chicken stock 21
chicken stock sauce 322
chicken in tomato sauce 217
chicken with tomatoes 218
chicken and tomatoes with black bean sauce 218
chicken with walnuts 220
chicken with water chestnuts 220
chicken wontons 221
chicken-stuffed melon 205
chilli-chicken curry 191
Chinese chicken curry 191
cooked chicken with pineapple 229
crispy chicken chunks 228
crispy chicken wings 221
crispy-fried chicken 224
crispy-fried spiced chicken 190
curried chicken with potatoes 192
deep-fried whole chicken 224
deep-fried chicken with curry sauce 192
deep-fried chicken with ginger 196
deep-fried chicken legs 192
deep-fried chicken livers 201
drunken chicken 193
Far Eastern chicken 195
five-spice chicken 225
five-spice chicken wings 221
five-spice chicken with potatoes 213
fried chicken with cucumber 190
ginger chicken 196
ginger and spring onion chicken 225
ginger-chicken with mushrooms and chestnuts 196
golden chicken 197
golden coins 198
grilled chicken livers 13

ham and chicken foo yung 195
han and chicken rolls 14
hoisin chicken drumsticks 223
honey chicken 199
hot-chilli chicken 188
kung pao chicken 199
lemon chicken 200
lemon chicken stir-fry 200-1
marinated chicken wings 222
marinated golden chicken stew 197
noodles with chicken 278
orange and lemon chicken 208
Peking chicken 210
poached chicken 226
poached chicken with tomatoes 218
quick cooked chicken with vegetables 219
quick curried chicken 191
red-cooked chicken wings 10
red-cooked chicken 213, 226
red-cooked spiced chicken 226
royal chicken wings 222
savoury chicken 214
savoury chicken with eggs 193
sesame chicken 229
sesame chicken salad 338-9
sesame roast chicken 226-7
sherry chicken 214-15
shredded beef with chicken and celery 102
simple chicken stir-fry 217
spiced chicken wings 223
spicy baked chicken 215
steamed chicken 227
steamed chicken with anise 227
steamed chicken with ham 198
steamed chicken with mushrooms 207
steamed omelette rolls with chicken filling 257
stir-fried chicken with chilli 188-9
stir-fried chicken with mushrooms 207
stir-fried chicken with peppers 211
stir-fried prawns with chicken 61
strange flavoured chicken 228
sweet and sour chicken livers 203
walnut chicken 219
Chilli
    chilli beef 103
    chilli prawns 61
    chilli-chicken curry 191
    green beans with chilli 289
    hot chilli chicken 188
    stir-fried chicken with chilli 188-9
Chinese cabbage
    Chinese cabbage with mushrooms 292

Chinese leaves
    beef and Chinese leaves soup 23
    braised duck with Chinese leaves 235
    Chinese leaf salad 339
    Chinese leaves in milk 295
    Chinese leaves with mushrooms 296
    Chinese leaves with scallops 296
    Chinese leaves with water chestnuts 296-7
    crab meat with Chinese leaves 82
    stir-fried Chinese leaves 295
Chinese mushrooms (see under mushrooms)
Chinese pickles
    beef with Chinese pickles 115
chocolate lychees 348
chop suey
    beef chop suey 104
    chicken chop suey 189
    pork chop suey 148
    prawn chop suey 62
Chops
    marinated pork chops 156
    roast pork chops 162
Chow mein
    beef chow mein 105
    chicken chow mein 189
    lamb chow mein 134-5
    pork chow mein 149
    prawn chow mein 62
    roast pork chow mein 149
    vegetable chow mein 309
Chutney
    pork with chutney 149
Clams
    asparagus with clams 283
    clam soup 26
    clams with bean sprouts 80
    clams with ginger and garlic 80-81
    pork stuffed clams 81
    steamed clams 80
    stir-fried clams 81
Coconut
    Chicken with coconut soup 25
    coconut cream and coconut milk 322
    coconut rice 266
Cod
    almond fish rolls 39
    Chinese fish cakes 41
    cod with bamboo shoots 39
    cod with mandarin sauce 43
    deep-fried cod 41
    fish fillets in brown sauce 40
    five-spice fish 41

ginger spiced cod 42
quick fried fish 44
steamed fish balls 45
Compote, pear 350
Courgettes
courgette stir-fry 297
courgettes in black bean sauce 297
prawns with courgettes and lychees 62-3
stuffed cougette bites 297
Crab
crab meat salad 339
crab balls with water chestnuts 13
crab cakes 82
crab custard 82
crab foo yung with bean sprouts 82-3
crab foo yung with mushrooms 263
grab with ginger 83
crab and ginger soufflé 261
crab lo mein 83
crab meat with Chinese leaves 82
crab meat and cucumber rings 339
crab meat with cucumber 10
crab meat rice 266
crab omelette with brown sauce 254
crab and scallop soup 26
crab soufflé 261
crab soup 27
deep-fried pork with crab meat 177
noodles with crab meat 278
prawns with crab 63
sautéed crab meat 84
stir-fried crab meat 84
stir-fried crab with pork 84
sweetcorn and crab soup 31
tofu with crab meat 317
Croûtons
hot-fried prawns with croûtons 68
sweet and sour prawns with croûtons 75
Cucunber
beef with cucunber 104
chicken with cucunber 9
crab meat and cucumber rings 339
crab meat with cucumber 10
cucumber with prawns 298
cucumber salad 340
cucumber salad with spring onion dressing 341
cucumber steak 105
cucumbers with sesame oil 298
fried chicken with cucumber 190
marinated cucumber 341
pork with cucumber 150
pork and cucumber soup 30

prawns with cucumber 63
shredded cucumber salad 340
smashed cucumber 340
smashed cucumber with spring onions 340
stuffed cucumbers 298
Curry
baked beef curry 106
braised curried beef 106-7
chilli-chicken curry 191
Chinese chicken 191
curried chicken with potatoes 192
curried onions with peas 303
lamb curry 135
prawn curry 64
prawn and mushroom curry 64
quick curried chicken 191
stir-fried curried beef 107
Custard
almond custard tea 360
crab custard 82
egg custard 250-51
egg custards 346
onion custard 304
Cuttlefish
deep-fried cuttlefish balls 84-5
Dandelion leaves
stir-fried dandelion leaves 299
dim sum 14
Dips
garlic dip 333
garlic dip with soy sauce 333
ginger dip 333
hoisin dip 333
hot chilli dip 333
mustard dip 333
peanut dip 334
rice wine dip 334
seafood dip 334
sesame dip 334
sesame and hoisin dip 334
soy sauce dip 334
soy sauce and mustard dip 334
tomato and chilli dip 335
Dressings
mustard dressing 335
oil and vinegar dressing 335
salad dressing 335
soy and groundnut dressing 336
soy and sesame dressing 336
soy and vinegar dressing 336
spring onion 341

Index

Duck
  braised duck 233
  braised duck with Chinese leaves 235
  braised duck with onions 238
  braised duck with pineapple 240
  crispy duck (peking) 240
  deep-fried steamed duck 234
  drunken duck 235
  duck with bamboo shoots 232
  duck with bean sprouts 232
  duck with exotic fruits 234-35
  duck fried rice 270
  duck with ginger 233
  duck with green beans 234
  duck with ham and leeks 236
  duck with orange 239
  duck with pears and chestnuts 239
  duck with pineapple and lychees 242
  duck with pork and chestnuts 242
  duck with potatoes 242-3
  duck with sweet potatoes 246
  duck with two mushrooms 238
  duck with vegetables247
  duck with wine 248
  five-spice duck 235
  honey roast duck 236
  moist roast duck 237
  orange-roast duck 239
  peking duck 240
  pineapple and ginger duck 241
  red-cooked duck 243
  rice wine roast duck 243
  savoury duck 244
  savoury duck with green beans 244
  slow-cooked duck 245
  steamed duck with celery 233
  steamed duck with rice wine 244
  stir-fried duck 245
  stir-fried duck with ginger 236
  stir-fried duck with mushrooms 237
  stir-fried duck with pineapple 241
  stir-fried duck with vegetables 247
  sweet and sour duck 246
  tangerine duck 246-7
  white-cooked duck 248
  wine vapour duck 248
Dumplings
  beef dumpling 126
  ginger soup with dumplings 28
  pork dumplings 17
  prawn dumplings with tomato sauce 65

Eel
  dry-cooked eel 46-47
Eggs
  asparagus with egg sauce 283
  braised chicken with eggs 194
  braised pork with eggs 151
  chicken egg rolls 194
  cooked egg roll skins 282
  deep-fried ham and egg balls 180
  deep-fried pork eggs 252
  egg custard 250-1
  egg custards 346
  egg roll skins 282
  egg soup 26
  egg yolk sauce 322
  fried eggs with vegetables 253
  fried rice with bacon and egg 269
  half-moon eggs 252
  mushroom egg drop soup 29
  noodles with egg sauce 279
  noodles with poached eggs 281
  poached egg rice 267
  pork egg rolls 150
  pork and prawn egg rolls 151, 176
  prawn and egg cups 65
  prawn egg rolls 66
  salted eggs 250
  savoury chicken with eggs 193
  scallop scramble with herbs 92
  scallops with egg 90
  soy eggs 250
  soy-sauce fried eggs 252
  steamed eggs 251
  steamed eggs with fish 251
  steamed eggs with ham and fish 251
  steamed eggs with pork 252
  tea eggs 250
eggs, see also omelettes, soufflés,
scrambled eggs, pancakes, foo yung

Fish
  almond fish rolls 39
  baked whole fish 35
  braised fish with mushrooms 36
  braised fish with tofu 46
  braised soy fish 35
  crispy-fried fish 41
  deep-fried fish with vegetables 34
  deep-fried marinated fish 55
  fish with bean sprouts 40
  fish in brown sauce 48-9
  fish fillets in brown sauce 40
  fish with gherkins 42

fish and lettuce soup 27
fish with pineapple 43
fish in rice wine 44
fish rolls with pork 44
fish sauce 323
fish souffle 262
fish soup 27
fish stuffed peppers 305
fish with vinegar sauce 46
five-spice fish 41, 49
fragrant fish sticks 42
hot-spiced fish 50
marinated fish steaks 57
marinated sweet and sour fish 45
pork stuffed fish 37
quick fried fish 44
sauce for fried fish 323
scrambled eggs with fish 258
sesame seed fish 45
soy fish with oyster sauce 35
steamed eggs with fish 251
steamed eggs with ham and fish 251
steamed fish balls 45
steamed fish roulades 51
sweet and sour fish 36-7
tofu and fish soup 32
west lake fish 53
Fish cakes
  Chinese fish cakes 41
Five spice mix 332
Foo yung
chicken foo yung 195
  crab foo yung with bean sprouts 82-3
  crab foo yung with mushrooms 263
  deep-fried egg foo yung 263
  egg foo yung 263
  egg foo yung sauce 322
  ham and chicken foo yung 195
  ham and egg foo yung 264
  pork and prawn egg foo yung 264
  prawn foo yung 66-7
  roast pork egg foo yung 264
Fools
  mango fool 348
  raspberry fool 352
French beans
  pepper and bean stir-fry 305
Fruit
  Canton fruit cup 346
  duck with exotic fruits 234-35
  fruits with almond cream 346
  precious fruit 352

rice pudding with candied fruits 353
Garlic
  beef with garlic 107
  clams with ginger and garlic 80-81
  haddock with garlic 49
  marinated garlic mushrooms 11
  plaice with garlic 54
  pork with minced garlic 152-3
  spinach with garlic 308
Gherkins
  fish with gherkins 42
Ginger
  beef with ginger 107
  chicken with ginger 12-13
  chicken and ginger soup 24
  clams with ginger and garlic 80-81
  crab with ginger 83
  crab and ginger soufflé 261
  deep-fried chicken with ginger 196
  deep-fried oysters with ginger 89
  duck with ginger 233
  ginger chicken 196
  ginger haddock with pak soi 50
  ginger soup with dumplings 28
  ginger and spring onion chicken 225
  ginger and spring onion noodles 280
  ginger-chicken with mushrooms and
    chestnuts 196
  ginger-spiced cod 42
  lychees with ginger 10
  mangetout with mushrooms and ginger 300
  mixed vegetables with ginger 311
  mussels with ginger 88
  pearl onions in orange ginger sauce 304
  pineapple and ginger duck 241
  prawns with ginger sauce 19
  red-cooked beef with ginger 108
  scallops with ginger 91
  spinach with ginger 309
  stir-fried duck with ginger 236
  stir-fried lettuce with ginger 299
  stir-fried pork with ginger 153
  sweet ginger balls 347
Ginger wine
  water melon in ginger wine 354
golden coins 198
grapefruit tea 360
Green beans
  bean and pepper salad 337
  beef with green beans 108
  chicken with green beans 228
  duck with green beans 234

green beans with chilli 289
lamb with green beans 132-33
pork with green beans 153
savoury duck with green beans 244
spiced green beans 289
stir-fried green beans 289

Haddock
fish in brown sauce 48-9
five-spice fish 49
ginger haddock with pak soi 50
haddock in black bean sauce 48
haddock with garlic 49
haddock plaits 51
haddock-stuffed peppers 48
hot-spiced fish 50
marinated fish steaks 57
steamed fish roulades 51

Halibut
halibut with tomato sauce 52

Ham
baked ham turnovers 14
chicken and ham 13
deep-fried ham and egg balls 180
duck with ham and leeks 236
ham and chicken foo yung 195
ham and chicken rolls 14
ham and egg foo yung 264
ham fried rice 281
ham and pineapple 180
ham sauce 323
ham and spinach stir-fry 180
omelette with ham and water chestnuts 254
poached prawns with ham and tofu 68
pork with ham and tofu 154
red-cooked ham with chestnuts 179
scallops with ham 91
sesame ham sticks 11
smoked ham rice with stock 271
steamed chicken with ham 198
steamed eggs with ham and fish 251
steamed ham 181
steamed lobster with ham 85
Szechuan soup 31

Herbs
scallop scramble with herbs 92

Honey
carrots with honey 294
honey bananas 345
honey chicken 199
honey-roast duck 236
vegetables with honey 310

Ice cream
ice cream puffs 347

Jelly
almond milk jelly with lychees 344

Kebabs
fried pork kebabs 154

Kidneys
pork kidneys with mangetout 179

kumquats, preserved 357

Lamb
baked lamb 141
barbecued lamb 132
braised lamb 133
fragrant lamb 135
grilled lamb cubes 136
lamb with asparagus 132
lamb with broccoli 133
lamb with cabbage 134
lamb chow mein 134-5
lamb curry 135
lamb with green beans 132-33
lamb with mangetout 136
lamb with mushrooms 137
lamb with oyster sauce 137
lamb and rice 142
lamb with spring onions 138
lamb stew 138
lamb with tofu 140
lamb and vegetables 139
lamb with water chestnuts 134
marinated lamb 136
mustard-roast lamb 140
red-cooked lamb 138
roast lamb 140
stir-fried lamb 139
stuffed breast of lamb 141
tender lamb steaks 138
willow lamb 142

Leeks
chicken with leeks 200
duck with ham and leeks 236
spare ribs with leeks 170

Lemons
lemon chicken 200
lemon chicken stir-fry 200-1
orange and lemon chicken 208
steamed lemon cake 355
trout with lemon sauce 56

Lettuce
braised lettuce 299
fish and lettuce soup 27

pork and lettuce rolls 16
stir-fried lettuce with ginger 299
Liqueurs
mandarin liqueur sorbet with lychees 348
Liver
Chicken liver with oyster sauce 202
chicken liver rice 266
chicken livers with bamboo shoots 201
chicken livers with mangetout 201
chicken livers with noodle pancake 202
chicken livers with pineapple 202
deep-fried chicken livers 201
grilled chicken livers 13
sweet and sour chicken livers 203
Lo mein
crab lo mein 83
Lobster
deep-fried lobster 85
lobster Cantonese 85
lobster with mushrooms 86
lobster nests 87
lobster tails with pork 86
omelette with lobster 255
prawns in lobster sauce 68
sauce for lobster 324
steamed lobster with ham 85
stir-fried lobster 87
lotus seeds, hot lotus tea 361
Lychees
almond milk jelly with lychees 344
chicken with lychee sauce 204
chicken with lychees 203
chicken with pineapple and lychees 212
chocolate lychees 348
duck with pineapple and lychees 242
lychees with ginger 10
lychees with papaya sauce 347
mandarin liqueur sorbet with lychees 348
prawns with courgettes and lychees 62-3
prawns with lychee sauce 69

Malt beer
shallots in malt beer 308
Mangetout
beef with mangetout 109
chicken livers with mangetout 201
chicken with mangetout 204
lamb with mangetout 136
mangetout with bamboo shoots 299
mangetout with mushrooms and ginger 300
mushrooms with bamboo shoots and
mangetout 301
mushrooms with mangetout 302

pork kidneys with mangetout 179
prawns with mangetout 70
turkey with mangetout 230
Mango chutney
prawns with mango chutney 71
Mangoes
chicken with mangoes 205
mango fool 348
mango pickle 357
Maple syrup
barbecued maple spare ribs 170
Marinades
barbecue marinade 328
chicken stock marinade 328
five-spice marinade 328
five-spice marinade with pork 328
garlic marinade 329
hoisin and chilli marinade 329
hoisin sauce marinade 329
hoisin and sherry marinade 329
honey marinade 330
orange marinade 330
pineapple marinade 330
rice wine marinade 330
soy and ginger marinade 331
soy sauce marinade 330
soy and wine marinade 331
spicey marinade 331
spring onion marinade 331
sugar marinade 332
Marrow
Chinese marrow 300
stuffed marrow 300
Mayonnaise
peanut mayonnaise 335
Meat
steamed meat cake 156
Meatballs
crispy meatballs 126
meatballs with sweet and sour sauce 128-9
pork and chestnut 17
steamed minced meatballs 168
Melons
champagne melon 349
chicken-stuffed melon 205
water melon in ginger wine 354
Meringue
Chinese nut meringue 356
milk sauce 324
Mince
fried rice with minced beef 269
minced beef with cashew nuts 127

steamed minced beef 129
steamed minced meatballs 168
steamed minced pork 176
stir-fried mince with oyster sauce 130
transparent noodles with minced pork 281
Monkfish
monkfish with broccoli 52
Mullet
mullet with thick soy sauce 53
west lake fish 53
Mushrooms
abalone and mushroom soup 22
abalone with mushrooms 79
asparagus with mushrooms and spring
onions 284
bamboo shoots with dried mushrooms 288
bamboo shoots with mushrooms 287
beef with bamboo shoots and mushrooms 97
braised beef with mushrooms 111
braised beef with mushrooms 36
cauliflower with mushrooms 294-95
celery and mushrooms 295
chicken and mushroom rice 266
chicken and mushroom stir-fry 206
chicken with mushroom and peanuts 206
chicken soup with Chinese mushrooms 25
Chinese cabbage with mushrooms 292
Chinese leaves with mushrooms 296
crab foo yung with mushrooms 263
duck with two mushrooms 238
ginger-chicken with mushrooms and
chestnuts 196
hot and sour soup 28
lamb with mushrooms 137
lobster with mushrooms 86
mangetout with mushrooms and ginger 300
marinated garlic mushrooms 11
marinated mushrooms 11
mushroom and cabbage soup 28-9
mushroom egg drop soup 29
mushroom sauce 324
mushroom soup 28
mushroom and water chestnut soup 29
mushroom with anchovy sauce 301
mushrooms and bamboo shoots 301
mushrooms with bamboo shoots and
mangetout 301
mushrooms with mangetout 302
oyster sauce mushrooms 16
peas with mushrooms 304-305
pork with chestnuts and mushrooms 148
pork and mushroom soup 30

pork with mushrooms 156
prawn and mushroom curry 64
prawns with Chinese mushrooms 70
red-cooked pork with mushrooms 157
scrambled eggs with mushrooms 258-9
spare ribs with mushrooms 171
spicy mushrooms 302
spinach with mushrooms 308-9
squid with dried mushrooms 95
steamed chicken with mushrooms 207
steamed mushrooms 302
steamed plaice with Chinese mushrooms 54
steamed stuffed mushrooms 302-3
stir-fried beef and mushrooms 110
stir-fried chicken with mushrooms 207
stir-fried duck with mushrooms 237
straw mushrooms in oyster sauce 303
stuffed mushrooms 15
tofu with Chinese mushrooms 316
turkey with walnuts and mushrooms 232
venison with dried mushrooms 249
Mussels
mussels in black bean sauce 88
mussels with ginger 88
steamed mussels 88
Mustard
cold pork with mustard 175
mustard-roast lamb 140
Noodles
beef noodles 278
boiled egg noodles 275
braised noodles 277
chicken livers with noodle pancake 202
cold noodles 276
dan-dan noodles 279
fried noodles 275
ginger and spring onion noodles 280
hot and sour noodles 280
noodle baskets 276-7
noodle pancake 277
noodles with chicken 278
noodles with crab meat 278
noodles in curry sauce 279
noodles with egg sauce 279
noodles in meat sauce 280
noodles with poached eggs 281
noodles with pork and vegetables 281
pork with noodle pancake 157
pork and prawns with noodle pancake 157
prawn and noodle rolls 19
soft-fried noodles 276
soup with porkballs and noodles 30-21

steam egg noodles 275
stewed noodles 276
stir-fried beef with noodles 111
tossed noodles 275
transparent noodles with minced pork 281
Nuts
Chinese nut meringue 356
roast spiced nuts 360
sugared nuts 355
Oil,
chilli oil 332
Omelettes
cauliflower omelette 254
Chinese omelette with bean sprouts 253
crab omelette with brown sauce 254
omelette with ham and water chestnuts 254
omelette with lobster 255
omelette with prawns 255
omelette with scallops 256
omelette with tofu 256
oyster omelette 255
pork stuffed omelette 256
prawn stuffed omelette 257
steamed omelette rolls with chicken filling 257
Onions
baked onions 304
beef with onions 112
braised duck with onions 238
chicken with onions 207
curried onions with peas 303
fried prawn balls with onion sauce 71
fried rice with beef and onions 270
onion custard 304
pearl onions in orange ginger sauce 304
scallop and onion stir-fry 92
stir-fried onion crackle beef 113
tomato and onion salad 343
Oranges
beef with dried orange rind 113
duck with orange 239
mandarin liqueur sorbet with lychees 348
orange and lemon chicken 208
orange tea 360
orange-roast duck 239
pearl onions in orange ginger sauce 304
spare ribs with orange 171
Oyster sauce
oyster sauce mushrooms 16
soy fish with oyster sauce 35
Oysters
deep-fried oysters 88
deep-fried oysters with ginger 89

oyster omelette 255
oyster pancakes 257
oysters with bacon 89
oysters with black bean sauce 90
pak choi 304
Pak soi,
ginger haddock with pak soi 50
Pancakes
chicken livers with noodle pancake 202
Chinese pancakes 282
noodle pancake 281
oyster pancakes 257
pork with noodle pancake 157
pork with noodle pancake 157
prawn pancakes 258
Peanut butter,
chicken with peanut butter 209
Peanuts
chicken with cabbage and peanuts 187
chicken with mushrooms and peanuts 206
chicken with peanuts 209
peanut crisp 349
pork with peanuts 158
spinach with peanuts 309
sweet peanut soup 350
Pearl onions,
pearl onions in orange ginger sauce 304
Pears
duck with pears and chestnuts 239
pear compote 350
steamed pears 350
Peas
beef and peas 112
chicken with peas 210
curried onions with peas 303
fried rice and peas 272
mandarin prawns with peas 72
peas with mushrooms 304-305
prawn and pea stir-fry 70-71
rice with peas 267
Pepper,
beef with pepper 114
Peppers
bean and pepper salad 337
bean sprouts and peppers 290
beef with peppers 114-15
carrot and pepper stir-fry 294
chicken with peppers 210
chicken with peppers and tomatoes 229
fish stuffed peppers 305
green pepper salad 341
haddock-stuffed peppers 48

pepper and bean stir-fry 305
pepper rice 267
pepper steak 114
peppers with tofu 319
pork with peppers 159
pork stuffed peppers 306
prawns with peppers 72
scallops with peppers 93
stir-fried beef shred with green peppers 115
stir-fried chicken with peppers 211
stir-fried peppers 305
turkey with peppers 231
vegetable stuffed peppers 306
Pheasant
    fried pheasant 248
    pheasant with almonds 249
Pickle
    mango 357
    turnip pickle 358
Pickles
    beef with Chinese pickles 115
    spicy pork with pickles 159
pine nuts, crispy 359
Pineapple
    braised duck with pineapple 240
    chicken livers with pineapple 202
    chicken and pineapple 211
    chicken with pineapple and lychees 212
    cooked chicken with pineapple 229
    duck with pineapple and lychees 242
    fish with pineapple 43
    ham and pineapple 180
    pineapple and ginger duck 241
    pineapple spare ribs 172
    pineapple tea 361
    plaice with pineapple sauce 54
    stir-fried duck with pineapple 241
Plaice
    fried plaice 53
    plaice with garlic 54
    plaice with pineapple sauce 54
    steamed plaice with Chinese mushrooms 54
Pork
    barbecue-roast pork 174
    barbecued maple spare ribs 170
    barbecued spare ribs 169
    barbecued pork 145
    bean sprout and pork soup 21
    bean sprouts with pork 291
    braised fragrant pork 152
    braised pork with eggs 151
    braised pork knuckle in red sauce 155

chicken with pork 212
Chinese roast pork 175
cold pork with mustard 175
crispy pork parcels 150
crispy prawn spare ribs 172
deep-fried pork balls 176
deep-fried pork with crab meat 177
deep-fried pork eggs 252
deep-fried pork fillet 152
deep-fried spare ribs 170
dim sum 14
drunken pork 177
duck with pork and chestnuts 242
fiery pork 151
fish rolls with pork 44
five-spice marinade with pork 328
five-spice pork 152
fried pork kebabs 154
lobster tails with pork 86
marinated pork 155
marinated pork with cabbage 147
marinated pork chops 156
noodles with pork and vegetables 281
pineapple spare ribs 172
pork with almonds 143
pork with bamboo shoots 143
pork and bean sprouts 144
pork with bean sprouts 177
pork with cabbage 146
pork with cabbage and tomatoes 146
pork with celery 147
pork and chestnut meatballs 17
pork with chestnuts and mushrooms 148
pork chop suey 148
pork chow mein 149
pork with chutney 149
pork with cucumber 150
pork and cucumber soup 30
pork dumplings 17
pork egg rolls 150
pork fried rice 271
pork with green beans 153
pork with ham and tofu 154
pork kidneys with mangetout 179
pork and lettuce rolls 16
pork with minced garlic 152-3
pork and mushroom soup 30
pork with mushrooms 156
pork with noodle pancakes 157
pork with oyster sauce 158
pork with peanuts 158
pork with peppers 159

pork with plum sauce 159
pork and prawn egg foo yung 264
pork and prawn egg rolls 151, 176
pork and prawn fried rice 272
pork and prawn wontons 168
pork and prawn wontons with sweet and
    sour sauce 20
pork with prawns 160
pork and prawns with noodle pancake 157
pork in red sauce 160
pork with rice noodles 161
pork salad 341
pork with spinach 175
pork with spinach and carrots 163
pork stuffed omelette 255
pork stuffed peppers 306
pork with sweet potatoes 164
pork with tofu 165
pork and veal rissoles 17
pork with vegetables 166
pork with walnuts 167
pork with water chestnuts 167
pork and watercress soup 30
pork wontons 167
pork-stuffed clams 81
pork-stuffed fish 37
pork-stuffed tofu 319
red-cooked pork 160
red-cooked pork with mushrooms 157
rich pork balls 161
roast pork chops 162
roast pork chow mein 149
roast pork egg foo yung 264
sautced spare ribs 174
savoury pork 165
scrambled eggs with pork 259
scrambled eggs with pork and prawns 259
slippery pork slices 163
soft-fried pork 165
soup with porkballs and noodles 30-31
spare ribs with black bean sauce 169
spare ribs with leeks 170
spare ribs with mushrooms 171
spare ribs with orange 171
spare ribs with rice wine 172
spare ribs with sesame seeds 173
spare ribs with tomato 174
spiced pork 162
spicy braised pork 144
spicy pork with pickles 159
steamed leg of pork 178
steamed eggs with pork 252

steamed meat cake 156
steamed minced meatballs 168
steamed minced pork 176
steamed pork 163
steamed pork buns 145
stir-fried crab with pork 84
stir-fried pork 164
stir-fried pork with ginger 153
stir-fried prawns with pork 72-3
stir-fried roast pork with vegetables 178
sweet and sour pork 164
sweet and sour spare ribs 173
Szechuan soup 31
transparent noodles with minced pork 281
twice-cooked pork 166, 179
Potatoes
    braised chicken with potatoes 213
    curried chicken with potatoes 192
    deep-fried potatoes and carrots 307
    duck with potatoes 242-3
    five-spice chicken with potatoes 213
    potato saute 307
    spiced potatoes 307
    steak with potatoes 120
Poussins,
    fried poussins 230
Prawns
    anise prawns 58
    barbecued prawns 59
    butterfly prawns 18
    chilli prawns 61
    Chinese prawns 18
    crispy prawn spare ribs 172
    crispy prawns 18
    cucumber with prawns 298
    deep-fried battered prawns 64
    deep-fried prawns 64
    deep-fried prawns with sherry sauce 73
    deep-fried prawns with tomato sauce 77
    deep-fried sesame prawns 74
    dim sum 14
    Far Eastern style prawns 66
    fried prawn balls with onion sauce 71
    fried prawns in sauce 67
    hot-fried prawns with croûtons 68
    mandarin fried prawns 69
    mandarin prawns with peas 72
    omelette with prawns 255
    Peking prawns 72
    poached prawns with ham and tofu 68
    pork and prawn egg foo yung 264
    pork and prawn egg rolls 150-1, 176

pork and prawn fried rice 272
pork and prawn wontons 168
pork and prawn wontons with sweet and sour
    sauce 20
pork with prawns 160
pork and prawns with noodle pancake 157
prawn balls 59
prawn chop suey 62
prawn chow mein 62
prawn crackers 18
prawn curry 64
prawn dumplings with tomato sauce 65
prawn and egg cups 65
prawn egg rolls 66
prawn foo yung 66-7
prawn fried rice 272
prawn fries 67
prawn and mushroom curry 64
prawn and noodle rolls 19
prawn pancakes 258
prawn and pea stir-fry 70-71
prawn soufflé 262
prawn soufflé with bean sprouts 262
prawn stuffed omelette 257
prawn tempura 74-75
prawn toasts 20
prawn wontons 78
prawns with almonds 58
prawns with asparagus 58
prawns with bacon 58
prawns with bamboo shoots 59
prawns with bean sprouts 60
prawns with black bean sauce 60
prawns and cauliflower 11
prawns with celery 61
prawns with Chinese mushrooms 70
prawns with courgettes and lychees 62-3
prawns with crab 63
prawns with cucumber 63
prawns with ginger sauce 19
prawns in lobster sauce 68
prawns with lychee sauce 69
prawns with manetout 70
prawns with mango chutney 71
prawns with peppers 72
prawns with tofu 76
prawns with tomato and chilli sauce 77
prawns with tomato sauce 76
prawns with tomatoes 76
prawns with vegetables 77
prawns with water chestnuts 78
sautéed prawns 73

scrambled eggs with pork and prawns 259
soft-fried prawns 74
stir-fried prawns with chicken 61
stir-fried prawns with pork 72-3
stir-fried prawns in their shells 74
sub gum 75
sweet and sour prawns with croûtons 75
Szechuan soup 31
tofu with prawns 319
Preserves
    Chinese pickled vegetables 358
    mango pickle 357
    pickled cabbage 357
    pickled celery 357
    preserved kumquats 357
    turnip pickle 358
Pudding,
    steamed meat pudding 129
Puddings
    pearl barley pudding 351
    rice pudding with candied fruits 353
    split pea pudding 353
    water chestnut pudding 353
Pumpkin,
    pumpkin with rice noodles 308
Raspberries
    raspberry fool 352
    raspberry sorbet 352
Rice
    almond fried rice 268-9
    beef balls with glutinous rice 128
    beef fried rice 269
    boiled brown rice 265
    chicken fried rice 270
    chicken liver rice 266
    chicken and mushroom rice 266
    chicken and rice soup 25
    coconut rice 266
    crab meat rice 266
    duck fried rice 270
    fried rice 268
    fried rice with bacon and egg 269
    fried rice with beef and onions 270
    fried rice with minced beef 269
    fried rice and peas 272
    fried tuna rice 274
    ham fried rice 271
    lamb and rice 142
    pepper rice 267
    poached egg rice 267
    pork fried rice 271
    pork and prawn fried rice 272

prawn fried rice 272
reheating rice 268
rice with beef 265
rice with peas 267
rice pudding with candied fruits 353
rice salad 342
salmon fried rice 272
Singapore-style rice 267
slow boat rice 267
smoked ham rice with stock 271
special fried rice 273
steamed oven rice 268
ten precious rice 273
white rice 265
Rice Noodles
beef with rice noodles 112
pork with rice noodles 161
pumpkin with rice noodles 308
Rice Wine
rice wine roast duck 243
spare ribs with rice wine 172
steamed duck with rice wine 244
Rissoles
chicken rissoles 214
pork and veal rissoles 17
Roulades,
steamed fish roulades 51

Salads
asparagus salad 337
aubergine salad 337
bean and pepper salad 337
bean sprout salad 337
carrot and celery salad 338
celery salad 338
chicken salad 338
chilled tomato salad 343
Chinese leaf salad 339
crab meat and cucumber rings 339
crab meat salad 339
cucumber salad 340
cucumber salad with spring onion dressing 341
green pepper salad 341
marinated cucumber 341
pork salad 341
rice salad 342
sesame chicken salad 336-7
Shanghai salad 342
shredded cucumber salad 340
smashed cucumber 340
smashed cucumber with spring onions 340
spinach salad 342
tomato and onion salad 343

tuna salad 343
Salmon
salmon fried rice 272
salmon with tofu 55
Salt,
Cantonese salt 332
Sauce
anchovy 301
beef 321
black bean 48, 60, 88, 90, 118, 169, 186, 218, 297, 315
brown 40, 48-9, 254, 291, 321
celery 321
chicken 322
chilli 316
curry 106, 192, 279
egg 279, 283
egg foo yung 322
egg yolk 322
fish 119, 323
for fried fish 323
ginger 19
ham 323
hoisin 198-9, 223
lemon 56
lobster 68
for lobster 324
lychee 69, 204
mandarin 43
meat 200
milk 324
mushroom 324
mushroom sauce with tomato 325
onion 71
orange ginger 304
oyster 16, 35, 80, 113, 130, 137, 159, 202, 208, 259, 288, 303, 318, 325
papaya 347
peanut 325
Peking 325
pineapple 54, 326
plum 155, 326
pork 326
red 127, 155, 160
sherry 73
soy 35, 53, 215, 227, 250, 252
sweet and sour 20, 36-7, 38, 45, 128, 327
sweet and sour egg 327
sweet and spicy 327
tomato 52, 65, 76, 77, 217, 313
tomato and chilli 77
vinegar 46

Index

Scallops
Chinese leaves with scallops 296
crab and scallop soup 26
omelette with scallops 255
scallop and onion stir-fry 92
scallop scramble with herbs 92
scallops with bamboo shoots 90
scallops with broccoli 91
scallops with egg 90
scallops with ginger 91
scallops with ham 91
scallops with peppers 93
scallops with vegetables 92
Scrambled eggs
Chinese scrambled eggs 258
scrambled eggs with fish 258
scrambled eggs with mushrooms 258-9
scrambled eggs with oyster sauce 259
scrambled eggs with pork 259
scrambled eggs with pork and prawns 259
scrambled eggs with spinach 260
scrambled eggs with spring onions 260
scrambled eggs with tomatoes 260
scrambled eggs with vegetables 260
Sea bass,
pseudo smoked fish 15
seafood *see* under fish and under individual
names of seafood
Sesame oil
bamboo shoots with sesame oil 288
chicken in sesame oil 214
cucumbers with sesame oil 298
sesame chicken 229
Sesame seeds
chicken sesame 10
deep-fried sesame prawns 74
sesame beef with broccoli 99
sesame chicken salad 338-9
sesame ham sticks 11
sesame roast chicken 226-7
sesame seed biscuits 355
sesame seed fish 45
spare ribs with sesame seeds 175
Shallots,
shallots in malt beer 308
Sherry
deep-fried prawns with sherry sauce 73
sherry chicken 214-15
Sorbet,
mandarin liqueur sorbet with lychees 348
Sorbets,
raspberry sorbet 352

Soufflés
chicken soufflé 261
crab and ginger soufflé 261
crab soufflé 261
fish soufflé 262
prawn soufflé 262
prawn soufflé with bean sprouts 262
vegetable soufflé 262-3
soups *see* under individual main ingredients
Soy sauce
braised soy fish 35
mullet with thick soy sauce 53
soy fish with oyster sauce 35
Spare ribs
barbecued maple spare ribs 170
barbecued spare ribs 169
crispy prawn spare ribs 172
deep-fried spare ribs 170
pineapple spare ribs 172
sauteed spare ribs 174
spare ribs with black bean sauce 169
spare ribs with leeks 170
spare ribs with mushrooms 171
spare ribs with orange 171
spare ribs with rice wine 172
spare ribs with sesame seeds 173
spare ribs with tomato 174
sweet and sour spare ribs 173
Spice
cinnamon spice 332
Spinach
bamboo shoots with spinach 288-9
beef and spinach balls 131
chicken with spinach 216
ham and spinach stir-fry 180
marinated beef with spinach 118
pork with spinach 175
pork with spinach and carrots 163
scrambled eggs with spinach 260
spinach with garlic 308
spinach with ginger 309
spinach with mushrooms 308-9
spinach with peanuts 309
spinach salad 342
spinach and tofu soup 31
tomato and spinach soup 32
Split peas,
split pea pudding 353
Sprats,
deep-fried marinated fish 55
Spring onions
spring onions 284

beef and spring onions with fish sauce 119
black bean beef with spring onions 118
celestial soup 24
cucumber salad with spring onion dressing 341
ginger and spring onion chicken 225
ginger and spring onion noodles 280
lamb with spring onions 138
scrambled eggs with spring onions 260
smashed cucumber with spring onions 340
stir-fried beef with spring onions 119
tofu with spring onion 320
Spring rolls
  chicken spring rolls 216
  vegetable spring rolls 312
Squid
  deep-fried squid 93
  fried squid rolls 94
  squid with bean sprouts 93
  squid with dried mushrooms 95
  squid parcels 94
  squid stir-fry 95
  squid with vegetables 95
Steak
  pepper steak 114
  steak with potatoes 120
  steak strips 121
  stuffed steak 125
  tender lamb steaks 138
Stew
  lamb stew 138
Stews
  beef stew 120
  marinated golden chicken stew 197
Stock
  chicken stock 21
  chicken stock sauce 322
  smoked ham rice with stock 271
  sub gum 75
Sweet potatoes
  duck with sweet potatoes 246
  pork with sweet potatoes 164
  steamed beef with sweet potatoes 122
sweet and sour sauce see under sauce
Sweetcorn
  chicken and corn soup 24
  sweetcorn and crab soup 31
Swordfish,
  sautéed swordfish 55
Tangerines,
  tangerine duck 246
Tea
  almond custard tea 360

grapefruit tea 360
hot lotus tea 361
orange tea 360
pineapple tea 361
walnut tea 361
toffee apples 344
Tofu
  battered tofu 315
  braised fish with tofu 46
  carp with tofu 38
  Chinese tofu 320
  cold tofu 11
  deep-fried tofu 317
  four-jewelled tofu 317
  lamb with tofu 140
  omelette with tofu 255
  Peng tofu 318
  peppers with tofu 319
  poached prawns with ham and tofu 68
  pork with ham and tofu 154
  pork with tofu 165
  pork-stuffed tofu 319
  prawns with tofu 76
  salmon with tofu 55
  shredded tofu-chilli beef 123
  spinach and tofu soup 31
  stir-fried beef with tofu 131
  tofu balls with vegetables 320
  tofu with black bean sauce 315
  tofu with chilli sauce 316
  tofu with Chinese mushrooms 316
  tofu with crab meat 317
  tofu and fish soup 32
  tofu with oyster sauce 318
  tofu with prawns 319
  tofu soup 32
  tofu with spring onion 320
  tofu stir-fry 320
tomato sauce see under sauce
Tomatoes
  beef with tomatoes 123
  braised aubergine with tomatoes 285
  chicken with peppers and tomatoes 229
  chicken with tomatoes 218
  chicken and tomatoes with black bean sauce
    218
  chilled tomato salad 343
  poached chicken with tomatoes 218
  pork with cabbage and tomatoes 147
  prawns with tomatoes 76
  scrambled eggs with tomatoes 260
  spare ribs with tomato 174

tomato and onion salad 343
tomato soup 32
tomato and spinach soup 32
Trout
deep-fried trout 56
trout with carrots 56
trout with lemon sauce 56
Tuna
Chinese tuna 57
fried tuna rice 274
tuna salad 343
Turkey
Chinese roast turkey 231
turkey with mangetout 230
turkey with peppers 231
turkey with walnuts and mushrooms 232
Turnips
red-cooked beef with turnips 124
turnip pickle 359
turnip soup 33

Veal
pork and veal rissoles 17
Vegetables
beef with vegetables 124
chicken with almonds and vegetables 183
Chinese pickled vegetables 358
deep-fried fish with vegetables 34
duck with vegetables 247
fried eggs with vegetables 253
fried spring vegetables 310
lamb and vegetables 139
marinated steam vegetables 310
mixed vegetables with ginger 311
noodles with pork and vegetables 281
pork with vegetables 166
prawns with vegetables 77
quick cooked chicken with vegetables 219
scallops with vegetables 92
scrambled eggs with vegetables 260
seaweed, crispy 293
simple stir-fried vegetables 312
squid with vegetables 95
stir-fried duck with vegetables 247
stir-fried roast pork with vegetables 178
sweet and sour mixed vegetables 313
tofu balls with vegetables 320
vegetable chow mein 309
vegetable soufflé 262-3
vegetable soup 33
vegetable spring rolls 312
vegetable stuffed peppers 306
vegetable surprises 312

vegetables with honey 310
vegetables in tomato sauce 313
vegetarian soup 33
Venison,
venison with dried mushrooms 249
Walnuts
chicken with walnuts 220
pork with walnuts 167
turkey with walnuts and mushrooms 232
walnut chicken 219
walnut tea 361
Water chestnuts
chicken with almonds and water chestnuts
182
chicken with chestnuts 188
chicken with water chestnuts 220
Chinese leaves with water chestnuts 296-7
crab balls with water chestnuts 13
ginger-chicken with mushrooms and chestnuts
196
lamb with water chestnuts 134
mushroom and water chestnut soup 29
omelette with ham and water chestnuts 254
pork and chestnut meatballs 17
pork with water chestnuts 167
prawns with water chestnuts 78
savoury chicken with water chestnuts 220
sweet puréed water chestnuts 354
water chestnut cakes 314
water chestnut pudding 353
Water melon,
water melon in ginger wine 354
Watercress
pork and watercress soup 30
watercress soup 33
Whiting
marinated fish steaks 57
Wine
duck with wine 248
fish in rice wine 44
wine-vapour duck 248
wine, rice see rice wine
Wontons
chicken wontons 221
pork and prawn wontons 168
pork and prawn wontons with sweet and
sour sauce 20
pork wontons 167
prawn wontons 78
wonton skins 282

Everyday Eating made more exciting

New Classic 1000 Recipes	0-572-02868-7	£6.99
Classic 1000 Chinese Recipes	0-572-02849-0	£6.99
Classic 1000 Indian Recipes	0-572-02807-5	£6.99
Classic 1000 Italian Recipes	0-572-02848-2	£6.99
Classic 1000 Pasta & Rice Recipes	0-572-02867-9	£6.99
Classic 1000 Vegetarian Recipes	0-572-02808-3	£6.99
Classic 1000 Quick and Easy Recipes	0-572-02909-8	£6.99
Classic 1000 Cake & Bake Recipes	0-572-02803-2	£6.99
Classic 1000 Calorie-Counted Recipes	0-572-03057-6	£6.99
Classic 1000 Microwave Recipes	0-572-03041-X	£6.99
Classic 1000 Dessert Recipes	0-572-02542-4	£6.99
Classic 1000 Low-Fat Recipes	0-572-02804-0	£6.99
Classic 1000 Seafood Recipes	0-572-02696-X	£6.99
Classic 1000 Beginners' Recipes	0-572-02967-5	£6.99

Foulsham books are available from all good bookshops; or you can telephone Macmillan Direct on 01256 329242 or order on our website www.foulsham.com